BELIEF AND
THE NATION

BELIEF AND
THE NATION

JOHN SCRIVEN

Foreword by
Andrea Minichiello Williams,
CEO of **Christian Concern**

WILBERFORCE
PUBLICATIONS

London

First published in Great Britain in 2013 by Wilberforce Publications
70 Wimpole Street, London W1G 8AX
All rights reserved.

Cover design by Lívia Halmkan Smiešna

ISBN 978-0-9575725-0-8

Printed in Great Britain by Imprint Digital, Exeter

"In and through Christianity the thinkers and writers and painters and moralists of two thousand years have struggled to make sense of life and the world and men. They have not struggled in vain. And they were struggling to find, not to fashion; to see how things are, not to mould them to a heart's desire. What is more, the life that they wrestled with is *our* life; the world they have portrayed is the world that *we* live in; the men they were striving to understand are *ourselves*."

John Renford Bambrough, *Reason, Truth and God,* based on the Stanton Lectures in the Philosophy of Religion given at Cambridge in 1963

"If there is to be reason in anything under the sun, God must be absolute. He alone must be eternal since no eternity of ours could furnish comprehensive rationality."

Cornelius Van Till, *Fundamentals in Christian Education: Theory and Practice,* 1953

"…In the last twenty years, we have realised that the heart of your culture is your religion: Christianity. That is why the West is so powerful. The Christian moral foundation of social and cultural life was what made possible the emergence of capitalism and then the successful transition to democratic politics. We don't have any doubts about this."

A member of the Chinese Academy of Social Sciences quoted by Dominic Lawson in his review of Niall Ferguson's *Civilisation: The West and the Rest*

FOREWORD

Over the last fifty years, perceptions of public truth have altered dramatically, though the particular changes have sometimes been imperceptible. The changes have sounded progressive and often kind, but the effects have been far reaching. In many areas of our national life, the wisdom of past generations has been discarded and ideas of radical personal autonomy and relativism have influenced public policy. Policy and law never stand still and, once heading in a direction, they can continue with unforeseen and unintended consequences. In recent decades, we have seen significant social and economic breakdown, although the full effects of past policies may not yet be apparent. Confidence in moral knowledge has fragmented and there is a crisis of authority in politics and in our institutions.

This book is about ideas and their effects. It is written for the Christian and the non-Christian alike. It explores the foundations of knowledge and the way in which different intellectual currents have shaped strands of political thought over the centuries. Ideas and the principles and laws derived from them, whether secular or Christian in origin, are interconnected. The book reveals the practical effect of these ideas on our politics. The book assumes no belief in God, but explains why Christian principles can form the basis of a flourishing society. Christian political thought is consistent with reason and encompasses a realistic but hopeful vision of what it means to be human and to live in community. In the light of Christian principles, recent developments in the law and current thinking, the book examines detailed policy issues and suggests changes which need to be made.

Christian thinking has shaped our nation's intellectual life — our culture, art, literature and music, our institutions and our laws. We are imperfect beings living in an imperfect world. We need the guidance of a creator God and the wisdom of the past. The application of Christian principles to politics may not always be straightforward and there are debates to be had. Freedom of belief and expression is a Christian principle and the basis of a free and democratic society. Respect for each individual is essential even, and particularly, when we disagree with their views. This book will help people, from whatever standpoint, to think through their beliefs and discuss them constructively with others.

Just as Christian communities exist for all members of society, particularly for the outsider, Christian values reflect the created order and are good for all people everywhere. Despite the challenges of public policy in a complex world, a Christian vision can transform people, communities and the nation. The vision is one where self sacrifice trumps self service, generosity replaces greed, compassion overcomes convenience, personal restraint mitigates self indulgence, hospitality vanquishes hatred and isolation gives way to interdependence.

It is my hope and prayer that this book may help us to make that transformation a reality.

Andrea Minichiello Williams,
CEO, *Christian Concern*

February 2013

CONTENTS

PART ONE: PHILOSOPHICAL FOUNDATIONS

PART TWO: PRINCIPLES OF GOVERNMENT

PART FOUR: SOCIETY AND THE MARKETS

PREFACE AND ACKNOWLEDGEMENTS

The book contains references to the writings of political philosophers. These are made to illuminate particular issues, rather than to analyse the work of these thinkers in a wider context. I apologise to anyone whose ideas I have absorbed but have not acknowledged in the text or the end notes. All good ideas ultimately come from God and, if this book is of any help to people, I am glad only to be able to articulate them. Much of the material is common currency and, to that extent, the book is an *aide-memoire* to matters already familiar. The book contains information taken from newspapers and other books, which have been referenced where practicable. This information has not been verified and may be inaccurate. I apologise if this is so, but the purpose is to illustrate general points rather than to provide an accurate historical record. Some of the examples given may be superseded by events. And the thoughts contained in this book are selective. For all these reasons, the book is a modest *tour d'horizon*, perhaps (to quote Churchill) with "much to be modest about".

I have been enormously helped by the encouragement and comments of colleagues in Christian organisations and by friends, both of Christian and other persuasions. I have not embarrassed them by naming them, particularly since they may not all identify with the thoughts expressed in the book, but without them the book might not have been written. I am also very grateful to those who have edited and formatted drafts of the book. As is customary, I admit that all errors and infelicities are my own. As ever, I thank my wife and children who have put up with the demands of my writing at unusual times.

This book is dedicated to those associated with *Christian Concern* and *The Lawyers' Christian Fellowship* and to my other friends.

February 2013

INTRODUCTION

It has been said that Christian principles represent a foundation for free and democratic politics, and for some people they are also the source of values that underpin a flourishing society. This book examines why this is so, with reference to political thought over the centuries and to current issues. The aim is to help readers explore perspectives in political thought and to look at how different ideologies are played out in contemporary politics. Politics is for everyone, because we all have a vote and can influence those who govern us.

The theological principles underlying the book are biblical and to apply these to political issues may be contrary to the spirit of the age. But the hope is that aspects of the book may resonate with people of other faiths, or of none, as we endeavour to make sense of the world in which we live. If Christianity offers truth, this must be so when applied to the challenges of human existence in a complex world. Differences of approach in relation to theory and practice abound in political thought and the book may serve as a starting point for discussion.

A theme of Christian thought is that there is an order in the world which reflects the character of its Creator. For Christians, the Creator has intervened in our world in space and time and given guidance for living which can help both individuals and society. Human beings have been given free will to choose belief and practice, and this freedom is a basis of democracy. Conflicts between personal interests are endemic in politics, but it is possible to rise above them and look to higher values. In the words of Jesus, we can "seek first the kingdom of God" and look for a 'kingdom' response to each challenge, however intractable.

Political theory can illuminate fundamental questions about the nature of mankind. This is because systems of political thought need to reflect the realities of the human condition. Christianity teaches that the perceptions of human beings as to what is good and their ability to practise that good are flawed. Human beings are not omniscient and they cannot predict the future. They often fail to understand themselves. But truth is a unity, though we may not comprehend all of it. Christian thought provides a context of rational meaning for what we can observe and understand, while acknowledging that human beings need both the revelation of what is good and help to perform it. Christian political theory allows for human imperfection in various ways, while holding that all government is subject to a higher law to which we are all accountable. And because of the mercy of God, Christian belief also holds out the hope of renewal both for individuals and for society.

The book endeavours to draw out some of the parallels between Christian and secular political thought. The similarities should not surprise us. We all live in the same world and can draw similar conclusions from the phenomena we observe. But there are limits to these parallels. Secular thinking does not provide a framework for the ultimate meaning of human existence. Secular theories tend to emphasise one strand of human aspiration at the expense of others and these conflict with each other. Christian political thought can be founded upon a more comprehensive understanding of human nature and the purposes for which human beings exist on earth.

Political thought and the business of politics do not represent the whole of the answer to questions of human wellbeing, but they are part of the answer. Institutions and laws set the parameters for our lives and influence human behaviour in numerous ways. Wrong ideologies can devastate families and lives down the generations. Good policies can set the framework for human flourishing. As a society we can (in the words of the King James Bible) "sow the wind and reap the whirlwind", or we can sow truth and reap goodness.

The book offers a Christian perspective on some of the issues which now face us as a nation. And for some readers it might also be an encouragement to explore the eternal truths of the Christian faith that have endured down the ages.

PART 1

PHILOSOPHICAL FOUNDATIONS

1
KNOWLEDGE AND MORALITY

1.1 KNOWLEDGE AND TRUTH

This book is about the structures of government and society, the ideas of political philosophy that explain them and current political issues in the light of those ideas. Before looking at theories of political philosophy, this chapter addresses questions about the nature of our understanding of the world we inhabit, with particular reference to moral judgements. This is because, as illustrated by Plato in *The Republic*, issues of political philosophy inevitably raise more general questions as to what we can know about our world and about ethical values, what constitutes a flourishing human life and how people should behave in society. Truth is a unity and we cannot easily separate questions of epistemology, metaphysics, ethics, psychology and constitutional theory.

"Does every question have a right answer?" This raises an issue about the foundation of knowledge and morality that is perhaps rarely articulated nowadays. However, all statements of whatever nature are based on the assumption that there is truth and untruth, and most qualitative statements assume that it is possible to come to a conclusion that some things are good and others are bad. If there were no such thing as truth, there would be no basis for making any statements of any kind, including those that hold that absolute truth does not exist. Without absolute truth, the only meaningful claims would be assertions about the personal perceptions of those making them. If conflicting views were equally valued, true or false, it would be hard to attach any meaning to them beyond the fact that they happen to have been chosen by one or more people. This would hardly be a basis for a rational debate since there would be no criteria, except perhaps some concept of majority rule, by which to evaluate different opinions.

Since the 18th century Enlightenment period, systems of thought that connect ethical judgements about behaviour with metaphysical statements about God have been challenged. Nearer to our own time, belief in the unifying secular systems of thought of the last century, such as Marxism and capitalism, has declined, although within the last half century the Christian faith has increased in many parts of the world, particularly South America and Asia. The book of Daniel in the Bible talks about knowledge increasing and people running to and fro in what he calls "the last days", and some people may believe that any kind of unified belief system is unattainable as greater volumes of knowledge flow into ever more diverse pools.

The nineteenth century poet, Matthew Arnold, who rejected Christian theology, nevertheless believed in Christian morality and he lamented, in his poem *Dover Beach*, the isolation that resulted from the "long withdrawing roar" of the "sea of faith". In the last century this loss of faith in a supernatural God even reached parts of the Christian church in the form of extreme liberal theology. This holds that religious belief is no more than a human idea necessary to make sense of the world we live in. It was popularised by Bishop John Robinson in the mid-twentieth century who, having called God "an idea in the mind of man", was described by the humorist Michael Flanders of *Flanders & Swan* (familiar to an older generation) as "an idea in the mind of God".

Some of the difficulties in finding a basis for objective truth in relation to morality have stemmed from an assumption that all knowledge is ascertainable in the same way and therefore equally accessible. But we would be wrong to conclude that because moral reasoning is different from other kinds of reasoning, there is no sense in pursuing it at all. Twentieth century logical positivism held that only empirically verifiable facts can be true, thus consigning to the realm of nonsense every absolute moral judgement and aesthetic notion. This thinking was, as the philosopher in Tom Stoppard's play *Jumpers* described it, "a deeply rutted garden path", since no meaning could be ascribed to anything, and morality was merely a matter of personal preference.

The statement that truth is conditional upon verification was self-contradictory, since the statement itself is not verifiable. There was also pride, or a lack of realism, in the assumption that human beings can prove all things that are true. Logical positivism provided a philosophical basis for relativism and this further widened the gulf between the doctrines of academic philosophy and the concepts required for practical living. The 20th century philosopher, Renford Bambrough,[1] gives the example of an American University where a student was thought to have been disciplined for a sexual offence, prompting a demonstration with placards stating that morality was a matter of personal choice. When it later transpired that the discipline was for blackmail and not for any sexual misdemeanour, there were no placards saying that blackmail was a matter of private preference.

1.2 THE LIMITS OF KNOWLEDGE

In practice, human beings act intuitively upon many assumptions about reality whose basis they may not fully understand. Science can explain some of the nature of reality but it has its limits too. Neurological analysis of the brain may not yield an explanation of moral reasoning or supernatural revelation. Though controversy surrounds near-death experiences, some would say that information can be received when the observable activities of the brain have closed down. Rupert Sheldrake, most recently in his book *The Science Delusion*,[2] invited us to consider phenomena which cannot be explained by known mechanistic processes. These include the memory of humans and animals and, curiously, a person's sense of being looked at by someone behind them and the ability of dogs to anticipate their owners' return.

There are limits to the capacity of the human mind. Certain aspects of our physical universe appear to be incomprehensible. Both the concept of infinity and bounded space are difficult to grasp. Infinity is now said to exist on many levels. There is said to be countable infinity with definite steps and a continuum of places on a straight line, together with other levels, although for most purposes this does not affect ordinary mathematics. (Recent work has highlighted the relationship between the levels of infinity in the hope that there may be one unifying theory of infinity.) Despite the efforts of scientists, the nature of ultimate physical reality remains mysterious. Kurt Gödel's incompleteness theory in relation to mathematics showed that there are some statements about sets and numbers that mathematicians cannot prove. It suggested that all systems of thought are incomplete so that you can make statements in them which are not supported by the system of thought itself. Harvey Friedman has discovered that number patterns do not always follow the usual laws of mathematics. The standard model of particle physics does not appear to be consistent with the Newtonian model, and there appear to be different laws which apply to subatomic and to macro reality. There is as yet no clear boundary between the two, nor is there a unifying theory which encompasses them both.

Quantum mechanics may be able to predict the behaviour of particles, but it cannot completely describe them, and it is not possible to measure the position of a subatomic particle and its velocity at the same time. Some cosmologists have concluded that the number of possible paths of these particles is infinite and that all quantum possibilities must be reflected in a multiplicity of parallel universes. Despite the calculations of theoretical physics, there is no observable evidence that multiple universes exist. The philosophical and moral consequences of the theory of multiple universes require reflection, and the espousal of this theory by scientists may illustrate the limitations of the compartmentalisation of knowledge. If all the universes are of equal value, does it matter if I take a wrong decision in one universe since I may take the right decision in another?

Hitler may have been a harmless painter in a parallel universe, but is this relevant? If a person has multiple personalities in multiple universes, is each of them the real person? The theory of multiple universes appears to undermine cause and effect and the continuity of time, upon which the intelligibility of the universe depend. The poet Larkin wrote that "Days are where we live",[3] and Einstein observed that time exists to prevent everything happening at once. Michael Brooks, surveying the different quantum theories in what he calls the "Quantum Zoo",[4] quotes Tim Maudlin, a philosopher of science at Rutgers University in New York who is not convinced that the idea of "many worlds" provides a good framework for explaining why some quantum outcomes are more probable than others.

To the extent that it is not founded upon observable evidence, cosmological theory is of a different order to conventional science. The theory of multiple universes, which is unverifiable by reference to scientific data, should be classed as philosophical speculation rather than science. And even where there is some evidence to support a conclusion, we cannot be sure that it is the only possible conclusion to be drawn from the evidence, since there may be other information which is not available to us which would alter that conclusion.

In any event, science, even if it can describe reality, cannot do so in a way that confers meaning upon it. Thomas Kuhn described science as puzzle solving, and its conclusions about physical reality leave open the questions as to what it means to be human, to live in society and to order good government — unless the answer to these questions is that there is no meaning, which is neither a necessary conclusion nor one that is capable of proof, not least because it contains an inherent contradiction. If there is no meaning, the statement that there is no meaning has no meaning itself.

The Greek philosopher Plato, the Apostle Paul in the Bible and the 18th century philosopher Immanuel Kant all recognised that there are limits to human perception. For Plato, this world was the shadow on the cave of the ultimate reality.

The Apostle Paul said that in this world, "For now we see through a glass, darkly".[5] Kant understood that our experience of reality does not correspond to reality itself — that there are things "in themselves" and also our individual experiences of them, and that these differ to some extent. Nearer to our own time, Wittgenstein, perhaps building on Augustine's thoughts about language learning, examined the boundaries of philosophical thought as a result of the limitations of language. Words are how we understand our world and how principally Christians come to belief in God. As the Apostle Paul said, faith comes from hearing the word of God. In Christian thinking, God has communicated with humankind in the eternal Word, the "logos", which came to earth in the person of Jesus Christ. Words are how thoughts are expressed and this is true even, as recent neurological research at the Helen Wills Neuroscience Institute at the University of California, Berkeley has shown,[6] for those who are unable, for instance as the result of a tragic accident, to express those words in a communicable form. But words may not always be able to express everything that we may wish to communicate.

Some people may also wish to make sense of what they perceive as mysterious messages from another world — for instance, numinous suggestions of the transcendent in our sense of awe at the wonders of the natural world. Christians would say that we have on earth the evidence of the unseen — in the well-known metaphor we "see the work of the invisible gardener". Many people understand that there should be another sphere of reality, but the way that this is perceived is different to the perception of the material world. In the Bible, Job acknowledged that he was not meant to understand everything and that mankind should have a degree of humility in the face of the wonders of a created order: "Surely I spoke of things I did not understand, things too wonderful for me to know."[7] He also had a personal experience of God: "My ears had heard of you but now my eyes have seen you",[8] and he knew that God had given him sufficient guidance to lead a good life.

A Christian perspective is that, although we may not be able to understand the ultimate nature of reality, the information we have been given should be sufficient for us to discover the purposes of our life on earth and how we, as individuals and as societies, should live.

1.3 PRAGMATIC RATIONALISM

Whatever our beliefs about metaphysics, we must all make assumptions about the nature and rationality of reality because we need to engage with the world as we find it. Alexis De Tocqueville quotes Montaigne who said: "Were I not to follow the straight road for its straightness, I should follow it for having found by experience that in the end it is commonly the happiest and most useful track."[9] As Kant explained, extreme scepticism about our own reasoning is self-defeating. He held that we must assume we have free will on the grounds that this is a condition of rational thought, whether or not we understand why this is the case.

Moral scepticism was a feature of the philosophical landscape of the twentieth century. Renford Bambrough described the phenomenon: "To speak of moral knowledge is already to be in conflict with many contemporary philosophers, according to whom morality is a matter of choice, decision, intention and commitment and allows no scope for discovery, knowledge, truth and falsehood."[10] This thinking may still linger in some academic circles, but it does not reflect the reality of our existence. As he put it over half a century ago: "… common sense and common language do not support those philosophers who dig deep gulfs or erect high barriers between facts and values: ignorance and knowledge, argument, judgement, opinion, reasons and conclusions, thinking, recognising — all these concepts and all their close kindred are as much at home in morality as in any other mode of enquiry or investigation."[11]

There is a qualification to the conclusion of the 18th century philosopher David Hume that facts do not lead to values and that an "is" can never entail an "ought". As a matter of logic by deduction this may be correct, but it is possible to infer the reasonableness of a moral or metaphysical belief from a number of facts, none of which would be conclusive proof of that belief. The existence of a creator God (if God does exist) and the fact of my proximity to my neighbour may suggest that there are duties to each of them. We live in patterns of coherence which suggest meaning. For some people, these patterns may appear to be intimations of a reality beyond the material world which T. S. Eliot described in *The Dry Salvages* in his *Four Quartets*.[12] For others, the coherence of our physical world may lead them to enquire whether there is a metaphysical reality which makes sense of it. Renford Bambrough compared the framework of knowledge required for the perception of our physical world with that required for reason and knowledge: "The supposition that there must be ultimate foundations for knowledge and reasoning is comparable with the idea that the possibility of locating objects in space requires some base lines or landmarks which underwrite the whole system of spatial relations without themselves being locatable within the system."[13] We explore these connections further in Chapter 4.

It is possible to over-emphasise the relationship between our observations about the physical world and moral values. Belief in absolute values about the physical world does not necessarily entail a belief in right and wrong as moral absolutes. The description of a flower as "yellow" means that it has an absolute quality of yellowness, but that does not tell you whether or not it is a good thing — that depends upon a judgement about its aesthetic qualities or the uses to which it is put. However, once we accept that there is truth and falsehood concerning material things, this suggests that these concepts may also apply to moral issues. And common perceptions support the belief that there are things which are right and things that are wrong. Some people may then wish to test the claims of theology, which seeks to provide a framework both for moral conclusions as well as for the nature of an objective reality. An important feature of absolute truth is that it is discovered as an objective phenomenon that exists outside ourselves rather than being constructed by human beings either individually or collectively. To the extent that we construct truth ourselves, we cannot expect to discuss it rationally or invite others to evaluate it objectively.

Christians believe in a supernatural creator God who is the ground and explanation of existence and, for them, this belief provides a basis for moral values. In the absence of a belief in God, however, most people entertain moral reasoning on pragmatic or other assumptions. The postmodern philosopher, Richard Rorty, rejects philosophy as a means to discover absolute truth in morality, but would judge behaviour as to whether it fulfils a particular purpose. Another philosopher, Alistair McIntyre,[14] who examined the different traditions of Greek City states, rightly associates ethical values with a coherent purpose, but would see this purpose embedded in the relativism of personal perceptions and the flux of changing cultural values.

Christopher Coker, Professor of International Relations at the London School of Economics, takes the view that there is a common purpose in moral rules, at least for each society, and that these reflect a view of our common humanity. Coker acknowledges that we may, like the 20th century French writer and philosopher Jean-Paul Sartre, reject the idea that we have been created by a master builder, but he is nevertheless able to conclude that: "We are condemned to being consistent. We should do nothing that in our own eyes, let alone the eyes of others, would devalue the stories we tell."[15] A system of moral principles or rules gives individuals guidance for specific decisions and makes sense of particular choices and judgements. Some kind of consistent moral framework is necessary to give coherence to human behaviour. Consistency is rational and a condition of human integrity, though it does not mean that the consistency is necessarily directed towards worthwhile ends. Consistency is a building block for the coherence which underlies the theory of natural law which is discussed in Chapter 4. Coker's notion of pragmatic ethics recognises that ethical principles should reflect the best of human nature in an integrated fashion in response to the practical challenges that human beings face. Thus in war, it is pragmatic to be magnanimous in victory since an enemy which knows it will be well treated is more likely to surrender and the treatment is more likely to be reciprocated. As Coker points out, the atrocities of both the German and the Russian forces on the Eastern front in the Second World War illustrate the folly, as well as the immorality, of abandoning the conventional ethics of warfare.

1.4   THE MAP AND THE TERRITORY

Not everyone perceives an ultimate source of moral values, but these values appear to exist in the intellectual landscape, and we debate their content and outcomes accordingly. Understanding the nature of moral values does not necessarily depend upon new information. As E.M. Forster pointed out in *Howards End*, connecting the facts we already have may be just as important. Moral values have a consistent pattern and the existence of that pattern itself suggests a meaning. An important question is whether that meaning is one which can be drawn out of a view of human nature which is consistent for all time and all places, or whether morality is relative to a personal situation or to the culture of a society. If we perceive that there is a universality in human nature, we may wish to explore whether there is a meaning in that universality and whether this indicates further possibilities or conclusions. Some philosophers have suggested the analogy of a map. We may not be able to locate the country, and we may have to assume it exists when we have no proof that it does, but we can ascertain the regions and landmarks in it and their relationship to each other. And, once we have done so, we may be better placed to find the country itself. In other words, once we recognise that there is a coherent pattern in moral reasoning, we may then be in a position to look for its source and ultimate significance. Other philosophers have likened theological belief to a child reading Greek — the information is on the page but connections need to be made and perhaps other knowledge acquired before the meaning in the pattern is discerned. As Renford Bambrough puts it: "One may have all the 'facts' and still have much to learn from thinking them through."[16] If a moral framework is coherent and consistent with human reason, then it makes sense to investigate both the usefulness of individual parts and also whether there is any explanation for it. And the pattern in the map may be more interesting than the territory of the human condition, to quote the title of Michel Houellebecq's novel, *The Map and the Territory*,[17] because the pattern conveys a meaning which is more intelligible than the sum of its parts.

1.5 RATIONAL DEBATE

Some Christians may be reluctant to debate ideas about ethics, politics and society within a secular framework on the grounds that ultimate truth can only be revealed within the context of their belief system. Cynics might say (as Renford Bambrough has suggested) that this is because they cannot lose a game that they have declined to play.[18] However, while a revelation born of faith may be valid for Christians as individuals, they will need to convince those who do not share their beliefs without recourse to the supernatural, and they may also struggle to persuade others to entertain their metaphysical beliefs without persuasive logic convincing them that the beliefs are reasonable.

Any belief system, such as the Christian faith, must make sense of the world we live in. The logic of the outworking of the Christian faith into practical propositions should be accessible to those who do not share that belief. Christian beliefs should explain reality as we all perceive it and also provide useful guidelines for individual behaviour and the organisation of society. While it may be convenient to compartmentalise knowledge, truth is indivisible and we should not expect two contradictory things to be true, even in different contexts. If

Christian belief is true and reasonable, it must be so when applied to the challenges of human existence.

1.6   PUBLIC AND PRIVATE MORALITY

Some secular thinkers, while acknowledging that moral values exist, draw a distinction in category between morality and personal belief systems, which are private, and the structure of society and its laws, which are public. This can be an unhelpful distinction. While we should distinguish between the matters over which the State should have jurisdiction and those for which individuals should be wholly responsible, there is no difference in the type of moral knowledge or values to be applied in the private and the public realm. The consequences of human action may be individual or may be collective. But human behaviour, whether it is individual or collective, has the same characteristics and is good or bad or neither of these. The State may or may not be right in imposing sanctions on any particular behaviour, but the ethical character of the behaviour itself, whether we think of it as public or private, is not different. Thus we may say that it is always wrong to lie, but only certain lies should attract civil or criminal penalties — not because they are a different type of act, but because the State should only have jurisdiction over certain matters. Cicero highlighted this in discussing whether the law should require a seller of property to reveal its hidden defects.[19] This may be a moral duty, but not necessarily one that the State should enforce.

We cannot say that the State should never interfere with "moral" matters. All human behaviour involves choices and these choices, even in relation to material issues, may involve moral considerations. For example, all governments and societies need to regulate, to some extent, the distribution of material goods and benefits, and this inevitably involves moral judgements. Nor should we say that a debate about a public policy matter should never entertain a perception about morality deriving from religious belief. It makes no difference to the intrinsic truth or falsehood of a moral statement (for instance, that it is wrong to lie) whether the conclusion derives from religious belief or from secular humanism.

Societies require commonly accepted values which can be objectively described. There may be more to virtuous behaviour than just doing what is right according to a set of principles. Gratuitous compassion is clearly good and it may not be possible (or even desirable) to make it rule-based. However, any concept of law, or consistently expected public behaviour, requires a sense of obligation. Unless we believe that the State has an absolute right to impose upon society any values that it chooses, those obligations must be set upon a foundation of values of some kind.

1.7 EXCLUDING RELIGION FROM THE PUBLIC DEBATE

Some secular thinkers maintain that religious values, and any policies that are connected with them, should have no place in the public square as a matter of principle. Baroness Mary Warnock expressed concerns that people of faith generally believe that they have a monopoly of moral values: "To regard such principles as the unique possession of people who hold certain metaphysical beliefs is to demean the status in society of those who do not hold such beliefs."[20] She wishes to "fend off the forces of theocracy."[21]

We should acknowledge that a belief in God, just as a belief in no God, is not common ground in a public debate. However, we should not arbitrarily exclude any perspective in that debate. A view of the absolute value of human life may be derived from pragmatic ethics, evolutionary ethics, a Kantian categorical imperative, an understanding of human nature, a belief in God or none of these, but the origin of that view should not disqualify anyone from expressing it. It is also helpful if the reasoning behind an opinion is transparent. Knowledge that a belief system underpins an opinion helps people to understand the opinion and can inform the importance that they attach to it.

If religious views were to be excluded from public debate, it would present further questions, since it would not be clear what views were being excluded. A religion may or may not involve a belief in a god. Zen Buddhism for instance does not involve a belief in a divine Creator, and the idea of a "god" or "gods" may be so diffuse as to be describing entirely different kinds of entities. At a low common denominator, a religion is a set of beliefs that endeavour to explain the purpose of human life and, in some cases, its source and ultimate destiny, in addition to guiding human behaviour. It would seem perverse not to allow these ideas to be aired in public debate since they can provide a framework for the principles that enlighten it and for specific policies.

The difficulty in excluding religion from the public square is highlighted by those in the US who say that, because humanism now has the same legal protections as religious faith, it too should be excluded from public debate to maintain the disestablishment of religion. The exclusion of religion from public life would also sever us from our history together with the understanding that this can contribute to the challenges of today. Carl Schmitt, writing in 1920s Germany, argued that "all significant concepts of the modern theory of the State are secularised theological concepts",[22] and Francis Fukuyama traced the origins of law in Western Europe in religious belief and religious institutions.[23]

1.8 VALUES IN SOCIETY AND PERSONAL VALUES

Societies should debate moral matters because, whatever beliefs individuals may have, societies function better within an ordered framework of commonly accepted values and rules, whether or not people believe these are connected to each other or to a higher reality. Furthermore, so long as we ignore the quest for truth, we are slaves to the spirit of the age or, as Keynes put it, the "theories of defunct theorists". Christian values should stand the test of examination. Those who favour pluralism of belief as a virtue in itself should be able to argue that this is good for society. Plato thought that there are certain beliefs, like that of the immortality of the soul, which governments ought to promote irrespective of whether or not they are true, since they encourage good conduct on the part of citizens. We may not agree with this, but he highlighted the link between belief and the cohesion of society. For many people, there are aspects of Christian moral reasoning that are valuable in themselves irrespective of any supernatural reality — though Christians would say that both the moral reasoning *and* the theological framework are objectively true, and that each is necessary to a full understanding of the other. If Christian thought expresses truth about the nature of the world and about humanity, it should be worth exploring and debating. This is true for those who do not believe in God. We study the poems and plays of ancient Greece that illuminate the human condition, whilst not subscribing to the mythological structure that underlies them.

In practice, governments need to make judgements about the rationality and acceptability of certain expressions of religious belief because they need to legislate on the outcome of certain expressions of belief — though, as we shall see, they should not regulate the freedom to hold a belief. Some expressions of belief are violent and some deprive others of commonly accepted basic goods, such as freedom of expression. Some expressions of religious belief may need to be restrained by the State, particularly to protect the vulnerable. For example, some beliefs can endanger those who have no choice (for instance minors) by imposing restrictions on medical treatment or by requiring harmful medical practices. Governments also have choices to make as to whether they should encourage a belief system by means of government policy, for instance by providing grants to faith-based bodies or conferring charitable status with its attendant tax benefits. They may therefore need to examine whether a belief system is good for the people for whom they are responsible.

On a personal level, individuals seek meaning for their lives, though their worldviews may reflect their experiences, feelings and individual life choices. This can lead to "designer ethics" — values moulded to fit the lifestyle of their proponents — since individuals are often reluctant to espouse a worldview that reflects adversely upon them. Expressive individualism, where people make sense of their own nature and destiny without objective guidance, can result in personal emotions and self-interest triumphing over reason and the common good. Restraint is often necessary in human behaviour and this requires a framework. Mountaineers climbing Everest, being aware that once they have reached a certain height their reason may be impaired by lack of oxygen, need to work out routes and potential decisions in advance. Similarly, we cannot expect to make rational decisions if we are guided only by our own perceptions about our own circumstances. Both individuals and societies require guiding rules that are based upon objective wisdom.

For many people, moral values are not taught in home or school as in the past, but are absorbed from culture or the media. The insights of literature illuminate the human condition but the focus can be more on sympathy for the individuals described as opposed to evaluating more general principles. Aristotle spoke of poetry as being more serious than history, and Ezra Pound noted that "art does not avoid universals, it strikes them all the harder, in that it strikes through particulars."[24] While this may be true, we also need to draw out general principles. However, these principles should not be born only out of personal perceptions. We cannot be sure that we will make rational choices when we are governed only by emotion or are motivated by what we perceive as our personal interests. We have an imperfect understanding of ourselves and of the effects of our actions, particularly in the longer term. As the novelist Anita Brookner once put it in relation to one of her central characters, we simply do not have the information. Human beings, whether individually or collectively, cannot predict or control the future. Moral principles are an aid to self-understanding and exist both to help people overcome human weakness and to address uncertainty, these being integral to the human condition.

The last century has seen great changes in much of what was formerly regarded as public truth. It would seem that, from the mid-twentieth century onwards, Western societies have sought to cast off restraints on behaviour that have been learnt over thousands of years and reinvent aspects of morality in their own image. For instance, fidelity in marriage can be personally inconvenient and, for some people, painful and difficult to maintain. However, this personal challenge, which inevitably not everyone meets successfully, should not have diluted the once generally accepted principle that infidelity is wrong. This used to be reflected in divorce law much more comprehensively than at present. Principles are not always adhered to and society and the law have to recognise this. However, if the principles in themselves are right, they should remain as the values of society. The difficulties in living up to those principles should not lead to their revision.

Over the past half century the response of opinion-formers in the media and the establishment has been to normalise the failure to meet some of these moral challenges. A feature of the intellectual climate has been a subjective approach to morality, perhaps influenced by an underlying fear of the imposition of moral rules. Renford Bambrough described the phenomenon: "Defenders of subjective and emotive and prescriptive theories of ethics are usually prompted also by a moral motive that some of them recognise and openly acknowledge: a liberal or individualistic outlook and a fear of moral dogmatism and authoritarianism. They are afraid that a recognition of the objectivity of moral enquiry, an admission that there is such a thing as moral knowledge, will lead to tyranny and inquisition."[25] Whether this fear is justified depends upon the customs and laws of the society in which those principles are applied and not upon the nature of the moral principles themselves.

Individuals may retreat into purely personal morality, but societies need to seek some common ground, without which they could ultimately fragment. The writer of the book of Proverbs said that, "Where there is no vision, the people perish,"[26] referring to the revelation of God for society. In another sense, a common vision of a future to which the whole of society can aspire is desirable for all societies. Socrates said that "the unexamined life is not worth living" and there is a truth here for societies. The business of politics is to implement policies that reflect the aspirations resulting from that examination. The vision for a society, a picture of a desired future state, should be built upon commonly accepted values and these require some rational coherence. Philip Allott put it like this: "It is a major task of the distribution of power within a society to organise a necessary unity of values, and a necessary defence of those unities. And the necessary structures of power include not only structures of policy making and legislation, the social processing of ideas with a view to willing and acting. They include also educational institutions, religious institutions, courts, bureaucracies, agencies for the protection of law and order."[27]

Jonathan Sacks quotes Bertrand Russell in the introduction to the *History of Western Philosophy* where he reflected upon the relationship between morality and social cohesion in Renaissance Italy: ".... the anarchy and treachery which inevitably resulted from the decay of morals made Italians impotent and they fell, like the Greeks, under the domination of nations less civilised than themselves but not so destitute of social cohesion."[28] As recorded by Peter Whittle, Robert Putnam, the Harvard sociologist "concluded from his research that communal trust decreases the more diverse a society becomes — not just between different ethnic groups but, interestingly, also within each of those groups."[29] While ethnic diversity may be a good in itself, a society characterised by that diversity should have a coherent set of values to which all ethnic groups can subscribe.

A plural society should allow different ideas to be discussed and debated, whether or not these ideas spring from religious beliefs. Preserving open and fair debate, free from gratuitous abuse, must be the aim of all rational people. There may be a plurality of philosophies in debate, but choices in policy still have to be made. A society and its laws will therefore inevitably reflect values of some kind, whether or not these are articulated, and whether they represent only a response to individual situations or reflect a coherent world view.

Those people with a religious faith will prefer the principles governing society to be consistent with the values taught by that faith. Others, for whom metaphysical beliefs may be problematic, will want those principles to be consistent with the world as they perceive it, or how they think it ought to be. We have a shared space and a shared language. As Wittgenstein pointed out, all language depends upon a common understanding. To be human is to be in relationship. We construct a framework for society by reference to our relationships, both personal and within society, and the common values that underpin them. This book suggests that values for society based upon Christian thinking are good for people because they are consistent with human nature and the world as we experience it.

2
THEORIES OF POLITICAL PHILOSOPHY

2.1 WHAT IS THE GOOD LIFE?

Theories of political philosophy need to make some assumptions (or provide a means of reaching a conclusion) about human nature, about what it means to be human and about what constitutes a "good life" for individuals and for society. Without this perspective, discussions can easily reach a dead-end. For example, if we say freedom is important, we should have some idea what that freedom is for. Is it a freedom to make arbitrary and meaningless choices, or do we expect the freedom to be converted into a "good", however we may define this? If we adopt a utilitarian proposition that a political system should deliver the greatest good for the greatest number of people, how do we decide what is good? Is mere happiness conclusive and, if it were, how would we define it? A political theory should therefore be founded upon a view of what constitutes a flourishing life for people, both individually and collectively, and this needs to be consistent with a rational perception of the human condition.

2.2 AUGUSTINE AND THOMAS AQUINAS

Classical political theory from the seventeenth century posited the "rational myth of the State" in which features of experience were extrapolated to create an imaginary State, explaining what should happen in an ideal world. The roots of this lay in the Greek philosophy of universals and in the understanding of the medieval theologian and philosopher, Thomas Aquinas, that although man's will was imperfect, his reason could nevertheless enable him to envisage a perfect political State. Aquinas' belief that divine grace does not abolish nature, but perfects it, laid the foundation for a rational political theory that could embrace the whole range of human activities and thought, distributing them in an orderly hierarchy. This philosophy can prove to be the basis for the best, and also the worst, political systems since it can be the justification for investing those at the apex of the political pyramid with absolute power. Aquinas himself recognised this: "Because both the best and the worst is to be found in monarchy, or government by one man, many people, knowing the evils of tyranny, regard the very name of king with hate."[30]

An alternative approach was favoured by Augustine, which may seem more relevant in the 21st century. Following the Apostle Paul, he accepted that both the will and the reason of mankind were imperfect, and he grappled with the question as to how much control we actually have over the forces that shape our political environment. As Kant put it, "Out of the crooked timber of humanity, nothing perfect can be built." The perception of evil in human nature is not unique to Christianity, though it conflicts with thinking that was thought to be progressive in the 20th century. The Stoic thinker Epictetus said: "Wouldst thou be good, first believe thou art evil."[31]

Augustine also recognised the need to satisfy the deepest needs of the whole human personality — the capacity to love and be loved. This finds an echo in Francis Fukuyama's theory that the motivation of human beings is connected to personal recognition of their identity, value and achievement.[32] It also connects with the Christian-based theory of "relationalism" today, espoused by Michael Schluter, which sees healthy personal relationships as the basis of a flourishing society and which, in evaluating a wide range of policies, looks at the effect that those policies have upon the network of relationships in society.[33]

The approaches of both Aquinas and Augustine have much to teach us. We should believe that mankind is capable of aspiring to rational ideals in political society, but we must also recognise the irrationality and evil in so much human behaviour and the need to adjust for this. Philip Allott put it like this: "All the grandeurs and all the miseries of human history and all the struggles of everyday life, stem from the ambiguous duality of the human condition, a duality which is not quite a duality. Human beings can behave as matter and as animals; and they can also behave as earth-born gods."[34] The 17th century philosopher, Blaise Pascal, summed up the paradox in the context of Christian belief: "Christianity is strange. It bids man recognise that he is base, even abominable; it also bids him desire to be like God."[35]

2.3   THE DANGERS OF UTOPIANISM

Attempts to bring in an ideal political state through the exercise of worldly power at the expense of fundamental liberties, whether inspired by religion, Marxism, fascism or revolutionary idealism, all founder on human imperfections, whether or not the aspirations are true and noble. Lord Acton's dictum that "power tends to corrupt and absolute power corrupts absolutely" continues to sound a warning against utopian political structures. Utopianism is frequently a feature of governments that oppress their people. Utopias are unattainable. It is dangerous for those possessed of a particular ideology to believe that the State has both the power and the duty to bring in a social system based on that ideology without consent. The imposition of a utopian ideal by government deprives the individuals in society of the freedom to choose and therefore oppresses them. The aims may be laudable, but the method used to further them is contrary to a fundamental aspect of natural law, namely the freedom of the individual. As we shall see later, only some moral laws should be enacted as laws of the State. Utopianism does not acknowledge the imperfection of human beings and the fundamental importance of free will. It does not see the need to separate the powers of the State from the ideological or spiritual realm. For utopians, totalitarianism — giving the State control over all beliefs and activities — becomes acceptable because the State and its functionaries are thought capable of determining and enforcing what they see as "good" in all aspects of life, including beliefs.

2.4   A COMMON VISION

While the structure of a political system needs to counter-balance the imperfections of human nature by avoiding undue concentrations of power, societies as a whole benefit from having a common vision of the absolute good to which a society should aspire. This common vision may be formed by what Bishop Michael Nazir-Ali has called a "grand narrative", a shared history and framework of values that encourages the cohesion of society. Jonathan Sacks has pointed out that dissolving national identity makes it impossible for groups to integrate because there is nothing to integrate into: "Without shared values and a sense of collective identity, no society can sustain itself for long."[36]

A government's specific policies can be tested against a vision for society, while individuals have the freedom to debate it and change it through the democratic process. Implementing policies which reflect a common vision may not be practicable in the short term, but the ideals should remain, despite the challenges of realising that vision in an imperfect world.

For individuals as well as for society, the outworking of Christian faith mirrors this tension between noble aspirations and the difficulty in realising them. On a personal level, Christians may be called to suffer and endure personal injustice (thus accepting the imperfection of the human condition) while at the same time loving their neighbours by holding out a vision of a better future in confronting injustice in imperfect political systems. God's reign, the kingdom of God, should be absolute in the lives of his people: "Love the Lord your God with all your heart, with all your soul and with all your strength" (Deuteronomy 6:5), but this reign can never be fully realised in the political structures of an imperfect world.

2.5   POLITICAL POWER AND BELIEF

The imposition of belief by political power deprives people of freedom and leads to oppression. Sadly, some of the history of Christianity has illustrated a failure to understand this. The political power of the Papacy in the Middle Ages and in later times has reflected something of this. An echo of this power survives today in that the Papacy purports to be a State with diplomatic functions and recognition. For Christians, it is a theological mistake (which fails to take account of human imperfection and human free will) not to recognise the limitations of political power to bring in the kingdom of God, which is God's rule in people's lives. To the extent that Islamic jurisprudence embodies the primacy of religious law that is to be enforced by government in all spheres above all secular and national law, it is flawed and potentially harmful to liberty and the freedom of belief and expression.

The principle of the division between the jurisdiction of the State and religious institutions — on the basis that the laws of the State must prevail in the laws of the land — reflects the principle that Christian institutions exist for the outworking of faith and not political power. Jesus declined a role in civil government when asked to decide an inheritance dispute (see Luke 12:13-14). There should be no private jurisdictions (including those based upon religion) and this principle was illustrated in the *Statutes of Praemunire* of 1353 and 1393, which prohibited Papal jurisdiction in England.

In 2011, the Irish Foreign Affairs Minister, Eamon Gilmore, believing that the Vatican had advised priests to cover up the evidence of child abuse, expressed the same principle to the Papal representative in Ireland: "I told him that the Government considers it unacceptable that Vatican intervention may have led priests to believe that they could in conscience evade their responsibility under Irish laws."[37]   In this case, the alleged actions by Roman Catholic priests were not acts of overt civil disobedience to an unjust law, but involved an alleged covert evasion of the jurisdiction of the Irish State. Similarly, when Muslims put up posters and distributed leaflets purporting to establish a Sharia-controlled zone in Waltham Forest, Tower Hamlets Council ordered their removal.[38] Baroness Cox's Arbitration and Mediation Services (Equality) Bill sought to address Sharia Councils and Muslim Arbitration Tribunals which enforce a religious law which may be contrary to the law of the State. These councils and tribunals purport to operate under the Arbitration Act 1996 which was intended to deal with civil (mainly commercial) disputes in a private forum. In practice they deal with matters of criminal and family law, which should be subject only to the jurisdiction of the UK courts. They may enforce decisions under principles of Islamic law that transgress human rights standards, particularly in relation to the rights of women. A Civitas report suggested that there are now at least 85 such entities acting in the UK (in addition to the five or so Muslim Arbitration Tribunals) and the Islamic Sharia Council had made over 7,000 judgments at the time that report was written. The operation of these Councils and tribunals and the intentions of Baroness Cox's Bill are discussed in Chapter 8.

During the late medieval period, Christian believers (who might be regarded as the forerunners of the Protestants) were persecuted by secular powers for their desire to read the Bible in their own language and to question the theology and authority of the Roman Catholic Church. Some Protestant rulers have also at times used the authority of the State to seek to impose religious belief and practice which we would generally regard as private. In the rule of Cromwell's Major-Generals, people could be punished for adultery (though it might be possible to argue that adultery ought to be an offence since it leads to family breakdown). However, the mainstream of Protestant Christian thought tends towards the freedom of the individual. While acknowledging the necessity of power structures in an imperfect world, it is wary of them and opposes policies that seek to govern belief or interfere with the liberty of the individual.

While the State should not impose belief, Christians as individuals have a calling to engage with the world and seek the well-being of the society in which they find themselves. Their engagement in politics will inevitably reflect their faith and what they believe is good for individuals and society. The Reformation theologian Martin Luther said that vocation is the work of faith and that it is worship in the realm of the world. All Christians are accountable to God for their engagement in public affairs. (In Chapter 7 we examine some of the tensions that can arise where the outworking of the Christian faith conflicts with current government policy.) Christians who promote what they believe to be the good of society should not expect success that can be measured in worldly terms, nor should they assume that others will come to share their beliefs. An essential element of Christian belief is that mankind has a large measure of free will. God does not force human beings in this life on earth to obey him, and faith is a freely chosen response of the mind and the heart.

2.6   RATIONALITY AND FREEDOM

Some Enlightenment philosophers and some more recent thinkers have viewed human action as being at the mercy of impersonal forces. They would see the human mind at birth as a blank slate that is subsequently imprinted with experiences and human decisions the result of an individual's genetic makeup, biological chemistry and environment. This leaves little room for moral responsibility or even actions that are characteristically human. An attempt to rescue humanity from the status of automaton was undertaken by Kant in his *Groundwork of the Metaphysics of Morals*, which argued that although there are limits to our perception, and our experiences can never fully explain or describe things as they really are, we are nevertheless moral beings with free will, enabling us to function beyond the requirements of necessity: "We have argued that in action rational beings must presuppose their own freedom."[39] Rationality depends upon free will. Intellectual freedom is essential in the search for truth, and this includes the freedom to disagree with culture and background, to reason about truth and to debate absolute values. Restraints on intellectual freedom may be both legal and cultural. If a particular culture is elevated above its rightful place, it can unduly influence personality, obscure reason and inhibit the discovery of truth.

2.7   ORDER AND PROTECTION

For some philosophers of political theory, the preservation of order and the need for a strong ruler trumps other considerations. For Thomas Hobbes, writing in the wake of the English Civil war, a State without authority resulted in the life of man being "solitary, nasty, poor, brutish and short".[40] This echoed the views of the Protestant theologian Calvin who, writing in the previous century in his commentary on Paul's Epistle to the Romans, said that God instituted civil government for specific purposes as a response to human sin, a principal purpose being that of protection. Martin Luther, one of the principal figures in the Protestant Reformation, saw this purpose illustrated in the protection by God of Cain in the book of Genesis in the Bible. For Calvin and Luther, the law and order of the State, as well as the personal responsibility before God of every individual to resist temptation, played a part in restraining the evil that is part of the human condition, and in promoting the common good. Calvin said that, "The usefulness of rulers is that the Lord designed by this means to provide for the peace of the good and to restrain the waywardness of the wicked... Unless the fury of the wicked is opposed and the innocent protected from their wilfulness, there will be universal destruction."[41]

Because those in government are appointed under the sovereignty of God, they have a duty to govern well. As Calvin put it: "They are not to rule for their own account, but for the public good."[42] Their power is both accountable and limited:

"Nor do they have unbridled power, but power that is restricted to the welfare of their subjects. In short, they are responsible to God and to men for the exercise of their rule."[43] Calvin did not believe that every individual government was approved by God, but rather that the institution of government was part of the divine plan: "Although dictatorships and unjust authorities are not ordained governments, yet the right of government is ordained by God for the well-being of mankind."[44] Hobbes' contemporary, Samuel von Pufendorf, in common with Aquinas, saw the natural reason of men as the foundation of an ordered society, with laws nevertheless required to deal with errant behaviour.

2.8 THE DIFFICULTY WITH HOBBES' PHILOSOPHY

Hobbes' philosophy has sometimes been associated with a justification of totalitarianism. While Hobbes rightly recognised the need for protection by the State (highlighted by earlier Christian thinkers), his thinking goes further in suggesting that there is no legitimacy in the organic order in society outside the State. In contrast, Christian thinkers, such as the Calvinist theologian Samuel Rutherford, acknowledged the natural order in domestic arrangements (the family being one).[45] We can recognise that human cooperation is necessary for survival and that this is part of our natural condition. For Christians, this is God-given: "It is not good for the man to be alone" (Genesis 2:18 NIV).

Hobbes did not ignore the existence of civil society, nor did he advocate a totalitarian State in which the government controls all aspects of society. He assumed that civil society would flourish in the spaces left by the limited operations of the State. But he did not believe that civil society has any natural legitimacy and held that there is no source of authority beyond the State. If there is no natural order, then society is only possible because of the imposition of order by the State. This can imply that the State should be invested with absolute authority over the activities of its citizens, since no other restraint on the lawlessness of individuals exists. This is wrong both theoretically, because it misunderstands human nature and the capacity for human cooperation, and in practice, because it fails to reflect empirical observation of how communities actually work.

Nor does Hobbes' philosophy accord a place to the continuing, or at least intermittent, consent of individuals given in free and fair elections that is required in a democratic society. This consent reflects the free will of citizens to choose how they should be governed. Consent is also necessary to avoid an abuse of power by rulers resulting from the exercise of the free will of the ruler. If the State is the ultimate arbiter, there is no accountability either to God or to the citizens of the State. And there is therefore no satisfactory answer, either in human or in metaphysical terms, to the ancient question: *'Quis custodiet ipsos custodes?' (Who will guard the guardians?* or *Who will watch the watchers?).* (We examine issues of accountability in Chapter 9.)

Finally, although the principle of protection is necessary in the theoretical justification of the powers of the State, it does not answer fundamental questions about what, apart from the maintenance of public order, is the common good that the State should be endeavouring to promote by its laws and through its influence over society.

2.9   THE SOCIAL CONTRACT

Although anticipated by earlier thinkers, Hobbes is one of the best-known philosophers, but not the first, to describe the social contract in which people willingly give up aspects of their autonomy in order to secure stable government. Aristotle begins Book I of *The Politics* by saying that: "We see that every state is a sort of partnership and that every partnership is formed to attain some good."[46] The author of the *Vindiciae, Contra*

Tyrannos, writing from a Christian perspective half a century before Hobbes, stated: "In the first place, it is clear that men are free by nature, impatient of servitude, and are born more to command than obey. They would not willingly have elected the command of another and renounced the law, as it were, of their own nature, in order to bear another's law, except for the sake of some great advantage."[47] Similarly, the Calvinist theologian Samuel Rutherford saw civil society as both natural and voluntary: "As domestic society is by nature's instinct, so is civil society natural *in radice*, in the root, and voluntary *in modo*, in the manner of its coalescing."[48] In this sense, the obligations to the State that individuals assume are therefore, at least in theory, voluntarily undertaken.

Other political philosophers have developed the theme of the social contract. In doing so, they have focussed primarily on the formation of political structure rather than the ultimate aims of the society that is created by it. The concept of a social contract rightly reflects the principles of equality and freedom for individuals. However, although it sets limitations on the power of rulers, it does not tell us to what ideals or values citizens, or society as a whole, should aspire. While a mechanism for the consent on the part of citizens to policies which affect them may pragmatically be the best way of ensuring good government, it does not define what good government actually looks like. In any event, consent and the way it is operated will be imperfect and is likely to fall short in reflecting the aspirations or expectations of all individuals in society.

Guiding principles are required. If the relationships between interest groups and people in society are solely a matter of contract and agreement, though this may be better than the law of the jungle that Hobbes warned against, the powerful may dominate and use these mechanisms to their own advantage. We can see this in a number of countries where minorities, often religious or ethnic, are persecuted. In these cases, the mechanisms of democratic consent have delivered power to those who believe they have the right to exercise it in favour of their own ethnic group, or those who share their ideology or religion. Institutional restraints founded upon moral principles, as well as the mechanisms of democracy and accountability, are required. These include respect for basic human freedoms, the impartial rule of law and the separation of the powers of government, which are addressed in later chapters.

2.10   THE SOCIAL CONTRACT AND COMMON IDENTITY

The contemporary philosopher Roger Scruton has pointed out that the social contract is a theoretical construct under which the citizens agree to be governed, but that the process of entry into the contract is based upon an assumption that the citizens enter into it as a body together and that they already have an identity of interest. As Scruton describes it, the US constitution assumes a common identity: "We the people…" "Which people?" "Why, us — we who already belong — whose historic tie is now to be transcribed into law?" The founders of the new social order already belong together. As he says: "There cannot be a society without this experience of membership. For it is this that enables me to regard the interests and needs of strangers as my concern."[49] There are dangers in extreme national exclusivity and a Christian response to this hazard, in terms of the overriding Biblical values of compassion and justice, has been explored in Miroslav Volf's *Exclusion and Embrace.*[50] Volf recognises the difficulty for those inside a particular tradition or interest group to see justice in universal rather than in particular terms. Nevertheless, people are made for relationships, both on a small and large scale, and so feel the need to belong to families, communities and national groupings. People in the same nation have multiple identities, for example, of belief, religion (for some), tribe, nationality, culture and class, and they need to coexist peacefully. The difficulties in addressing different aspirations in terms of law and rights are addressed in later chapters.

A common identity is necessary in relation to those matters over which the State has jurisdiction, such as national allegiance and a system of law. Cicero defined a "commonwealth" as "a multitude united in association by a common sense of right and a community of interest",[51] and Augustine a "people" as "the association of a multitude of rational beings united by a common agreement on the objects of their love".[52] The 18th century philosopher David Hume emphasised the necessity for shared practices rather than shared beliefs, stating that these practices should be such that enable people to live together under a common government. But practices are derived from beliefs and this brings us back to the need for common values, and the importance of identifying what these should be and how they are to be discerned. A requirement for consent cannot determine either the purposes of a political structure or the values that should underpin it.

2.11 RIGHTS THEORY

Some political philosophers have looked to the existence of inalienable rights as a source of objective values. This raises fundamental questions such as: who confers the rights, to what creatures they should be given and how conflicts between different rights are to be resolved. These issues continue to surround the theory of human rights today. The US constitution holds certain truths to be "self-evident" and, for a Christian society, they may have been. However, without a belief in a higher power it may be difficult to explain why these things should be so. Some secular thinkers have held that human rights spring from human nature, but this poses the question as to what human nature is and where it comes from. For instance, if we believe in Darwinian evolution by chance and the survival of the fittest, rather than in life being conferred by a creator, it may follow that there is no reason to believe that all human beings have inherent equal value. If individuals do not have any inherent value, then there may be no basis either for human rights or for democracy.

The various freedoms that people seek (which can often be expressed in terms of "rights") conflict with each other because people have different aspirations, yet have to coexist. Freedom to manifest a belief, or to exercise what might be described as a right, can result in incompatible aspirations, simply because human beings are imperfect and are inevitably (to some extent) self-interested. Rights may appear absolute but, upon closer inspection, may turn out to be circumstance-specific or are put forward to promote the interests of a particular group. This is partly because the concepts are simply too generalised. For instance, a right to family life is capable of manifold interpretations. It may also be impossible to distinguish between rights and interests, particularly when the subject matter of the right or interest is a matter of economic welfare. Moreover, since rights are generally perceived as absolute, when human rights are framed in terms of law, there may be no scope for a compromise between conflicting rights, resulting in the winner taking all in any dispute.

Whilst there are concerns both about the theoretical basis of human rights and about certain aspects of their application, the concept of human rights is in some respects consistent with Christian thinking. The concept of human rights assumes the existence of a universal moral framework that applies to all people everywhere. This conflicts with the relativism of some 20th century philosophy. As a practical matter, human rights are useful because they are capable of defining basic values that can be used to assess the behaviour of governments. Furthermore, the idea that these rights are derived from a view of the nature of a common humanity is consistent with the premise that political ideas should be based upon a view of human nature, which Christian thinking explains in the context of a belief in a creator God. The strengths and limitations of human rights theory and practice are discussed further in Chapter 7.

Although some would promote animal rights, these cannot be similar to human rights, not least because it is assumed that we expect to be able to treat mammals differently from insects and parasites. Animals do not share common characteristics in the same way as human beings, nor can they understand, express or assert their "rights".

2.12   UTILITARIAN THINKING

Utilitarianism, perhaps unconsciously subscribed to by many people today, can be regarded as an attempt to answer the fundamental question as to what society is for.   Utilitarian thinking focuses on the results of an action and assumes that those results should reflect the aspiration of human beings to gain happiness. Jeremy Bentham believed that a political system should produce the greatest good for the greatest number. The term "good" generally meant "pleasant" whilst "bad" meant "painful": "By utility is meant that property in any object, whereby it tends to produce benefit, advantage, pleasure, good or happiness, (all of this in the present case comes to the same thing) or (what comes to the same thing) to prevent the happening of mischief, pain, evil or unhappiness to the party whose interest is considered."[53] The aim is therefore the greatest happiness of the greatest number of individuals.

Although Bentham's theory can in some ways be a useful way to begin looking at public policy issues, it reflects an incomplete picture of the breadth of the aspirations that spring from our human nature.   For many people, purely mechanistic reasoning, devoid of moral value, produces neither a compelling vision nor a coherent outcome.   The concern is that the description of happiness as the aim of human existence is either so subjective as to be meaningless or so shallow as to be valueless.   As Herbert Schlossberg records in his book *The Silent Revolution and the Making of Victorian England*,[54] Leslie Stephen was himself a free thinker and utilitarian "but came to wonder about the shallowness of the philosophy, its valuing of comfort above all, it producing 'a quiet ignoble littleness of character and spirit'."[55] Even taken at face value, calculations based upon human sensations alone cannot be addressed as a balance sheet or a profit and loss account. Nor can they alone provide a useful guide to the enduring value of the range of human experience. As the poet Hopkins put it, "Sheer plod makes plough down sillion shine",[56] and hard and perhaps temporarily unpleasant work is necessary for so much creative or worthwhile endeavour. For example, competition may not be comfortable, but in an imperfect world it appears to be necessary to encourage a degree of economic efficiency. Competition between artists can spur them on to greater achievements. As Giorgio Vasari pointed out in his *Lives of the most Eminent Painters, Sculptors and Architects*, competition between Florentine artists was "one of the nourishments that maintain them".

The focus upon the human senses in utilitarianism was a retreat from the wisdom of classical civilisation as well as from Christianity. Towards the end of Plato's dialogue *Protagoras* Socrates invites Prodicus to agree that what is pleasurable is good and what is painful is bad (Bentham's formulation). Bentham need not have taken this at face value, since Socrates goes on to question how this principle can apply to the virtue of bravery, and the ancient philosophers were familiar with the concept of *akrasia* — weakness of will, where there might be an immediate pleasure in doing what is wrong. Utilitarianism might be plausible in an ideal world where the knowledge of truth and goodness is easily attained and put into practice, but we know that this is not so in the world in which we live. Plato's later dialogue *Meno* explores whether the practice of goodness can be taught. The paradox of a person doing something they know is bad, because they desire it, is explained by the imperfection of human nature. This encompasses a lack of knowledge of the future and an inability to weigh up long-term consequences against perceived short-term benefits, together with the irrationality and emotion that cloud so much human judgement. Morality may be a matter of knowledge but, as the Apostle Paul taught, to know what is right is different from doing it.

Utilitarian theory does not provide a justification of higher values such as love, fidelity and self-sacrifice, nor even for social ideals such as liberty and equality, though much utilitarian thinking suggests social responsibility. The 19th century philosopher John Stuart Mill developed utilitarian theory by recognising that there were different kinds of "happiness" which included, for instance, a claim to justice. Mill, in exploring the benefits of freedom from compulsion, held out the prospect that this freedom would provide a context for cooperation in civil society. John Locke, writing earlier, had also prioritised choice and believed that this would lead to a consideration of the effect of one person's choices on those of others. But this thinking fell short of Aristotle's belief that all human activities have a natural end and that these need to be ordered together towards a flourishing society. Nor does utilitarian thinking pay sufficient attention to Plato's perception that rulers need to encourage moral thinking in their citizens so that they will make just and moral decisions that benefit the common good.[57]

Later utilitarian philosophers, such as G. E. Moore, expanded the view of the common good to include intuitive values, but without providing a framework for the validity of those values. More recent refinements to utilitarian thinking which have highlighted particular aspects of it, such as "consequentialism" (prioritising results), "welfarism" (looking at collective outcomes) and "sum ranking" (looking at total benefits), have only served to illustrate its fundamental limitations. Utilitarian thinking fails to deal with issues of the unjust distribution of benefits, where the greatest good of the greatest number can result in substantial inequality. It also fails to provide an answer to the questions as to: why it would be wrong to punish an innocent person to deter others from committing crimes (assuming this is proven to be effective); or to maintain public order (as Pilate did when condemning Jesus to death), and why it would be wrong to reduce crime by simply eliminating serial wrongdoers for the benefit of the rest of society.

There is also a danger that utilitarianism can be used to support totalitarianism. The State could be thought to be rational enough to determine what constitutes happiness for individuals and to bring it in irrespective of the wishes of its citizens. This denies both human imperfection (in the State determining what is good) as well as any aspirations beyond the material, and it reduces human nature to a collection of mere desires. On the other hand, it should be acknowledged that on a practical level much utilitarian reform has been valuable. In the 19th century utilitarian programmes of social reform, for instance in relation to the prisons, had much in common with Christian initiatives, though their philosophical foundations were very different.

A concern with utilitarian thinking is that it can assume a proposition as to what constitutes the public good without examining the assumptions that lie behind the proposition. The Christian writer Nick Spencer records a conversation with Baroness Mary Warnock in which they discussed the unintended consequences of legislation.[58] The Baroness believed in looking rationally at the consequences of legislation in a utilitarian fashion, and took the view that those with religious beliefs are concerned only about irrational religious principles. Spencer suggested that legislation allowing euthanasia in Britain might lead to unintended consequences, in the same way that a permissive application of the 1967 Abortion Act has resulted in a huge number of abortions (over seven million) since its enactment. However, Baroness Warnock responded that the consequences of abortion legislation were not necessarily a bad thing since teenage mothers were unlikely to provide adequate care for their children, leading to "awful" social consequences. Spencer concluded that: "Consequentialism is simply too pliable to see us through the moral maze" and that it is "a slippery beast. So sensible, so reasonable, so scientific, it is, in reality, endlessly malleable, a leaf for every ideological wind that blows. Why did Spartans throw weak babies off cliffs? Why did Romans 'expose' infants (especially girls)? Why did intelligent people fight for the slave trade and against the Factory Acts? Because each believed that the consequences of letting weak or 'unwanted' children live, or undermining the national interest, or interfering with free trade, would be deleterious for society. Perceived consequences have a habit of moulding themselves around our existing concepts of the good."[59]

Furthermore, some absolute values have to be espoused — irrespective of utility — simply because, in an imperfect world and with the limits on human knowledge, reason and wisdom, it is impossible to evaluate outcomes comprehensively, or predict the consequences of policies in an uncertain world. This is one of the pragmatic reasons (apart from issues of principle) why the ends cannot justify the means. Even if we were to accept that the ends could justify the means, we cannot predict the future and so we cannot be certain what all the consequences will be. Christians may be comforted by the broad sweep of prophetic history in the Bible, and some may relate aspects of history to biblical prophecy. However, in relation to the near future, "None of us knows what is going to happen and there is no one to tell us", as the writer of Ecclesiastes put it.[60] Christian reasoning says that we must always do the right thing according to a set of moral absolutes, and then leave the outcome to the sovereignty of God. Human beings might want to believe that they can disregard these principles, because they believe that they know what is best and what the outcomes of their choices will be. However, in Christian thinking, this would be to usurp the role of the Creator who has given humankind consistent guidelines for behaviour. These guidelines hold true whatever the outcome, although the results may not always be congenial according to human understanding. Aquinas, in defending the necessity for the divine law, refers to the "uncertainty of human judgement".[61]

The application of clear principles may involve hard decisions in particular cases. For instance, we may think that a "mercy killing" is indeed merciful, but this course should not be open to us since we cannot know whether a person's continuing life, or their death, would be more merciful to them, or indeed to others. Even if we were to agree that such killings should be made lawful in the UK, judgements would still have to be made about the motives of those involved — was the motive really one of mercy or was there, for instance, personal advantage at stake? In practice, it may be impossible to make these judgements in such a way as to achieve the objectives of an impartial law. The Christian view is that there should be an absolute rule against the killing of another. This embodies a fundamental principle about the nature of life and the act of killing itself. It also reflects the fact that we are not omniscient and all wise, so the law given by God prohibiting the taking of life has a pragmatic purpose which is necessary for our protection.

2.13   MEANS AND ENDS

Implicit in utilitarian thinking is the idea that the outcome of an action is the determining factor in deciding whether that action is right or wrong. This denies the absolute moral quality of an action irrespective of the outcome. The Romans had a saying "Fiat iustitia, pereat mundus": "Let justice rule, though the world may perish", thus advocating principle above utility. One of the difficulties with utilitarian thinking is that if we base a decision only upon our view of the expected outcome, we necessarily compare that outcome with the alternatives which appear to be available. This is a wrong approach because all of the perceived alternatives may be wrong, though one outcome may be less harmful than the others. In focussing on outcomes, there can be temptation to say that the less harmful outcome is right because it is the lesser evil. This is similar to saying that the end justifies the means, since in this case the "end" is the less harmful outcome and the "means" is the wrong action which achieves that outcome.

If the concepts of right and wrong exist, what is right must *always* be right and what is wrong must *always* be wrong, irrespective of the alternatives. It is wrong to argue that an unjust solution to a situation is justified simply because it is better than a third (more unjust) solution, since the proposition is based upon the limited range of options that appear to be available. A person should not believe that he has the choice only between two wrong courses of actions on the basis that a limited choice is given by others or imposed by the circumstances surrounding the situation. In either case, a person has a choice not to act, so long as there is an absence of duress. Furthermore, in any event, the situation could change so that the consequences of not acting may turn out to be different to those foreseen. However, even in circumstances where there is no apparent possibility that the situation at hand will change, to behave as though there is no other choice than to do the lesser evil is only justifiable in extreme circumstances, i.e. where there is duress.

However hard it may be in practice, where there appears to be a choice between two wrong acts, the right course of action is not to do either of them. We should be compassionate in situations of duress where individuals are forced by others to engage in wrong behaviour (by torture, for instance). The presence of duress does not alter the objective nature of the act itself, though on a subjective level it does absolve from guilt the individual who is forced to act against his will. In some cases individuals nevertheless believe that it is right to choose the lesser of the two evils, even where no extreme circumstances exist. In principle the range of options available cannot determine what is right or wrong. Governments as well as individuals must hold to absolute principles, irrespective of the circumstances. Policy makers should have a clear idea of the vision they are seeking to implement and the criteria against which what is "good" can be judged, even if the options appear limited because the desired outcomes are not immediately attainable.

Here are two examples of an individual choosing to do wrong because he is under the false impression that the existence of an apparently limited number of choices justifies choosing a wrong course of action. One example is a judge in Nazi Germany who orders the death of a person for dissent because he honestly believes that he can save the lives of others as a result. Another example is a judge in the UK who believes that abortion (except to save the life of the mother) is morally wrong because it amounts to the murder of an innocent human being. This judge nevertheless orders an abortion (for example, for a mentally disabled mother) because he honestly believes that by doing so he will remain in post and as a result will have the opportunity to do good in other ways. He may reason that the abortion would in any event be sanctioned by another judge, and so his refusal would make no difference to the sum of human happiness. In each case, the options available may appear to be limited. A Nazi judge who refuses to act as expected may be killed in a concentration camp and a judge in the UK who declines to administer the current law may face dismissal. However, if the taking of life is wrong, it will always be wrong regardless of the motive. For the Christian, the perceived limited options, or any perceived benefits that might ensue from the death, cannot justify the wrong act. We have a personal responsibility for our own actions, but not generally for the actions of others and we cannot predict what they will do. This personal responsibility is based upon our free will and we cannot absolve ourselves on the grounds that others would perform the wrong act were we to decline to do so. In both cases the judges assume that they will have the opportunity to do good by staying in post. They may be right in their perception that what they intend to do is good, but whether they will be able to carry out their intentions is not within their control since they cannot predict the future.

There are countless examples — prophets in the Old Testament and John the Baptist in the New Testament, as well as other individuals in history — of those who risked or gave their lives to confront evil in high places. The world may be imperfect but, where behaviour is wrong in principle, it cannot be justified, though there may be mitigating circumstances which engender our sympathy for the perpetrator. David Hall, in his book on the political thought of Calvin, comments: "Of the need for resistance to a totalitarian power that wrongly attempts to command the conscience, Calvin noted that 'Daniel could not obey the edict [that made his prayer a crime] without committing an atrocious insult against God…'."[62] For the prophet Isaiah, God is the judge, lawgiver, king, saviour and the ultimate authority (see Isaiah 33:22) and many characters in the Bible, for example Joseph, Esther, Daniel and the Apostle Paul, concluded that it is better to serve God than man (see Acts 4:18-20).

2.14 PERSONAL LIBERTY

John Stuart Mill championed liberty as he sought to defend the sanctity of individuals against what he saw as unjustifiable interference by society and the State. In his *Essay on Liberty* he said that: "The only purpose for which power can be rightfully exercised over any member of a civilised community against his will, is to prevent harm to others. His own good, either physical or moral is not a sufficient warrant."[63] In highlighting the need for freedom of belief and toleration, Mill's philosophy is valuable, but it is incomplete. While a utilitarian belief in the greatest good for the greatest number poses the question as to what constitutes the "public good", Mill's emphasis on liberty and tolerance as aims in themselves (rather than as the means to an end) allows the co-existence of contradictory ideas about what is "good" without a common understanding as to how conflicts are to be resolved. In this sense, Mill might be regarded as the father of modern diversity theory, though he would have been shocked by the enforcement in our own time of particular manifestations of that diversity. Mill thought that in matters affecting members of the public, society only has the right to interfere with individuals for the purposes of advancing the welfare of society as a whole. This rightly indicates a limited role for the State, but it raises the question as to which matters actually do affect society. In this regard, family breakdown is an example of a private matter which has wide social ramifications. Also, there are matters over which the modern State has now taken jurisdiction and from which it may not be practicable in the short term for it to retreat, even if this were desirable.

More recently, the philosopher John Rawls has followed Mill in prioritising liberty and choice. In doing so, he has recognised matters beyond the material, though there will be material consequences of the ideas associated with liberty. Rawls also believed in "certain fundamental intuitive ideas" as being necessary for the operation of a democratic society. The liberty of the individual requires a framework of law which regulates some aspects of human behaviour. As Archbishop William Temple put it in his *Christianity and the State*: "It [law] is not only a means by which I restrain the liberty of others to injure me; still more fundamentally it is the means by which I secure my own liberty to live as a good citizen against my own occasional desires to act otherwise."[64]

Some secular thinkers would regard human tradition (particularly in the form of religious beliefs) as inhibiting the full development of human potential, and would elevate human autonomy above laws or values requiring restraint. However, in Christian thinking, freedom without the restraint of a moral structure places an unsustainable burden on imperfect individuals and, when manifested in political systems, is likely to result in disorder and oppression.

2.15   POLITICAL IDEAS AND OUTCOMES

While we should be wary of purely utilitarian thinking because of its exclusive focus upon outcomes, it would be wrong to separate political ideas from their practical outcomes. Political ideas are theoretical constructs but they affect behaviour. In examining the ideas, we need to look at how they work in practice, particularly if one ideal is emphasised at the expense of others. For example, the concept of freedom should not be separated from the consequences of the exercise of the rights that might be said to flow from it. An undue emphasis on freedom in the form of personal autonomy may not result in a good outcome for an individual, since that will depend on the manner in which choices are exercised and the limitations of the surrounding circumstances. History abounds with examples of mass crimes pursued to promote ideologies (such as fascism and communism) irrespective of their practical consequences for individuals. No political ideology should be elevated above a fundamental moral rule. For example, democracy is an admirable ideal, but we should not torture citizens to advance it.

Christian thinking should not separate theory and practice. The Bible teaches that good works are the necessary product of faith (see James 1:22-2:26). Christian belief is both metaphysical and down to earth. The first commandment: "Love the Lord your God"[65] is balanced by the second very practical one: "Love your neighbour as yourself".[66] So Christians should not claim to love God whilst endeavouring to advance his cause by persecuting individuals. As Dr David McIlroy has pointed out, the two commands complement one another. If Christians love God, they should want to love their neighbour because they want to obey God, and they will look to God's grace to enable them to do so.

God's commandments can help to interpret secular political philosophy by putting them in the right perspective. The contemporary English philosopher Roger Scruton has pointed out that the divine commandments do not replace the secular law, but rather constrain it. As he puts it: "They [the commandments] set limits upon what the secular power may command."[67] While principles of secular political philosophy may not be wrong, Christians would not ascribe an ultimate value to them. To do so would be what Christians would describe as "idolatry", which is the worship of something in place of God.

2.16   THE ORGANIC SOCIAL ORDER

Edmund Burke, writing in the 1790s, crystallised his thought in his *Reflections on the Revolution in France*.[68] He held out a vision of society that supports and enfolds the individual in an ordered community, acknowledging that mankind is by nature a social being. As a result, his philosophy valued the structures of society that had grown organically to reflect the wisdom accumulated over the ages, and specifically those that reflected a moral order. For Burke, the practical outcomes of ideologies and different forms of government indicated pragmatic conclusions based upon human nature. While there is value in traditions formed over time, the longevity of ideas and political structures does not confer legitimacy. History and the present day are littered with examples of unjust regimes that have endured for long periods. Burke valued the wisdom of the past, but he saw this as reflecting a natural order and concluded that liberty "cannot exist at all without" order and virtue. Burke was a natural law theorist who acknowledged an "immutable pre-existent law" which he saw as interpreted by the common law of England which had developed over time. He advocated a political system that reflects the aspirations of its people in the form of local organisations and small groupings as opposed to a top-down structure. Burke's vision valued the "little platoons" (small and local associations of people) as bastions of liberty against an over-mighty State. But he might not have been sympathetic to those minority groups today which exercise undue influence in the public sphere by virtue of their activism.

In recognising that the compact between rulers and citizens must include the deceased and the unborn as well as the living, Burke questioned the chronological snobbery implicit in progressive thinking that assumes that modernity is inherently superior to older wisdom. The Bible frequently counsels a return to the "ancient paths" and the value of the unchanging moral law: "He decreed statutes for Jacob and established the law in Israel, which he commanded our forefathers to teach their children, so that the next generation would know them, even the children yet to be born, and they in turn would tell their children" (Psalm 78:5-6, NIV and see also Deuteronomy 6:7 and 11:19).

Burke also pointed out that private licence in moral behaviour leads to public repression — as is witnessed by the mountain of law and regulations in modern Britain. As we have seen in the financial markets, where there is no self-restraint, governments will seek to regulate behaviour by law leading to what the contemporary political thinker Phillip Blond has called "the regulatory arms race."[69]

2.17 THE CHALLENGES OF FREEDOM AND CHOICE

The French sociologist Emile Durkheim, writing at the end of the nineteenth century, analysed the consequences of personal freedom unconstrained by traditional social values and limits on individual free will which results in the abyss of "anomie". This has sometimes been taken to mean loneliness, anonymity and a lack of identity. It has these connotations, but it literally means "A-nomie", a lack of law. The loosening of social constraints and the evaporation of group values creates lawlessness in some people, with no limits on their personal desires. This, according to Durkheim, can cause psychological problems such as "egoism" which can, in extreme cases, lead to suicide. He observed that, as collective life diminishes, there is an increase in certain types of suicide. Freedom without restraint is harmful not only to society, but can also be deadly to certain types of personality.

Jean-Paul Sartre said that we are "condemned to freedom". Since, for Sartre, we create our own reality and moral framework, he might have agreed with Christopher Coker's conclusion (mentioned in Chapter 1) that we are also "condemned to being consistent".[70] In Christian thinking, free will is an irrevocable gift and the great responsibility of humankind, at least until the day of our judgment. At the same time, Christians believe that the gift of free will comes with the guidance of an objective and consistent moral framework given by God. Christians believe that they can look to God's help in their often inadequate endeavours to live within that framework.

Just as the existence of choice does not guarantee that it will be rightly exercised, Fareed Zakaria has shown that there are difficulties in relying solely on democratic mechanisms which seek to transmit the free choice of a mass of people to produce rational and good results.[71] The illiberal democracy in Russia and the popularity of extremist Islamic movements in some countries are evidence of this. Democratic governments may also behave irrationally in reacting to public pressures or concerns. Dambisa Moyo has compared the rational way in which Chinese authorities reacted to a pneumonic plague with Britain's irrational response to the outbreak of swine flu where authorities, because they were afraid of public criticism, distributed anti-flu drugs against the advice of experts who had warned that the virus may mutate and return in a more devastating form if the drugs were made widely available.[72]

While Christian thinking suggests the need for systems of law and accountability that restrain governments, guard the liberty of the citizen and protect the vulnerable, much will also depend upon the values of those populating these structures. If they are defective, the systems may fail. For example, if in the UK jurors are influenced by wrong values in society, they can be responsible for unjust results. Public good is affected by private morality, even if this cannot and should not be enforced. The old adage that "people get the government they deserve" reflects Aquinas' view that a cause of tyranny can be the sins of the individuals in society and that in such cases, "for the scourge of tyranny to cease, guilt must first be expiated".[73]

Although laws cannot make individuals good, they can nevertheless restrain evil and encourage right behaviour. The reverse is also true, in that laws can change people's perceptions of what is acceptable. Once boundaries in the law are moved, there can be calls for further movement, and we see this in changes in legislation over recent decades. For example, the ease with which abortions are available under the law has normalised the procedure in people's perception and encouraged calls for further liberalisation.

2.18   DEBATING THE PUBLIC GOOD

What amounts to the "good" that governments should seek to promote needs to be debated. It is widely accepted that purely economic calculations, such as gross domestic product, are inadequate indicators of well-being. This is because they fail to take into account significant areas of human experience, such as the preservation of the environment, safety, law and order, and educational and cultural values. These are the "goods" that economic activities are capable of promoting, but it is equally possible that wealth may be channelled into worthless or even malign activities. Some may regard significant areas of contemporary culture in this light. Choices about expenditure are made by governments and individuals, but they may not be the right ones. Secular political thinkers have explored a number of good but often incompatible aims. As illustrated by history, the trio of liberty, equality and fraternity conflict in an imperfect world. Equality, at least of outcome, requires some restrictions on liberty. Fraternity may not be best achieved by equality, and liberty gives rise to inequality. More recent refinements of political "goods" such as fairness, natural justice and distributive justice can result in similar conflicts.

Aristotle associated happiness with individual virtue. At the beginning of his *Nicomachean Ethics* he explains: "A life of making money is contrary to nature; it is clear that wealth is not the good we are seeking; it is merely acquired with a view to something else."[74] For Aristotle, we are moral beings with a purpose and we can only enjoy liberty (legitimate free will) if we live in a community with rules which enable those purposes to be fulfilled. Some objective notion of human flourishing is necessary. For Plato, the virtues of wisdom, courage, temperance and justice are the values of the soul that enable human beings to flourish. This is echoed by many Christian thinkers, particularly Aquinas, who took the view that "the object for which a community is gathered together is to live a virtuous life".[75]

Christian thinkers have highlighted the difference between rule-based virtue and Christian virtue, with the latter being a transformation of the whole personality by the grace of God and in humble dependence upon him. For Christians, human flourishing is about the creation in human beings of something of the character of Jesus — of humility, self-sacrifice and love. This should be more profound (in terms of a change in character) and more effective (in its results) than the observance of moral rules, however good those rules may be. In this way Christian thought can acknowledge the value of much secular wisdom, but transcends it.

2.19   CONCLUSIONS

Secular political philosophy has much to offer in identifying aspects of society and government which need to be accommodated in any political system. The contrasts between the various theories mirror the incompatibility of different human aspirations. They also reflect the central paradox of the human condition — the aspiration to idealistic values and the failure of imperfect humanity to live up to them. Some theories prioritise ideals such as freedom, but they founder upon human imperfection. Other theories focus on a mechanism such as consent, or they concentrate on the necessity for public order, while failing to provide a compelling vision as to what society is for. In the next chapter we look at how contemporary secular thought has sought to address some of these issues, and reflect upon some of the theoretical and practical challenges that have resulted.

3
SECULAR THOUGHT

3.1 COMMON GROUND WITH CHRISTIAN THOUGHT

This chapter examines a number of aspects of secular thinking and their outworking in society. Some secular beliefs conflict with Christian values, but there are also a number of valuable elements in secular thinking which are consistent with Christian thinking. A belief in absolute and rational truth is a foundation of Christian thought and this also underlies much secular philosophy. Christians can acknowledge the value of much of the thinking of the 18th century Enlightenment which encouraged a spirit of enquiry and debate. The Christian view of the State has in common with secular liberalism the perception that the State must not govern the discovery of truth because the State should be a reflection of that truth, not its arbiter.

Neo-Kantian thinkers, who may be secular in their outlook, nevertheless believe in absolute moral values. For them those values are derived not from a creator but from a categorical imperative which is based upon the logical consistency of reciprocal moral obligations. Human rights theory assumes the existence of absolute values which are universally applied. Some secular thinkers derive those absolute values from the nature of our common humanity. Others value the framework of Christian thought and ethics in our historic heritage as an organic expression of common identity, while finding the metaphysics of Christian belief problematic.

Many people of a secular outlook are, in common with Christians, troubled by modern social experimentation with new family structures, perhaps on pragmatic or economic grounds. A number of secular activists have been disturbed by attempts (in legislative proposals and the use of the current law) to restrict freedom of speech, and they have worked with Christian activists to defend free expression. Christian thinking has parallels in secular thought and secular allies in relation to a number of issues.

However, in some secular thought we see conflicts with Christian values, and it can be helpful to explore the assumptions and beliefs which underlie this kind of secular thinking. It is these assumptions and beliefs, rather than the secular thought which has common ground with Christianity, which are the principal focus of this chapter.

3.2   AUTONOMY AND TRUTH

A characteristic of some currents of secular thought is the denial that there exist any absolute values or objective truth which should govern human behaviour, except perhaps for a number of beliefs generally consistent with human autonomy. There is a positive value in a degree of human autonomy, since it reflects a fundamental feature of the human condition that Christians would recognise as free will. However, the manifestation of this free will cannot be unbounded and peaceful societies require that it is restricted by morality, culture and law. Many societies do not recognise autonomy as a primary condition of human flourishing (as in some Asian countries). The practical requirement for constraints on autonomy indicates that it should not be an overriding value in any system of political thought.

A belief in autonomy rests on the foundation that the natural inclinations of individuals are to be encouraged. This does not take account of mankind's capacity for evil as well as for good. Some human inclinations are harmful to individuals and to wider society, and therefore need to be examined against an objective standard as to what amounts to "good". There can be reluctance on the part of some secular thinkers to encourage or discourage particular forms of private behaviour, such as sexual behaviour, which are said to be private moral issues. Thus, some have campaigned successfully for the age of consent for sexual relations to be lowered and have encouraged free choice. This reluctance to restrict individual autonomy in some areas does not extend to other matters previously beyond the reach of State regulation, such as smoking, hunting and, as highlighted more recently, obesity.

The current law has permitted freedom in a number of areas of behaviour, reflecting the changes in social attitudes over the last fifty years. Developments in the law, as well as in education and the media have also contributed to those changes in attitudes. A psychologist in his sixties, quoted in Rob Parsons' book *Teenagers*,[76] reflected on the changed climate which had resulted from this, stating: "When I was a teenager it was as if I was walking down a corridor with doors on either side. The doors had labels: 'Alcohol', 'Gambling', 'Sex', 'Drugs'. But all the doors were locked. Occasionally I would hear of one of my friends who had gone through one of the doors into one of the rooms, but if that happened it was a big deal. Today's teenager walks down the same corridor, but all the doors are open — and their friends are in the rooms shouting out 'What are you doing out there? Come on in!'."[77] James McConnell, writing in *The Telegraph* about his 18-year old son, Freddie, who died from a drug overdose, warned that: "The fact is, if you've got teenage children, it is inevitable that they have taken drugs. After Freddie died, his friends opened up to me. They told me of 15 year olds selling mephedrome (also known as meow, meow or MCAT) to 13 year olds."[78]

There is an inconsistency in the thinking of those who would emphasise the necessity for State intervention in economic matters but not in areas associated with personal morality. If mankind's natural and autonomous instincts were good, intervention in economic affairs would not be necessary. Christian thought, on the other hand, takes account of what Miroslav Volf has called "the background cacophony of evil" which "permeates institutions, communities, nations, whole epochs...."[79] This describes a fundamental characteristic of the human condition and highlights the need for constraints on human behaviour, while suggesting that there may be limitations as to how far evil can be restrained by human agencies.

3.3   JOHN RAWLS

Some secular political thinkers subscribe to a utilitarian approach expressed in terms of what is good for society as a whole. The challenge for them has been to find a coherent framework to resolve the conflict between liberty (or autonomy) and the need for a framework of values and laws to embody that sense of "good". Adam Smith, the 18th century Enlightenment thinker who is best known for his economic thinking,[80] developed a number of theories surrounding morality in his book *Theory of Moral Sentiments.*[81]   Adam Smith explored the idea of the "objective bystander" or "impartial spectator" where an objective view of morality could be understood through what an impartial individual, without a personal interest in the situation, would have concluded. This has something in common with Kant who sought universal rules by reference to the logic of reciprocity.

The 20th century philosopher John Rawls developed the idea of the impartial spectator as a basis for a theory of justice.[82] He put forward a utilitarian theory of justice based upon what is objectively good for all. He believed that this would minimise disadvantage in society but preserve equality of opportunity. Rawls invited us to imagine what would be good for society from a standpoint where we disregard all our personal characteristics of race, gender, class, wealth etc. He hoped that rational people would agree in what he called an "overlapping consensus" about democratic values such as liberty, freedom of speech, assembly, conscience and personal property, but he did not offer a foundation for those values. Rawls was striving for an impartial notion of justice without a source of that justice. It is difficult to describe justice merely in terms of a mechanism for achieving it, such as a means of reaching a consensus, because that may result in different outcomes depending on the people involved. And if you were part of the people seeking to achieve consensus, you would need to have a basis for arguing that your idea of justice was worthier than the ideas of justice espoused by others.

Rawls, like Kant, assumed that human beings are rational and can view themselves objectively. But whereas Kant used the logic of universality to form a rational morality based upon the illogicality of a person prioritising his own needs above those of others, Rawls declined to form any absolute view as to what constitutes human flourishing. He was concerned that any attempt to define this would conflict with the liberty of the individual to define it for himself. This approach is inconsistent with the universality of human nature and of reason. The existence of free will and the importance of political liberty do not mean that all opinions are of equal value. They merely mean that we have the ability to make choices about them. The thinking of Rawls does not provide a basis for determining what the common good is, nor does it provide a means of resolving conflicts between opposing interests and ideas. It is still necessary to give priority to one proposition rather than to another, and to have a basis for doing so.

A concept of justice must be capable of being reflected in human behaviour or implemented by law. If it is to be coherent, it will need to reflect some substantive principles. Rawls was right to acknowledge that in practice there are a variety of competing world views which influence the way people think about fundamental issues, such as justice and freedom, and that these need to be respected in a free society. But the issue as to how we handle disagreements in a free society should not be confused with a relativism about the content of the matters about which people disagree. Freedom of thought is good, but also a means to an end, not the end itself. The free choices that people make are a precarious foundation for a theory of justice and more is required. The Harvard University professor and Reith lecturer Michael Sandel recognised this when he said that,

"It's not possible to decide these big questions of policy, law, justice and rights without presupposing some account of the good life."

Smith's theory of an "objective bystander" and Rawls' "veil of ignorance" assume a degree of rational consensus which is not borne out by the lessons of history or our present experience. People with different world views and different backgrounds of loyalty (to family, community or country) may not agree. The result can be competition or conflict. Ideas of justice from different cultural and political traditions may have radically different implications. Rawls hoped that "a fair system of cooperation" between free and equal citizens would emerge. He was optimistic that people could in practice be guided by a criterion of reciprocity derived from objectivity, but he did not hold reciprocity to be a categorical imperative in the manner of Kant. Nor did he acknowledge this reciprocity as an eternal moral rule, as in the teachings of Jesus Christ. The idea of the objective spectator may appear to be a plausible one, but human imperfection prevents us from acquiring Thomas Nagel's "view from nowhere". For Christians, only God has a truly objective and comprehensive perspective, and some of this is communicated to humankind in the Bible and to those who seek God's wisdom.

3.4   MORAL VALUES ARE DIFFICULT FOR PEOPLE

Moral values are personally challenging. For some secular thinkers, any systems of thought that suggest absolute and objective values in personal behaviour, rather than personal choice, can be regarded as prejudice. If these beliefs are associated with metaphysical religious belief, they can also be called irrational. It is understandable why absolute moral values, such as those found in Christian thinking, are so challenging for many people. There can be a profound tension between human desires and obligations.

The narrative of the Bible illustrates the attempt by human beings to be independent of God and free of moral constraints, and it is a part of human nature to want this freedom. Moral autonomy may appear to be attractive, but it allows the potential for the outworking of imperfection (and what Christians would call evil) in human beings, though in practice people may still be constrained by the disapproval of others.

3.5   THE CHALLENGES OF RELATIVISM

Some of the antipathy on the part of secular thinkers to Christian values may be traced back to some 18th century philosophers who blamed religion for wars, coercion and violence. The 19th century French philosopher Auguste Compte, and more recently the contemporary English writer Alain de Botton, have proposed a universal religion of humanity based upon reason, but without doctrinal belief, in the hope that this may unite people who have different beliefs.[83] Apart from the fact that the beliefs may be inconsistent, if no absolute truth resides in any of the beliefs, a commitment to rationality is merely one belief amongst many and its meaning (if there is any) is only conferred by society. Richard Rorty's saying that "truth is what your peers will let you get away with"[84] may not have been wholly serious, but it expresses a truth about the relativism of post-modernism. When post-modernists say that objective moral reality does not exist, they echo the beliefs of logical positivist philosophers of the mid 20th century. Post-modernist thinking suggests that perceptions of reality differ and, if there is no creator and no logic in creation, there is no ground for one belief being superior to another.

A feature of some post-modern thought is that the world is simply not intelligible and that it is therefore necessary for human beings to create their own meaning. (The notion that objective truth is impossible is an old one which dates back to classical times and the school of sceptic philosophers, for instance Pyrrho of Elis.) However, even on the assumption that meaning is created by human beings in their communities, Christian belief is often not accorded a valid place in the pantheon of possible beliefs, even though its meaning is conferred (in the secular way of thinking) by the Christian community.

Post-modernist thinkers may attack the belief that objective truth exists and that individuals are capable of ascertaining it on the grounds that it necessarily implies intellectual pride. This would appear to confuse the nature of a belief with the attitude of those holding it and is an example of the *ad hominen* argument, which is a logical fallacy. In any event, the reverse is true. The existence of objective truth requires humility because it exists in fact. It is discovered, not created, by those who hold to it. Furthermore, Christian belief requires humility because both mankind's reason and ability to follow that truth and to do right are imperfect. Christians should have a dependence upon God as well as a confidence in him.

3.6   ELITES

One of the features of some intellectual secular thinking is that it can be the preserve of an elite which is remote from ordinary people. For example, most people do not relate to a relativistic way of thinking where there are no moral absolutes. The average person knows that lying is generally wrong and cannot understand intellectuals who say that this is merely a matter of individual choice or collective societal preference. Nor does the concept of individual moral autonomy provide a compelling vision of a better society.

Some people believe that secular thinking which holds that there are no moral absolutes is promoted by an elite which has concluded that, where there are no moral constraints, individuals and society will be weakened. The logic is that, devoid of constraints, people will be less able to resist the encroachments of the State and will become dependent upon it, and this dependency will in turn increase the power of the State and the elites in charge.

This may not be the intention, but it can be a consequence of moral relativism. In totalitarian states, the traditional structures of society, which are capable of resisting the power of the State, are weakened. Aldous Huxley's *Brave New World* illustrated the relationship between personal licence and the power of the State. Hannah Arendt, writing in the 1950s, recognised the breakdown of communal structures and a weakened society as a precondition of totalitarianism: "What prepares men for totalitarian domination in the non-totalitarian world is the fact that loneliness, once a borderline experience usually suffered in certain marginal social conditions like old age, has become an everyday experience of the ever-growing masses of our century."[85]

Some liberal left thinking can be traced back to pre-Stalinist Communist ideology. Following the Russian Revolution, the State sought to undermine the organic structures of society, particularly the family and the traditional values associated with it. It took control of schools, separated children from their parents and gave them value-free sex education, and encouraged abortion. In 1920s Russia a range of sexual activities were deemed to be natural and good. The collapse of the family led to social instability and increases in crime. When Stalin came to power, he restored more traditional values. Abortion and divorce were made more difficult and the liberalisation in relation to sexual activities reversed. From the 1960s, the new left in Western countries adopted the original social agenda of Marxism with considerable success under the auspices of such concepts as freedom, diversity, tolerance and 'safe' sex which denied a traditional moral framework. The homosexual rights movement has been particularly successful in undermining the biological and natural distinctions between the sexes in the promotion of same-sex marriage and homosexual adoption of children. It is a feature of totalitarian regimes that enemies of the State are labelled and abused without a rational examination of their opinions. The naming of those who oppose a liberal left agenda in relation to sexual ethics as "bigots", "fascists" or "homophobes" may be perceived to have something in common with this phenomenon.

3.7 DIVERSITY AND TOLERANCE

While tolerance within appropriate limits may be a valuable principle to enable people to coexist peacefully in society, for the State to encourage diversity of belief and practice as an end in itself is problematic both in theory and in practice. It assumes that the State both can and ought to be neutral in relation to different belief systems. Whilst a tolerant society is desirable in the sense that freedom of expression and debate ought to be encouraged, the notion of diversity for its own sake, and not just as a means to an end, suggests that there are no absolutes and no standards against which rules and behaviour can be judged. If all beliefs are equally valid, none can be prioritised in public policy. Those who regard diversity of belief as an end in itself may view any absolute belief as a threat to cohesion and therefore undesirable before its merits or demerits have been examined.

Equality of beliefs is a meaningless idea unless the beliefs themselves have no meaning. Those advocating a diversity agenda may believe that they themselves are neutral, whereas in fact they represent a particular belief system. The tendency to regard widely differing beliefs as equal may reflect a concern that, if qualitative differences between beliefs were to be acknowledged, it might lead government to impose one belief and restrict the expression of another. But although governments need to make choices about policy and these may be more or less consistent with different belief systems, the State should not impose belief or unnecessarily restrict the liberty of the individual to manifest a belief. In Christian thinking, while Christian beliefs may be taught and encouraged, they can never be imposed.

It is understandable that people are reluctant to stand in judgment upon belief systems. But we should not elevate this into a philosophical principle by saying that it is impossible. Richard Rorty has said that even rationality cannot float free of the educational and institutional patterns of the day. This conclusion follows logically from the assumption that there are no absolute values, since rationality is one of those values.

Christians have some sympathy with a reluctance to stand in judgment since, although they have firm beliefs which are inconsistent with the beliefs of others, only God is the judge over those people. Christians also acknowledge the flawed nature of human reasoning and the capacity for this to be coloured by deception and self-serving aims. However, in Christian thinking, human imperfection does not point to an equal value for all beliefs or to the impossibility of belief in any absolute values, but to a need to seek the truth in God's revelation to mankind. Some secular modernists who reject absolute values may nevertheless aspire to stand outside history and society and come to an absolute judgement on moral issues. However, they are unable to do so without a framework of values, and this requires knowledge as to the source of those values.

3.8   DIVERSITY CAN DIVIDE

Those seeking to understand the motives of those who promote diversity as a principle have noticed that diversity categorises people into groups and regards these as homogenous. Miroslav Volf focuses upon the importance of the identity of people as members of ethnic and religious communities and is aware that these influences can shape thinking on issues of justice.[86] While an understanding of backgrounds can enhance self-understanding, it may be unwise to overemphasise this perspective. A focus on the importance of community identity and categorising people by reference to their group or culture can, as Savitri Hensman has pointed out in *The Guardian*, lead to the most powerful being treated as the most representative. It can also militate against personal relationships across cultural, ethnic and religious groups. As she says, "Personal reconciliation...can... be hindered by an emphasis on collective identities".[87]

Government and regulatory surveys have invited regulated professionals to disclose their ethnic origins, religion and sexual orientation as if these were defining characteristics, and the requirement for these surveys was reinforced by the Equality Act 2010. While some people may accept this, an Irish person or a homosexual person may resent their categorisation by the State into a separate class of persons on the basis of what may be, for them, an unimportant characteristic which is not relevant in most situations. The tendency to class individuals having certain characteristics into arbitrary so-called "communities", where none exist, enables people to be more easily manipulated, even if this may not have been the original intention. These "groups" can be spoken to as entities and accorded minority rights. Political parties supporting the rights of those groups may be rewarded at the ballot box by the beneficiaries of those rights. Those who promote diversity tend to reject individuality in favour of a series of collective cultures that trump the rights of the individual and discourage individuals from assessing the values of their culture against absolute values. In some cases, the cultural values may be oppressive and encourage unequal treatment. Further, in the absence of any absolute values, it is these cultures and so called "communities" that confer meaning and legitimacy, even though their respective beliefs may be mutually inconsistent. Perhaps fortunately, the commercial world has taken the concept of "community" beyond parody. An issue of *Private Eye* quoted references in publicity to the "lighting community", the "signalling community" and the "armoured vehicle community".

3.9 COMPETITION FOR INFLUENCE

It has been said that each system of government has a guiding principle (what Plato would call a "virtue") — that of a monarchy, loyalty — that of a military dictatorship, honour — that of a bureaucratic dictatorship, efficiency — and that of a socialist system, fraternity. A philosophical belief in diversity connects with the view that there are no guiding principles because there are no absolutes. The effect is that the values of society are determined by a competition for influence. There can be no rational debate about what beliefs are good for society, since there are no moral or philosophical absolutes by which to judge them and it may be thought discriminatory to do so. The difficulty with this approach is that, while the State should allow freedom of conscience, its laws are bound to reflect some belief system. The belief that there are no absolute values is itself a belief system, though it is self-contradictory and possibly meaningless to believe in something that you do not think is objectively true. A free market of ideas reflects the free will that individuals have been given. However, for choice to mean something, there needs to be an understanding that there are absolute values against which choices can be judged, even though people may disagree about the values.

Secular liberal democracy rightly values the principle of consent. It can nevertheless produce interest groups, for instance social, industrial and intellectual, that compete for power. When power is achieved, it brings with it the ability to influence future generations through law, the media and education. While this may be inevitable, politics can be a playing field where the winning side is able to change the rules and entrench its influence. Changes in culture and society resulting from this influence may be slow or may be swift. Despite twenty years of ANC rule in South Africa, much of the wealth of the country remains in the hands of the white elite and most of the black population remains impoverished. In other cases, such as the UK in the 1960s, change can be very rapid as Callum Brown, a secular sociologist, has chronicled in his book *The Death of Christian Britain*.[88] The re-education of the German consciousness after the Second World War is acknowledged to have been similarly rapid, though entirely welcome.

The socially conservative commentator Peter Hitchens has depicted a current liberal consensus in this country as being a "new permanent government of Britain" promoting left-wing social values. One aspect of this consensus is the use of words by government and the media to import new values. For example, "unmarried mothers" are now referred to as "single parent families". Although this change reflects the fact that there are unmarried couples with children, it also equates unmarried single parenthood (which is likely to have been chosen) with divorced parenting (which may be involuntary), as if there were no difference. The increased acceptability of unmarried mothers has been reflected in government welfare over the past decades, with an increase in the State subsidy to fatherless families and an increase in the number of children suffering the poor outcomes associated with single parent families. (Issues surrounding family policy are discussed in Chapter 14.)

The absence of a commonly accepted framework of public truth, whether or not reflecting a Christian outlook, increases the competition between interest groups, each seeking to promote their own interests or agendas by means of law and policy. In practice, those interest groups that are most vocal or most influential in the media can disproportionately influence government policy. Some secular thought tends to reject authority, preferring the autonomy of individuals. Inevitably these autonomies clash, but secular thinking provides no framework of authority to decide the resulting issues. Human rights theory provides a framework of objectives but it contains inbuilt contradictions, since there is no means of determining what the hierarchy of rights should be. For example, if there is no belief that human beings have an intrinsic value under God, aspects of humanity that should be protected as a priority, such as the right to life or freedom of expression, can be disregarded in favour of other so-called rights, such as non-discrimination. These issues are discussed further in Chapter 7.

3.10   ARBITRATING DIVERSITY

Those who believe in diversity as an end in itself may hope that concepts such as justice or human rights can regulate the conflicts that ensue. The concept of human rights rightly recognises the difficulty in separating private and public identities and acknowledges the universality of moral rules. There is therefore an inherent contradiction between the basis of human rights (which elevates absolute values above personal preference) and a belief in diversity as an end in itself. Diversity requires not only the coexistence of conflicting values, but the equal recognition of those values in laws and society. But in practice it is necessary to accord to some human rights a priority over others.

The definitions commonly given to concepts such as justice and human rights are neither self-evident nor free-standing. They can reflect a value system that informs decisions as to which human rights, or particular expressions of them, are to be given precedence over others. Lord Justice Laws illustrated this way of thinking in his judgment in the *McFarlane* case.[89] He emphasised that no belief system should have priority over another, while at the same time making a choice between two positions based on different belief systems, thus prioritising one over the other (in this case the secular one over the Christian). To encourage all belief systems equally would, even if it were possible, be an abdication of the responsibilities of government. Neutrality is impossible. In practice, liberal secular humanism, which is in many ways as much a matter of faith as Christian belief, is promoted in schools and reflected in legal judgments. The State has determined that some values are bad for society and that others are good. Secular thought can also assume that human beings have no need for a religious dimension. It can also imply that all religions are necessarily irrational and that, as a result, only secular knowledge should define the terms of the debate.

Secular thought may indicate that, in order for people to live together in a society, it is necessary either to accord equal value to all belief systems (even if they are mutually incompatible) or to ascribe no value to any of them. But if all religions are equally irrational, there are no grounds on which to assess their benefits and shortcomings. Tolerance is an admirable aspiration for individuals and for society, but tolerance should not be confused with lack of belief. True tolerance recognises the differences between beliefs and requires understanding and respect for those with whom there are disagreements, together with a willingness to engage in rational discussion with grace and generosity of spirit.

Some current philosophy focuses on the procedural aspects of equality and justice, and explores how diverse viewpoints are to be managed in society. However, it cannot resolve some of the more fundamental questions, such as the ultimate source of moral authority. If we differ about the nature of the good for society, we are likely to differ about the rights and concepts of justice that underpin the social order. Without underlying principles and values, the operation of a system of justice cannot ensure the impartial arbitration of disputes. Equalities and freedoms inevitably conflict. For example, equality of opportunity is likely to lead to inequality of outcome. Freedoms can be incompatible because people have different aspirations and they seek to exercise those freedoms in ways that conflict with the freedoms of others. My privacy may be your secrecy, and vice versa. Individuals are imperfect and often self-interested. We cannot all have everything we want, even if that were desirable. Conflict in society is inevitable and it must be resolved on the basis of rational principle.

Secular values cannot form the basis of a neutral arbitration between diverse values, which has been described as "procedural secularism". This neutrality may seem plausible, but objectivity requires a concept of absolute truth. That truth may be found in theological concepts, or it may not be found there, but a supposed neutrality between different belief systems which seeks a position of objectivity necessarily sets itself up as higher than the beliefs which it arbitrates. This neutrality inevitably assumes a position of truth and that purported truth must be invested with some values. For this reason procedural secularism can never be neutral. Procedural secularism assumes that secular values will be the basis for managing the different views and is therefore bound to be "programmatic". This means that the values of secularism influence people in a particular direction of belief or lack of belief, whether or not this is the intention. This should not surprise us. Any system of regulation cannot fail to reflect some values and these are bound to mean something.

3.11 VALUE-FREE LAWS AND THE GENERAL WILL

The legal positivist theory that the laws governing society are in theory, as well as in practice, no more than a reflection of the will of the ruler and that there are no values by which they are to be judged, may to some extent reflect reality, but not one to which we should aspire. The theory can imply that whatever the State requires of individuals must be done, because there are no higher values and there is no higher authority which can overrule a law that transgresses a moral principle. The notion of the positive law of the State as the ultimate authority which must be obeyed in all circumstances is a characteristic of totalitarianism. During the Nüremberg trials, Rudolf Höss, the commandant of Auschwitz, was asked whether he ever considered disobeying Himmler's orders regarding the so-called "Final Solution". "No," replied Höss, "from our entire training, the thought of refusing an order just didn't enter one's head".[90]

The theory that law should only be a reflection of the "general will" as put forward by Rousseau, although seemingly attractive, is no less problematic. Who is to determine the "general will" and what if the body whose will is enacted reflects the worst of human nature? In any event, any individual or group aspiring to give effect to the "general will" will inevitably need guidelines and boundaries. What these should be takes us back to the question as to what is good for people and to the question posed by moral philosophers down the ages (and the title of a book by Charles Colson, the former Watergate attorney and Christian writer), *How Now Shall We Live?*

3.12   CONCLUSION

Any system of government and its laws must reflect some view of human flourishing and what behaviour a society or its rulers deem to be acceptable. Even for those for whom there are no moral absolutes, society must be regulated by laws and social norms which mirror approval or disapproval of attitudes and actions. Secular liberalism has sought in vain for a plausible source of authority, but can only offer the several and often contradictory meanings conferred by diverse cultural and intellectual traditions.

The issue as to what behaviour should be allowed in a free society must inevitably be addressed in the context of a belief in absolute values, since there are inherent contradictions in relativistic thinking. People may have freedom of belief but, for that freedom to mean something, they need to be able to live out that belief in society. Questions surrounding the expression of belief are discussed in Chapters 7 and 15.

4
NATURAL LAW

4.1 OUR CONFUSING WORLD

Whilst laws should both reflect shared values and claim the allegiance of society in the source of their authority and their outcomes, how are we as citizens, to judge what laws are good, and why should rulers obey laws rather than invent them? The ancient question mentioned in Chapter 2 *"Quis custodiet ipsos custodes?"* raises the issue as to whether there is higher law to which rulers are accountable, both for the formulation and for the enforcement of their laws.

The sum of all the inventions of the scientific age has resulted in what is, to many, a puzzling and mysterious society. As its parts become more ingenious and minutely calibrated, the whole becomes less easy to understand and control. The dream of reason has indeed produced monsters, whether these be the atom bomb, credit derivatives or the mass media society with its scope for manipulation and demagoguery. The society enabled by technology has reduced much skilled manual labour to automation and has distanced people from the processes that affect their lives. Functional rationality in the means of mass production has separated many people from the creative processes of work. Weber's theory of "bureaucratic rationalisation" characterised by the increasing power of the State staffed by efficient technocrats was over-optimistic to the extent that the modern State can be both oppressive and inefficient. However, complex as reality now is, human nature is surprisingly constant and topical issues are frequently similar to those in the past. Commentators refer to the credit crunch of 1294 and the different policies adopted by France and England at that time, which find echoes in the policies of governments in our time. Philip Allott reflected on the universality of human nature which is a foundation of political theory when he said that, "The unity of the human condition, of human nature transcends the diversity of socially organised ideas."[91]

4.2   NATURAL ORDER AND NATURAL LAW

It is not the place of this book to rehearse the arguments for and against evolution by chance and intelligent design but, in whatever way reality came to be as we now experience it, we may struggle to escape the conclusion that there is order in the universe and in our perception of it. Rationality presupposes a consistent framework of reality. We are able to reason about the world both because we are rational creatures and because there is order in it and we are capable of discerning this order. The world is intelligible because it is intelligent. We see this order in art, literature and music. Paradoxically, the apparent meaninglessness of some modern expressions of art and music illustrates this point. Even where there is no apparent idea or meaning, our natural instincts are to seek them in the artistic objects, whether or not any meaning was intended by the artist. In our appreciation of art, as in life, we look to make sense of our experience and to express rational thoughts about it.

If there is a natural order in the world, it is plausible to extrapolate from the existence of a mathematical, physical or an artistic order to a moral order. Theists would say that this represents the character of the Creator, while others may perceive that moral laws can be inferred from the nature of reality and its internal order. The concept of natural law as expressed by Cicero, and later by many other thinkers, is that laws follow from the nature of the world as it has been created. As Cicero puts it, it is "right reason in agreement with nature; it is of universal application, unchanging and everlasting….It is a sin to try to alter this law."[92] Cicero recognised that the source of the natural law lies beyond the material world: "according to the best authorities, law was not thought up by the intelligence of human beings, nor is it some kind of resolution passed by communities, but rather an eternal force which rules the world by the wisdom of its commands and prohibitions. In their judgement, that original and final law is the intelligence of God, who ordains or forbids everything by reason."[93] The concept of natural law is based upon reason and is consistent with Philip Allott's perception that rationality is itself a moral category.[94]

For Thomas Aquinas, natural law had both a moral and a theological dimension: "As though the light of natural reason, by which we discern good from evil, and which is the natural law, were nothing else than the impression of the divine light in us."[95] For Aquinas, human laws may or may not be a reflection of the natural law: "...Every human law has just so much of the nature of law as is derived from the law of nature. But if in any point it deflects from the law of nature, it is no longer a law, but a perversion of law."[96] Aquinas' theory of natural law was founded upon the existence of a rational Creator: "Since then, the eternal law is the plan of government in the supreme governor, all schemes of government in those who direct as subordinates must derive from the eternal law. Consequently, all laws, so far as they accord with right reason, derive from the eternal law."[97]

For Aquinas there were three types of natural law — an inclination to self-preservation, an instinct to live in relationship and an instinct to do good in a rational way. Some Christian thinkers, such as Karl Barth, have suggested that human imperfection is so all-encompassing that there is no truth outside theological revelation. As a result Barth rejected the idea of natural law. This thinking is over-pessimistic. While the effects of human sin are far-reaching, the Bible recognises that human beings have been given the gifts of reason and conscience which enable them to discern right from wrong, though they may struggle both to know and to do the right.

Gratian, in a collection of canon law compiled in the twelfth century, described natural law as follows: "Natural law is common to all nations because it exists everywhere through natural instinct, not because of any enactment. For example, the union of men and women, the succession and rearing of children, the common possession of all things, the identical liberty of all, or the acquisition of things that are taken from the heavens, earth, or sea, as well as the return of a thing deposited or of money entrusted to one, and the repelling of violence by force. This, and anything similar, is never regarded as unjust, but is held to be natural and equitable."[98]

When the American founders held some truths to be "self-evident," they were pointing to the fact that certain primary truths are necessary to other matters that are commonly accepted. C.S. Lewis described the law of nature as intuitive: "This law was called the Law of Nature, because people thought that everyone knew it by nature and did not need to be taught it."[99]

4.3   THE RECIPROCAL BASIS OF A MORAL LAW

The concept of virtue as a general quality which can be applied to particular cases requires a degree of universalism and consistency in its application. Otherwise, we would not know what it means to be virtuous since there would be no common characteristics that are shared by a number of actions and that are necessary for us to understand what the concept means. Aristotle reminds us that a concept is not the same as its definition, but the manifestations of a concept must nevertheless correspond to a common meaning. Natural law recognises this type of generality in a more extensive system of morality and perceptions about people in society. We shall see that there are some limitations in devising this moral system only from human nature as we observe it in the past and in the present. Human nature is mixed and some human inclinations are destructive. But the universality of human nature has proved an enduring basis for ethical values, which is consistent with much secular as well as Christian thought.

In Christian thinking, the moral order derives from a moral Creator. This is consistent with the concept of a moral law which reflects a universal reciprocity. This reciprocity, which finds an echo in the philosophy of Immanuel Kant, is at the heart of Jesus' teaching: "Do to others as you would have them do to you."[100] Thus, what applies to your treatment of me also applies to my treatment of you. There are no exceptions and no privileges. This is a fundamental characteristic of the nature of law, since law must be impartially and equally applied to everyone.

Kant took up the theme of the necessity of consistency as a basis for the moral order. A moral rule is one which we understand should be applied equally to our actions and those of others: "Act only on that maxim through which you can at the same time will that it should become a universal law".[101] Kant gives the example of a person who acts only out of self-love as a basis for a decision to commit suicide and concludes that this can never be a universal law of nature since life is a condition of collective existence. He also gives the example of a person who borrows and promises to repay money he knows he cannot repay. If promises were as a rule broken, then they would not be promises.[102] Another example given by Kant is that of a person who acts selfishly. Kant's view is that it cannot be a general rule for a person to act selfishly because, if the selfish behaviour were generally replicated, it would be against that person's self interest. Michel Houellebecq describes the perception of timeless morality by his central character: "...Kant only served to confirm what he already knew: that perfect morality is unique and universal. Nothing is added to it and nothing changes in the course of time. It is not dependent upon history, economics, sociology or culture; it is not dependent upon anything. Not determined, it determines. Not conditioned, it conditions. It is, in other words, absolute."[103]

Kant, in contrast to Aristotle and Christian thought, did not believe in the value of moral emotions and the need for education in them. Nor did he believe that compassionate actions derived from emotion were an indication of true goodness. Instead, he believed that there was a motivation for performing self-evident moral principles which he called "duty". That sense of duty was derived from a reasoned understanding of the logic of reciprocal moral obligations. He explained it in this way: "… An action done from duty must wholly exclude the influence of inclination … But what sort of a law can that be, the conception of which must determine the will, even without paying any regard to the effect expected from it? … As I have deprived the will of every impulse which could arise to it from obedience to any law, there remains nothing but the universal conformity of its actions to law in general, which alone is to serve the will as a principle, i.e. I am never to act otherwise than so that I could not also will that my maxim should become a universal law".[104] This concentration upon the importance of the will echoes the Stoic philosophers, for instance Epictetus who said that, "The nature and essence of the good is in a certain disposition of the will."[105] It also reflects the teaching of Jesus that evil comes out of the heart (see Matthew 15:19).

Kant took the universality of human nature as the ground of ethics. I am no different from other people. If this is so, it is illogical for me to prioritise my own wants above those of others. This reflects the teaching of Jesus who requires us to love our neighbour as ourselves. Kant's rational reciprocity, Adam Smith's impartial spectator and Rawls' objective justice (see paragraph 3.3 above) invite us to consider a rational basis for morality based upon consistency. If I admit that pain is bad for me, there is an argument that I cannot logically deny that it is bad for you. If all human beings are equal, then it may follow that the concerns of others should be of concern to me.

While a symmetry derived from universality is consistent with a duty to behave in a particular way and may even suggest it, the logic of reciprocity is not conclusive of that duty. If there is no purposeful created order and the universality of human nature is mere chance, why should there be a duty not to be selfish? People may have common characteristics but, if this is only a consequence of a random process, there is no reason to regard this as relevant to behaviour. In Christian thinking, the justification for reciprocity lies in the heart of the creative purposes of God, for it is God who has created all people equal in essential nature and dignity. For the Christian, the duty to love the neighbour derives from a transcendent law that reflects truths about the purposes of human life on earth and which has been articulated in the instructions for living that God has given.

4.4 THE LIMITATIONS OF REASON AND BELIEF IN GOD

We reflected in Chapter 1 that there are limits to reason and the human mind. We may also perceive that not everything can be explained by deductive reasoning. For Plato, the idea of goodness was a universal metaphysical value which existed irrespective of its manifestation in the material world. Other thinkers have sought to provide a theory of everything connecting matter and metaphysics. Spinoza, writing in the 17th century, believed that it was possible to construct ethical conclusions by logical deduction from self-evident premises. He attempted to deduce the existence of one unifying substance of God, which he equated with nature, and he denied the authenticity of the Bible and rejected belief in a Christian God. Leibniz took a different approach and concluded that there were an infinite number of substances that were held together by a pre-existing harmony, which he attributed to God. Kant, on the other hand, thought that it was wrong to believe that it was possible to discover the ultimate nature of reality by reason alone. An extreme extrapolation of this view was exemplified by the conclusion of J. M. E. McTaggart (a 20th century philosopher) in *The Unreality of Time* that, because human conceptions of time contain insuperable contradictions, it must be unreal. This might suggest that because we cannot understand something it does not exist.

But we would be wrong to define rationality solely by reference to what human beings can understand. We should know that there are things which we cannot understand. To limit the concept of rationality to the understanding of human beings could be regarded as what the ancient Greeks described as *hubris*, a manifestation of human pride. A Christian perspective is that we live within time and therefore we cannot completely understand things outside time. It is doubtful that we can ever know how we will experience eternity. But if God is the Creator, he must be outside time because he created everything, including time (see Psalm 139: 4-6). And, if God is outside time, he can be omniscient and his character cannot change. He must also be the arbiter of moral standards because he created them.

Kant believed that there had to be what he called "*a priori*" (necessary to other propositions) and "*synthetic*" (not demonstrable) truths because (as the philosopher A.J. Ayer put it)[106] their existence was "necessary for the world to become an object of our experience",[107] thus making the assumption that experience is in fact real. Reflecting on the limitations of rational philosophy and illustrating the need for some fundamental assumptions, Ayer commented that, "The more factual content a deductive system appears to have, the greater the likelihood that factual assumptions are concealed in the axioms or definitions".[108] Mathematics requires assumptions about the existence of both space and time and these "*a priori*" propositions point to a reality beyond the material and observable. The notion that there has to be some sort of *a priori* knowledge is found in Plato's dialogue *Meno*. Once a geometrical problem is explained, it is understood by a person without prior knowledge. Plato suggested that mathematical truths, and the rationality that explains them, exist outside the experience of individuals. Plato applied this to moral knowledge which he thought was pre-existing and could therefore be discovered. (He doubted, however, that the teaching of moral knowledge would be effective to change character and in *The Republic* he favoured rule by people of wisdom and virtue rather than democracy.)

Kant held that things in themselves exist independently of our perception of them, and this can lead to scepticism about our ability to perceive things as they truly are. This is consistent with the Christian perception that in this world we cannot understand the whole of reality. Christian thinking is that perceptions can be flawed and the scope of logic is limited. Paradoxically, the perception that the ladders of deduction or induction from observation can only take us some distance in the direction of a belief in God is reasonable. If the ideas connected with God were merely reflections of our common sense view of the world as we experience it, a specific belief in the existence of God would be adding little to our perception of reality. We would not be making any statements about existence beyond what we already know. The 17th century theologian Samuel Rutherford reflected upon the imperfection of mankind as a reason for revelation from God. He believed that "scripture's arguments may be drawn out of the school of nature" but that our ability to understand the truth from it is limited: "Had man's conscience been a faithful register, there should have been no need of a written bible".[109]

A belief in a natural law that is founded upon a belief in God explains reality, but does not merely reflect it. As Kant perceived, we need some "*a priori*" assumptions against which we can then test reality as we perceive it. Adam Smith stated that: "The doctrines of revelation coincide ....with those original anticipations of nature".[110] God's revelation, as we shall explore further in this chapter and Chapter 5, provides a framework which makes sense of the world as we encounter it, apart from any justification based upon the historical nature of the Christian faith.

Natural law, as the description of an aspect of a created universe, is consistent with a belief in God and reason. Although some philosophers have concluded that either we infer natural law from our surroundings or we decide upon it for ourselves, the existence of a natural law (as Aquinas argued) suggests a lawgiver. The existence of a law giver means that there is logic and order in the universe — both physical and moral — and that creation is not a matter of random chance and selfish genes. Science is still struggling to explain a designed universe without a designer. Harvard geneticist, Richard Lewontin, (quoted by Melanie Phillips) has admitted that some scientists "take the side of science in spite of the patent absurdity of some of its constructs" because "they cannot allow a divine foot in the door".[111] Instinctively we sense that we live in a rational universe and the reverse is difficult to imagine. And, if absolute truth exists, it needs to be consistent with what is rational.

4.5   THE ARGUMENT FROM DESIGN

A. J. Ayer rejected the "argument from design" as an indication of the existence of God. This is the notion that there is a design in the universe and that there must therefore be a designer. Ayer asks us to think of the universe as a play with an author, since he cannot attach any meaning to the idea that a creator might exist outside time, and continues: "But now the question arises whether the character of the world as we know it gives any support to these analogies. The fact that regularities are detectable in it is not sufficient, for we have seen that no describable world can fail to exhibit some regularity. Neither is it sufficient that some processes within it are goal-directed, for the fact that ends are pursued and sometimes attained within a system is not proof that the system as a whole is directed towards any end. What needs to be shown is that the entire universe presents the appearance of a teleological system."[112]

A difficulty with Ayer's argument, and one perhaps for Christians also to consider, is that this universe is the only one we have — there is no "control universe" in the experiment. We cannot compare this universe with other universes which might or might not exhibit the greater degree of evident purpose which would satisfy Ayer. That there is a significant degree of order and logic in the universe is observable and Christian thought holds that this could not have occurred by chance. Christians cannot prove that what they believe constitutes the teleology that Ayer was looking for, although their belief does provide a framework of meaning for existence and confers purpose upon human lives on earth.

4.6   THE COHERENCE THEORY OF TRUTH

Closely connected with the theory of natural law is the coherence theory of truth. This theory is based on the assumption that rationality exists and invites us to evaluate propositions on the basis of whether they are consistent with one another. It suggests that the consistency and coherence of phenomena are themselves indications of truth. The coherence theory of truth has its limitations. Just because things fit together does not mean that they are necessarily true. And some philosophers, in common with Christian theologians, would argue that we can describe phenomena without relating them to other phenomena because they accept that there is an objective framework of reality outside the collection of objects that they are describing. As Plato perceived, there exists a world which is independent of representations of it, so the aim should be to describe the world as it is (though this may not always be achievable), not just to relate aspects of it to each other.

Nevertheless, there are difficulties in describing phenomena without a consistent and rational framework and this assumes that it is possible to relate phenomena to each other. Statements and ideas which are consistent with each other are more likely to be true than those which are mutually inconsistent. Otherwise the world would not be rational. It should therefore be possible to consider whether one set of ideas better explains what we perceive as reality than another set of ideas. Paul Dirac (incidentally, an atheist) who won the Nobel Prize in 1933 jointly with Erwin Schrödinger for their work on quantum physics, is credited with the view that if an equation was not beautiful, he would choose to disregard it.

Renford Bambrough, writing in a vein contrary to the intellectual climate of the 1960s which he inhabited, gave an interesting perspective on the coherence theory of truth. He reflected that, "Philosophers who are so prompt and so perfunctory with their refutations of the coherence theory of truth might usefully reflect on the notorious difficulty of sustained, continuous and consistent lying. No doubt it is theoretically possible to produce an account that the world is both false and internally coherent but there is theoretical significance in the enormous practical difficulty and indeed impossibility of doing so."[113] This idea of coherence is fundamental to a justification of natural law. The coherence theory of truth accords with Kant's theory of universal and consistent moral laws of action. We have seen that these reflect Christian teaching that we should treat others as we ourselves would wish to be treated. The coherence theory of truth is also in harmony with Aquinas' Christian perspective that moral laws exist as part of the created order and that human beings have been given reason by God in order to understand the rationality of those moral laws.

We can and therefore should debate whether moral notions are compatible with human nature, whether they are logical and whether they are consistent with each other. If we conclude that they are, then we should acknowledge that they may also be objectively true. And if we concede that there is such logic and consistency, we should not be reticent in applying it in individual cases. So, for example, we may be discussing the point from which the life of an unborn child should be protected, for instance, from conception, or from fourteen days after conception, or when the child is capable of surviving outside the womb. Logical consistency would indicate that it can make no sense to draw the line when physical birth actually occurs, since that is merely an accident of positioning and no essential characteristics have changed. It would therefore follow that to allow abortion in the case of disabled children up to the time of birth must be logically and therefore morally wrong, unless one takes the view that it is right to kill disabled babies after birth, for which a separate justification is required. The view that if an unborn child is wanted, it is thought of as a "child" but, if it is not wanted and is aborted, it is referred to as an unwanted "foetus", is inconsistent. It is an offence against logic as well as, for many people, an offence against humanity.

4.7   NATURAL LAW AND UTILITARIAN THINKING

Inherent in a theory of natural law is a notion that individuals and societies are disadvantaged by transgressing it — in that things will not go well for them — quite apart from whether they are punished by a temporal power. To this extent, there is common ground with utilitarianism. As Christopher Coker explains in the context of warfare (though the reasoning extends more widely), there is a pragmatic utility in moral laws: "We have evolved rules for a reason: they work, they help limit war. As a species we are rule bound; rules do not constrain our freedom, they make it possible to be free. Laws make life simpler and can be liberating for that reason."[114] Nevertheless, natural law theory differs from utilitarian thinking in that the focus of utilitarian philosophy is on the consequences of actions rather than general principles which evaluate the character or nature of an action. The basis of natural law theory is different from utilitarian theory in that natural law proposes unchanging principles, not ones which can be adapted depending upon the circumstances. Natural law reflects the way things are within the consistent framework of a designed system. The idea is that natural laws are as internally necessary to the structures of reality as the laws of mathematics, the harmonies in music or the logic of language.

Reflecting on the differences between the two idea systems of natural law and utilitarianism, it can be said that Aristotle and Cicero rejected utilitarianism before it was formulated by Jeremy Bentham. Cicero said that some acts are either so repulsive or so wicked that a wise man would not commit them, even to save his country. In other words, irrespective of the ends which an action might achieve, if the means by which the end is achieved (in terms of the nature of the action) is unacceptable, then the action should not be countenanced. Cicero gave as examples Themistocles' plan to set fire to the Spartan fleet when in harbour and the promise of a deserter to poison King Pyrrhus. An acquaintance of the French revolutionary Robespierre echoed the same thought at a time when people were being summarily tried and executed by the guillotine: "In a free country he is a traitor if he employs a means contrary to liberty, even if it is to save his homeland." In our own time, we might apply this principle to the bombing of non-combatants in war or the torture of prisoners in possession of intelligence. We might also recall George Smiley's promise to Ricki Tarr in *Tinker, Tailor, Soldier, Spy* to save Irina when he knew she was dead, thereby engaging Ricki's cooperation for a good purpose. Cicero was reflecting Aristotle's proper distinction between things that are right or wrong in themselves — issues of fundamental moral principle — and things that are right or wrong only as a means to an end, such as most political judgements, and there may be a difference of opinion as to what that end should be in any particular case.

4.8   NATURAL LAW, FREE WILL AND LAWS IN HISTORY

Free will and human imperfection mean that human behaviour, although to some extent constrained by natural law, is not determined by it. An illustration of the operation of the natural law and its interplay with human freedom was given by Edward Hugh Henderson, Professor of Philosophy at Louisiana State University, reflecting on the oil spill in the Gulf of Mexico in 2010. Echoing the thinking of Austin Farrer, a 20th century Oxford philosopher who advanced the theory of "double agency", Henderson commented: "God does not smash in from the outside to overthrow creatures, to put out of gear the order of nature that God has over eons of evolution brought to its present state. What the oil is doing to the Gulf and its denizens is what oil, being oil, would do. It's at the level of human freedom that you can distinguish between action that is or isn't underwritten by the... divine will."[115]

Henderson's comments illustrate the relationship between causal laws and the exercise of free will in the course of human behaviour. Herodotus reflected a partial truth when he said that very few things happen at the right time and others do not happen at all. Tolstoy, at the end of *War and Peace,* said that free will would negate scientific laws: "If there is a single action due to free will, then not a single historical law can exist, nor any conception of historical events".[116] But historical laws, in the sense of scientific laws, are not necessary to understand the patterns of history. As Mark Twain said, history does not repeat itself, but sometimes it does rhyme. There are no predictive laws in history that explain events in terms of what must necessarily happen, as is the case in science. This is both because we do not have all the information about the past that we would need and also because the free will of individuals and the occurrence of chance events leave open a number of possibilities. Reflecting on the information available, the philosopher of science C. G. Hempel has pointed out that we can study various aspects or characteristics of historical events and that there is no limit to the number of them we can insist on taking into account. Because of this fact, it is impossible to have a complete description of an event and "it is impossible to give a complete explanation of an individual event in the sense of accounting for all its characteristics by means of universal hypotheses...."[117]

The consequences of human action may vary widely depending upon a whole series of unconnected circumstances. We might call this the "Sliding Doors" phenomenon after a film of the same name, which describes two parallel stories where the quite different outcomes depend upon a trivial chance event. Thomas Nagel has reflected on the phenomenon of "moral luck" where individuals are praised or blamed out of proportion to the nature of their acts because of other circumstances beyond their control. For example, careless drivers who cause injury or death are punished far more severely than those who do not.

Humankind's free will provides a further layer of complexity in addition to the multiple possibilities of chance circumstances. The historian I. D. Jones, in describing the confusion in the year between the fall of Richard Cromwell and the return of Charles II, refers to the combination of events that "produce a tangled skein of desperation, irresolution and treachery which needs a psychologist's rather than a historian's analysis."[118] An article in *The Washington Post* of 4th February 2011 outlined three possible scenarios for the future of the Egyptian revolution — an Islamist dictatorship similar to that which took the reins in Iran in 1979; a messy transition to democracy, as in Indonesia in 1998, or something in between, with the *status quo* reasserting its power, as in Romania in 1989. The description of these parallel events provides a framework of explanation that may help to provide an analysis of causes and outcomes. However, in any given situation we cannot know all the relevant factors so as to take them all into account; we cannot predict human behaviour, and there may be random events. So it was not possible to predict at the time that the article was written which, if any, of the three outcomes would transpire.

4.9   EVOLUTIONARY AND BEHAVIOURIST ETHICS

Recently, some secular academic analysis of ethics has focussed on an evolutionary basis for moral decisions and has reflected upon the basis for instinctive perceptions of right and wrong. But evolutionary ethics do not satisfactorily address the question of the source of moral values. Some have held that moral values are inherited genetically, but there is no adequate scientific evidence for this. Others have concluded that moral values are transmitted culturally. This is partially true in any society, but it does not account for the instinctive sense of right and wrong which is not taught.

Some behaviourist ethics are helpful in posing questions, for instance, as to why we recoil more against doing wrong to our known neighbour than we do in relation to others more distantly known to us. Or why do we conclude that positive harmful acts are morally more wrong than omissions? Law in the UK has generally made a distinction between positive acts on the one hand and omissions on the other, so that a duty to act only arises where there is a statutory duty to do so or, in common law, where reasonable reliance should be placed upon a person so acting. While the law does not determine what is morally right, the distinction between acts and omissions is a good one in helping us to identify our responsibilities since we are all guilty of an infinite number of omissions, most of which exclude one another. Time is limited and we cannot be in two places at once; priorities have to be determined and choices made. We owe ourselves and those around us a duty to preserve our mental and physical health but also to look to the welfare of others; doing this will be an imperfect process in an imperfect world. The issue of omissions may be easier for Christians to deal with, since they believe that there is a creator God with whom they can have a relationship, and that he can help in the task of making choices as individuals and societies face increasingly complex challenges.

Some neuroscientists and scientific behaviourists would minimise human responsibility for our actions on the grounds that all behaviour is determined by mechanistic processes and instincts over which we have little control, and that self-consciousness is therefore insignificant. Dr Henri Laborit, a French biologist, collaborated with Alain Resnais on one of the most memorable films of the 20th century, *Mon Oncle D'Amerique*. The film traces, through the lives of the characters in different stressful situations, the characteristics of human nature that we share with the animal world, and poses some fundamental questions (illuminated by Frederic and Mary Ann Brussat in their online review): "Does the human mind free us from enslavement to nature's laws? Can free will liberate us from the manifold external forces that seem to control our lives?"[119] Conrad's *Lord Jim* indicates that we may never wholly understand free will. Marlow says at the end of the book: "We ought to know. He is one of us...." But we cannot predict human behaviour and scientific determinism cannot tell us, because free will and choice operate in a realm which cannot be reduced to chemical and biological processes. Jim was not the only white officer who deserted the *Patna* but, because of the choices he made, the act defined his life thereafter.

Chemical and biological processes themselves do not indicate a moral framework and confer no meaning beyond the expectation of prediction. If human decisions were only the product of scientific reactions, there would be no free will and therefore (as Kant indicated) no scope for either reason or morality. We would be automata, bound by the past and prisoners of our nature. A curiosity of a deterministic view of consciousness is that it can be applied selectively. So the behaviour of criminals, for instance, is held to be conditioned by experience, which may to some extent be true. But, for some determinists, the conditioning which governs behaviour does not apply to the thinking of sociologists and criminologists who assume that they are entirely rational when they analyse the behaviour of the criminals. Kant's perception that free will is a condition of rational thought illuminates the inherent contradiction in determinism.

Christian thought indicates that there are common characteristics of human nature which are played out in the moral perceptions, the choices and the actions of human beings. Human beings have the free will to make choices, but they need to understand the tendencies (which may be derived from their experiences) which can draw them to one way or to another, whether these be moral weaknesses or instincts to do good. Christian thinking is that human beings can look to their Creator for change and renewal and to help them overcome the moral challenges that they face.

There is no doubt much more to understand about the mechanisms of human consciousness and choice. The research of Professor Sir David Baulcombe (Regius Professor of Botany at Cambridge) into epigenetics, suggests a mechanism by which human choices are reinforced by neural changes. Epimutations involve changes, for instance, neural changes that are not genetic and are not random. Epigenetics may explain why choices become reflected in more permanent desires and characteristics. Professor Baulcombe describes it colourfully in terms of human emotions: "Epigenetics might also change the popular song. Instead of 'I love you because it's in my DNA', it would be more appropriate to sing 'because I am epimutated'. The lyrics could explain that a visit to Birmingham in 1959 had affected the epigenetics of a neural stem cell, and that this change had altered brain circuitry to create, finally, an obsession with Aston Villa, sad-eyed ladies of the lowland, or whatever the song is about".[120]   If this view of epimutations is correct, it provides support for training in moral emotions, which is discussed in Chapter 13. It also makes sense of the disciplines of good habits which, over time, may become desires. To this extent, for better or for worse, we become what we think and what we do.

In Christian thinking, the instinctive perception of good and evil in the consciousness of human beings is part of the created order. Professor Paul Bloom, a psychologist at Yale University's Infant Cognition Centre has said of some recent research: "A growing body of evidence…suggests that humans do have a rudimentary moral sense from the very start of life. With the help of well-designed experiments, you can see glimmers of moral thought, moral judgement and moral feeling even in the first year of life. Some sense of good and evil seems to be bred in the bone."[121]   In this we are different from animals, which have no sense of morality or of moral obligations. Thus we may disapprove of the behaviour of an animal, but it would make no more sense to speak of "bad" (meaning morally defective) sheep than it does to blame an inanimate object. Some secular thinkers may explain conscience purely in social terms, but this analysis cannot confer any absolute value on it. They may struggle to explain why they disapprove of any particular behaviour except in terms of their personal preferences, or in terms of some concept of majority rule or consensus, which are fragile foundations for moral judgements.

4.10   THE PHILOSOPHER'S MAP AGAIN

The existence of moral values points to a created order and a creator but does not in itself justify a belief in a Christian God. We return to the philosopher's map. We do not all know or agree upon where the country is (where the values come from), but the landmarks (the values themselves) are clear and we can look for clues about their location (the origin of the values). For example, everyone would agree that genocide is wrong, but we also need to understand why. Similarly, we may ask "Why do lives matter? Why is might not right? Why are some human beings not inherently superior to others? Why is liberty important?" If we do believe in moral absolutes such as these, then we should also wish to know where they come from.

Secular thinkers may recoil from the metaphysical. However, any moral system is necessarily metaphysical in the sense that it recognises or constructs a rule that applies generally and can therefore be used to determine what should be the outcome in a particular case. If a rule exists outside of its subjects, it exists as an idea or a generality in a different dimension to the facts which constitute its subjects, and it must therefore in this sense be metaphysical. If this is the case, the question arises for the secular thinker as to what is the basis for a moral rule. We may agree that it arises from human consciousness at an individual and a collective level, as observed by Philip Allott,[122] but this does not explain the origin of the human nature which gives rise to that consciousness.

4.11   THE CREATOR OF THE MORAL LAW

If we acknowledge that there is morality built into the created order, the challenge is then to discern what the content of that moral law is. If we believe that the moral order is derived from a created order, then we may want to discover what we can about the Creator and his purposes. Christianity provides a narrative which explains these, but Christian belief may not be necessary to appreciate the truth of the values that Christianity promotes. This is because these values are true irrespective of a belief in God, because they reflect a coherent system of truth that explains human nature. But an appreciation of the truth of the values may encourage investigation into Christian belief as the source of those values.

John Locke, writing in the seventeenth century, acknowledged the universal values of Christian belief: belief in God is the "foundation of all morality" and without morality we are incapable of society.[123] For Locke, a belief in God was a translation of moral duty: "The idea of a Supreme Being, infinite in power, goodness and wisdom, whose workmanship we are, and on whom we depend; and the idea of ourselves, as understanding, rational creatures, being such as are clear in us, would, I suppose, if duly considered and pursued, afford such foundations of our duty and rules of action as might place morality amongst the sciences capable of demonstration: wherein I doubt not but from self-evident propositions, by necessary consequences, as incontestable as those in mathematics, the measures of right and wrong might be made out, to any one that will apply himself with the same indifference and attention to the one as he does to the other of these sciences."[124]

Like many political philosophers, Locke also recognised that an understanding of the nature of man was necessary to construct a political theory about society: "To understand political power aright, and devise it from its original, we must consider what estate all men are naturally in, and that is, a state of perfect freedom to order their actions, and dispose of their possessions and persons as they think fit, within the bounds of the law of Nature, without asking leave or depending upon the will of any other man."[125]

4.12   THE DISCOVERY OF THE MORAL LAW

If we have a view about the source of moral law and have concluded that it proceeds from a creator, we need then to reflect upon how the moral law is discovered. The Christian perspective, which we explore in the next chapter, is that the Creator has interacted with humankind in history and the historical record of that interaction is to be found in the Bible. God's communication through the Bible is the primary way in which God speaks to us, though it does not exclude other ways in which God makes himself known. The Christian view is that the Bible is objective truth that is communicated so as to be personal to each human being. Central to the Protestant Christian view is the perception that, although divine revelation is given in the Bible, it is discovered by the body of the people from the Bible and not handed down by a sovereign or decreed by an all-powerful institution. As we shall see in later chapters, this is foundational to our Western heritage of democracy and freedom.

5
GOD'S LAWS AND HUMAN LAWS

5.1 GOD'S COMMUNICATION

Christian ethical principles are based on a view of what it means for people to flourish, which means to fulfil the purposes for which they were created. For the Christian, these purposes can only be fully understood in the revelation of the Bible. If there is a creator who has made rational beings, it would be reasonable to expect this creator to communicate with the creatures he has made. Human knowledge and reasoning is imperfect and human beings are prone to deception by others and self-deception, as well as to pride and folly. They need some help in pursuing the truth.

5.2 THE BIBLE

For Christians, the Bible is the record of God's interaction with mankind through the people of Israel, in the life, death and resurrection of Jesus Christ and in the activities of Jesus' direct disciples shortly afterwards. The knowledge given in the Bible supplements and undergirds the principles of natural law. In Christian theology, God is the Creator and sustainer of the universe and he created humankind in his image. As well as the law revealed in creation, Christians believe that God's nature and His purposes for humankind are revealed more explicitly and more specifically in the divinely inspired Bible and in the person of Jesus Christ, the "image of the invisible God" as the Apostle Paul put it (Colossians 1:15 NIV).

Many Christians would say that there is also supernatural wisdom which, though rational and accessible to reason, can only be fully perceived when a supernatural person, the living

Spirit of God, fills individuals who believe and trust in Jesus Christ, God's ultimate revelation to mankind. The truth of the Bible centres upon the need for individuals to be reconciled with God and to accept the lordship of Jesus Christ in daily life. For the Christian, the Holy Spirit can also bring personal meaning to the words of the Bible as a guide for daily living. This requires humility, particularly intellectual humility, and repentance (the admission of wrong actions and turning from them), which may seem far from current cultural norms. While political structures and human behaviour should reflect the will of God for the common good of all, Christians would say that only the renewal of people's individual hearts and minds can restore them to a relationship with God. Some Christians would also say that only the Christian faith in individual lives will achieve the right kind of change in a community or a nation.

The idea of revelation from God can be difficult for some people. But it is good that revelation is necessary since, if people could find the truth by their reason alone, they might become proud, and humility is a personal and a social virtue. From the Christian perspective, revelation from God is also necessary because at the heart of the character of God is his desire for a personal relationship with the human beings he has made. This personal relationship requires an acknowledgement that God has communicated with humankind and a response by individuals to that communication. For Christians, the relationship becomes personal when individuals acknowledge the truth about God as revealed in the Bible and the need to submit the course of their lives to the authority of God and his guidance.

Christian faith can make sense of personal lives and explain some of the apparent contradictions we encounter. We have mentioned the human capacity for both good and evil, for nobility and degradation. There are other contrasts in the moral world. Humility is praiseworthy, restraint can result in self-fulfilment and giving is rewarding. And there are further apparent contradictions in the Bible, for example where uneducated disciples teach the most learned men in the community (see Acts

4:13). The ultimate and profound paradox is the cross of Jesus Christ, where an act of disgrace leads to glory and where God, the maker and judge of all mankind, pays the price of wrongdoing in the death and separation of Jesus from his Father.

5.3   GOD AND HUMAN NATURE

Christian principles of political theory are both transcendent and immanent. They are transcendent because they are a function of a metaphysical (though objective and universal) reality, namely the character and wisdom of God as revealed in the Bible. They are immanent in the sense that these principles reflect the existing natural order of the world that God has made and the character of the people he has created to inhabit it. Christianity teaches that human beings are made in "the image of God" (Genesis 1:27). They therefore have the capacity to discern good and evil and, though imperfect, have the free will to do both good and evil. Human beings are equal in worth irrespective of age (including the unborn), nationality, gender, human status, ability or any other characteristics. They are also made for relationships, reflecting something of the self-giving love revealed in the relationships in the triune God of Father, Son and Holy Spirit. The Christian view of what it means to be fulfilled as a human being includes a right relationship with God, since Christians believe that each human being was created with this purpose.

Christianity recognises the individual and collective shortcomings that have the potential to cut human beings off from God. Systems of thought that do not recognise the existence of both the good and the evil tendencies of human beings are bound to be limited, because they fail to address a fundamental aspect of the human condition. Some realism about our flawed human nature is necessary. It is through repentance and belief in Jesus Christ as Saviour and Lord that Christians are forgiven and enabled to come into a relationship with God. That relationship with God through Jesus Christ gives them the resources to overcome the evil in themselves and to realise their potential as eternal beings with an eternal destiny. Jesus defined this as "abundant life" or "life to the full".[126] Extending this principle from individuals to societies, Christian teaching suggests that societies flourish to the extent that God's standards are reflected in their laws and customs and in the beliefs and behaviour of their citizens. "Righteousness exalts a nation, but sin is a disgrace to any people", as the writer of the book of Proverbs put it (Chapter14:4, NIV).

5.4   THE BIBLE AS A BASIS FOR TRUTH

The Christian narrative about the nature of reality and the place of mankind in it, the interaction between God and mankind down the ages, and the moral law revealed by God in the Bible is based upon objective historical truth. Beliefs derived from the Bible can act as Kant's "*a priori*" assumptions which can be tested against history and reality as we encounter it and from which we can draw further conclusions. This book is based upon the premises of traditional biblical Christian teaching. There are other interpretations of the Bible that impact upon a range of questions. These matters include issues in relation to the beginning and end of life, and the family and its implications for society. Not all those professing to be Christians will share similar conclusions. However, Christians would generally agree that the Bible contains the truth that God has intended as a guide to flourishing lives for individuals and for societies, as well as a way to personal faith.

5.5   NATURAL LAW AND REVEALED LAW

A Christian perspective would suggest that, since God created mankind with reason, and since he created a world that operates according to rational laws, God's moral standards will be consistent with a rational understanding of the natural order revealed in creation. Much of Christian thinking can therefore be endorsed by those who have no belief in God. For instance, because mankind was, according to Christian belief, created in the image of God, the value of each person is intrinsic and not conferred by any human power. Every human being matters to God, and therefore should matter to each of us, irrespective of race, creed, gender, age, disability, wealth or any other external thing. This value is an absolute because it reflects the character and order of the Creator, and is not dependent upon changing cultural values.

5.6   THE STRUGGLE BETWEEN GOOD AND EVIL

The Bible teaches that all people have fallen short of God's standards and, to a lesser or greater extent, have chosen to go their own way instead of obeying the Creator's laws. This resulting dislocation has left the world, as the Apostle Paul put it, in "bondage to decay" (Romans 8:21 NIV), so not everything we see in ourselves, in others, or in the world, reflects God's nature and his intentions for mankind. A consistent theme in Christian teaching is the struggle between good and evil and the potential for good and evil within every person. Christians believe in the power of the cross of Christ to deal with the consequences of evil with perfect justice, perfect mercy and perfect love. Civil laws should reflect both the potential in human beings for evil and the possibility of redemption. Mankind was created to love, to appreciate beauty and to enjoy creation. Following the maker's instructions is what it means to be authentically human. Whilst the moral law derived from these instructions should set the boundaries for human behaviour, what Christians call grace (the undeserved gift of God) enables them to reflect in some degree God's characteristics of compassion, mercy, forgiveness and self-sacrifice, which were supremely shown in the life and death of Jesus Christ, the Son of God.

5.7 WHAT THE BIBLE MEANS FOR POLITICS

The Bible teaches that the original creation plan has been degraded by human imperfection. Nevertheless, the timeless principles of God's law can be seen in the natural order as well as in the moral law and the lessons from history in the Bible. These principles can also be derived to some extent (since this can be flawed), in the sense of right and wrong given to all individuals in their consciences, which Christians explain as "common grace".

The Bible teaches, for instance, that murder is wrong, and this rule must extend to any living human being, whether born or unborn. It also teaches a number of things about personal morality, particularly in relation to social justice and gender issues, which have repercussions in the political realm. For example, to form a public policy on adoption, it is helpful to understand whether homosexual unions are part of the God given natural order for flourishing families or whether they are a characteristic of an imperfect world that is not as God would wish it (see Chapter 14). To form a policy on the environment, it is helpful to have a framework informed by God's purposes for creation as described in the Bible (see Chapter 20). To form a policy on education, we can learn from the instructions given to the ancient Israelites (see Chapter 13). The Bible contains specific teaching on the nature and purposes of government and on the wise stewardship of resources (see in particular Chapters 17 to 21). And we will explore other examples in later chapters. But in all cases, Christian political thought should be consistent with an understanding of the nature of mankind, the relationship of each individual with the Creator and their purposes on earth. There are many issues which the Bible does not address explicitly, but we can seek to draw out conclusions from the general principles that it contains.

A particular example of biblical teaching which impacts on politics is that concerning the family. The value of the natural biological family as a fundamental building block of human existence is both a sociological fact in history and affirmed in the Bible (see Deuteronomy 6:2; 28:4, 15 and 41; Psalm 78:5-6; and Mark 10:7-9) as the best environment in which children are to be raised. This has political consequences and, by way of example, two are mentioned here. First, the family is where values are taught and shown by example and where human character is developed. In political terms, the nature of the character formed will either lead to self-control, self-reliance and personal independence, or to a lack of self-restraint and a consequent dependence upon external help and/or control. This will have important implications for the lives of communities and in the realm of public order. Secondly, for Christians, the God given nature of the family and the primary responsibility of parents for raising their children also have consequences in education. For Christians, it is not the ultimate responsibility of the State to educate the moral consciences of children. One consequence of this is that parents should be given the right to withdraw their children from moral teaching that they believe is wrong or unhelpful, or which they believe is given at the wrong stage of development.

5.8   GOD'S LAWS AND THE LAWS OF THE STATE

Cicero said that human laws "were devised to ensure the safety of citizens, the security of states and the peaceful happy life of human beings"[127] and not all of God's laws should be reflected in a society's criminal and civil laws. God has given mankind free will to obey him or not, and free expression, within boundaries that protect others, should reflect these principles. Marsilius of Padua, writing in the 14th century, recognised that there are limits to human law: "For there are certain acts that a legislator cannot regulate by human law."[128]

Much Christian scholarship has addressed the way in which the principles of the laws given by God in the Bible should be applied to modern society. In the Old Testament, elements of God's laws were seen as good for both the people of Israel and for those of surrounding nations (see Deuteronomy 4:7-8), and in the New Testament these were for the law abiding and the lawless (see 1 Timothy 1:8-10). Calvin believed that there was a clear threefold division of the Mosaic laws in the Bible into the ceremonial, the judicial and the moral, and that only the moral remains binding today. Calvin saw the role of the civil law as a guide for Christian conduct and as an encouragement to respond to God's grace.

These divisions of the Mosaic laws have been extensively addressed in academic theology, most recently in Philip S. Ross's book *From the Finger of God.*[129] Christopher J.H. Wright has proposed five categories.[130] Michael Schluter and his colleagues at the Jubilee Centre in Cambridge have sought to draw out from a wider range of Old Testament laws (for example those relating to inheritance, land and commerce) how the character of God is revealed in those laws and the general principles that can be applied today, although the laws were made for a particular people at a particular time.[131] Schluter's perception is that the law is based upon relationships — the relationship between human beings and God and the relationships between individuals themselves. This reflects Jesus' summing up of the law when he said that we should love God and our neighbour (see Matthew 7:12 and 22:37-40) and connects with theories of justice which are founded upon right relationships.

In modern societies there is much legislation that is not intended directly to reflect an unchanging moral principle, but is enacted simply to regulate the affairs of people so that they can coexist peacefully. Road traffic regulations are an obvious example. Aquinas recognised the need for "*lex humana*" to regulate matters left unresolved by the law of God. However, such regulations should nevertheless have a rational purpose and be directed towards the common good.

5.9 FREE WILL, PROTECTION AND RELATIONSHIPS

While there may be consequences for the well-being of the individual in this life if he or she transgresses the natural law, the law of the land should as far as possible respect the free will of individuals whilst also protecting society, and particularly the vulnerable within it. While good laws cannot make people good, or ensure the right decisions are made in the lives of individuals, laws provide social norms of expected behaviour. Laws can and should restrain evil. And they can also, as the Apostle Paul taught (with reference to the Jewish religious law), prompt people's consciences to recognise what is right and what is wrong. On the other hand, if the law promotes or even allows a form of behaviour, such behaviour may over time meet with general approval.

The laws of God that need to be reflected in civil laws are mainly those that relate to the relationships between people and between people and the State. They should relate to behaviour and not to intention alone or to belief, since freedom of belief reflects God given free will (see Chapter 15). However, as the poet John Donne put it, "No man is an island"[132] and most of our actions affect others in some way. Personal decisions, such as those relating to divorce or suicide, can leave trails of social and psychological devastation behind them in the lives of others stretching down the generations and can also impose significant burdens on society. An edition of the *London Evening Standard* on 2nd March 2010 focussed on poverty and illustrated its "dispossessed" theme, with a report on a lady who is dependent on welfare benefits and lives in shockingly sub-standard conditions with her eleven children fathered by five different men.[133] Personal morality, when it affects behaviour and lifestyle, is not only personal in its effects.

5.10   LAWS AND THE COMMON GOOD

The extent to which a society will want to translate Christian principles into its laws will reflect the beliefs of that society. Whatever those beliefs are, biblical principles are nevertheless considered by Christians to be true for all people for all time, because they reflect the character of the God who created all human beings.   However, Christians should not expect to be able to persuade people who do not believe in God that this is the basis upon which these principles should be implemented. In these situations, Christians will need to convince those who do not believe in God that the laws that they propose are good in themselves, in that they are consistent with the world as it is experienced, and that they reflect a view of human flourishing to which all can relate.

The common law of England is based upon principles derived from the Bible and Christian teaching.   It was first established in the Saxon kingdoms, notably under King Alfred, whose legal code included the Ten Commandments and Mosaic laws from the book of Exodus.   It was then adopted by the Norman and Plantagenet kings, in particular Henry II who established a court system applying "common law" throughout the kingdom.   Although the common law has now in many areas been supplanted by statute, the concept of common law is that law should evolve by applying general principles (originally derived from Christian thought) to particular situations, thus creating precedents.   The common law thus preserves both general principles and the ability to adapt to changing circumstances.   The law, however, can be influenced for better or for worse by the values of the judiciary.   These values were at one time predominantly Christian but in many significant respects are now no longer so.   Human systems, however good, are always affected by the persons who populate them.

As Edmund Burke articulated, a basis of the common law is the liberty of the individual which is founded upon the Christian belief in free will.   This limits the power of government.   As Burke put it in his speech on the trial of Warren Hastings: "We have no arbitrary power to give, because arbitrary power is a thing which neither any man may hold nor any man can give". In Christian thinking the belief in freedom is informed by an aspiration to further the common good. The preamble to the Magna Carta illustrates the connection between the laws of the land and the purposes of God for the common good: "John, by the grace of God, king of England ... Know that by the inspiration of God and for the good of our soul and those of our predecessors and heirs, to the honour of God and the exaltation of the holy church, and the improvement of our kingdom. ... Since, moreover, for the sake of God, and for the improvement of our kingdom... we have made all these concessions."[134] For the Calvinist theologian Samuel Rutherford, writing in the 17th century, the purpose of the law was *salus populi*, the good of the people. This had a spiritual dimension. As John Coffey puts it: "This common good included both secular ends (justice, peace, safety, lives, liberties) and religious ends (the godly life, the salvation of souls)."[135]

The principles of Roman law which are applied today in many countries are derived from the period of the Christian Roman Empire (particularly in the law of Justinian, the *Corpus Juris*), as well as from classical Roman thought. Many systems of law in continental Europe are derived from these traditions of Roman law, which was codified during the period of Napoleonic rule. Roman law is more prescriptive than the common law since it was derived from autocratic, rather than consent based, systems of government. Marta Andreasen MEP has described the difference in the character of the two systems of law: "The British people have a highly evolved legal system good enough to have been the basis of the legal system of a large part of the rest of the world. It is very strong because it is based upon the needs and actions of a reasonable and rational individual. On the contrary, the continental or Roman system is prescriptive; you follow the rules and you do not question them too much. So it comes down to this. In my opinion and from my experience in dealing with European legislation, the Europeans are afraid of freedom and liberal laws unlike in the UK."

5.11   THE LIMITS OF HUMAN LAW

Human law will always have limitations. Just because something is permitted by law does not mean that it is morally good and need not be questioned, though this can easily be wrongly assumed in relation to many laws and regulations. Where there are no generally accepted ethical standards, law can readily be regarded as a proxy for those standards so, if something is permitted, people may assume that it is morally good. Good laws cannot make people morally good by commanding the virtues of love, mercy or forgiveness. The Christian gospel is that God, by coming to earth in human form and bearing the consequences of human wrongdoing, made his forgiveness freely available. This opens up the possibility of a relationship with God which should enable people better to reflect his character of goodness, love and mercy in their dealings with others.

For Christians, final judgment is reserved by God for the end of this age. While Christians should seek to do good on earth in representing God's character, they see themselves as citizens of another country, the kingdom of God, in which God reigns supreme and in which truth, justice and goodness rule. Christians pray: "Your will be done on earth as it is in heaven". But they know that this kingdom in which God's will is done can only be implemented in a fragmentary manner in the human structures of power on this earth, and that human beings alone do not have the power or the ultimate responsibility to bring this kingdom in. Jesus did not seek political revolution, but to introduce the values of the kingdom of God into the lives of individuals. These values are a reversal of worldly standards of behaviour and they affect everything, both private and public. The prophets of the Old Testament did not hesitate to denounce the wrongdoing of secular rulers.

As we have noted, Christian political philosophy is sceptical of utopian visions and of attempts to implement them by political power. Mankind is imperfect and all political systems should allow for those imperfections. (This perception underlies much of the discussion in this book, in particular that relating to impartial justice and the separation of powers in Chapter 8, accountability and democracy in Chapter 9 and freedom of expression in Chapter 15.) Humility and servant-hood on the part of legislators seeking to create laws that reflect the Creator's design are also essential, as is sound morality amongst the citizens of the nation.

PART 2:

PRINCIPLES OF GOVERNMENT

6

LIMITED GOVERNMENT, PERSONAL RESTRAINT AND WELFARE

6.1   LESSONS FROM THE BIBLE

Whilst Jesus said that his kingdom was not of this world and demonstrated that it is not to be brought in by force, the Bible is the story of God's interaction with mankind and human societies. We can therefore draw on the Bible for indications about the purposes of government and the best forms of government. Ancient Israel was the people to whom God revealed his laws, which would be a blessing to them and serve as an example to surrounding people: "Keep his decrees and commands, which I am giving you today, so that it may go well with you and your children after you and that you may live long in the land the Lord your God gives you for all time" (Deuteronomy 4:40 NIV). As we have seen, the Apostle Paul in his letter to the Romans reminded his followers that the institution of government, though not the actions of any particular government, is part of the God given order for the world. Governments, he said, have a duty to God to restrain evil and to encourage good so that, as he puts it in his letter to Timothy, people may lead "peaceful and quiet lives in all godliness and holiness" (1 Timothy 2:2 NIV).

6.2   HUMAN IMPERFECTION AND THE LIMITS OF POWER

According to the Christian perspective, only God is perfectly just and omniscient and his rule, when it comes, will be absolute. Meanwhile, the kingdom of God on earth is where the will of

God is done and people willingly submit to His rule. The rule of God on this present earth is not coercive. Similarly, earthly government must reflect the free will that God has left to people in terms of the liberty of the individual. It must also reflect the imperfection of human beings and the ever present danger of an abuse of power, which is a reflection of the operation of that free will. In the Old Testament, the people of Israel wanted a king, a "*melech*", an absolute ruler. The prophet Samuel warned them that earthly kings would exploit and overtax them, and the subsequent history of Israel bears out his warnings. In the Old Testament and in European history there have been kings personally submitted to God who sought God's will for their earthly kingdoms. The most notable in British history was King Alfred, the only king to bear the title "Great". Obedience to God brought blessing on the people of his day, though in every age evil still resides in individuals and human political structures and there is invariably a struggle for right to prevail.

As David W. Hall has explained,[136] Protestant thinkers of the sixteenth and seventeenth centuries explored the Old Testament models to set out the basis of governmental power and its limitations. As he says, "A century after Calvin, Samuel Rutherford used this same Mosaic pattern in his 1644 *Lex Rex* to argue for a republican…form of civil polity. Indeed, most of the Reformation-era political tracts (e.g., by Calvin, Beza, Bucer, Knox, Buchanan, Ponet, Althusius, etc.) devoted extensive commentary to the Old Testament patterns of government. These reformers viewed Old Testament precedents as applicable to the politics of their own settings, and these same ideas were drawn upon later by an American tradition that nourished its founders."[137] Calvin, in addressing the power of governments, taught that: "There are limits prescribed by God to their power, within which they ought to be satisfied: namely, to work for the common good and…direct the people in truest fairness and justice; not to be puffed up with their own importance, but to remember that they also are subjects of God."[138]

As quoted by David Hall, Johannes Althusius, reflecting Calvin's thought in his *Politica Methodice Digesta, Atque Exemplis Sacris et Profanis Illustrata* (which when translated from the Latin reads: "Politics Methodically Digested, Illustrated with Sacred and Secular Examples") (1603) summed up the Christian thought on the origins and limits of political power. "All power", he noted, was "limited by definite boundaries and laws. No power is absolute, infinite, unbridled, arbitrary and lawless. Every power is bound to laws, right and equity...".[139] The ruler "exercises not his own power, but that of another, namely, the supreme power of the realm of which he is the minister."[140]

Arguments for democracy do not defeat those for limited government. John Stuart Mill warned of the tyranny of the majority and concluded: "The limitation, therefore, of the power of government over individuals loses none of its importance when the holders of power are regularly accountable to the community, that is, to the strongest party therein."[141]

6.3   NO ENFORCEMENT OF BELIEF

The earliest statement of belief for Christians was that "Jesus is Lord". Declaring this could cost a believer his life since it denied the affirmation required at one time under Roman law that "Caesar is Lord". God is the ruler of the universe and one day all earthly powers on earth will submit to Jesus. However, the extent to which God's rule on earth can be implemented by governments and human structures is limited by the imperfections of human beings and by God's design that individuals have free will. Individuals may submit to God's rule but, because of human imperfections, they will inevitably fail to reflect this fully in their lives.

Totalitarian governments, and governments that seek to enforce private belief or proscribe certain beliefs by force of law, are inherently wrong, whether or not one agrees with the content of the beliefs that they seek to impose. When faced with a similar dogmatism in the early Church, the Apostle Paul's response was: "Let each be fully convinced in his own mind" (Romans 14:5 NIV). In other words, it is right to hold strong convictions, but not to require others to hold them. The historian monk Bede, writing in about 700AD concerning the conversion of King Ethelbert to the Christian faith circa 600AD, recounted that "he [the king] learned from his instructions and guides that the service of Christ must be accepted freely and not under compulsion."[142] Freedom of thought and the non-violent expression of those beliefs reflect the use of God's gift of freedom to mankind, whilst oppression and violence are evidence of its abuse.

6.4   LICENCE AND OPPRESSION

Edmund Burke observed in the 18th century that an absence of personal restraint by individuals (as in revolutionary France) leads to the need for repressive measures in government. Conversely, as Alexis de Tocqueville noted about America in the 19th century, democracy cannot function without a restraining moral framework. A common understanding and application of the moral law allows limited government to function properly. Christian thinking recognises, as Burke did, the link between individual behaviour and political freedom. Personal restraint is necessary for individuals to cooperate in society and an absence of restraint can lead to oppressive government. In Christian thinking, forgiveness helps people to move on from past wrongs and Christian hope enables them to look positively to the future. The call of Christ upon the lives of individuals requires obedience and enables the transformation of character. It should result in what Christians regard as virtue — desirable characteristics such as self-restraint, goodness, grace and the courage to do what is right. Evidence of dramatic changes in character can be seen in Christian revivals, such as the Welsh revival of 1904 which resulted in decreases in crime.

Self-governance is a Christian duty and it relieves the secular power of the need to govern behaviour by coercion. On the other hand, where self-restraint is lacking and where support from other institutions in civil society is weak, people expect the State to fill the void and they are likely to acquiesce in its increasing power to prevent disorder. Self-restraint is good in matters both great and small. There is currently a Government campaign to reduce obesity. It may be that the growing incidence of obesity in our society today can be attributed less to a lack of exercise (though it is good to have a healthy lifestyle and this will reduce the chances of other illnesses) than to a lack of restraint in eating too much or eating the wrong kinds of food.

Peter Hitchens, who is regarded by some as being overly pessimistic in his description of current British society, painted a bleak picture of a society where moral restraint has evaporated to be replaced by armies of State functionaries. He recorded the increase of recorded crime from 103,000 crimes in 1921, when large sections of the population were (compared to today's living standards) in poverty, to 5,200,000 crimes in 2001.[143] Hitchens commented that: "The wicked, the selfish, the loud, the oafish, the inconsiderate and the bully are freer to behave as they wish than at any time for a hundred and fifty years."[144] He asked: "Why have all that high taxation, those regiments of social workers, and that maze of targeted benefits, not to mention the bureaucracies needed to organise them, if they do not actually make people more content and better behaved?" We may not all share Hitchens' pessimism or identify with his colourful language, but his argument supports the contention that the intervention of the State is inadequate to ensure good behaviour. Laws are necessary, but laws in themselves, even if they are good laws, do not make people good.

Nevertheless, in the absence of personal restraint, laws are still required. The less self-restraint there is, the greater will be the need for the restraint of the law. John Mack, the former chief executive of Morgan Stanley, acknowledged the need for regulation in the absence of personal or institutional restraint:

"We cannot control ourselves. You have to step in and control [Wall] Street".[145] That the regulation was badly needed (in the absence of personal restraint) was evidenced in the behaviour of Fabrice Tourre, the Goldman Sachs trader who sold toxic asset-backed securities, collateralised debt obligations and wrote to a girlfriend: "More and more leverage in the system… the entire edifice threatens to collapse at any moment. Only potential survivor, the fabulous Fab…standing in the middle of all these complex, highly leveraged, exotic trades he created without necessarily understanding all the implications of those monstrosities."[146] The need for regulation, as well as personal restraint, in financial markets is explored in Chapters 17 and 18.

6.5   INDIVIDUAL RESPONSIBILITY

Despite the requirement for regulation where this is necessary, Government intervention should wherever practicable be limited, since it is a Christian principle that people should have the freedom given by God to take decisions within a framework of law, and this freedom is both a private and a public good. That freedom brings personal responsibility which is part of being human. Aspects of the panoply of health and safety legislation in the UK remove this responsibility and substitute for it the bureaucratic control of the State, which is inevitably cumbersome and expensive. Where individuals are able to exercise responsibility, the discretion which flows from that responsibility is best exercised by those who have been encouraged to take decisions for themselves and for others, and this discretion requires good education and training.

Government may step in to fill a void left by the apparent inability of people to take responsible decisions. But the intervention of government in prescribing rules and procedures may at the same time relieve people of their responsibilities and reinforce their original behaviour. The "harm reduction" medicine can make the condition worse. Brendan O'Neill has highlighted the dangers of a therapeutic culture in which people are absolved of personal responsibility by psychologising what was once regarded as bad behaviour.[147] Thus promiscuity is labelled as 'sex addiction', gluttony as 'chocolate addiction' and so on. Carol Sarler records a four year old child in the US being given Ritalin following his parents' painful divorce resulting in him being a complacent zombie boy.[148] Hard situations can result in painful emotions. These have to be lived through and can also build self-reliance. Teaching self-reliance and self-restraint and providing a framework of law that encourages these qualities are the subjects of later chapters.

The issue of personal responsibility is not a new one. One of the characters in Margaret Kennedy's *Ladies of Lyndon,* written in 1923, remarks: "Dolly thinks that our much vaunted civilisation is too much preoccupied with palliatives. She's very strong upon the folly of substitutes for godly living as she calls it. She thinks we concern ourselves too much with averting the consequences of our own acts instead of eradicating folly and vice itself."[149]

6.6   LIMITED GOVERNMENT

Christianity does not prescribe a form of government, but Christianity teaches that human beings are imperfect and Christian thinkers have taught that, whatever the form of government, there must therefore be limits to its powers. Excessive power on the part of the State is likely to lead to an abuse of power, just as a lack of restraint on the part of citizens will cause that power to increase. While, for Christians, the answer to a person's individual predicament may be faith in Jesus Christ and the forgiveness of sins, institutions need to safeguard against the ongoing imperfection of flawed human beings and their schemes on earth. The Christian principle is that the relationship between the State and the citizen will be enhanced when they both acknowledge the authority of a higher law.

Augustine described the two realms that Christians inhabit, the earthly city and the heavenly city. A Christian owes duties to each of them, but they are not the same. Jesus said "Render therefore to Caesar the things that are Caesar's, and to God the things that are God's", and on another occasion advised payment of the temple tax (see Luke 20:25 NKJV and Matthew 17:24-27). But the earthly city cannot determine an individual's eternal destiny. This must be the choice of the person concerned, and so there should be a place for conscience in every person that must be protected from political control. Society is indeed different from the State (as David Cameron has articulated) and it follows that there are private realms into which the State should not trespass. If it does so, the State is tyrannical. Where the State requires the collaboration of its citizens in the execution of tyrannical laws, there may be a moral duty to disobey the State (while submitting to the punishments that the State imposes).

Laws need to be imposed for the protection of the vulnerable and for the good of society. Behaviour which some might regard as justified by a principle of freedom may need to be restrained for the common good. There is no freedom to do physical harm to others, whether by personal violence or, for instance, corporate pollution of the environment. Freedoms, particularly if too widely framed, may conflict and regulation is required so that people can coexist fairly in society. But laws should not extend to all areas of human activity. God has given free will to mankind to choose to obey his moral laws, or to ignore them, though the State needs to reflect some of these moral laws in its secular laws for the protection of individuals and the wellbeing of society. Christians recall that God did not enforce obedience in the Garden of Eden, though he could have done so.

Tacitus observed that the more numerous the laws, the more corrupt the State. A multiplicity of laws points to an overbearing government, a lack of consent and common values, a breakdown of law and order, or a combination of these. Under the Blair government, twenty-seven new laws were introduced each month and under the Brown administration this rose to thirty-three.[150] C.S. Lewis in an article in the *Observer* as early as 1958 reflected: "The modern State exists not to protect our rights but to do us good or make us something. Hence the new name 'leaders' for those who were once 'rulers'. We are less their subjects than their wards, pupils or domestic animals. There is nothing left of which we can say to them, 'Mind your own business'. Our whole lives are their business."

As we shall see in a number of the following chapters, the current UK State, in common with governments in many countries, has assumed jurisdiction over a number of areas of life that in previous generations have been in the charitable or private domain. For those without the means to buy private education, there is only one provider, which is the State. There is a plethora of documentary guidance. The instructions given to State schools issued during the Labour government's tenure about dealing with disruptive pupils ran to six hundred pages. Under the present government it has now been replaced with only fifty-two pages. Once power is assumed by the State, the degree of interference can increase. Some may attribute this to the self-interest of the state functionaries. Their personal prospects can depend upon the scope of their powers and the volume of their activities. More civil servants are required for more control. The Free Schools scheme, modelled on the "charter school" movement in the US, frees schools from local authority control. The move to give greater freedom to schools reflects concerns about the effects of excessive State control in terms of the ideological ethos commonly promoted by public authorities and in relation to teaching methods, once thought to be progressive, but now perceived to be ineffective (see Chapter 13). The hope is that the greater freedom given to Free Schools, by giving schools more responsibility and accountability to the parents, will encourage both an aspiration to excellence and impatience with failure.

In the West, some of the arguments about limited government may now be academic. Theoretical arguments about the limits of the State could become less relevant as it becomes clear that the socio-economic model of most Western economies has only been sustainable by debt and that major structural reforms are necessary to reduce government expenditure. The activities of government will have to shrink because they cannot be paid for. The deficits of past years which have been financed by excessive government borrowing and eased by wealth destroying inflation are unsustainable and must at some point come to an end. However, it is possible that the wrong activities could be cut. The public debate will need to focus upon the important functions of government that must be maintained and upon the policies which need to be adopted. These need to reflect the right purposes of government and these are a theme of this book.

6.7   ENCOURAGING GOOD BEHAVIOUR

Since society is the sum of the collective acts and omissions of individuals, the State, whilst not coercing individuals, may nevertheless need to influence individual choices in limited areas. As advocated by the Apostle Paul (see Romans 13:3) and Calvin, governments should encourage good behaviour in certain areas. This may be done by a "nudge" (favoured by the Chicago University professors Richard Thaler and Cass Sunstein) which can take the form of incentives and disincentives. People may need to be encouraged to do things that will improve their long-term well-being, whether it relates to their health or their financial future. This reflects the thinking of Aquinas who said: "Those who are just rule not out of a desire to dominate, but because it is their duty to give counsel."[151]

Whilst the encouragement of certain types of good behaviour is an obvious requirement for governments with programmes of social change, it is also true to an extent of any kind of government, even one that believes that government should have a limited role. All governments should have a vision of what kind of society is desirable and, by implication, what type of social character they wish to encourage in their citizens. Thus taxation policy can be used to encourage families to stay intact, whereas in the UK it currently disadvantages them compared with single people living together (see Chapter 14). In France larger families are encouraged by reductions in income tax. However, only some means are permissible to encourage a change in behaviour and only some areas should be regulated by government. The enforcement of one-parent families in China is an example of the State overstepping these limits. Some people may also be concerned that, although human behaviour is frequently irrational or foolish (as Christians and students of behavioural economics would agree), it is not the business of the State to decide what makes people happy and to load the dice accordingly by incentivising certain types of behaviour. The distinction should be one between those actions that are solely a matter of private happiness and ones that will affect the relationships between people in society, or that tend to impose burdens on the State. Thus, while it may be right for reasons of public health and order to discourage the consumption of alcohol by levying excise duty or by imposing minimum prices, it would not be good to deprive people of the freedom to drink by banning alcohol altogether. And it would not be appropriate to discourage the purchase of harmless but excessive fashion accessories or luxury foods, even if the purchase of these is not thought to be a responsible use of resources.

6.8   CHANGES IN CULTURE AND THOUGHT

Because the character of a person may determine their behaviour to a greater extent than the law, a change in the culture of thought in society may be more important as an agent of change in society than government policy reflected in legislation. Aquinas held that the object of human society is a virtuous life. While we may accept this, the State should not impose (rather than encourage) virtue, however we may define "virtue".

Protestant Christian thinking emphasises the importance of the personal accountability of individuals to God without the need for intermediaries, so that people make their own choices within the limits of the law, guided by moral principle. For Christians, these principles will be informed by an understanding of the truths revealed in the Bible, and they should be reluctant to accept teaching only because it is handed down by an authority, whether that authority is secular or church-based. A Christian accustomed to checking whether a pastor is theologically correct is unlikely to accept uncritically the pronouncements of those holding political power, whom they know to be vulnerable (as the Bible teaches that all human beings are) to self-interest, self-deception, pride and error. Truth and virtue are objective realities, but need to be discovered subjectively.

6.9   THE IMPORTANCE OF CIVIL SOCIETY

We have seen that there should be limits on the scope of the authority of government. Further, as a practical matter, many other structures and associations influence human behaviour. Society is made up of a number of institutions and bodies: family, social networks, associations, churches, the voluntary sector, schools and universities and the media, all of which influence people. Abraham Kuyper, the Dutch theologian and Prime Minister (1901-1905), formulated a number of spheres of activity that have a right to exist within, but separate from, the State, reflecting the dispersal of power in the Old Testament society. It follows from the theory of limited government that government should not attempt to control these bodies or to dictate to them what their beliefs should be or whom their membership should include, unless they promote unlawful behaviour. Kuyper held that for government "To take over the tasks of society and of the family therefore lies outside its jurisdiction."[152] Freedom of association in these bodies is a reflection of the freedom given by God and has always been part of the bedrock of a free and democratic society. In the UK, anti-discrimination legislation relating to sexual orientation can be used to limit this freedom where, for instance, the law does not allow a religious organisation to decline to employ a person who does not share the organisation's beliefs as to sexual ethics. (These issues are discussed in Chapter 7.)

6.10 EXCESSIVE GOVERNMENT

The scope of some anti-discrimination monitoring has represented a significant use of resources. Philip Davies, the MP for Shipley, described in 2011 the implementation of the Equality Act as "a blizzard of extra bureaucracy."[153] It was reported that the Department of Energy and Climate Change examined whether homosexuals in civil partnerships had been unfairly treated by the suspension of a £300 million home insulation scheme. The Department of Transport issued a study into harassment and discrimination on ships and hovercraft, which included a study of its impact on transsexuals. And the Department for Environment, Food and Rural Affairs (DEFRA) investigated the impact that boosting fish stocks would have on, amongst others, Chinese and Welsh speakers. Philip Davies has said that the equality laws are "ludicrous and pointless" while Dominic Raab MP referred to them as "divisive."[154] There is also a concern that public authorities might withhold services from people or discriminate against them by reason of a failure to complete diversity surveys. Eric Pickles, the Communities Secretary, issued statutory guidance which clarifies that there is no requirement for local authorities to carry out "lifestyle or diversity questionnaires".[155] However, this may not prevent them from doing so. In November 2012 David Cameron announced that he wished to dispense with impact assessments under the Equality Act, though the provisions of the Act remain in force and the Act was supported by his party when in opposition.

Minette Marrin commented on the projection by the charity, the Trussell Trust, that by the year 2015 500,000 people would be fed by food banks: "How can this be when we are spending £110 billion a year on welfare (along with £121 billion on healthcare and £122 billion on pensions)?" She concluded that social services should abandon all work not dealing with a lack of the most basic social care, a safe home and, above all, food. "If people have to turn to charity for food, what point is our elaborate welfare state?"[156]

Excessive regulation can be deadly. Simon Burgess, a charity worker, drowned in a three foot deep pond after the emergency services refused to rescue him because the water was higher than ankle deep. A lady onlooker said to a fireman "You're having a laugh" but he replied "No, that's health and safety".[157]

6.11   PROPAGANDA

The exercise of excessive State power is often accompanied by government propaganda, which has long been a feature of totalitarian regimes. But the distinction between propaganda and the justified dissemination of public information can be blurred. Heather Brooke records that the average UK local authority spent twice as much (£971,985) on publicity in 2007-8 as it did in 1996-7 and that twenty councils together spent more than £100 million. In 2006-7 the deprived borough of Tower Hamlets spent £2,354,000 on public relations, an increase of 86.2% on ten years before.[158] Brooke comments that the information tends to be self-congratulatory with fulsome references to the achievements of local councillors and officials while scandals are ignored. Central government employs at least 709 public relations personnel.

6.12 OUR PERSONAL DATA AND THE POTENTIAL FOR MISUSE

In the UK at the present time, government entities have access to significant amounts of personal data which potentially gives them power over individuals. Crime and terrorism related legislation in recent times have included control orders (replaced in January 2012 by Terrorism Prevention and Investigation Measures), ASBOs (to be replaced by Crime Prevention Injunctions) and detention without charge for terrorism offences. Concerns on the part of the population in relation to terrorism can lead people to prefer security over liberty. Human beings are flawed and discretionary powers will almost inevitably be misused. This was illustrated when powers of surveillance given to public authorities to prevent terrorism were then used by local government for purposes that were not intended by the legislators. Benjamin Franklin's saying that "Any society that would give a little liberty to gain a little security will deserve neither and lose both"[159] is familiar, and it highlights the need for absolute principles to underpin a free society.

There are, as Helen Brooke records in *The Silent State*,[160] at least six national databases containing details in relation to children. Databases can easily be misused to defame or vilify (without their knowledge since there may be no criminal proceedings) those whom the State finds inconvenient but who have committed no offence. Brooke details the case of Jane Clift who, when she complained about a Council employee, was put on a database designating her as a "medium threat" on a par with a violent criminal. Fortunately she was later able to win a case in defamation. A mother who left her four children to play while she bought her fifth child an ice cream returned to find her four children being interviewed by the police. She subsequently discovered that she had a record on the Criminal Records Database when she applied to become a voluntary Sunday school teacher. Robert King, a teacher who was cleared of sexual offences, was unable to work because the allegations continued to appear on a Criminal Records Bureau (CRB) check. (There are currently calls to reform the CRB.) Primary school children have had their names recorded on "hate incident" registers. In the period 2008 to 2009 more than 10,000 incidents of primary school children making homophobic or racist remarks were recorded. School heads were told to keep records of racist incidents in 2002 and in 2007 were advised to include disability and homophobic incidents.[161]

Philip Johnston in his book *Bad Laws* referred to a Joint Parliamentary Committee on Human Rights which expressed concern that a children's database contained a category relating to "the existence of any cause for concern" about a child.[162] Johnston quotes Professor Ross Anderson, an expert on database security, who says that: "There will always be bent insiders. If you connect all these systems up and you've got a million professionals needing to access this every day, it will all get out. Paedophiles, for example, can use the database to find out which children in their neighbourhood are vulnerable and where they live."[163] Current concerns (as of 2012) include the Communications Data Bill which would require internet service providers to store details of electronic communications and make them available for inspection by government agencies.

6.13   GOVERNMENT POWER AND SOCIAL JUSTICE

The extent to which social justice should be brought in by law or left to the operation of structures in society that encourage moral behaviour is one that will be different for each society. Change may need to be either incremental or revolutionary, and the starting points will be different for each society at any given point in time. The UK at the present time is heavily socialised with relatively high rates of taxation, even of the relatively poor, and has extensive social welfare arrangements. Before the Second World War, rates of taxation, particularly for the poor, were much lower or non-existent, but welfare provision was left to a much greater extent to voluntary agencies. It seems unlikely that in the short or medium term voluntary agencies could provide the services on the scale that the State currently provides. But, in the longer term, as long as the uneven nature of voluntary welfare can be remedied (since not all areas will have the same voluntary resources), voluntary agencies may provide a more just and efficient way of caring for the disadvantaged than government run arrangements, since they can better encourage self-sufficiency and human dignity.[164]

Welfare policies that discourage initiative and deprive people of responsibility for their own future prevent them from realising their full potential. God means people to flourish and to be fulfilled in relationships and in community. Whilst the vulnerable and weak need protection and help, and others may need assistance at particular points in their lives, long term dependence on the State (except where it is necessary, as in the case of disability) can undermine the incentive for people to take responsibility for their lives and flourish as they should.

6.14   THE CHALLENGES OF WELFARE

In the UK, if welfare provision is to be affordable now and in the future, particularly with the demographic changes that will result in fewer working people supporting more pensioners, fundamental change is required. Sheila Lawlor has made the case for a genuine insurance system based upon Beveridge's original idea of contributions paid into a fund by the worker, the employer and the State in exchange for benefits if earnings ceased because of sickness, unemployment, retirement or bereavement. The insurance fund could be ring fenced or have a state guaranteed rate of return linked to inflation. For those who are unemployed and have built up no contributions over the years, it would be necessary for there to be a basic subsistence sum, but contributors would build up higher levels of benefit. In this way, there would be an incentive to seek work.

The current proposed reform is to introduce a universal credit. This rationalises and restricts the current patchwork of benefits which can result in people being better off out of work than in work. (It has been estimated that the lower paid can have an effective tax rate of 90% on earnings taking into account the effect of benefits.)[165] The proposed welfare reforms do not incorporate a link between contributions and benefits in the provision of State benefits, though this link is recognised in occupational pension schemes, which are to become compulsory for most employees. It is this link that encourages people to take responsibility for their lives. Their actions at one point should affect their position at another. If some people choose not to work or save (and for others there may be very good reasons beyond their control why they are unable do either), it is a moral principle that the results of that choice should be recognised. The Apostle Paul expressed the principle rather starkly when he said: "If a man will not work, he shall not eat" (2 Thessalonians 3:10, NIV). The State or private bodies may need to intervene to help those in need as a matter of charity, but it is part of the moral order that actions should have their consequences and that entitlement be connected with responsibility. Sweden has a welfare system which recognises contributions in the form of insurance premiums, with a lower level of income support (which can be difficult to obtain) for those who have no record of payments.[166]

As of 2011 the number of households in which every adult has never had any paid work stood at 370,000, a rise of 5 per cent on the previous year (it stood at 284,000 in 2008). Some people may not be much better off taking a job than staying on benefits. If this is the case, they cannot be blamed for not working and taking the best advantage of the system. Since 1997, a single mother of two children has seen her benefits rise by 85 per cent. People respond to the economic incentives of the welfare system. It was reported that in 2011 there were approximately 70,000 people who could not get a job, and were therefore entitled to benefits, because they could not speak

English. In September 2011, the Prime Minister suggested that, for these people, attending an English course should be a condition of receiving benefits. While it may not be possible, for instance in relation to people coming from the EU, to restrict entry into the country on the part of those who do not speak English, the economic incentives to do so could be adjusted by limiting benefits in these cases.

The State is wrong to remove from people the incentive to work and thereby to relegate a vast number of people to unfulfilled lives. Until the recent recession, many jobs were created in the UK, but the statistics suggest that a very significant number of them were taken by those from overseas. During the last decade, five-and-a-half million people entered the country looking for jobs and homes. In the six years since Poland became a full member of the European Union, the number of Polish nationals working in the UK rose from 50,000 to nearly 400,000. More than 100,000 foreign nationals registered to work in Newham when the Olympic facilities were being built. At the same time, some 5 million people are currently on out-of-work benefits. According to the Office of National Statistics, of the 1.8 million rise in employment from 1997 to 2010, 99 per cent was due to immigration, though this was reduced to 82% between 2010 and 2011.[167] This is not to suggest that the unemployed were necessarily in a position to take jobs, or that they would have been selected for them if they had applied for those jobs. It is likely that the overseas workers were employed because they were better trained or qualified, had a better attitude to work, had better experience or were more mobile. In 2011 only 75% of children reached the required Level 4 at Key Stage 2 in maths and English when they left primary school at the age of 11, though this improved to 79% in 2012. Many of these children do not achieve much better literacy at secondary school and leave school functionally illiterate and therefore unqualified for most jobs.

According to James Bartholomew, in Sweden, after the financial crisis of the 1990s, unemployment increased "until there were simply too many well-remunerated claimants for too few taxpayers".[168]   More than one in five people of working age were on one benefit or another.   As in most countries, parts of the UK are more dependent on the State than others. The Centre for Economics and Business Research estimated in 2011 that State spending accounts for 57% of output in the North East and 63 per cent in the North West.[169] Essays edited by the American libertarian academic Tom Palmer, published as *After the Welfare State*, take the view that the current welfare systems will bankrupt Western economies.[170]   James Bartholomew records that in Sweden the benefits system was reformed in the 1990s — unemployment benefits and the length of time during which it could be received were reduced and claimants were required to take menial jobs. Similarly, in Germany in 2005, Gerhard Schröder pushed through Parliament a programme called "Agenda 2010".   Although he was defeated in the subsequent election, the programme survived and reformed the German welfare state by reducing unemployment benefits and regulation. It was also agreed with trade unions that wages would be held down in return for job security through a short work scheme under which workers' hours were reduced to avoid lay-offs and the government covered part of the lost wages. 1.5 million Germans benefited from the scheme and it cost €4.6 billion at its peak in 2009. According to an OECD report, it saved 500,000 jobs though, according to an International Labour Organisation report, real earnings dropped by 4.5% over the decade.

The provision of money alone by government to those in poverty may be a short or longer term necessity, but it is no more the answer to long-term poverty in the UK than it is in relation to overseas aid. In overseas aid it is now recognised that the aim should be sustainable economic self-sufficiency (see Chapter 21). Similarly employment of some kind must be the overriding objective of welfare for those who are able to work. Only recently are "welfare to work" schemes being undertaken in the UK. Those providing the services report that a significant proportion of clients have problems of various kinds which the programmes are designed to overcome. These include basic literacy and numeracy, drug or alcohol problems, lack of transport, lack of self-esteem, and a need for skills, training and experience. Long-term unemployment de-motivates and de-skills people. The National Institute for Economic and Social Research estimated in 2001 that 320,000 people had permanently withdrawn from the workforce.[171] One in six children grows up in a workless household[172] and poverty is passed down the generations. The challenges are huge.

Changes in public attitude are required. The virtues of thrift, familiar to older generations, need to be rediscovered. As Charles Moore has pointed out,[173] governments have disincentivised self-reliance by allowing inflation (which destroys savings), by tax (the changes to the pensions regime) and by welfare. Moore quotes Samuel Smiles, the author of *Self Help* (written in 1875) who highlighted the dangers of dependency: "Give a man money without working and he will soon claim it as a right." Saving is the responsibility of all wage earners and the Victorians established an economic framework and institutions by which this could easily be done. Today, both the bank and Government savings schemes offer individuals rates of interest well below the rate of inflation, which constitutes a disincentive to potential savers. Some may suggest that in the current recession the Government is right to encourage consumption, not saving. But this would be to take a short-term view. It is in the interests of government that it encourages people to take responsibility for their finances. By allowing negative real interest rates (interest rates lower than the rate of inflation), the government oversees the erosion of the value of savings year by year. Further, it then requires savers to pay tax (subject to tax allowances) on the inadequate nominal interest (which does not compensate for inflation) paid on saved earnings that have already been taxed. The government should offer State guaranteed savings accounts at inflation linked interest rates, and interest on savings accounts should only be taxed on any gain above the rate of inflation.

6.15 CONTRACTING OUT PUBLIC SERVICES AND UTILITIES

The UK government and some overseas governments have been seeking to reduce the size and cost of the State and to find new ways of providing public services. The new models could include the corporatisation or mutualisation of activities previously run as State enterprises and the hope is that increased competition will result in efficiencies. But the imperfection of human nature suggests that caution is required. Any transfer of public activities to the private sector can result in conflicts of interest and/or the enrichment of individuals, and such transfers may be irreversible. Furthermore, effective competition may be impossible to achieve, as in the water industry, where inevitably monopolies continue in the private sector and the industry needs to be regulated (admittedly with some past success in the UK). In the UK, energy companies compete but the array of complicated tariff options, which many people do not have the time to investigate, effectively limits competition. In November 2012 the government announced that they would be introducing a compulsory simplification of the tariffs with the possibility of compulsory switches to the cheapest option, but (as at January 2013) implementation has been limited.

The privatisation of infrastructure presents challenges. A suggested plan that the maintenance and the expansion of the motorway network be transferred to private operators would be complex since, as with water, there is a built in geographical monopoly (water cannot be easily and cheaply transported). Monopolies require regulation by contract or by laws and these can be flawed to a greater or lesser extent. Moreover, any system of regulation is likely to be inadequate to ensure good behaviour.

Where current arrangements for privatised utilities are already embedded, it may not be practicable to make radical changes, even if those arrangements are not ideal. Taking the water utilities in the UK as an example, the existing regime (which involves licences under which the assets have been transferred on a long-term basis to a company listed on The Stock Exchange) effectively limits the government's options for the future. If the government were to decide that it would be better to grant concessions on a competitive basis for a limited period in the same way as a railway operating franchise, it would be necessary to compensate the existing shareholders.

While competition can be an incentive to efficient commercial behaviour, it may not be the best motivator of those providing a public service. William T. Muhairwe records the transformation of the National Water and Sewerage Corporation of Uganda from an extremely inefficient state body to an effective and dynamic organisation by inspirational leadership and rigorous management.[174] It is difficult to regulate many kinds of performance by contract, as the Private Finance Initiative (PFI) programme in the UK has illustrated. The new programme, called PF2, launched in December 2012, aims to address some of the flaws, but the capacity of contracts to deal with complex commercial realities is limited. Payment mechanisms (which deduct amounts from the contract price for failure to perform specific functions) may be too lenient or too harsh and it is difficult to calibrate them in advance. In any event these mechanisms can only cover a selection of indicators of contractual performance. Commercial companies recognise this fact and in practice rely upon the trust built up in long-term relationships, but with short contractual periods, since purely contractual remedies may be inadequate. It may be necessary to end a contractual relationship even where there is no clear non-performance which constitutes the necessary legal ground for termination due to breach of contract. The changes to the PFI model embodied in PF2 seek to address some of the limitations of a long-term contract by taking many of the services out of the contract, but the need for the capital development to be funded by private finance on a long-term basis and the requirement to use a wide range of standard documentation inevitably build in a degree of inflexibility.

The limitations inherent in contracts, particularly those which incorporate payment by results, attend the arrangements for the welfare to work programme, the intervention contracts for families with multiple problems and the contracts for the services of mentors to those leaving prison. Payment by results may seem to be a good principle, but its conversion into contractual terms is problematic. The actual results may be the outcome of a large number of variables and risks, many of which are unconnected with the good (or otherwise) performance of the contract. This has been recognised in many government contracts to the extent that only a proportion of contractual payments are dependent upon results.

A concern about the contracting out of government functions is that in some areas, for instance the defence sector, different performance standards may be required to those in the private sector. In some cases failure may need to be insured against in a manner which is not compatible with conventional risk allocation. There are private sector areas, for instance in relation to aircraft, where the risks of failure are very high and systems have been developed to address them. But it can be difficult to reduce these to contractual terms while creating a fair allocation of risk, and contractual inputs may be uncertain and outputs difficult to quantify.

Tendering procedures for public contracts, particularly those governed by the UK's procurement Regulations derived from European Union Directives, can also be inflexible and bureaucratic. Evaluation procedures need to be carried out in accordance with the methodologies in the tender documents (which can be difficult to prepare, particularly for new types of contract) and strict adherence to those methodologies can sometimes result in the wrong bidder being awarded the contract.

The introduction of elements of competition into public services is challenging and this is apparent in the 2012 health service reforms. Even competition in relation to quality may be problematic, since some facilities will have a built in advantage, for example because they are more up to date or because of their location. The purposes of the State in providing a high standard of public service may also be deflected by commercial competition since competition can incentivise the wrong kind of behaviour. Commercial competition can also dilute the motivation of members of staff who would prefer to see themselves primarily as servants of the public good and not as commercial managers. On the other hand, rigorous standards, efficient management and a culture of excellence need to be maintained. A limited element of competition, for instance in relation to reputation, together with efficient management and effective systems of accountability, rather than a commercial competitive framework, can encourage the achievement of these goals.

Attempts to ensure good performance solely by contract are limited in a similar way to the manner in which laws are limited in their effect, though these are necessary. Good contracts, though they may contribute to good performance, cannot ensure it. Other motivations for performance, such as long-term relationships with customers, good management and healthy relationships within the organisation, a strategic vision and an ethical framework for doing business, may be more significant.

6.16   THE PURPOSES OF GOVERNMENT

If government should be limited in its aims, what should those aims be? In Christian thinking, it is the common good of all of society where the formulation of this "good" is informed by what the Christian perceives as the Creator's best plan for human beings. There is the primary purpose of protection and order, enabled by just laws impartially applied, which allows people to lead free and flourishing lives. In Christian thinking, an aspect of a flourishing life which also serves the common good is the freedom for individuals to come to a conclusion about the purpose of a person's life on earth and his or her eternal destiny. For the Apostle Paul, writing to Timothy, governments need to create the means by which people could lead "peaceful and quiet lives" (1 Timothy 2:2 NIV). This idea was echoed by Hobbes, but Paul had a purpose in mind — that people should be in a position to come to understand the truth about God.

Paul also said that the law (referring to the Jewish law) is a "schoolmaster" in that it teaches right and wrong and enables people to see their need for repentance and divine rescue. Some Christians would extend this principle to include civil laws, particularly those which reflect a moral principle. The criminal law should restrain evil and therefore protect society. It should also represent a set of values that society recognises as a reflection of right and wrong. The criminal law should inform people's consciences although, in a post Christian society, there may be occasions where the criminal law conflicts with what Christians perceive to be a fundamental moral law.

For the Christian, Government should protect those things that have been given to a person by God and it should not be within the power of a human being to take them away. Secular thinkers may refer to some of these matters as the subject of human rights, and the concept of human rights (discussed in the next chapter) has some similarities with Christian teaching. Christians would see some obligations that are perceived in secular terms as the subject of man-made human rights as the function of duties owed to God. This confers upon them an ultimate value, since they derive their nature from the character of an eternal God who created mankind in his own image. For the Christian, it is possible to reach conclusions about what those duties are and the ways in which the rights that flow from those duties should be protected. Christian principles provide a framework for exploring what it means for an individual to lead a flourishing life and what should be the role of the State in protecting people as they aspire to lead that life in our complex and multi-layered society. Later chapters explore more specific areas of policy in the light of Christian political thinking. The following chapter looks at some of the tensions between the powers of the State and the freedom of the individual which have arisen in recent years.

7

CONSCIENCE, RIGHTS AND THE PUBLIC GOOD

(A large part of this chapter first appeared in *Religion and Law*, edited by
Nick Spencer, published by Theos in 2012)

7.1 HUMAN RIGHTS THEORY

Much of modern thinking in relation to issues of equality and
discrimination is based upon human rights. Human rights
theory is helpful in asserting that there are universal values and,
for many rights theorists, these are derived from the nature of
human beings. However, there remain significant theoretical
and practical difficulties with a secular view of human rights.
There is no common agreement as to the source of the rights. If
we cannot agree how rights arise or how they are conferred, it
is difficult to agree what they should be. Furthermore, there is
no common basis for a discussion about the way in which rights
should be applied, in particular in relation to the precedence to
be accorded to conflicting rights.

In Christian thinking, rights exist either as the expression of
a gift from God upon which human beings must not trespass,
for instance the right to (or sanctity of) life, or as a function of
obligations that are owed to others. These include the duties that
human beings owe to their creator. The utilitarian philosopher
Jeremy Bentham held that rights are merely "the fruits of the
law, and of the law alone" and that there are "no rights anterior
to the law". For him, rights were only the product of man-
made legal obligations. There is some logic in this, since a right
cannot exist without an obligation and it can be argued that the
obligation must exist before the right arises. If this is correct,
the question is how an obligation arises. For the Christian, the
obligations stem from the duties of a human being to love God
and to love the neighbour. The good behaviour (to act in ways
that respect and benefit others) which results from those duties

may be regarded by secular theorists as the subject of rights, but the theoretical foundation of those rights in secular thought is fragile. There is no agreement as to the source of the rights or the basis of any duties which might give rise to them.

Some issues about the exercise of belief that surface as matters of conscience for believers concern the welfare of people generally. The ban on Sunday trading was not only about allowing believers to go to church, although in the UK employees must resign their employment to exercise their right to worship on Sunday if there is a conflict.[175] More importantly, it was also about whether it is good for there to be one day when families are able to gather together for rest and relaxation and to strengthen family bonds. Christian teaching indicates that a communal day of rest is part of the created order. In this case, the debate should not have focussed primarily on the principle of freedom of religion, but on the issue of the public good. The fact that the issue involved a Christian principle for individuals made it easier for those in favour of Sunday trading to represent the arguments against it as those of a minority group.

7.2 THEORETICAL AND PRACTICAL DIFFICULTIES WITH HUMAN RIGHTS THEORY

The assertion of rights without recognising the duties from which they flow can lead to injustice. Human rights theory can fail to draw out adequately the distinction which Cicero makes (quoting Zeno) between things which are materially advantageous for individuals and things which contribute to the common good.[176] Rights by their nature, whether they are defensive (to stop others doing something), or are in the nature of a claim to an interest or a good, are a reflection of human autonomy. They are centred upon individuals and their personal treatment. This means that the rights need to be asserted and enforced by those who have been prejudiced by an infringement of the rights. This can automatically disenfranchise those who, because they are weak or vulnerable, are unable to assert the rights. In a number of cases, a concept of rights is not appropriate because it is impossible for the person affected to exercise a right. Those who are mentally incapacitated, or who are in a coma, cannot assert their rights, though others may nevertheless have duties towards them. Although beneficiaries under wills can be said to have rights which are enshrined in law, it is more satisfactory to explain why it is right to carry out the wishes of a dead person in terms of a duty to honour those wishes rather than a human right, because the person who is dead cannot have a right in theory or exercise one in practice. Whether or not there is agreement upon the content of rights, there are conceptual limitations built into the concept of human rights and these inevitably spill over into issues surrounding their exercise.

In practical terms, even on the assumption that it is appropriate to define particular aspirations for human beings in terms of rights, some so-called "rights" may at particular points in time be simply undeliverable. For example, it does not make sense to claim that there is an absolute legal right to food and water in circumstances where, immediately following a natural disaster, no-one is physically capable of delivering them. There would, however, be a moral duty on others to do all they can to deliver humanitarian aid and that aid may extend beyond the provision of food and water. There may also be humanitarian duties to provide welfare in the form of economic benefits to people in some circumstances which, for others in different circumstances, might be regarded as a gift or a privilege and not a human right.

Because rights are personal, they can be released by consent. But such consent may be wrongly given. An elderly person may consent to relinquish the right to life because they do not want to be a burden on their relations (while not being coerced in any way). But they may make the wrong choice in purely human terms (apart from any Christian belief in the sanctity of life or in the life hereafter), both for themselves and for their close family.

The perception that duties precede rights connects with the belief in a creator. Duties do not exist unless they are owed to a person. For the Christian, duties are owed to the Creator as well as to other human beings. Human beings may be able to absolve others of their duties towards them and relinquish the rights that stem from those duties. But duties owed to God cannot be so easily disposed of. By way of example, for Christians there is a duty to God, as well as to other people, to live and to sustain life. The reflection of this duty is the right to life. But if the duty to live is owed to God, that duty cannot be released either by a person who commits suicide or by those who might be adversely affected by the suicide, even if they could all be identified and were able to give their consent (some may be unborn). In Christian thinking, the duty is owed to God and it is absolute. In theological terms it is therefore more satisfactory to speak of a "duty to live" and a "duty to sustain life", rather than a "right to life".

Whereas Christian principle holds that there is a duty not to kill an unborn human being (whether or not that human being has any rights or the means to exercise them), human rights legislation does not recognise that a human being has any human rights until birth. This is illogical, since a foetus is capable of living outside the womb after 22 or 24 weeks and often does so. The necessity of asserting a right in law rather than requiring compliance with a duty means that the beneficiary of the right needs to have the status in law of a person. The current law does not recognise an unborn child as having the human rights of a born child.

It can be difficult for those without substantial financial resources to assert their rights. In the UK the Equality and Human Rights Commission, other State bodies and well-funded lobby groups are capable of funding actions in law and claiming substantial costs from the losing side. In practice this can prevent people defending claims of alleged discrimination. The resolution of issues that arise from conflicts of beliefs by reference to rights may enrich some lawyers, but can result in an "inequality of arms" where one side is better resourced and can therefore intimidate the other.

7.3   LIVING OUT BELIEFS

Christian thinking is based upon the gift of free will by God who gives individuals the choice as to what to believe. This foundational principle supports the free expression of beliefs and opinions. Christian teaching is that government is also given for the purpose of protection. So in some cases, where a manifestation of belief causes harm to others, it may need to be curtailed. So the expression of a belief accompanied by physical violence, or the threat of physical violence, is wrong and the criminal law is needed to restrain it.

A person's ability to hold a belief, as opposed to acting upon it, should normally be unquestioned. An exception might be oaths of obedience to the State or its sovereign by service personnel, though these can relate to the execution of a common purpose (the defence of the State) and need not extend to particular beliefs. As we shall see, the principle of freedom of belief has been significantly eroded in the case of UK public servants.

Issues in relation to the manifestation of a belief can be complex. It can be said that nearly all belief requires some manifestation, if only that of gathering with others to share the belief. In practice, the requirements of a religion go beyond this. As James (the brother of Jesus) put it, "faith without works is dead" (James 2:20 KJV). According to the European Convention on Human Rights (ECHR), freedom of thought, conscience and religion is a right that can be limited by governments "in the interests of public safety, for the protection of public order, health or morals, or for the protection of the rights and freedoms of others".[177]

In practice, the State has to make choices about which manifestations it is prepared to allow, and it should have a rationale in terms of the public good for its conclusions. There has been some inconsistency in the policy of the UK government. The law has allowed the manifestation in dress of a Sikh's belief in that Sikhs have a right to wear a turban at work or a *kara* bangle to school. But, until the judgment of the European Court of Human Rights (the European Court) on 15th January 2013 in the case of *Eweida and Others v The United Kingdom*, the judgment of the UK courts (which was argued by the UK government in the case before the European Court, but which was overruled by the Court) was that Christians could be prohibited from wearing a cross at work on the grounds that this was not a generally recognised form of practising the Christian faith.

To take another kind of manifestation of belief, the General Medical Council brought a case against Dr Richard Scott who was accused of sharing his faith with a patient in a one to one consultation.[178] (The facts of this case are a little unclear, because at the hearing the complainant did not appear, so Dr Scott had no opportunity to cross-examine the complainant about what was actually said, which is contrary to the principles of natural justice.)

7.4   DISCRIMINATION AND THE PUBLIC GOOD

The next sections look at recent development of the law in relation to non-discrimination as it affects public functions, employment and the provision of services. But first we reflect upon some general considerations relating to a right not to be discriminated against.

Arguments expressed in terms of secular human rights and non-discrimination focus on the effect on those affected by the alleged discrimination. They can therefore by-pass issues of the public good. Human rights are seen as absolute. Once they are invoked, they automatically trump other concerns. Since a right of non discrimination may conflict with other rights and can inflict significant burdens on others, it should only be introduced where there is an overwhelming need in terms of the public good. A group should only be accorded protection in law from discrimination by virtues of its characteristics or beliefs where it has been decided, after examination of all the evidence, that those characteristics and beliefs are good, or neutral, or beyond the control of those who have them (such as disability). Even if this test is passed, it must also be in the public interest to provide specific legal protection for those characteristics or beliefs.

The relative values to be attached, on the one hand, to the freedom to act in a certain way towards a person (for instance to decline to offer a benefit such as employment or a service) and, on the other hand, to the right or interest of a person to receive the benefit should be assessed in terms of the public good. The weight attached to the right or interest may depend upon the circumstances in any particular case. For instance, if a person is denied work by one person, but work is freely available from other sources, the effect on that person may be insignificant. On the other hand, where a person is denied work by all providers then the effects will be more serious. So if a significant proportion of red haired people were deprived of work, there might need to be a law to protect them. But if this occurs hardly at all, there is no need for the law. At present any person may be discriminated against on account of the colour of their hair since this is not a characteristic which is protected in law.

Even where a policy of non-discrimination in relation to the provision of goods and services to certain classes of people is justified prima facie on the grounds of the public good, it does not necessarily mean that the persons affected should never be refused goods and services. There may be a good justification for the refusal. There may be another right or interest that should take precedence over the interests of those who would otherwise receive the services. For instance, disabled people are entitled to reasonable access to facilities. But this is not an absolute right. There are still a large number of buildings that they cannot easily access and where they have no legal rights of redress. This is because in some cases it would be unreasonable to require building owners to undertake expensive works (which might put them out of business) in order to provide access for disabled people.

Incidentally, the example of disabled access illustrates the point that a policy of non-discrimination need not necessarily approve the condition of those who might be discriminated against. A policy of non-discrimination in favour of disabled people does not mean that we should celebrate disability as a good in itself, as opposed to the courage, resourcefulness and good humour of the individuals who overcome disability. Although exceptional people have found personal growth in disability, for instance in renewed compassion, disability is an aspect of an imperfect world.

A legal right not to be discriminated against (if there is one in any particular case) may conflict with the exercise of conscience. It may be helpful to separate three strands in the issue of conscience. The first one is the freedom to believe that a practice is wrong and the right to exercise that belief. Not all beliefs may be manifested, since some may adversely affect the legitimate interests of others, for instance if they are violent or if they conflict with other laws, for instance health and safety. Thus, for instance, a Hindu may not have a funeral pyre in a public place. Muslim nurses may have to wear close fitting rather than free flowing hijabs for health and safety reasons.

Secondly, there is the issue of public good. A belief may be irrational and may lack the support of any recognised framework of belief, or the framework of belief may be damaging to society. It is necessary to have some criteria to decide whether a belief is irrational or damaging. These may be informed by a perception as to whether the belief system is generally good for society. Where the State makes a fundamental change to laws and customs and then gives a non-discrimination right to those who support the change, this right may conflict with the conscience of others. In this case the State should have a considered view, based upon evidence and backed by public consensus, that the change is good for society. For example, in the case of relationships which are endorsed by law, it needs to be determined whether these relationships are good for those who might be encouraged to enter into them and for those who may be affected by them.

Except in cases where the original laws or customs that are superseded by a change in law are dangerous, the State should endeavour to accommodate those people who believe that the changes are wrong. The issue was discussed in the Joint Partly Dissenting Opinion of judges Nicolas Bratza and David Thor Bjorgvinsson on 15th January 2013 in the case of *Eweida and Others v The United Kingdom* before the European Court. The judges made the point that Lillian Ladele's disinclination to perform civil partnership ceremonies should be accommodated since the legislation for civil partnerships was introduced after Ms Ladele's appointment as a Registrar. It is inconsistent that a person can be educated by the State to believe that a certain kind of behaviour is wrong (particularly if it was, until recent times, illegal) but that person can subsequently, as result of a change in government policy, be penalised for believing what they have been taught.

Thirdly, there is the role of the State and the question as to whether the law should be intervening at all to support a particular practice or belief by providing a non-discrimination right. Where a type of relationship or behaviour is to be endorsed by law, it must be clearly demonstrated to be unambiguously good and sufficiently good, both for individuals and for society, for it to be appropriate for the State to promote the relationship or behaviour by legal sanctions. It should also be the subject of widespread consent. (We explore substantive questions of the public good in relation to certain legal relationships in Chapter 14.)

UK law has a legal requirement of non-discrimination in employment on the grounds of gender, race or colour on the grounds that this contributes to social cohesion. It also has a legal requirement of non-discrimination in relation to religion or belief. But religion and belief are different from gender, race or colour. Belief is not a permanent defining characteristic similar in nature to ethnic origin. Ethnicity cannot be changed, but beliefs may be debated and altered. In some rare cases, even discrimination on the grounds of race may possibly be justified, when for instance the casting of a play or film requires persons of a certain race or colour to portray the relevant story convincingly.

7.5   EMPLOYEES OF THE STATE AND PUBLIC FUNCTIONS

In the UK those holding certain public offices have not been allowed to hold beliefs and act upon them, when these beliefs are contrary to government policy on civil partnerships. An example is the case of Lillian Ladele.[179] The issue in the legal case centred around whether Ms Ladele, a registrar, had a right to decline to perform a civil partnership ceremony on the basis of a religious belief. It was decided that she could not do so and therefore was not unfairly dismissed for being unwilling to perform the ceremony. Part of the reasoning of the Court of Appeal in that case was that to decline to act was discrimination against the persons who required the ceremony. Although this had a legal basis in the relevant Regulations, this was the wrong approach, since it was the public authority that was providing the service and not Ms Ladele herself in a personal capacity. Thus only the public authority, and not Ms Ladele, could fail to provide the service and discriminate against a person for not doing so.

If the public authority had found a replacement for Ms Ladele, then there would have been be no discrimination, particularly since those affected need not have been aware of Ms Ladele's disinclination to perform the ceremony. Any disciplinary proceedings against Ms Ladele for failing to carry out a duty should have been decided by reference to her employment arrangements. The issue should have centred upon the latitude that employers should reasonably allow to employees in relation to the issues of conscience in general and Ms Ladele's beliefs in particular. The issue of discrimination should not have been relevant, since she personally could not have been discriminating. So, although the Court applied the relevant law in terms of discrimination, the substantive question should have been whether a public servant should be allowed to hold the belief that homosexual unions are wrong and decline to perform the ceremony. Medical doctors are currently permitted in law to refuse to perform abortions, but this ability to exercise freedom of conscience does not extend to issues in relation to civil partnerships.

In the case of Ladele, given the existing law in relation to discrimination, the Court of Appeal may not have been in a position to consider some of the wider questions of the public good and the role of the State. The law had determined that civil partnerships were valid and the issue of whether civil partnerships are good for society was not revisited by the Court. However, had the Court been able to consider the issue of conscience in terms of the public good, it might have been in a better position to conclude that Ms Ladele's beliefs should have been accommodated. Ms Ladele's views represented those of a rational and traditional set of beliefs and values. If the law had not been changed to allow civil partnerships, the issue for Ms Ladele would never have arisen. The Council could have found others to perform the functions so that gay couples were not prejudiced. In the event, the argument in relation to freedom of conscience was raised and rejected. Lord Justice Laws said that in a multi-faith society no religious belief was worthy of any particular protection since to provide such protection would be "deeply unprincipled".

The Court in the *Ladele* case did not examine whether there was a wider public good in Christian values or whether it was in the public interest not to exclude people of Christian belief from public service. In giving evidence in the case Lord Carey (the former Archbishop of Canterbury) made a point in relation to freedom of conscience which was not received sympathetically by the Court. He pointed out that 2 billion Christians worldwide would support the beliefs of Lillian Ladele, and that to regard such views as discriminatory was wrong. Lord Justice Laws expressed the view that discriminatory conduct need not be disreputable. This is difficult to accept, because it disconnects the law from morality. Where discrimination is legislated against, this should be because the discrimination is wrong and it adversely affects society. People assume (not unreasonably) that this is the reason why the discriminatory behaviour has been made unlawful. If a non-discrimination law is reasonably assumed to be morally right, it was inconsistent for Lord Justice Laws to say that behaviour which is unlawful by reason of that law can be morally acceptable.

In Ms Ladele's appeal to the European Court, the Court stated that the requirement for Ms Ladele to conduct civil partnership ceremonies had a "particularly detrimental effect upon her because of her religious beliefs" but held (by a majority of four to two) that the policy of the local authority in "requiring all employees to act in a way which does not discriminate against others" was justified on the grounds that it protected same-sex couples from discrimination. The judgment of the Court recited "rota difficulties" caused by Ms Ladele's refusal to conduct civil partnership ceremonies. However, it did not consider in detail whether the local authority's actions in dismissing Ms Ladele were proportionate to achieve the goal of non-discrimination against same-sex couples or whether it was necessary to put Ms Ladele in a position where she might be regarded as discriminating.

The European Court reached a similar decision to that in relation to Ms Ladele in the case of Gary McFarlane who was employed as a counsellor by Relate Avon Limited (Relate). Mr McFarlane was dismissed from his employment because he refused, on the grounds of his religious belief, to commit himself to providing psycho-sexual counselling to same sex couples. The Court held that his employer was justified in dismissing him in order to protect others from discrimination. The rehearsal of the facts of the case in the judgment implies that Court did not believe that it was possible to achieve this end without dismissing Mr McFarlane. The Court also held that Mr McFarlane had voluntarily entered into a contract of employment knowing that it would have an effect upon the manifestation of his religious beliefs. However, it is not clear from the judgment of the Court that the relevant part of the Code of Ethics and Principles of Good Practice dealing with non-discrimination (to which Relate subscribed) was in force when Mr McFarlane began his employment in May 2003.

Another example of the power of the State to require a person to hold a belief is the case of the Johns, who were husband and wife and experienced foster carers. The local Council delayed in approving them as respite carers of children while questioning them about their Christian beliefs concerning homosexuality.[180] (The legal processes surrounding the case were somewhat complex, since the parties sought a declaration in the form of answers to defined questions, though the matter was framed as a judicial review of a decision that had not yet taken place.) The effect of the Court judgment was that the local authority has the right to determine its own diversity policy with the effect that people may be disqualified from being foster carers by virtue of their belief that homosexuality is wrong.

It is right that the State should have regard to the interests of the child and seek to put a foster child in a suitable family. In doing this it is reasonable for the State to consider the beliefs of the foster parents as one of the matters to be taken into account. If, for instance, the Johns had been neo-Nazis or violent extremists, the local authority would have been right to decline to place a child with them. In this case, despite some prompting from Counsel for the Johns, there was no examination in the judgment of the Court as to whether the Christian beliefs of the Johns were in fact (taking into account the whole of their beliefs) good for the children, who should have been the primary concern. The judge said that: "We sit as secular judges serving a multicultural community of many faiths…. The aphorism that Christianity is part of the common law of England is mere rhetoric." It was assumed that the Council's policies in relation to diversity must be agreed by the Johns without any examination by the Court of the merits of those policies. Even on the assumption that the policies were reasonable, there was no consideration in the judgment as to whether it was proportionate for the State to require compliance with the policies by foster carers in terms of the benefits or otherwise as far as the children were concerned. And the wider effect in terms of the public good of the State requiring a belief to be held, which could result in the exclusion of Christians from the provision of foster care, was not considered. It can also be noted that the Johns, though they were remunerated by the local authority for their foster care, were private individuals offering foster care in their own home, and not public servants performing a public office. They were therefore in a different position to public servants who might be said to owe particular duties to the State.

The cases considered here illustrate the differences between Christian thinking and the current law and also suggest that the law and the courts in some instances have failed, whether intentionally or otherwise, to consider some of the relevant issues.

7.6   DISCRIMINATION IN EMPLOYMENT

The Equality Act 2010 requires non-discrimination in appointments on the grounds of religious belief and sexual orientation. There is a limited exemption in the case of religious belief where the employer has "an ethos based on religion or belief". There is also is an occupational requirement relating to the type of duties of the employee that allows employment to be restricted to a person with the relevant beliefs. The exemption is narrow and may be confined to those employees performing teaching functions or rituals. The exemption does not take into account the fact that those working for a Christian organisation in a non-teaching capacity, for instance administration, are motivated by their Christian belief to uphold certain standards and that they want to work together with other Christians. Both employees and the organisation for which they work should have the freedom for Christian belief to be shared by all employees and for this to be reflected in the practices of the organisation.

There is also a limited exclusion in relation to discrimination on the grounds of sexual orientation which applies to employment for the purposes of "organised religion" where the requirement is necessary to comply with the "the strongly held religious convictions of a significant number of the religion's followers". The scope of "organised religion" is restrictive since this is not the same as a religious organisation and therefore the term only applies to established religious denominations and not, for example, to a Christian charity.

The requirements of the Equality Act conflict with the principle of freedom of association which is generally recognised as a public good. This is the ability of private citizens to associate with whom they please. It is particularly relevant here, since the bodies affected are private and not public organisations. An anomalous aspect of the law is that discrimination is permitted in the case of beliefs that do not qualify as religious, such as political or other ideological beliefs. A political organisation, in selecting whom to employ, is allowed to discriminate against a person who does not hold the beliefs of that organisation. However, a religious organisation is limited in its ability to do the same thing. It would not be reasonable to expect the Labour Party to be compelled to employ a Conservative voter. According to the same principle, a Sikh temple should not be compelled to employ a practising Christian. Similarly, a church which believes in sexual relations only within marriage should not be required to employ (in any capacity) someone who does not believe and practise that belief. But such compulsion is the effect of the current law. A feature of the law is that, for the purposes of the regulations which forbid discrimination on the grounds of sexual orientation, sexual practice by homosexuals is assumed to be an inevitable consequence of a homosexual orientation. However, a requirement of abstinence from sexual activity outside marriage is not recognised by the law as the manifestation of a Christian belief even though this is an established part of Christian teaching.

7.7   DISCRIMINATION IN SERVICES

Non-discrimination requirements also apply to the provision of services. It has been held that Christian bed and breakfast proprietors cannot reserve double beds exclusively for married couples.[181] They are not permitted to do so on the grounds that they would be discriminating against homosexual couples, even if they would behave in the same way towards unmarried heterosexual couples. In this case, it makes no difference to the legal analysis that the homosexual couple alleging discrimination could have easily obtained the relevant facilities elsewhere, so that in practice the exercise of the ability of the homosexual couple to manifest their orientation was unhindered. As a practical matter, no one should be refused accommodation at short notice having previously arranged it. If Christian homeowners offering accommodation wish to reserve double beds only for married or heterosexual couples, but not same-sex couples, they should make this clear on any website and to all who make bookings. In this way same-sex couples can make arrangements with those who welcome their behaviour and should not be inconvenienced.

The effect of the legislation is to render the manifestation of a certain belief unlawful, in this case the exercise of the Christian belief, without reference to the practical effect of the manifestation of the belief on those affected, which may be immaterial. Equality legislation which is framed in terms of human rights and non-discrimination does not balance the interests of those alleging discrimination against the benefits of freedom of belief in the context of the wider public good.

7.8   REASONABLE ACCOMMODATION OF BELIEF

There is a current proposal by a number of Christian organisations that there should be reasonable accommodation for issues of conscience. The intention is to balance fairly the conflicting rights of the different interest groups. The proposal appears to be a pragmatic one in a society that has rejected a number of Christian values. However, giving Christian or other faith groups reasonable accommodation in the expression of their beliefs does not address the more fundamental question, which is whether the relevant belief is consistent with the public good. If the proposal were adopted as law, it might be difficult for the Courts, which have now taken the view that no belief system has any particular value compared with another, to resist calls for a multiplicity of beliefs to be accommodated. For example, a Muslim believer employed in a supermarket might object to handling pork on the grounds that it is a matter of religious belief and that others could be employed to perform these tasks. It could then be argued that this is comparable with a doctor declining to perform an abortion and that his belief should be accommodated. While the concept of reasonable accommodation may be a helpful means to achieve compromises in practice, it is still necessary for there to be some criteria to determine which beliefs are acceptable and, where there are conflicts, how these should be resolved.

7.9   FREEDOM OF EXPRESSION IN PUBLIC

The Public Order Act 1986, much amended by the last government, has been used to prosecute or to intimidate those whose behaviour is deemed "insulting". This law has been invoked to convict a person expressing, in public, beliefs which are critical of homosexuality. It has led to the arrest of Christian street preachers, though two have been awarded damages for wrongful arrest, unlawful imprisonment and breach of human rights by the police. It has also been the grounds for the questioning by the police of Mrs Pauline Howe (aged 67) when she objected privately to the Council about a homosexual rights march at which she claims she was verbally abused,[182] and for the arrest of a girl burning a *Qur'an* on YouTube.

These and similar cases raise the issue as to how far the State is justified in preventing the expression of a belief because it conflicts with government policy or may offend other people. The purported justification for these restrictions on freedom of speech may be on grounds relating to non-discrimination because people might be offended, or for reasons of public order because people may react violently. However, the principle of free speech means that there should be no ground for legal complaint if a belief is criticised. There should be no legal right of any person not to be offended, however morally wrong the nature of the insult or misguided the belief that prompts it. This should even extend to instances where the insult (provided that it is not violent) relates to characteristics that the recipient cannot change, such as shortness of height, red hair or even possibly race, as well as religion (which should be the subject of reasoned debate). Insults may be morally wrong, but it is not the business of the State to outlaw them, unless they are an intentional provocation to physical violence.

There has been a campaign to remove the word "insulting" from the Public Order Act 1986 and the House of Lords voted to do so by 150 votes to 54 on 12th December 2012. On 14th January 2013 it was announced that the government would accept the amendment. Whether the removal of the word would be effective to stop the police using the Act to prevent free speech is doubtful because the words "threatening" and "abusive" would remain in the Act. (Freedom of expression is discussed further in Chapter 15.)

7.10   A LEVEL PLAYING FIELD?

Some Christians might say that all that is required is a "level playing field" in which all beliefs coexist and compete in the formulation of laws on an equal basis. The level playing field may be problematic for Christians where a law is passed which requires them to act against their conscience. A number of Christians have strongly held beliefs and their consciences do not permit them to do things which are inconsistent with those beliefs. For instance, if Christians hold the view that a particular action is necessarily wrong in itself (rather than merely likely to result in a wrong state of affairs), then they should not participate in or promote that wrong action. So if, as a result of free and fair debate, it became compulsory in law for a Christian doctor to perform an abortion where there is no risk to the life of the mother, then he or she would not be permitted by Christian belief to do it. The State therefore has to decide whether a doctor or nurse has the right to hold a belief, for instance that abortion is wrong, and to express that belief in action.

The difficulty with the view that all that is required is a level playing field for the equal expression of different views is that beliefs conflict in practice. Some people believe that abortion is a public good or represents an important freedom for women and others believe that it is akin to murder. Public authorities need to have a view as to what is a permissible belief and what is objectively good. Christians may hold that their beliefs are good for society as a whole. But if society decides otherwise and the State requires them to act contrary to their beliefs, their consciences will not permit them to cooperate.

7.11   A LIBERTARIAN PERSPECTIVE

Libertarians argue that anti-discrimination legislation, as well as trespassing upon some fundamental freedoms, is always liable to be inadequate in fairly defining the cases where discrimination is or is not justified. They point out that, even where discrimination is outlawed on the grounds of unalterable characteristics, anti-discrimination legislation can have perverse effects. For example, they would say that the benefits given to women in pregnancy and the possibility of claims for harassment and discrimination in the workplace can result in companies declining to employ women, resulting in further attempts to regulate these defensive practices by government quotas. They say that in a free market companies will seek to protect their commercial interests and that, if talented women are not being employed when they should be, there will be a commercial explanation which should not be interfered with.

A libertarian approach to legislation is that the State should generally refrain from interfering in what are essentially private acts, even if the private acts have consequences for other people and moral implications for those responsible for taking the decisions. Libertarians say that attempts to regulate by law the kind of behaviour which should be subject only to moral constraints imply that the State has a right to regulate opinions and beliefs. The difficulty here is that the dividing line between public and private acts is hard to draw, since many private acts have public consequences. Racial discrimination is irrational and it is also damaging to society as a whole. It is therefore right that it is unlawful to discriminate on the grounds of race. This highlights the need for a clear view of the public good and the role of the State in promoting it.

Some US libertarians, although they abhor racism and support the banning of discrimination in governmental activities, nevertheless believe that a strict interpretation of property rights means that it is a matter of private morality, and not a matter for government intervention, whether a private business operates racial segregation. Christian libertarians may argue that the purpose of the law is primarily to restrain evil and to protect individuals, but they would not regard that protection as including a freedom from discrimination. They would equate legislation in relation to racial discrimination with the State requiring a certain view of virtue. They would say that for the State to require virtue, as opposed to restraining evil, is to restrict the exercise of free will and that it therefore falls beyond the legitimate scope of government.

All people would agree that arbitrarily and irrationally depriving a person of the opportunity to work on the grounds of an unalterable characteristic is wrong. The issue is whether certain types of behaviour of this nature should be prohibited by law. As we have seen, it is not an offence under the law to decline to employ someone because they vote Labour or Tory. It is also not an offence to discriminate against a person irrationally because they have red hair, though dismissal from employment on these grounds would in qualifying cases allow the dismissed employee to claim compensation for unfair dismissal. Governments have determined that racial cohesion and the right to be fairly considered for employment irrespective of race are public goods of sufficient importance that discrimination on the grounds of race in prospective employment should be unlawful. This is right in the case of racial discrimination. However, the State should be reluctant to intervene in private choices except when there is a public necessity or a fundamental right which should override the freedom of the individual.

While discrimination on the grounds of race is unacceptable, discrimination on the grounds of characteristics that relate to behaviour and belief (which are choices) should be allowed. For the State to intervene in these cases is to deprive a person or a business of the choice of person with whom they wish to associate on grounds that may, or may not, be rational, and it is not for the State to determine with whom citizens choose to do business. The jurist Dicey, writing in 1904, argued it in this way: "If X or Y or Z may each of them lawfully, as is certainly the case, cut A because of his political opinions, they may all it would seem agree to cut him."[183] Whilst choosing not to employ someone on the grounds of race is always irrational or wrong and also may deprive a person of an important right or interest, it may be rational to choose not to work with someone who has particular beliefs or who exhibits certain types of behaviour. Thus, as we have seen, the Labour party is not bound to employ a Conservative party member and vice versa.

7.12 THE DIFFICULT QUESTIONS OF SEXUAL ORIENTATION AND BEHAVIOUR

Many of the controversial issues in relation to discrimination and freedom of conscience have been concerned with sexual orientation and behaviour. Some people might regard these issues as a distraction from the central Christian message, or they may wish to avoid them on the grounds that the traditional Christian position can alienate people from Christianity. Christians have been criticised for placing too much emphasis on issues of sexuality, and it can be helpful to understand why these are of such concern in some Christian circles.

In Christian thinking, the biological nature of male-female relations is a fundamental feature of the natural order which is reinforced by biblical teaching. There is particular concern in Christian circles about the Lesbian, Gay, Bisexual and Transgender (LBGT) movement. As Bishop Michael Nazir-Ali has pointed out, bisexual relations require infidelity. Transgender identities are a denial of what Christians regard as the God-created order. Until the middle of the last century, the Christian view was assumed in Western thinking. Individuals may for different reasons have not lived within this framework but, until recent decades, their choices have not met with the approval of the law and their preferences have not been endorsed by legal structures. Christians should always be sympathetic to the personal struggles of those who find that they feel the need for love from someone of the same sex, or who cannot feel emotions for people of the opposite sex. Nor is it necessary to assume that homosexual or any other sexual inclinations can always be changed. Human beings carry many unwelcome burdens in their time on earth. Christian teaching is that they cannot expect to shed them all in this life, nor can they expect that their feelings and desires will always coincide with what is right and good for them.

Christians are bound not to encourage something that they believe is not the creator's design (and therefore not in the best interests of the individuals concerned), and which they believe will take those individuals further away from a right relationship with their creator. However, while Christians believe that the State should not encourage homosexual practice, few Christians would believe that these should be criminalised, except in the case of minors who require protection. They would say that in purely private acts which do not affect others people should be able to exercise free will. For similar reasons, the law does not prohibit marital infidelity as a criminal offence. However, just because a practice is permitted by law, it does not follow that public policy should encourage it. Thus, while homosexual behaviour may be lawful, Christians may argue that is not a public good that government and society should promote. They would say that government should not celebrate homosexual practice in legal structures, as has happened with the passing of legislation for civil partnerships. (The implications for society of the approval of same-sex relations are discussed in Chapter 14.)

The proposal of reasonable accommodation for Christian belief, as mentioned above, might suggest that all groups should support each other in accommodating the manifestation of their beliefs. However, in some cases, the exercise of conscience may prevent a Christian from supporting others in their expression of a belief on the grounds that to do so would be wrong and would not be good for the person concerned. Thus, for instance, in a country where homosexual couples are not permitted to occupy double beds in a hotel, Christians may have difficulty in actively supporting those couples in their claim to do so, though they would not want to prevent them from arguing their case.

7.13   UK GOVERNMENT VALUES

Whether or not this is articulated, current UK Government policy in practice favours, or does not favour, the values associated with a particular belief system, whether secular or religious. It enacts laws which are either consistent with a belief system or inconsistent with it. For instance, educational values and government sponsorship of cultural events may, or may not, encourage a particular belief system. Christians have perceived an asymmetry in the current law which allows the expression of secular beliefs, but not some expressions of traditional Christian moral teaching. Diversity policies require that the sexual practices of every person must be respected, regardless of orientation or gender expression. But, according to the current interpretation of diversity, the religious beliefs and moral convictions of every person need not, and indeed should not, be respected.

To some people "respect" means "agreement" and this deprives others of the freedom to express a contrary opinion. Logically, it does not make any sense to respect beliefs as such, rather than to respect the people who hold them, which all people should do in any event. If we are required to respect a belief rather than the person who holds it then, on some interpretations, we cannot question whether that belief is good for society. Tolerance, according to current secular thinking, requires an acceptance of a diversity agenda. This means endorsing an agenda that requires approval of a wide range of sexual practices celebrated by the LBGT (lesbian, bisexual, gay and transsexual) movement. In the case of the companies that promote diversity, the sexual preferences of their employees should be irrelevant to their businesses. Provided that there is no discrimination against individuals on the grounds of their sexual preferences, it should be immaterial whether an employee espouses a particular sexual preference or disapproves of that preference out of a religious belief. The diversity agenda can have the effect of a form of censorship in the expression of beliefs in the workplace which some might regard as having something in common with that of a totalitarian state.

While freedom of belief is essential, aspects of belief that affect issues of law and social organisation should be debated as public matters. It is not the business of the State to persuade people to adopt a particular belief. However, in its policies the State is bound to encourage, or place restrictions upon, practices that reflect a belief system. The State cannot be neutral in relation to matters over which it exercises jurisdiction (whether or not ideally it should do so) or in relation to matters which it influences. These affect the nature of the society that it governs. Thus the State has a view, which is reflected in law, on matters which are the subject of religious belief. These include, for example, polygamy, arranged marriages of persons under the age of consent and whether girls should be educated in the same way as boys.

7.14 SOME CONSEQUENCES OF THE GOVERNMENT'S VALUES

Where the State has a choice that it should exercise (or that in practice it does exercise), it needs to have a view as to what behaviour it regards as desirable and what behaviour it views as undesirable. Although Christians believe that education is the primary responsibility of parents, in practice in the UK the State, rather than private or charitable organisations, is the main provider of education and can control the curriculum. While providing wide ranging sex education, the State declines to teach sexual abstinence and marital fidelity. In 2011 Nadine Dorries MP proposed a Bill to encourage the teaching of sexual abstinence for children aged between 13 and 16, but it was dropped for lack of support.

The State allows and encourages the adoption of children by homosexual couples. Here the freedom to manifest a belief (that of some adoption agencies to decline to support adoption by same-sex parents) may appear to be the immediate issue, but it is not the principal one. The most important issue is whether it is the business of government to promote a particular kind of sexual behaviour and, if it does so, whether or not that behaviour is good for individuals and society. Some public authorities have, as a matter of policy, decided to encourage homosexuality. For example, this policy extends into areas of education. The institution of a "lesbian, gay, bisexual and transgender history month" as part of the history curriculum changes the ordinary standards of history teaching in order to promote a policy unconnected with history. At a community school in West London a sociology teacher said: "In history they learn how gay people were treated in the Holocaust, in psychology we looked at how gay people used to be "cured", in geography they looked at different countries and their attitudes to homosexuality. In RE they looked at different religions' attitudes to gay parenting."[184]

The State has chosen to endorse certain behaviour by conferring upon same-sex couples a legal status in civil partnership and the privilege of the opportunity to parent children. Same-sex relationships have not been unlawful for some time (since 1957), but for the State to afford those relationships a legal status amounts to the State pronouncing that they are good. The issue is generally considered in the context of a right of a person not to be discriminated against. This implies either (i) that homosexual behaviour is morally neutral and those who choose a homosexual lifestyle are "victims" who are powerless to change their behaviour and/or (ii) that homosexual practices are worthy of encouragement by the State and approval by the law. Behaviour, which is a matter of choice, is often equated with race, which is not. The difficulty here is that the assumptions behind the issue of non-discrimination are rarely examined in public debate because to do so would be perceived as personal attack. Other kinds of sexual relationships are not recognised by the law, and some are prohibited. Here it is not said that those who advocate these relationships are being discriminated against, because the relevant sexual practices are not regarded as a public good. In these cases, sexual behaviour that is regarded as wrong is not said to flow naturally from a sexual orientation, and those with the relevant sexual inclinations are expected to restrain them.

Even if it were right to conclude that homosexual relationships are good for those involved in them, this conclusion does not justify same-sex parenting. This should be considered in the context of what is good for the children and for society. To frame the debate in terms of "discrimination" is to make prior assumptions which are generally unexamined in public debate. (The substantive issues of the public good in relation to the education of children and the adoption of children by same sex couples are discussed further in Chapter 14.)

Libertarians may take the view that the State, in undertaking education and wide ranging welfare schemes, is stepping outside the boundaries of its legitimate role. They would take the view that it would have been preferable not to have to debate some of these issues in the context of government policy, and this was not necessary when government intervened less in these matters. In the past many of the activities now promoted by government were regarded as private matters. The activities of the UK state are so wide ranging that it needs to take a view on matters of sexual ethics. Government activities include the funding of many programmes undertaken by charities which promote a variety of sexual relationships and behaviour. There is a need for a debate about these issues as they affect government policy. This should consider whether the activities that are encouraged by the State are natural and good or whether they are harmful to the health of individuals and to society. Issues of non-discrimination and equal treatment are important, but a discussion of government policy should not bypass the important questions as to what is the proper role of the State in these matters and what amounts to a public good. Policy makers have a responsibility to ensure that the behaviour that they are encouraging is not harmful to individuals.

7.15 DISCUSSING FAITH SYSTEMS

It is a matter of public policy whether the particular values of major religions such as Christianity, Islam or Hinduism that affect social behaviour and the organisation of society are good for people or are consistent with the values which a society holds or the State promotes. For instance, public policy does not endorse the practice of the caste system in Hindu belief or approve the legal status of women under Islamic Sharia law. These matters affect public policy in the same way that a view about the rights and wrongs of capitalism, communism or fascism are relevant to politics.

A focus in France has been on a particular manifestation of belief, the face covering, and it was argued that a ban was contrary to freedom. Another way of looking at the issue would be to examine whether the face covering, or any other manifestation of Islamic belief, in practice restricts the freedom of individuals (in this case women) and prevents them from playing a full role in society.

Freedom of debate is important. A person who speaks against Islam may be called an "Islamophobe". The reference to "phobia" indicates an irrational fear. However, it is in the interests of the common good to debate those manifestations of the Islamic faith that affect society. There may be reasons for the reluctance to debate aspects of the Islamic faith in terms of the public good. One is that the overarching system of Islam is, like Christianity, based upon metaphysics and it may be felt that this is not something that is appropriate to debate in the public realm. This is understandable, since public policy is generally concerned with outcomes and not with belief as such, so it is sensible for debate to be centred on policy and not on metaphysics. However, knowledge of a belief system is helpful in understanding its manifestations, and it is sensible for public discussion to consider belief.

Another reason for the reluctance to criticise the Islamic religion is the conflation of religion with race and identity. Criticism of a person or a group on the grounds of race or identity is irrational and wrong. Religious beliefs gain much support from communities, since communities nurture and transmit belief systems. However, this does not mean that the beliefs are the same as the ethnic identity of the people holding those beliefs. Beliefs can be changed either individually or collectively and anyone can convert to Islam, Christianity or Buddhism. While most people from Pakistan are followers of Islam, there are many Christian believers in Pakistan and many people of Pakistani and other Asian origins practising the Christian faith in this country. To equate belief with community and culture and to define people by the group to which they belong, or appear to belong, is to devalue the personhood of the individual and their freedom to choose. The thinking that elevates culture over the freedom of belief of the individual is not consistent with Christianity, which teaches that each individual is accountable to God personally for their beliefs and their actions.

7.16   BELIEF AND THE STATE IN ISLAM

The Christian doctrine of free will, and the limits on the powers of the State that this implies, should prevent the imposition of belief by the State. Nevertheless, Christians would argue that a society and a State based upon Christian principles are good for people. Not all religions have the same view as Christianity about the relationship between the religion and the State. Islam treats issues of private belief and its manifestation differently to Christianity. Islam acknowledges the sovereignty of Allah over all but does not in its foundational documents recognise a distinction between the spiritual and the secular realms. Historically, Mohammed's kingdom was, unlike that of Jesus, a kingdom of this world. Territorial conquest, principally of Christian territories, was the result. (It is sometimes forgotten that, whatever the rights and wrongs of the Crusades, the Christian lands that the crusaders sought to reclaim had, before their conquest by Islam, been Christian for longer than the period of Islamic rule before the Crusades.)

The concept of the Muslim Calif is that of Allah's vice-regent on earth with power over all creation. While there are manifestations of Islamic belief that in practice moderate the more extreme Islamic approach to secular law, it is helpful to look at the way in which countries with a predominantly Muslim population restrict the expression of other beliefs, and restrict the freedom of Muslims to be converted to those other beliefs, for instance to Christianity. For Christians, freedom of belief is important not just because God requires it, since forced belief is no belief at all, but also because human beings are imperfect. If beliefs are imposed, they may be wrong or they may be enforced in the wrong way. In Christian thinking, free will and imperfection are linked. Freedom leads to imperfection because human beings can choose to do wrong. And the imperfection of human beings necessitates political freedom, since no human ruler can be all wise and completely just.

7.17   FREEDOM OF ASSOCIATION AT UNIVERSITIES

In the US, the Supreme Court held that Hastings College of Law at the University of California could not grant facilities to a Christian Legal Society which, following traditional Christian teaching, excluded those students practising unrepentant homosexual conduct.[185] This exclusion by the Christian group was compared by Justice Anthony Stevens with excluding Jews, blacks and women and he said that a free society must not tolerate such Christian groups. The majority of the Supreme Court rejected any distinction between homosexual behaviour and homosexual orientation, thus classifying homosexual conduct as inevitable and unchangeable, and equating it with a racial identity. It would have been more logical, although wrong, for the Court to have decided that homosexual behaviour is a public good and that this overrode the principle of freedom of association. But the issue was not addressed in these terms. Justice Samuel Alito in his dissenting judgment said: "I do not think it is an exaggeration to say that today's decision is a serious setback for freedom of expression in this country."

There have been similar issues in relation to societies at universities in the UK, and compromises have been reached. In practice there is no reason why a person should want to join a society or organisation that has a belief or an ethos with which they do not agree. They are always at liberty to establish a new society and do not have to disrupt an existing one. Socialists do not generally want to join the Conservative Party. The defining feature of a Christian organisation is its ethos. If a person or group does not agree with Christian belief, the only reason that they may have for wishing to join the organisation may be to disrupt it, or to modify or even suppress one or more of its beliefs. They may even want to destroy the organisation with its distinctive belief system. Even if the State has legitimate reasons for requiring its public servants to express, or refrain from expressing, certain beliefs in the performance of their duties, individuals should be free to choose their beliefs and to associate with whom they choose.

7.18 CONCLUSION

Issues of discrimination and human rights throw up fundamental questions relating to the public good and the role of government in allowing the manifestation of belief and the exercise of conscience. A coherent view of the public good can provide the context for a fair balance to be struck between the competing interests which may be viewed as human rights, particularly in relation to non-discrimination. Christian belief in the duties to a creator and love of neighbour in community provide a basis for examining what is the common good. A secular view of human rights focuses upon the interests of individuals and provides a rationale for governments to require beliefs (framed, for instance, in terms of diversity) to be held by its citizens. A Christian concept of the common good can address some of the structural weaknesses in the theory and application of secular human rights and is a more coherent framework than human rights for dealing with the issues of conscience that affect the individual.

8

IMPARTIAL JUSTICE AND THE SEPARATION OF POWERS

8.1 HUMAN IMPERFECTION

It follows from the imperfection of human beings that laws are required and that these must function objectively. In an imaginary world of perfect justice administered by those possessing perfect wisdom, it might be reasonable to allow a wide discretion to judges in calibrating the severity of the punishment for a crime so as to take into account many factors other than the crime itself. The punishment would not fit the crime, but the person who committed it. Whilst systems of law may allow some variation in punishment for the same crime depending upon specified circumstances, a system of law by its nature requires objectivity. This means that the criteria for punishment should be applied impersonally on the basis of the nature of the crime, taking into account (where appropriate) only limited matters relating to the background of the criminal. Objective criteria for law enforcement are necessary because human beings have neither the wisdom nor the information to make perfect judgements. It is a feature of police states that discretion is exercised by the State to decide whom to punish and how to punish them without reference to an impartial law.

There is a concern that changes in the law that are too rapid may not be fair or impartial because they respond too quickly to particular circumstances and do not rest securely upon general principles. There is a difference here between a general system of constitutional law, to which governments should be subject, and the particular legislation enacted by governments. In Book VII of Plato's *Laws*, the Athenian stranger warns that, "Change, as we shall find, except in something evil, is extremely dangerous."[186]   David W. Hall points out that, "Calvin also alluded to the necessity for fixed laws and universal norms, warning that 'many are necessarily injured, and no private interest is stable unless the law be without variation; besides, when there is a liberty of changing laws, license succeeds in place of justice. For those who possess the supreme power, if corrupted by gifts, promulgate first one edict and then another: thus justice cannot flourish where change in the laws allows of so much license.' "[187] Some might perceive this phenomenon today where governments respond too hastily to the pressures brought to bear by minority interest groups. Philip Johnston's book *Bad Laws* characterises a "frenzy of law making" in modern Britain as "interfering in our lives to an extent that is neither healthy nor wanted."[188] The UK gets 25,000 pages of new legislation each year.[189]

8.2   IMPARTIAL LAW AND ENFORCEMENT

The rule of law must be applied without fear or favour. This is an essential element of a just and free society. Where enforcement is selective or based on criteria other than objective law, privilege can become entrenched and individuals persecuted. An example in the UK was a set of guidelines issued by the Association of Chief Police Officers (a publicly funded body), which required the interrogation of people who committed no crime, but who objected to aspects of a diversity agenda. While the police do need to exercise limited discretion in relation to certain matters, the content of the law which they enforce should be the law of the land democratically decided and not other rules invented by those in positions of power.

Some law enforcement is governed by policy manuals, not by the law. To give a bizarre example, a Hate Crime Guidance Manual issued by the Association of Chief Police Officers was given to officers warning that they must ignore "doggers", those committing sexual acts in public (contrary to the law), because it can cause them to suffer Post Traumatic Stress Disorder (PTSD) if they are admonished.[190] It stated that even though outdoor sex is unlawful, people who take part in these activities have rights that protect them from becoming the victims of hate crime. The effect of this guidance not to enforce the existing law was discretionary law creation by a body other than Parliament. As one officer (who did not want to be named) commented regarding the "Managing Public Sex Environments" policy: "It's getting to the stage that people who break the law have more rights than the normal man or woman on the street, and as for them suffering from post-traumatic stress, what about the people who witness these exhibitions and are shocked by it? What about their rights?"[191] This kind of general guidance needs to be distinguished from the proper discretion which the authorities exercise in relation to prosecution in individual cases which needs to depend upon the strength of the evidence in relation to the crime in question.

ASBOs (anti-social behaviour orders) are capable of creating an array of unspecified new criminal offences since a wide range of behaviour can be deemed to be anti-social (without the requirement for a law to define that behaviour) and can become the subject of an ASBO. It is a criminal offence to contravene the ASBO by repeating the behaviour. Similar concerns apply to the proposed replacement for the ASBO, the CPI (crime prevention injunction). Breach of a CPI would be a contempt of court, the punishment for which could be imprisonment, normally of up to two years, or a fine. The same considerations may also apply to the proposed CBO (criminal behaviour order) which could be attached to a criminal conviction. Breach of a CBO could result in a prison sentence of up to five years. While anti-social behaviour must be dealt with, it should be addressed through the framework of criminal law with specified offences.

To achieve impartial justice, it is essential that the forces of government are under the control of the law. Plato, who rejected Athenian democracy and in the *Republic* advocated rule by the most capable, nevertheless held that rulers should be under the rule of law. This principle has long been a foundation of Western freedoms. In some countries the police appear to be outside the law or are in practice unaccountable, and are a law unto themselves. In the UK the behaviour of the police in confrontations with demonstrators where the police declined to identify themselves could be regarded in a similar light, since the relevant police officers evidently believed that different standards of behaviour applied to them compared with those that applied to ordinary citizens. Police officers should not be permitted to exercise powers without being willing to identify themselves personally, thus enabling them to be accountable. The Tomlinson case was a particular example of this.[192] In 2012 the exposure of police behaviour in the Hillsborough disaster, the relationship of police officers with the *News of the World* and the resignation of a government minister, Andrew Mitchell, as a result of false evidence given by the police, undermined public confidence in the impartiality of the police.

A report by the think tank Civitas, entitled *A New Inquisition: Religious Persecution in Britain Today,* highlighted the possible influence of a Crown Prosecution Service Staff Association called the National Black Crown Prosecution Association in affecting the impartiality of the Crown Prosecution Service. It concluded that there was clear evidence of biased application of the law and mentioned the case of a Muslim man only prosecuted for criminal damage, not a religiously or racially aggravated offence, when he sprayed "Islam will dominate the world — Osama is on his way" and "Kill Gordon Brown" on a war memorial.[193]

8.3   THE SAME JUSTICE FOR EVERYONE

The justice system also needs to be based upon uniform laws and practices that apply equally to every person in the land. Sharia Councils and branches of the Muslim Arbitration Tribunal now operate in many parts of the UK. These councils and tribunals dispense justice that is based upon principles and values different from those of English law. A Civitas report has suggested that there are 85 bodies of this nature acting in the UK. Parties to a commercial arbitration are, under the Arbitration Act 1996, free to choose a law other than English law (invariably that of a country) to govern the resolution of their dispute by an arbitrator. Sharia Councils, in deciding upon issues such as divorce, effectively replace the authority of the English Courts and apply law that is contrary to English law. Those presiding call themselves "judges" and the parties may be asked to sign an agreement to abide by the decisions of the Council. There will be social pressure to comply with a ruling and English family courts may even be willing to uphold and enforce "agreements" reached by "mediation" in a Sharia Council. There are many legal difficulties with Sharia Councils. Sharia law provides, for instance, that a woman's testimony is worth half that of a man's; that for certain crimes including rape, only the testimony of four male witnesses will be sufficient; that a man may have four wives and may divorce any of them by a simple triple declaration; and that sons are entitled to a double portion of an inheritance compared with daughters. The testimony of a non Muslim counts for little and the standards of proof required can be inadequate. Swearing on the *Qur'an* multiple times may be taken as conclusive. Although many of the sanctions of the Sharia penal code are unlawful in the UK, it provides for death for adultery, homosexual behaviour and apostasy, and amputation for theft. Sharia law also excludes wife-beating and marital rape from its definition of domestic violence. In Western thinking, Sharia law encourages the oppression of women.[194] In 2010 Baroness Cox introduced a Bill[195] into the House of Lords that seeks to ensure that Sharia Councils and Arbitration Tribunals do not arbitrate on family or criminal matters, and that they operate in accordance with equality legislation. If they do not, their decisions would not be upheld in the civil courts. The Bill may be further pursued in Parliament.

Impartial justice may sometimes be sacrificed to further political ends. Concerns have been expressed that an investigation into the alleged involvement of a person in a crime committed while he was part of a terrorist organisation may have been shelved in order to advance the Northern Irish peace process.[196]

8.4 THE SEPARATION OF POWERS

Where the State needs to exercise public duties, no one body should have excessive power. This principle underlies the doctrine of the separation of powers, where the executive, legislative and judicial functions of government are undertaken by different entities. The requirement for clear boundaries between these functions reflects Christian thinking about human imperfection.

In the Old Testament, Jethro persuaded Moses to delegate judicial functions while he retained executive power. Israel in the Old Testament was a theocratic state in the sense that its laws were intended to reflect the laws which God had given. There was, nevertheless, a distinction between the different roles of the ruler, the priest and the prophet. The priests had an important function but they had no worldly wealth (see Deuteronomy 18:1). It was expected that the prophets would seek to hold the rulers to account in the light of God's standards, as the prophet Nathan did in the case of King David when he denounced the king for intentionally bringing about the death of Uriah (see 2 Samuel 12). The separation of powers reflects the Christian understanding that human institutions of government are imperfect and that the different functions of government are subject to an overriding, higher law. The judges' continuing practice of wearing robes can be seen as a reminder of the religious origins of their office, where clerics were able to exercise restraint upon the executive rulers under the authority of God. In 390 A.D. the Emperor Theodosius, after being confronted by the bishop Ambrose, did public penance for the massacre of the citizens of Thessalonica.

The principle of the separation of powers was developed further by Montesquieu, which proved a basis for the American constitution. As Montesquieu stated: "When the legislative and executive powers are united in the same person, or in the same body of magistrates, there can be no liberty."[197] Those who make the laws should be different from those who enforce them.

The principle can be applied to the operation of the criminal law so that the investigating authorities are separate from those deciding on the guilt or innocence of an accused person and from those who pass judgment in handing down penalties for a crime. The principle of the separation of powers has been preserved to a large extent in the English constitution though, as we shall see below, there are bodies in the UK that exercise two or more functions.

In the Westminster Parliament there are too many members of Parliament who are either members of the executive branch of government, or are aspiring to join it, so that the executive is not properly held to account. The increased influence of the select committees of MPs over recent years is a welcome development. When it was proposed that the number of MPs be reduced, it was not clear that this would be matched by a proportionate reduction in the number of ministers (as was proposed by one Conservative MP), so the legislature would have been weakened in relation to the executive.

John R. Bradley described in February 2011 the likely constitutional arrangements in Egypt if the Muslim Brotherhood were to take power and he outlined a possible system in which there would be little separation of powers. He contrasts this with those in Western countries: "the Brotherhood will make political participation of individuals in society subject to the principles of Sharia. In the West, the legislative and judicial branches of government monitor State actions to ensure they conform to democratic rules. The three branches of government keep each other in check. In the Islamist set-up the Brotherhood aims to establish, actions of the State would be monitored by, well, the Muslim Brotherhood, ensuring they conform to Islamic law. In other words, the Islamists would monitor themselves."[198] Bradley's concerns were borne out by the assumption in November 2012 of additional powers by President Morsi which put his decrees put beyond legal challenge, although this change was withdrawn in December 2012.

The justice system must contain checks and balances. It needs to be independent of a potentially powerful State. The jury system, and the rule that a person can be tried only once for the same offence, were designed to protect the individual from being pursued by the State in the courts for political reasons. The rule that a person can be tried only once has now been abolished where there is new evidence. This appears reasonable, but the concern is that it could allow the State to pursue a series of retrials with different juries until it obtains the result it desires. Trial by jury and the principle of one trial only for the same offence were hard fought for liberties, not least in the seventeenth century, when Britain was threatened by attempts at absolute rule on the part of two monarchs, Charles I and James II, who were removed. These principles were enshrined in English law in the Bill of Rights of 1689.

The jury system is an important element in the separation of powers that prevents the executive arm of government from enforcing criminal laws in a way that the ordinary person would regard as wrong or oppressive. Lord Justice Leveson has questioned whether all defendants accused of theft should have the right to require trial by jury. Lord Justice Moses has been sceptical of the ability of juries to understand the summing up of evidence by the judge, or directions to the jury. Juries may be flawed but, like democracy, they are the least bad system and in the past have provided a vital protection against an over-mighty State. Juries also represent, both symbolically and in fact, the consent that is necessary for the respect which law should have in a democratic society. The idea of a social contract between government and the people may appear to be a theoretical construct, but there are moments when it is grounded in reality. The operation of jury trials and the casting of votes in elections are examples of these moments.

A principle of the separation of powers is that judges should only administer and not make the law, and that they should interpret it fairly and rationally. The more general the definition of the principle that a judge is interpreting, the easier it is for a court judgment to create law. This can reflect the intellectual milieu that the judge inhabits. An example of this might be the judgment of Mr Justice Blake (which was overturned on appeal) that Rocky Gurung, convicted of what the Sunday Telegraph described as a "an extremely unpleasant instance of manslaughter", could not be deported because he had a right to family life under the European Convention on Human Rights. In this case, what was in effect law creation by the judiciary (had it not been overturned on appeal) could have compromised one of the fundamental purposes of government, which is to protect the people. Another example might be a prisoner's right to vote, which was not included specifically in the European Convention on Human Rights, and so could be regarded as law creation by the European Court of Human Rights.

8.5   NATURAL JUSTICE

Although there are now some regrettable exceptions to the rule (upon which we shall reflect in paragraphs 8.6 and 8.7 below), the tradition of English law has been that, where a governmental authority acts in a judicial capacity, principles of natural justice should apply. Elements of natural justice are reflected in the European Convention on Human Rights which provides (in Article 6) that, "In the determination of his civil rights and obligations or of any criminal charge against him, everyone is entitled to a fair and public hearing within a reasonable time by an independent and impartial tribunal established by law." A requirement of natural justice is that the judge or tribunal should hear both sides in a fair and unbiased way. Each side should have the opportunity of independent legal representation and access to the relevant information. Counsel should be able to cross examine witnesses presenting evidence for the other side. The judge should be free from bias and should administer the law impartially. If the judge has inadequate information or it is presented in an unbalanced way, or if there is no proper examination of the evidence, the trial may not be fair. Hearing both sides fairly is at the heart of the adversarial nature of court proceedings in common law jurisdictions. Advocates representing each side are able to present the perspective of their client and it is the task of the judge (or in criminal cases, the jury) to decide the truth. This procedure acknowledges human imperfection in that one person alone should not be able to administer justice. Objective truth should emerge, not from the wisdom of one person, but from the process of a number of people with different roles presenting, listening to and evaluating the evidence.

A flaw has been perceived in the administration of the adversarial system of criminal justice in the courts in the UK. The evidence for the prosecution is generally provided by the police who investigated the case. The legal team for the defence in a criminal trial may need to disprove the allegations of the prosecution by establishing other facts. But there may be limited scope in practice for the defence team to conduct a separate investigation of the case. There may also be opportunities for the police to withhold from the defence team evidence which favours the defence.

In December 2012, the government proposed reforms which it hoped would reduce the number of judicial challenges to the decisions of public bodies. Judicial review of certain administrative acts of government entities can be sought if decisions are made that are outside the relevant powers of the government entity, if the decisions are not made in accordance with the proper procedure or if they are beyond the bounds of reasonableness (which is widely construed). The proposed changes involve increasing the costs of judicial review and altering the limitation period during which an action can be brought. Judicial review has a positive effect in incentivising public authorities to reach decisions in a proper way. While it is unlikely that the changes will make much difference in practice, governments should not fear accountability.

8.6   CHILD PROTECTION IN THE UK

Social workers in child protection who assess the fitness of parents to look after children exercise more than one function. They report what is, in effect, treated as criminal behaviour (see below), they investigate the situation and they then decide on the evidence to be brought before a judge. Legal restrictions on the disclosure of information can prevent parents from informing other people who could provide evidence in their favour, and the legal representation of parents is often inadequate. As a result parents may not be able to mount a defence to the allegations made against them.

The system of child protection gives the State the power to deprive a person of a basic human right — the right of a parent not to have a child permanently taken away — without having first been convicted of a criminal offence in a trial which complies with the principles of natural justice. Clause 39 of the Magna Carta of 1215 provides that the sovereign cannot deprive any person of life, liberty or property except after they have been found guilty in a trial by a jury of their peers.[199] For a parent or family member to be deprived by the State of the right to look after a child falls within the spirit of this provision.

Under the current system a child can be taken away from parents where the burden of proof used in civil litigation has been applied. This means that whatever is alleged is decided "on the balance of probabilities". This means that the test is whether the alleged wrong is more likely than not to have been committed, or the parents are more likely than not to be unfit. For a criminal conviction, the offence must be proven "beyond all reasonable doubt". The circumstances which are said to justify removal of children fall short of criminal activity and can relate to the perception of the professionals involved of the fitness of the parent or family member to look after the child. The result is that children have been removed from families, in some cases immediately after birth, because the parents are deemed to be unfit. Whereas the criteria for criminal behaviour are in theory clear, a judgement by social workers about whether a parent is unfit could be reached on ideological grounds where, for instance, a family has beliefs with which those prosecuting the case do not agree, and this could colour the evidence put before a judge.

Another feature is that children are taken away from parents by social workers before there is any hearing at all. They can then be held for as long as a year before the matter is determined by a court. Justice is denied because it is delayed. The State has the right to take a child away from its parents for periods of over a year in cases where it is later bound to acknowledge that it had inadequate grounds for doing so. As of February 2012, the average childcare case took 15 months to reach the courts. The government has undertaken to reduce the period during which a child can be held before a hearing. However, a period longer than a few weeks is still too long, particularly since the removal of a child can devastate a family and cause the mental health of a parent to deteriorate. The length of time before a hearing (in effect a trial of the parents) should be regarded as a breach of Article 8 of the European Convention on Human Rights which requires respect for family life and a breach of the principles of natural justice embodied in Article 6 (as mentioned in paragraph 8.5 above). Where children are in immediate physical danger they should be removed from their parents before a full hearing, but a court order obtained on a fast track basis (like an injunction) should be necessary for this to occur. The court order entitling the public authority to retain the child should be discharged (i.e. become ineffective) if the full hearing does not take place within a specified period of time (which should be short) and this should be specified in the court order.

A consequence of the removal of a child for a long period is that a mother who is in a stable and good psychological condition before the child is taken away may, after a number of months following the removal of the child, be so distressed by the removal of the child that she is in a seriously depressed condition. At the hearing she can then be deemed unfit to look after the child because of her emotional condition. Christopher Booker, who has been an outspoken critic of the child protection regime, has drawn attention to a study by Professor Jane Ireland for the Family Justice Council which examined 126 psychological reports and found that two thirds of them were "poor" or "very poor" and that 20% of their authors had no proper qualifications.[200] One woman lost her children on the basis of a report written by someone who had not met her while, in another case, the social workers employed successive psychologists before finding one who would designate the woman as having "a borderline personality disorder". Two children were removed from their parents by social services after doctors diagnosed a broken arm as a pulled muscle which social services attributed to child abuse.[201] A mother was said to be a danger to her child by a psychiatrist who had never examined her, despite reports from other professionals stating that the child was happy and thriving and that the mother was no risk to anyone, including the child.[202]

The absence of criminal trial procedures can deprive parents of the ability to defend themselves adequately. They may not know the charges which are effectively being brought against them and they may not be able to cross question those giving evidence against them, for example those who have prepared psychological reports. The secrecy of the proceedings, which are supposed to be for the protection of the children involved, then prevents injustices coming to light.

Christopher Booker and Ian Josephs (who runs a website from Monaco called *Forced Adoption*) have highlighted a series of issues. They point out that: (i) parents often forfeit their rights by "failing to engage with the professionals" (which itself provides evidence of unfitness); (ii) solicitors tell their clients to agree to interim care orders (or they risk never seeing their children again); (iii) parents are routinely forbidden to call witnesses and are forbidden (on pain of imprisonment for contempt of court) to speak about their case; (iv) friends and family are often prevented from entering the court; (v) statements are read from witnesses who cannot be cross-questioned because they are not in court; (vi) parents are often given only one or two hours' notice to appear in court; and (vii) the children themselves are denied the right to be heard. Children are taken away for any unexplained injury, or if they are on the balance of probabilities "at risk of emotional abuse" — a test that can easily be passed, particularly when the grief of the parents when a child is taken away can be used as evidence that they are emotionally unstable.

Fortunately, in a small number of cases some of the effects of these unjust procedures are now coming to light. Lord Justice Thorpe said in a case in 2011: "I am completely aghast at this case. There is nothing more serious than a removal hearing, because the parents are so prejudiced in proceedings thereafter. Once you have lost a child, it is very difficult to get a child back."[203] The hearing lasted only 15 minutes after a doctor "expressed the opinion" that bruising in the ear of one of the three children in question looked as though it was caused by pinching. In a 2010 case Lord Justice Wall said that he found the closed mind of the authority "wholly contrary to good practice in care proceedings and unduly adversarial" and that it was "quite shocking" that a local authority could behave in such a way.[204] However, notwithstanding English and European case law in relation to care proceedings which sets out some of the requirements for a fair trial and despite the possibility of appeal in individual cases, the framework of the law and practice allows abuses to continue.

Even proven miscarriages of justice may not be reversed. The courts have ruled that, even when a parent has been deprived of a child on the basis of injuries alleged to have been the result of parental violence but which were later accepted to be due to a medical condition, an adoption order will not be set aside since it has been lawfully made.[205] This can give the State effective immunity suit and leave falsely accused parents with no redress.

The Family Justice (Transparency, Accountability and Cost of Living) Bill was introduced into the House of Commons on 26th October 2012, but failed to pass second reading. In particular, the Bill sought to: (1) ensure transparency and accountability in care proceedings; (2) ensure that professionals giving expert opinions are properly qualified and open to scrutiny; (3) ensure that family members are given an adequate opportunity to look after the child; (4) improve procedures for regulating the way children in care are looked after; and (5) require judges to provide specific grounds for forced adoptions.

There is more that could be done. A comprehensive reform could: (i) set down the precise grounds of unfitness that must be proven against parents before a child is taken away (there may be cases where the child would be better off elsewhere, but parents have a right to parent); (ii) allow children to be taken away before a full hearing only when they are in danger of physical harm, but otherwise to leave them with parents until the full hearing; (iii) in the case of (ii) above, ensure that the case comes before a judge for an interim hearing within, say, 14 days, and that the full hearing takes place within, say, 60 days; (iv) provide that the burden of proof in proceedings be beyond reasonable doubt, not on the balance of probabilities; (v) allow adoptions to be reversed where the grounds are later proven to be unfounded; (vi) ensure that all witnesses and those providing expert evidence for the authority are present at the hearing and can be cross examined; (vii) ensure that adequate legal aid is available to all those at risk of having a child taken away; and (viii) provide for punitive damages where an authority is wilfully, recklessly or negligently in breach of the law.

Although good decisions may be taken by conscientious people in the current system of child protection, the rules of the system itself offend against the principles of natural justice. The extent of the discretionary powers given to the bodies of the State, the absence of the proper separation of functions, the lack of speedy due process, the lack of the protection for the accused which exists in a criminal trial procedure, the secrecy surrounding the court processes and the wrong burden of proof constitute serious breaches of the principles of natural justice. While some children may be protected, the breach of these principles must inevitably result in miscarriages of justice and traumatised parents and children.

Although senior members of the judiciary are now alert to the possibility of injustices in individual cases, the underlying issue is the structure and general operation of the system, rather than its failure to respond appropriately in particular cases. This raises the issue as to whether lawyers should have declined to take part in the legal proceedings on the grounds that they are contrary to the principles of natural justice. Lawyers in other countries may be more familiar than those in the UK with the notion that there can be unjust laws where it would be morally wrong to collaborate with those administering them. Wide ranging changes are urgently required to the law and the practices of the courts and to the guidance and oversight of social workers.

8.7   OTHER AGENCIES

An example in the UK of a body which exercises a number of functions is the Charity Commission. The exercise of combined functions is a feature of a regulatory body which both investigates the behaviour of the entities that it regulates and decides upon the penalties to be applied in the case of infractions of the relevant rules. The Charity Commission is the statutory regulator and registrar of charities under the Charities Act 2011. It may receive complaints and it can investigate a charity if it decides to do so. It can instigate a statutory inquiry into the charity and interview the charity's officers. It can effectively act as prosecutor, judge and jury in coming to a conclusion as to the guilt or innocence of those concerned. It can then decide the sentence, which may involve vesting charity property in the Official Custodian for Charities, removing trustees or appointing an administrator to take over the charity's assets. Apart from the issues arising from the lack of the separation of the functions, a potential issue is the subjective nature of some of the judgements involved, for instance whether the charity's aims are principally political (which is not allowed) or whether the political activity is incidental to its charitable aims (which is allowed).

There is a concern that the requirement that a charity must produce "public benefit" (a criterion that applies to all charities), may be applied with subjective or politically motivated views about what amounts to "public benefit". This appeared to some people to be a merely theoretical concern until November 2012 when the Charity Commission denied charitable status to a Plymouth Brethren church in Devon on the grounds that it did not meet the test of public benefit. The issue was raised by Fiona Bruce MP in the House of Commons, but there is little that Parliament can do without a change in the law in relation to the criterion of public benefit or in the statutory system of regulation. The law no longer provides that the practice of the Christian religion is in itself a public benefit and decisions of the Charity Commission can only be challenged in the courts on the grounds that they are contrary to law. (There is a possibility that the church could take its case to the European Court of Human Rights.)

HM Revenue and Customs (HMRC) have wide ranging powers which are not subject to the appropriate limitations. Officers of HMRC can detain those suspected of infringements and enter business premises without a warrant. There have been concerns that HMRC can effectively close down a business before a trial of the issues, thus enforcing a penalty without due process. In November 2012 it was reported that HMRC had applied to be on the list of emergency services entitled to break speed limits.

8.8   AUTHORITIES OUTSIDE THE LAW

Some public agencies appear to encourage members of the public to act outside the law or imply that they are able to do so. A minor example would be authorities who urge complaints without explaining what the law provides and protects. The Bath and North East Somerset local authority has said in its literature that "Everybody has the right to live their life free from violence, fear and abuse…to be protected from…exploitation."[206] Whilst we may agree with the morality which these sentiments express, the matters described are not all a subject of the criminal law. The relevant terms are not defined and so they could be interpreted at will by public authorities, and they may not involve criminal behaviour. Yet individuals are encouraged: "If you have seen or experienced something you want to stop, here are some numbers you can call…" Some public authorities, like the police who investigate "hate incidents" rather than crimes, believe that they have the right to intervene and question people even if the alleged behaviour is lawful.

8.9   EXTRADITION

Extradition laws which allow deportation without the examination of any evidence, for instance the European arrest warrant procedure or the extradition treaty with the US, are a breach of natural justice. Where extradition is allowed in relation to offences predominantly committed in the UK, this is also a denial of sovereignty. The arrangements with the EU and the US can permit extradition of a person from the UK without examination of the evidence against them. A person can also be extradited from the UK for actions which are lawful in the UK. A person in a foreign country is inevitably at risk of arrest in accordance with the laws of that country. However, once a UK citizen is in the UK, he should be entitled to the justice of this country.

The principles of natural justice and sovereignty indicate that person should not be extradited unless: (i) there is an examination by a court in the UK of the prima facie evidence against that person; (ii) the crime was committed in the country to which the person is being extradited; (iii) the offence would also be an offence in the UK; and (iv) there is likely to be a fair trial.

8.10 ACCESS TO JUSTICE

An important part of a fair justice system is access to justice. The UK public authority responsible for the courts, H M Courts and Tribunals Services states (on its website) that it aims "to ensure that all its citizens receive timely access to justice according to their different needs". While the courts may be capable of delivering justice, most legal action requires legal advice and representation and this is expensive.

Legal aid is available in the UK only to those with very limited income and assets, but this excludes the majority of people. In an endeavour to reduce the legal aid budget, The Legal Aid, Sentencing and Punishment of Offenders Act 2012 (as of November 2012 not fully in force) excludes significant categories of legal advice and action from legal aid. These include: education (except special educational needs); welfare (except legal issues); debt; housing (except where a home is at risk); employment; negligence (except in limited cases of medical negligence); and family law (except for some child protection issues). Reductions in legal aid fees are likely to result in inadequate service in many cases and many law firms offering legal aid are going out of business or ceasing to offer legal aid.

Public bodies can in practice spend large sums in legal actions at the taxpayer's expense, and companies may have the ability to do so at the expense of their businesses. For individuals, many types of legal action are prohibitively expensive and in practice most legal action is unaffordable for the majority of people. "No win no fee" arrangements (where the lawyer is only paid where the action is successful) can provide access to justice in some cases, but the scope for these arrangements is limited. There are also concerns that these arrangements can encourage less than fair and honest practices on the part of lawyers whose fees are dependent upon them. Even where "No win no fee" arrangements are possible, individuals with assets may not be able to put them at risk or risk bankruptcy when they face the possibility of paying the legal costs of the other party (who may be the government or corporations) if they lose the case.

Poor policy making by government and unclear and unnecessary laws have contributed to the need to litigate, or to defend litigation brought by others, and to the costs of doing so. Complex laws have been introduced, while the ability of people to protect their interests by taking or defending legal action, particularly against well funded public bodies, has diminished as the legal costs increase.

There are no easy solutions to the issue of access to justice. The principal challenge in the issue of access to justice is the cost of legal representation. Lawyers will generally require to be paid although there is some scope for work to be done *pro bono* (without charge). The challenge is therefore to limit legal costs without compromising the principles of natural justice. In many cases one party is better funded than the other and the other party has to employ similar resources if it is to remain on equal terms, which it may not be able to do. This is referred to as an "inequality of arms" and typically occurs in cases involving a well funded state or commercial entity and an individual or a charity with limited resources. This inequality could be alleviated by limiting the amounts spent by public bodies on legal fees or by limiting the costs recoverable from the losing side if they win. The number of barristers or counsel engaged and the amount of legal costs incurred by either side could be restricted in cases where one party, typically an individual, has limited resources. (There would not need to be any limit where both sides are well funded organisations.)

In cases of public interest, for instance those relating to civil or religious liberties, a losing party should be responsible for its own costs, but a losing party in these cases should not have to pay the costs of the successful party. Or these costs could be limited. The prospect of being responsible for the successful party's costs can be a significant disincentive to the bringing of a legal action even if the prospects of success in the case are good.

In relation to legal aid, the State could make graduated contributions dependent upon wealth. The "all or nothing" approach of the current legal aid arrangements disadvantage those who narrowly fail to qualify for legal aid.

Solicitors could be given rights of audience in all courts and tribunals except the appeal courts, thus avoiding the necessity for a litigant to employ both a solicitor and a barrister. Barristers can now advertise direct access to their services (not via a solicitor) in the same way that solicitors are able to do so, and instructions from clients direct to barristers are increasing in volume.

The courts have had some success in encouraging mediation in civil cases, but there may be scope for more streamlined procedures in a wide range of non criminal cases. For most disputes relating to commercial construction operations in the UK (for instance, building houses and infrastructure) there is a mandatory system of adjudication. This is an interim but binding dispute resolution process by which an adjudicator hears evidence and decides a case in a short period of time. The adjudicator is bound by the rules of natural justice, for instance to hear both sides fairly, but is not bound by the rules of court procedure. The decisions of the adjudicator in these disputes are enforceable pending any appeal, but they can be appealed on any grounds in court or arbitration proceedings (whichever is chosen under the contract). In practice, however, there is often little incentive on the parties to make an appeal. The costs of adjudication proceedings are normally significantly less than those of a case in court. A similar system of adjudication could be extended to other civil cases, possibly with the right of appeal limited to points of law, as is the case with appeals from arbitrations (unless appeals are excluded).

Legal aid charities can be set up which could be resourced by the donation of either time or money by lawyers. The Access to Justice Foundation provides funds to organisations which provide *pro bono* legal advice and which support legal advice centres. The Law Society (representing solicitors) and The Bar

Council (representing barristers) could encourage lawyers earning over a certain amount per annum to donate a fraction of their income or an equivalent amount of time to *pro bono* work. It is important that the bodies deciding which cases should be funded are independent and represent a fair spectrum of opinion. Some people regard The Law Society as inappropriately politicised. (In 2012 The Law Society declined to let its premises to be used for a conference on the merits of conventional marriage on the grounds that it was inconsistent with its diversity policy.) The CLEAR projects, which operate in a number of African countries, are an example of legal aid charity work. In these projects The Lawyers' Christian Fellowship works in partnership with local Christian lawyers' organisations to deliver free legal education, advice and representation.

9

ACCOUNTABILITY AND DEMOCRACY

9.1   FREEDOM AND AUTHORITY

In Dostoevsky's *The Possessed*, Shigalyov says "Starting from unlimited freedom, I arrived at unlimited despotism".[207] An extreme belief in liberty places a heavy burden upon the moral responsibility of individuals and does not adequately recognise the structural evil that arises in human systems. Freedom can lead to injustice where that freedom is exploited by those in positions of power to further their own interests. Without a framework of restraint, autonomy does not nourish tolerance but leads to oppression, because those who have power can exercise it for their own ends.

In the absence of a sense of accountability to God, rulers may have no reason not to abuse their powers. Without that accountability, a combination of democratic processes, social constraints, an acknowledgement of accountability to the people and common decency may in practice operate as constraints. But these influences do not restrain all rulers, and for many people they do not represent any absolute values. Where there is no perception of accountability, either to God or to other people, there may be little meaning in any moral or social order. The Roman centurion whom Jesus met recognised that authority can only be exercised because it is given (see Matthew 8:5-13). Jesus says to Pilate that: "You would have no power over me if it had not been given from above" (John 19:11 NIV). Edmund Burke articulated the link between divine law and accountability: "If then, all dominion of man over man is the effect of divine disposition, it is bound by the eternal laws of him who gave it."

Democracy, the least bad system of government, can confer some legitimacy in human terms, but can nevertheless deliver oppression to both minorities and majorities. The authority of a higher law is required. Hannah Arendt recognised that the absence of an acknowledgment of divine law and accountability provided the setting for totalitarian tyranny in the twentieth century: "In the new secularised and emancipated society, men were no longer sure of these human rights which until then had been outside and guaranteed, not by government and constitution, but by social, spiritual and religious forces."[208] All rulers need to know that they will be held to account not only in this world, but also in the next.

Totalitarianism does not recognise accountability either to God or to the people in democratic processes. There is no authority except that of State. Totalitarian regimes presuppose the absence of a natural moral and social order and thrive on the abolition of civil society. These regimes seek to break down the distinctions between people which are part of the natural order. Totalitarian justice is not seen as giving people their rightful due, but assumes that all people, apart from the rulers, should be treated exactly the same. This radical equality agenda can also be also seen in recent secular movements, for instance those which purport to equate same sex unions with heterosexual marriage. Extreme collectivism, which is a feature of communist totalitarian regimes, seeks to replace the natural social order. This collectivism is made possible by a radical autonomy which seeks to reshape human relationships. Radical autonomy rejects any notion of absolute values outside the material world and denies that there is a pre-existing organic order outside the State. This leaves the State as the ultimate arbiter of public truth.

9.2 THE PRINCIPLE OF ACCOUNTABILITY

According to Christian thinking, the laws of a State should be consistent with God's laws. All people will need to give an account to God in the life to come on the day of their judgment and those who are responsible for creating and enforcing the law will need to account for their actions. In this world, however, the objective of Christian laws should be achieved by consent. All human beings have been given freedom, but responsibility necessarily follows from this freedom. In the Christian perspective, the existence of God and objective moral laws provide the basis for a structure of accountability in human government.

The Roman centurion understood that you have authority over others because you have been given it and that a person cannot be trusted with authority unless he or she is prepared to submit to it. It follows that the governed can also hold their rulers to account by reference to objective moral standards, since these are an inherent part of the created order. Deuteronomy 17:14-20 reminds those in authority to obey the law of God, to remain humble and to maintain a restrained lifestyle. The prophets of the Old Testament, guided by God's laws and standards, held their kings to account. No ruler has the right to interpret what God requires without being accountable to others. Imperfection can easily result in mistakes and self-deception. The old doctrine of the divine right of kings was wrong because it implied few constraints on the authority of rulers. This held that kings were appointed by God and were accountable to him, but had no duty to account to their subjects. In practice, rulers who are able to act without systems that limit their power are liable to abuse it.

The biblical model of leadership is one of service, which Jesus modelled. This, not self-importance, admiration or status, should be the guiding principle for all leaders. President Mubarak of Egypt and President Mugabe of Zimbabwe achieved great power and acquired great wealth to an extent that it was impossible they would have a prospect of enjoying a fraction of it. But they forfeited the love and respect of their people. The Old Testament is replete with histories of kings who oppressed their people, as predicted by the prophet Samuel. Charles I, who held to the doctrine of the divine right of kings, was conscientious and sincere. But he exceeded his powers by arbitrarily imposing taxes and seeking to rule without the consent of Parliament. Following two civil wars (and the possibility of a third), which showed his unwillingness to compromise, he was executed. All citizens have a duty to be politically active in questioning their rulers as to whether they are exercising their powers rightly.

The concept of accountability to God is not just a means of encouraging good government and restraining bad rulers. It answers a more fundamental question as to why subjects or citizens should obey governments at all. Unless governments are accountable to a higher authority, it may be difficult to construct an argument beyond the merely pragmatic as to why they should be obeyed and to determine in what circumstances (if any) they should be disobeyed. The theory of the social contract between the governors and the governed (discussed in Chapter 2) indicates that rulers are accountable to the people with whom they have contracted. But social contract theory presents questions associated with democracy and majority rule. For instance, what kind of consent is required and how should it be expressed? And what if even democratically elected rulers behave unjustly or oppress minorities? Thomas Jefferson was perhaps unduly pessimistic: "A democracy is nothing more than mob rule, where fifty-one per cent of the people may take away the rights of the other forty-nine", and James Madison thought that democracies "have ever been spectacles of turbulence and contention". Democracy, if it is solely the rule of the people and there is no established rule of law and systems of accountability, may serve to reflect only the collective autonomy of those who populate it.

9.3   ACCOUNTABILITY AND OBEDIENCE

Law should apply both to the rulers and to the ruled. This is a function of the accountability of governments both to those whom they rule and to a higher authority. Governments or the people may enact or consent to oppressive laws. But there has to be a standard of "good law" that supersedes human law, however we define that "good law". There should be some sort of accountability to a person or body responsible for protecting that law. Human institutions may represent that authority, but they will be flawed. Christian teaching recognises the ultimate authority of the Creator as the source of human authority to whom all rulers and all people are accountable, both in the making of laws and in their application. The freedoms that the English people fought for in the seventeenth century were founded upon the belief that the monarch is subject to the customary law of the land which was based upon a higher law. Many constitutions still recognise the ultimate authority of God. The Canadian constitution does so, though in some instances the priority of God's law has not been adhered to in Canada in recent years.

Conscience should prevent a person from participating in an evil act even if required by secular law, but Christian thinking holds that it is generally right to obey the civil powers in other cases. The Apostle Paul, who suffered badly at the hands of Roman rule, nevertheless taught that civil government was ordained by God for people's protection. For the sake of order and peace governments should be obeyed unless they act oppressively. But the thinking that governments are accountable to God provides an ultimate answer to the question: "*Quis custodiet ipsos custodes?*" This accountability rests upon the authority of God's law being above human law.

There will therefore be limits to the obedience of citizens when the State transgresses the boundaries given to it by God and requires its citizens to act in a way which is, by its nature, necessarily wrong. In the book of Acts (17:6-7 KJV), the Apostle Paul and his followers were described as revolutionaries because they were more accountable to God than to an earthly power: "These that have turned the world upside down have come hither also; whom Jason hath received: and these do contrary to the decrees of Caesar, saying there is another king, one Jesus". The jurist Blackstone wrote: "Any law which is contrary to the scripture is no law at all and not to be obeyed". For instance, the State should not have the power to order the execution of a person without justification. A Christian has a duty to God not to participate in, and to speak out against, such an act. However, even in such cases, there is Christian teaching that resistance should not be violent, except perhaps (as the Reformation theologian Melanchthon held) in the case of self-defence.

The 17th century political theorist John Locke summed up the accountability we all have to God: "For, ultimately, all obligation leads back to God, and we are bound to show ourselves obedient to the authority of his will, because both our being and our work depend on his will...."[209] Christians should remember that their primary duty is to obey God, not man (see Acts 4:19). The dying words of Cardinal Wolsey, Henry VIII's Chancellor, echo down the years: "Had I but served God as diligently as I have served the king, he would not have given me over in my grey hairs. But this is the just reward that I must receive for my incessant pains and study, not regarding my service to God, but only to my prince."[210]

9.4   DEMOCRACY, HUMAN DIGNITY AND RATIONALITY

Democracy is based upon the premise (which is consistent with Christian belief) that every individual has an innate dignity and the ability to decide between what is right and wrong. This assumes that the concepts of right and wrong exist. If they do not, then the decisions collectively made in the democratic process have no rationality. While (as Philip Allott has observed) rationality is a moral category, morality is also necessary to a rational outcome in politics. If there were no objective standards of ethics, this would leave open the argument either that an arbitrary ruler with a coherent but misguided ideology knows better than the people what is good for them, or that nobody does, in which case "might is right" because there are no moral absolutes to say that might is wrong.

While many people without a belief in a rational God and a created order believe in moral absolutes, Christian thought provides a coherent explanation for the origins of the values that underpin democracy and the values that restrain those in power from abusing it. The accountability to God of both voters and governments is essential. Alexis de Tocqueville, writing about America in the 19th century, recognised that the institutions of civil society and its laws, particularly free expression, were vital to the health of a democracy. He put a particular value upon the Christian faith: "Despotism may govern without faith, but liberty cannot".[211] Echoing the Athenian stranger in Book VII of Plato's *Laws*,[212] he emphasised the importance of the unwritten laws — the habits of the nation: "Laws are always unsteady when unsupported by mores; mores are the only tough and durable power in a nation."[213] Democracy depends upon a shared sense of rationality; a belief that objective truth exists and that it can be discovered, and that each human being possesses a dignity and a right for his or her opinion to be heard and taken into account.

9.5 ACCOUNTABILITY AND DEMOCRACY

The principle of accountability to God is also expressed in the accountability that governments have to their people in democratic countries. Democracy is a vital safeguard against oppressive and corrupt government, but it does not necessarily ensure that the government is good, for example that it respects basic human freedoms or the rule of law. The participants in the democratic process, particularly the voters, need to espouse these values and reject any government that seeks to undermine them. Christians would say that the voter has the right and dignity (being made in the image of God) to decide how he or she should be ruled, but must do so by reference to the absolute values that are given by God. Voters should not seek to invent these values or to absolve themselves of responsibility by conferring unlimited power upon a ruler. Hannah Arendt has said: "The ideal subject of totalitarian rule is not the convinced Nazi or the convinced Communist, but people for whom the distinction between fact and fiction (i.e., the reality of experience) and the distinction between true and false (i.e., the standards of thought) no longer exist".[214]

9.6 DEMOCRACY AND THE BIBLE

Although the Bible does not prescribe democracy or any particular institutional arrangement as the only legitimate form of government, it is a strong theme in Christian thinking. As pointed out by Vishal Mangalwadi: "Lincoln knew that the Bible was the true source of American democracy, justice and integration. His definition of democracy as the 'government of the people, by the people, for the people' came directly from the preface of the Wycliffe Bible."[215] William Barclay has observed that the Greek word "*ecclesia*" is the term used in the New Testament to describe the Christian church: "The ecclesia was the convened assembly of the people (in the Greek City States). It consisted of all the citizens of the city who had not lost their civic rights.... It elected and dismissed magistrates and directed the policy of the city...it was a true democracy. Its two great watchwords were 'equality' (*isonomia*) and 'freedom' (*eleutheria*). It was an assembly where everyone had an equal right and an equal duty to take part."[216] The Apostle Peter referred to believers as a "holy priesthood" (1 Peter 2:5 NIV) and there developed the concept of the "priesthood of all believers", equal in status together before God.

Marsilius of Padua, writing in the 1320s, believed that the common will of the people was the human source of political authority, since the people were the best judge of the common good: "The absolute primary human authority to make or establish human laws belongs only to those men from whom alone the best laws can emerge. But these are the whole body of the citizens or the weightier part thereof which represents that whole body."[217] He held that the "authority of the legislator" was "established by election".[218] This conclusion was based upon his view of the nature of mankind: "For most citizens are neither vicious nor undiscerning most of the time; all or most of them are of sound mind and reason and have a right desire for the polity and for the things necessary for it to endure, like laws and other statutes or customs...."[219] Marsilius understood from the Bible the limits of government, and that civil government must respect freedom of conscience: "This was also the view of the Apostle in 2 Timothy 3:16, when he said: 'All scripture is divinely inspired and is useful for teaching, for reproof, for correction and for instruction in righteousness'. But never did the Apostle say: 'for coercion or punishment in this world.'"[220]

Calvin, in commenting on Deuteronomy 1:14-16, stated: "Hence it...appears that those who were to preside in judgment were not appointed only by the will of Moses, but elected by the votes of the people."[221] Later, the *Vindiciae, Contra Tyrannos*, written in about 1579, records that the people of Israel in the Old Testament covenanted with God and with their kings to establish a righteous commonwealth. George Garnett, the editor of the English edition of the *Vindiciae* (1994), calls this a "tripartite covenant between God, king and people."[222] As the author of the *Vindiciae* put it: "There was a twofold consent at the inauguration of kings: the first between the king and the people that the people should be a people of God; the second between the king and people that while he commanded well he would be obeyed well."[223] 2 Kings 11:17 (KJV) records that "Jehoiada made a covenant between the Lord and the people that they should be the Lord's people; between the king also and the people." The Protestant theologian Samuel Rutherford, writing in the 17th century, said that the people delegate their powers to a king: "They measure out, by ounce weights, so much royal power, and no more and no less. So they may limit, moderate and set banks and marches to the exercise."[224]

The anointing of King David by the prophet Samuel should remind rulers that, although they may be confirmed in their office by God's representative, they rule by the consent of the people. David remained in Hebron until all the tribes of Israel came to him and asked him to be king (2 Samuel 5:1). When David faced a rebellion, his friend Hushai defected to his son Absalom who asks him: "Is this the love you show your friend? Why didn't you go with your friend?' Hushai said to Absalom 'No, the one chosen by the Lord, by these people and by all the men of Israel — his will I be and I will remain with him' " (2 Samuel 16:17-18 NIV). But there was a qualification for leadership. As Moses instructed: "Take you wise men and understanding, and known among the tribes, and I will make them rulers over you" (Deuteronomy 1:14 KJV).

In English history, the progress towards democracy and civil liberties was slow. The Anglo Saxon Witan and the medieval parliaments represented a limited but increasing degree of consent to legislation and the exercise of royal power. The principle of consent to government was reinforced in the Civil War period in the 17th century and in the Glorious Revolution of 1688 which removed James II. There was also a movement in civil liberties. During the Reformation in the 16th century the structural certainties of hierarchical religion began to dissolve and historians have seen this as paving the way for the pluralism of later times. In the 17th century people in England began to associate religious liberty with civil liberty. Toleration, which for Oliver Cromwell began with the acceptance of all Christian believers whatever their denomination, began to be extended to other religions, and the Jews were granted freedom to return to England in 1656.

9.7   CHRISTIANS AND THE AMERICAN REVOLUTION

At the time of the American Revolution, contemporaries noted that the resistance was based on Christian thought. As quoted by David Hall, the Reverend William Jones wrote: "This has been a Presbyterian war from the beginning as certainly as that in 1641"[225] and Captain Johann Heinrichs called it an "Irish-Scots Presbyterian Rebellion."[226] Indeed, when Cornwallis surrendered at Yorktown, all the colonels in the Colonial Army but one were Presbyterian elders. This does not mean that Christians are necessarily more likely to rebel against established governments, since they are enjoined by the Apostle Paul to obey secular powers, but the Christian belief that it is more important to obey God than to obey human commands provides a framework for resistance to what Christians perceive as tyranny. As late as the middle of the last century Dietrich Bonhoeffer could write: "The American democracy is not founded upon the emancipated man but, quite the contrary, upon the kingdom of God and the limitation of all earthly powers by the sovereignty of God."

9.8   THE LIMITS OF DEMOCRACY

Democracy is important in restraining rulers, but as an expression only of the will of the people it is not a guarantee of good government, as is discussed in Fareed Zakaria's *The Future of Freedom*.[227] Democracy can deliver dictatorship, demagoguery or theocratic government, all of which may restrict fundamental freedoms. Both Socrates and Plato were critical of the theory and practice of Athenian democracy. As Renford Bambrough puts it, "They took the view that to decide questions of political principle by the vote of an ignorant assembly was no better than to allow the skilled navigator of a ship to be overruled by a majority of crew untrained in navigation and ignorant of the stars and sea routes."[228] Plato nevertheless believed that the rulers should be accountable to the people by the operation of law, so that they could be tried for misgovernment. Sadly, some 20th century political philosophers, such as Carl Schmitt, justified dictatorship as an expression of the will of the people. Plato's concerns about the lack of knowledge of the people suggests both the benefit of an element of delegation from the people to qualified representatives and also the need for fundamental principles to guide the will of the majority and to constrain it in case it becomes oppressive. In Christian thinking, these principles need to be derived from the created order and the Creator, and the government must be subject to them.

The current government of China is seeking ways of promoting a harmonious state. It perceives divisions in Chinese society, for instance between the rich and the poor and between the cities and the countryside, and it does not trust the people to operate democratic processes. The transition to democracy, if there is to be one, is likely to be slow. An interim step would be for the rulers, like Plato's governors, to be subject to an objective rule of law, impartially enforced, which would punish corruption and address misgovernment. Bernard Mandeville described this in his *Fable of the Bees* (1714) where he said of the bees that "They were not slaves to tyranny, Nor ruled by wild democracy, But Kings who could not wrong because, Their power was circumscribed by laws." Laws may not be able to ensure good government, but they can restrict the scope for rulers to abuse their power. They can punish corruption and enforce the impartial administration of justice.

Alexis De Tocqueville, writing in the 19th century, worried about the self-interest of voters. He had good reason to do so in the light of the burden of debt that is building up in the Western world for future generations to deal with. He was pessimistic about the ability of people to vote in the long-term interests of the country and took the view that a democracy cannot exist as a permanent form of government. It can only exist until voters discover that they can vote themselves largesse from the public treasury. Then the majority always votes for the candidates promising the most benefits.[229]

In a democratic system the people, in approving policies and governments, need to act rationally in their own self-interest and in the interests of the wider common good, and also in the interests of subsequent generations. The legal system should operate impartially and without corruption, and there needs to be law, order and security. As can be seen currently in Russia and the Ukraine, democratically elected governments can abuse their powers, usually with the intention of prolonging their time in office. In particular, the legal system can be subverted by the use of fabricated legal charges against opponents and their conviction by judges beholden to the ruling party. The treason law introduced in Russia in November 2012 could be used to further stifle dissent.

Democratic governments can be expected to reflect the standards and values of the population as well as the state of the civil society and the other institutions of the country. De Tocqueville warned that democracy could lead to excessive materialism and selfish individualism, and the history of the late 20th and the 21st century has justified his concerns. Democratic systems in the West are imperfect. They involve party organisations (which can limit choice), expensive campaigns and reliance upon funding by organisations which have vested interests. We can see the limitations of democracy in the Middle East, but unaccountable and undemocratic rule may be worse in the long term.

9.9   CONSTITUTIONAL MONARCHY

The contemporary political writer Phillip Blond has defended constitutional monarchy, saying that it provides some protection against the imperfections of democracy. In the past, the monarchy and its advisers constituted the executive branch of government which was held to account by the legislature which had the power to approve taxation as proposed by the monarchy. In more recent times, the monarch has had no executive power and this has enhanced the ability of the monarchy to be a symbol of allegiance to a higher power and higher values. The monarchy can be regarded as a living symbol that can educate people in virtue. The monarch represents accountability to God. In the coronation oath the Queen swore to uphold the

Christian, and specifically Protestant, biblical faith, though she cannot in practice prevent, and formally is bound to approve, the passing of laws which undermine it.

Although they may be regarded as quaint or romantic echoes of a distant past, the symbols of monarchy remain as vestiges of a faith which was woven into the fabric of the constitution. They recall a time where our laws were still designed (albeit imperfectly) to reflect the laws of God. The orb, representing the world, and the sceptre, the symbol of royal power, are surmounted by a cross to show that God is the ultimate authority. The royal regalia include two saltcellars, salt being a biblical sign of a covenant, as a symbol of the tripartite covenant between God, the sovereign and the people. It is also possible to see in the constitution of the UK (which allows for some bishops to sit in the House of Lords) a reminder that laws should reflect eternal values. This representation is largely symbolic, for the Lords have relatively little power (though some influence) and, while some members of the House of Lords have taken a stand for traditional Christian principles on the more controversial issues, many bishops have been absent from the relevant debates.

9.10 SUBSIDIARITY

Although the concept of "subsidiarity" is used by the European Union to justify a top-down authority, it can be helpful if it is divorced from its European context. The principle prescribes that decisions should be taken at the lowest possible level. However, while the European Union would regard the idea of subsidiarity as a framework for the delegation of functions from the higher power of the Union, power should instead be thought of as being originally invested as of right in the people. Thus only those powers that need to be exercised by a higher authority should be handed over to it. This reflects both the principle of limited powers for government authorities and the need for those authorities to be accountable to those from whom they receive their power.

The Localism Act 2011 is described as seeking to devolve more decision making to local bodies. The new "community rights" may give local organisations the opportunity to purchase locally important assets, but it remains to be seen whether the planning provisions will give neighbourhoods greater control over planning decisions. A concern is that the general power of competence given by the Act to local authorities will extend their powers and result in greater intrusion into the lives of the people.

9.11   DEMOCRACY IN THE MIDDLE EAST

The establishment of democracy in the Middle East presents particular challenges. Timur Kuran (a professor of economics and political science at Duke University and author of *The Long Divergence: How Islamic Law Held Back the Middle East*), writing in the *New York Times* summed up some of the challenges: "Democracy requires checks and balances, and it is largely through civil society that citizens protect their rights as individuals, force policy makers to accommodate their interests, and limit abuses of State authority … The preconditions for democracy are lacking in the Arab world partly because Hosni Mubarak and other Arab dictators spent the past half-century emasculating the news media, suppressing intellectual inquiry, restricting artistic expression, banning political parties, and co-opting regional, ethnic and religious organisations to silence dissenting voices. But the handicaps of Arab civil society also have historical causes that transcend the policies of modern rulers. Until the establishment of colonial regimes in the late 19th century, Arab societies were ruled under Sharia law, which essentially precludes autonomous and self-governing private organisations."[230]

Whilst there are functioning Arab democracies such as Indonesia and Turkey (though in the case of Turkey, the ruling party is reported to be attempting to suppress dissent and entrench its powers), the challenges of transition to democracy in the Middle East are considerably greater than they were for the countries of Eastern Europe following the fall of the Berlin Wall. Freedom of expression and freedom of association are essential building blocks for a healthy democracy and these were evident in the Facebook communications between protesters during the initial uprisings in Tunisia and Egypt. However, these democratic rights should be embedded in constitutional settlements which provide redress against those (whether in or out of government) that oppose their exercise and seek to prevent their practice.

9.12   CONCLUSION

Democracy connects citizens with the processes of government. This, as James Bartholomew has found in the research of Professor Bruno Frey of Zurich University, makes people happier irrespective of whether it delivers better government.[231] It embodies the social contract and provides a mechanism for accountability. It also reflects the freedom and responsibility that each person has individually and in the communities of which they are a part. While accountability in human institutions mirrors the principle of accountability to God, the imperfection of those institutions and of those who populate them highlights the need for all rulers to understand that they are ultimately accountable to God for the discharge of their duties. Democracy cannot by itself guarantee good government. Other institutions, particularly those embodying the effective rule of law and impartial justice, are required. And these need to be supported by guiding moral principles that are embedded in the fabric of civil society and the values of the people.

10
EQUALITY AND SOCIAL JUSTICE

10.1 EQUALITY OF STATUS

A consequence of the Christian belief in creation is the universality of the characteristics given by God to human beings. This transcends all differences of creed, colour, race and any other differences. They are the same for all people because all human beings are made "in the image of God". For the Apostle Peter, each Christian believer is part of a "royal priesthood" — equal in status despite different roles in the church (1 Peter 2:9 NIV). Although early Christian teaching acknowledges the existence of a system of bondservants, often referred to as slaves, it was different from slavery as it was practised in other places and times, for example in America in the eighteenth century. A bondservant had a number of rights, and often a responsible position, and was able to earn his freedom after long service. Moreover, when explaining the early church's attitude to equality, the Apostle Paul said that in Christ, "There is neither Jew nor Greek, there is neither slave nor free, there is neither male nor female; for you are all one in Christ Jesus" (Galatians 3:28, NKJV).

Paul, in his letter to Philemon, urged him to take back his bondman as a free man. Gregory of Nyssa, preaching in 379 AD, condemned slavery as an institution on the grounds of equality before God, saying that: "all of us are equal, prey to the same frailties, capable of the same joys, beneficiaries of the same redemption, and subject to the same judgment" and that "it lies not even in God's power to enslave men and women".[232] Christian faith was the motivation for the abolition of the slave trade and slavery in the British Empire in the nineteenth century. In contrast, the German philosopher Nietzsche believed that, once God had been dispensed with, there would be no rational basis for equality. Equality of status is a reflection of the principle that all human beings are subject to a universal moral law that applies to all persons. In this respect Christian belief provides grounds for what most people intuitively believe.

Alexis De Tocqueville was concerned that radical equality can erode the bonds of society which depend upon, and support, the structures of authority. His perception was that if each person's desires are of equal value, then all people may conclude that they can do as they please (which is anarchy), or one person might assert a right to rule based upon power because no other person can assume a right based upon a higher authority (which is tyranny). This underlines the need for all people, both the rulers and the ruled, to be subject to a higher authority (as discussed in Chapter 9).

Equality in Christian terms is about intrinsic worth and dignity. It is neither primarily about equality of opportunity in society, though this is important, nor is it about ensuring equality of outcome, though extreme inequality should be reduced. Equality of opportunity may mean little to those who are already disadvantaged, who may need not just the opportunity, but also proactive help, to lead a more fulfilled life. Further, it is difficult to provide equality of opportunity for children without imposing a more radical equality of outcome upon their parents, which is likely to be perceived as unfair. An all-party Parliamentary report has highlighted research showing that half of all children in the UK will share the economic and educational prospects of their parents, compared with only 15% in Denmark.[233] However, equality of opportunity can be greatly improved by good education and by support for parents.

All societies have always been unequal in terms of the economic outcome for individuals. The issue for politics is the extent to which inequality should be tolerated and the means by which inequality should be addressed, bearing in mind the effect of the policies used to address it. The flawed nature of humankind leads to structural imperfections in economic systems. Government policies, as well as private charitable action, are required to address the hardships that can result. The aim should not be equality in material terms, but flourishing human beings who are able to use the skills and talents they have been given to realise their potential. Equality of outcome can only be enforced by a powerful State. Communist governments purporting to promote equality of outcome have only succeeded in creating new, usually unaccountable, elites which have exploited and oppressed their populations. As we have seen in Chapter 6, where welfare programmes result in inadequate incentives for people to work, this can diminish personal responsibility and initiative. This is neither healthy for the individuals concerned nor is it good for society as a whole.

While policies that enforce equality of outcome are likely to be oppressive and uneconomic, extremes of inequality should be restrained. The pay of chief executives has increased from £300,000 in 1987 to £4 million in 2011, after allowing for inflation.[234] There are positions in the banking industry where large salaries and benefits are paid to those who have no unusual talent and who benefit disproportionately from the positions that they occupy. They are easily replaceable and others could be trained to do the same job. The viability of a number of retail banks in the UK relies upon the implicit guarantee by the government of their solvency for the benefit of their depositors. It follows that the benefits paid to their executives, particularly in those institutions which are now majority owned by the government, should reflect to a greater extent the levels of salary appropriate for government employees. The mechanisms of corporate control are one way to moderate these inequalities, and there are signs that some changes in corporate law and governance may be implemented to enable this to happen. For instance, each element of the corporate pay packages for senior executives could be set out in detail and voted upon separately in a general meeting of shareholders. Where corporate mechanisms fail, there may be a case for taxation to play a limited role, though taxation could not distinguish between rewards for failure and rewards for success.

Inequality of upbringing, which is characterised by relative poverty, is a serious challenge in the UK. Children in better off families are likely to have better schooling and more personal attention than those who are materially deprived. They will also probably live in a culture where learning is encouraged and achievement valued. But it can be argued that there should be no necessary connection between material poverty and the basics of child development, for example the ability of a child aged five to read simple sentences, to get dressed, to take turns in a conversation and to know some of the alphabet, which are the criteria highlighted in Professor Marmot's 2012 report *Fair Society Healthy Lives.*[235]

The nature of the parenting is an issue, particularly for children in families affected by family breakdown where the parents do not have the money to compensate for the inevitable challenges of lone parenting. While the principle of limited government and the importance of private charitable welfare should remain as aspirations, government may need to resource those organisations seeking to support parents. Young children who are slow in developing can be left behind at school and are more likely to end up in the "NEET" category of those not in education, employment or training. The aim of intervention should be self-reliance and independence, not continuing dependence. In Chapter 13 we look at some of the challenges facing state schools. Over past decades, the gap between attainment levels at independent schools and state schools has widened, reducing equality of opportunity, though there are some indications of improvement in the state sector.

Even equality of opportunity cannot necessarily always be regarded as the "*summum bonum*" (the highest good) for the purposes of public policy making. There are other goals to which individuals properly aspire, which governments may wish to promote and these may in practice conflict with the goal of equality. Excellence in education or in medicine, which is ultimately for the common good, may only be achievable by concentrating resources on particular groups of people and this may disadvantage others. Also, though it is just for individuals to be able to realise their full potential, Michael Young has observed that equality of opportunity can transfer talented people from poorer neighbourhoods to richer ones, and this can reinforce geographical class stratification.[236]

10.2   THE RESPONSIBILITY TO GIVE

Since commercial transactions entered into freely are an expression of freedom given by God and this free will is the framework for individual action, the primary duty to share wealth is that of the wealthy themselves. Plato said that a city some members of which are very rich, whilst others are very poor, is a city divided against itself. Those who are rich have heavy responsibilities. Andrew Carnegie said that "the man who dies rich, dies disgraced."[237] The Old Testament prophets consistently berated the rich for accumulating wealth at the expense of the poor. Jesus said that it is not possible to serve both God and Mammon (a symbol of wealth) and he taught that riches were to be used for the service of God and others. The Apostle James, Jesus' brother, emphasised the need to meet people's material needs as well as their spiritual needs and Christian charities do this throughout the world. Christians know that they have received everything they own as a gift from God and that they are temporary stewards of their wealth. The Charities Aid Foundation's 2011 Market Tracker report recorded that religious people donate twice as much to charity as those without a faith.

For individuals and charities, the relief of poverty has always been a Christian principle, but it needs to be directed at relieving the real need. Poverty may not be merely a lack of money, though this may be a symptom of it. There may be a need for education, community support, practical help and friendship as well as money. If money were the only answer to issues of social justice, there would be no need for the government's troubled family initiative which provides a dedicated social worker to help families with multiple problems. Christian charities are involved in debt counselling, pregnancy counselling with a view to helping women to make the right decision in relation to abortion, post-abortion counselling, the provision of second hand household goods to those with low incomes, restorative justice programmes, programmes to help those with alcohol, drug and other addictions and dependencies, and many more. The aim of these charities is not simply to relieve the symptoms of poverty or need on a temporary basis, but to help individuals reach a point where they can operate independently.

10.3   TAXES

Jesus advised payment of taxes and these are necessary for maintaining the government. Governments may need to intervene to deal with extreme inequality of outcome and to ensure that the poor are cared for. Market economies can create great disparities of wealth and these should be moderated. Where individuals and the structures of society fail to achieve this, governments have to act. However, a lack of personal responsibility or social restraint can lead to excessive government intervention, as a result of what Phillip Blond has referred to as the "regulatory arms race",[238] with legislation and avoidance, in this case tax avoidance, leapfrogging each other as the legislation and schemes to avoid it become ever more complicated.

While those paying tax usually wish to minimise their tax burden, just because something is legal does not mean that it is morally good. However, governments should not attempt to enforce morality except where this is reflected in the law. Governments should not blur the distinction between law and morality. Law must be objective and clear and impartially enforced and taxes legally due must be paid. One of the issues which Greece has to address is the unlawful evasion of tax. In 2011 two thirds of Greek doctors were reporting incomes of less than 12,000 Euros a year.[239] But issues of morality, where an action is lawful (even if it is morally reprehensible) are the responsibility of the individual. For instance, a person who believes that the State is wasting resources may legally avoid tax and then give a high proportion of their income to charitable causes. For governments to intervene in moral issues where the activity is lawful can amount to discretionary law enforcement. This, as we have seen in Chapter 8, is a feature of totalitarian regimes.

High taxation can inhibit commercial enterprise. The extent to which this is the case depends upon the motivation of individuals and this may not be only the pursuit of greater wealth. While more limited State activity in some areas is desirable (as discussed in Chapter 6), in the short term some higher taxation of the wealthy may be necessary to reduce a government's deficit. In the US in 1970 the wealthiest 1% of the population took home 9% of the nation's income. This is now 24%, the highest since 1928. 22,000 households earning more than US$1 million pay less than 15% tax. The income gap between rich and poor in the US has increased. In 2010 half the nation's income went to the top 20% of the population, nearly twice as much (compared with the bottom 20%) than in 1967, which was the highest disparity recorded.[240]

In the UK there may be scope to increase taxes on the very rich. About 550 people earning more than £1 million a year were paying a lower average tax rate than those with an annual income of £20,000.[241] Although the top 1 per cent of earners contribute 28% of total income tax, the very wealthy could pay some higher tax, for instance in the form of a 'mansion tax' in respect of houses where, in real terms, the Council tax is much less than what it was some years ago. But there may be less scope to increase the tax paid by the larger group of middle and above average earners, referred to as the "squeezed middle". HM Revenue and Customs believed that in 2011 almost 27 out of 30 million taxpayers in the UK would contribute less than £6,000 per head in income tax. Dennis Sewell concluded that those who have a child in school or who make substantial use of the NHS are likely to be net takers, rather than contributors.[242] But there are other taxes which, directly or indirectly, affect most people. Income tax makes up only 43% of government revenues. The rest comes from VAT (17%), council tax, which is paid out of taxed income and therefore is a double tax (4.5%), business rates (4.5%), corporation tax (8%), excise duties (8%) and other (14%).[243] Merryn Somerset Webb quotes the Tax Payers' Alliance in giving the example of a £60,000 earner who buys a pair of shoes for £40. Adding together income tax, VAT and employee's national insurance means that he would have to earn £81.93 to buy the shoes, 59.32% of which would have been taken in tax.[244]

The UK's corporate taxation system is dysfunctional. It allows companies to load up subsidiaries with intra group debt so that the interest is deductible against gross profits. It permits companies to pay royalties on intellectual property to offshore group companies in low tax jurisdictions. It even allows some companies to record sales in a low tax jurisdiction where the goods are sold to people in the UK. One possibility (suggested by the City commentator Allister Heath) is to tax all net distributions, including dividends, debt interest payments and shareholder buy backs (royalties could also be included) to any parties, including group companies.

Whatever our views about the social justice of taxation, it appears that in practice there may be limits to the proportion of the gross domestic product (GDP) which the government can take in tax. Higher tax rates do not lead to proportionately higher tax revenues, as the wealthy find legal ways to avoid tax or, because of disincentives, are discouraged from creating the wealth that produces it. The increase in the higher income tax rate to 50% did not greatly increase (if at all) overall revenue. Matthew Lynn cites the 'Laffer Curve', named after the American economist Arthur Laffer, which indicates that, at some point, the more a government taxes the less it raises in tax.[245] In the UK in recent times that point appears to be about 36% of GDP.

The tax take in 1982 and 1984 was 38.2% of GDP, but in the years of the Labour government it did not rise above 36.4% and usually it is about 36%.

Lower overall rates, with fewer reliefs and exemptions, would be more efficient than the current tax system which is extremely complex. In particular, the combination of allowances and thresholds can result in the poor having higher marginal rates of tax than the rich. The Nobel prize winning economist Sir James Mirlees has suggested a progressive and steady increase in marginal rates of income tax,[246] which would be fairer than the current system.

10.4   THE MARKET

Those justifying the large bonuses of bankers, for example, can refer to the operation of "the market" as if it has some ultimate authority. Although restricting the operation of the market may have adverse effects upon a nation's economy and may reduce wealth, this does not mean that the market is necessarily "right" in the sense that it always produces a right outcome or that it has any intrinsic moral justification. Christian thinking indicates that the mechanisms of the market that place a value on resources reflect the collective imperfection and irrationality of mankind, as well as the free will God has given to human beings. Although some attempts to intervene in the market may in practice be unwise or counterproductive, this perception does not confer any moral authority on the market.

The book of Revelation in the Bible contains strong passages condemning the excesses of wealth produced by the market system and the low value placed on the "bodies and souls of men" (Revelation 18:13 NIV). The market facilitated and provided a justification for the exploitation of underage workers in Victorian England (before reforms that were initiated principally by Christians) and this kind of exploitation continues in some less developed countries today. The requirements of the market and free trade were used to justify the continuation of slavery and the slave trade which were abolished after campaigns led by Christians. Though in some cases intervention by the State in the processes of the market may not be productive or right because of the loss of freedom for individuals and the increased power of the State involved in that intervention, the criteria by which we judge whether social justice is being achieved must be driven by a standard higher than the dictates of the market.

To regard the market as inevitably just is to forget the commandment to love God and one's neighbour. Social justice should reflect a framework of behaviour which flows from good relationships, and the market may not deliver these. It is also foolish to rely upon the market, since the market is only the operation of mass movements of resources in response to the decisions of individuals. The outcomes may not be rational or predictable, as recent events have proved. Individuals simply do not have the information about the future and they may not know what other options are available to them. James, the brother of Jesus, put it like this: "Come now, you who say, 'Today or tomorrow we will go to such and such a city, spend a year there, buy and sell, and make a profit'; whereas you do not know what will happen tomorrow. For what is your life? It is even a vapour that appears for a little time and then vanishes away. Instead you ought to say, 'If the Lord wills, we shall live and do this or that'…" (James 4:13-15 NKJV).

The extent to which it is right to restrict the operation of the market in the light of any adverse consequences is an issue that needs to be addressed pragmatically. There are differences between the approach to moral absolutes, such as the right to life, and the approach to relative wealth. Where there is excessive inequality of outcome, the aspiration to achieve a greater degree of equality of outcome has moral force. But this is not in the same category as absolute moral boundaries such as the prohibition against murder. Jesus said that it is the love of money which is the root of evil, and money may be used well or unwisely. Also, in an imperfect world, when dealing with economic outcomes rather than moral absolutes, it may be necessary to choose between the lesser of two undesirable outcomes, where otherwise the worse outcome may occur. Enforced equality of outcome, as in an extreme communist state, deprives people of the free will to be generous as well as restricting other liberties and benefits. Generosity, or indeed any kind of giving, is only possible if people own possessions that they can give. The people of the early church were able to share their possessions because the possessions were theirs to give. People can be generous with their own money, but not with other people's. Generosity in charitable giving can be contrasted with expropriation of property by the State, for instance the forced collectivisation of the farms which occurred in Russia between 1928 and 1940.

10.5   EQUALITY AND DISCRIMINATION

Equality has been the banner under which a number of issues of discrimination or purported discrimination (discussed in Chapter 7) have been addressed. The Equality Act 2010 imposes an equality duty upon public bodies to "advance equality of opportunity,"[247] which has been interpreted by the Equality and Human Rights Commission as a duty to "promote equality,"[248] specifically in the form of promoting the rights of groups who have what the Act (and the "Draft Code of Practice: Higher and Further Education", which runs to 250 pages) call "protected characteristics". The assertion of some of these rights may conflict with a Christian view of the common good.

Equality legislation illustrates the proposition that the basis of thinking in terms of human rights (which underlies the legislation) fails to deal with the issue of competing rights and does not address the underlying issue as to what is a public good that is worthy of protection and encouragement by the State. The application of the concepts of "equality" and "human rights" can impose duties upon other individuals and bodies without the necessary scrutiny as to whether these duties are reasonable, proportionate or desirable in the context of the good of society as whole, or for the good of the individuals affected by the exercise of such rights. The incorporation of the concept of "diversity" into equality policies can over emphasise the differences between groups of people and is therefore liable to be inconsistent with equality of treatment for all people. The promotion of the rights of those with "protected characteristics" can relatively disadvantage those who do not posses them. (These issues are discussed further in Chapter 7.)

The requirement for equality of treatment should be interpreted in a rational and proportionate way. Being equal does not mean being the same. Men and women are different, not least in childbearing and this is reflected in the legal requirement for maternity leave. It does not make sense to afford the same benefits to men. Employees caring for young children, who are mainly women, should benefit from the ability to work flexible hours. Although flexible working is desirable for all employees where it is practicable for the business, it makes sense for employers to be able to discriminate in favour of carers, without being vulnerable to claims for sex discrimination. It should not be assumed that men and women have the same physical qualities, though this is not adequately recognised in the law in relation to sex discrimination. Andrew Rogers, a 62 year old disabled man suffering from a rare blood disease and osteoporosis, who was a male model for artists, won a case of sexual discrimination against an art college because a woman was given work and he was not.

The requirement of non discrimination between men and women in car insurance premiums as a result of a European Court of Justice decision (where there are good rational and commercial reasons for that discrimination), is likely to increase premiums for women. The insurance industry has taken the view that women drive more safely than men. There are good statistical reasons for this view.[249] The insurance industry should have the freedom to take a commercial decision and women should have the right to benefit from it. These freedoms are more important than the right of a section of the population (in this case men) to have lower insurance premiums merely because another group (in this case women) is benefiting from a rational difference in treatment. At stake here is not a fundamental human right, or even the ability to drive a car on the roads, but merely the cost of driving. The difference in costs does not represent the deprivation of a human right and it is not more important than the right of the women to receive a commercial service at the price freely offered.

10.6   SOCIAL JUSTICE

Since God values all people and requires right conduct from them, justice is a recurrent theme of the Bible. The Old Testament prophets consistently inveighed against those in positions of power who prospered by acting unjustly. Isaiah, for instance, attacked the large landowners who forced small farmers into debt and bought their land, rulers who made unjust laws and a corrupt judiciary.

The Old Testament prophets, in speaking against injustice on the part of rulers and those in authority, directed their condemnation against the personal behaviour of those involved. They attacked a number of practices, such as bribery and duress, which are rightly categorised as criminal offences in Western culture. They advocated acts of mercy and compassion and they appealed to the rulers and the wealthy to act justly and generously. For them, as David McIlroy has shown, justice is a positive intervening concept that includes what we would regard as acts of mercy and compassion. The prophet Micah summed up the responsibilities of mankind as follows: "To act justly and to love mercy and to walk humbly with your God" (Micah 6:8 NIV). For him they are all connected. Justice and mercy are intertwined and, for Christians, God's grace enables them to be realised.

Domitius Ulpianus ("Ulpian") defined justice as follows: "*Iustitia est constans et perpetua voluntas ius suum cuique tribuens*"[250] and this concept was echoed in Justinian's laws. This maxim can be translated as: "Justice is the unchanging and continuing will to give to each person what he is entitled to." However, the question posed by the definition is: "What are the entitlements, and from whom or what are they derived?" Ulpian's definition is helpful when a society has established by custom and agreement what the entitlements are, but it does not enable us to define the nature of the entitlements. The nearest we come to agreeing what each person is due in today's thinking is the concept of human rights. As we have seen, there are questions about the nature of the rights, who confers them, and how to address the issue of competing rights.

The idea of entitlement, from wherever those entitlements are derived (and Christians would say they are given by God), is one way to address what should be the nature of the relationship between people in society under a system of government. Society and the operation of its government and economic system provide the framework for people to obtain benefits. These include: work and payment for it, the ability to own property, access to justice and the right to make legally binding agreements which are enforced by the State. The concept of human rights rests upon the proposition that some of these benefits may be regarded as entitlements in the nature of fundamental freedoms or rights which should give rise to legal rights of redress against those who infringe them. But principles are required to underpin what those benefits and entitlements should be.

10.7 THE IMPORTANCE OF RELATIONSHIPS

At the heart of any system of justice and rights of redress should be the right relationship between people. Good relationships in society mean that trust should not be abused, power should not be exercised oppressively and wrongs must be put right. The 17th century jurist Grotius distinguished between "*iustitia communitaviva*", the justice that rectifies wrongs and "*iustitia distributiva*", which regulates the relationships between individuals in society. There is a public and a private element to all questions of justice. Just laws are the framework that enables there to be right relationships between people and encourages the ordered behaviour that follows from those relationships.

Right relationships are a key to understanding justice. An essential element in Christian thinking about justice is the right relationship between people and their God. For the prophets, "justice" was God's justice. They preached the necessity for a change of heart towards God which they called repentance and which would result in a change of behaviour. To the prophets, injustice could take the form of unjust laws, the failure to execute laws in the courts impartially because of bribery, corruption or self-interest, or it could be the misuse or abuse of power. The Old Testament concept of justice involved both a system of obligations and a means of enacting them in society. Justice is therefore both a standard of right and the implementation of that standard in an act of rectification or vindication of the wronged party.

Forgiveness, preached by Jesus, assumes that a wrong has been done. Otherwise there is nothing to forgive. Mercy and forgiveness go beyond the requirements of justice, but they do not make any sense without absolute standards of right and wrong. For Christians, without loving God first, it may be difficult to forgive and perhaps impossible to love one's neighbour in a truly selfless way. "Keep on loving each other as brothers", as the writer of the letter to the Hebrews puts it (Hebrews 13:1 NIV). Human beings constantly fail and the ability to forgive is important, both for leaders in domestic politics and international relations and for all individuals in families and communities. Jesus taught the need for repentance and for forgiveness by God. A theme of the parables of Jesus, summarised in the prayer he taught his disciples (the Lord's Prayer), was that those who have been forgiven so much by God must be ready to forgive others. The sense of God's grace in the forgiveness received from God may enable the change of heart necessary to forgive and cooperate with others. Ian Paisley was questioned by the broadcaster John Humphreys as to how he could cooperate with Martin McGuinness, previously an IRA commander. Paisley acknowledged that he himself was "a sinner saved by grace", who needs the forgiveness of God. Paisley could work with McGuinness in the politics of Northern Ireland once McGuinness had renounced violence.

10.8   VOLUNTARY ACTION AND THE STATE

The aspiration to social justice is the motivation behind countless acts of goodness. Some of these may be voluntary, by individuals or charities, and others may be the result of intervention by the State. The idea behind David Cameron's "Big Society" was that individuals should be motivated to play their part in constructing a society where community action reflects the right relationships between people. The Cabinet Minister David Willetts described it in this way: "Civic Conservatism…proceeds from deep-seated individual self-interest towards a stable cooperation. It sets the Tories the task not of changing humanity but of designing institutions and arrangements that encourage our natural reciprocal altruism."[251]

Others, tending towards a more socialist view, have seen the State as the primary engine of social justice. The Trade Union and Socialist Leader Kier Hardie, writing in 1907, put it thus: "It would, however, be an easy task to show that Communism, the final goal of Socialism, is a form of Social Economy very closely akin to the principles set forth in the Sermon on the Mount."[252] However, the subsequent history of the twentieth century has shown the dangers of giving the State powers to deprive people of freedom in the interests of enforcing social transformation. Christian sharing in the early church was voluntary and not enforced by the community. We return again to the importance of free will in Christian thinking. Christ does not in this mortal life on earth compel obedience. If it is good to give to the poor, this should be done with a generous heart: "God loves a cheerful giver", as the Apostle Paul put it (2 Corinthians 9:7 NIV). Inner transformation is necessary. The Pharisees were castigated by Jesus for the hardness of their hearts, even though they were scrupulous and disciplined in their outward observance of the Jewish law and the additional regulations surrounding it. The widow's mite given with love was more valuable than the substantial sums given by the wealthy without compassion (see Luke 21:2-4).

10.9   THE BASIS OF CHRISTIAN SOCIAL JUSTICE

The teaching of Jesus is in some respects the antithesis of material utilitarianism. Jesus is not primarily concerned with results in material terms, but with the transformation of people's characters and their relationships with God and with other people. But great achievements are the product of transformed hearts and minds. The right relationship with God brings humility and dependence upon God, rather than pride and self-aggrandisement, and this attitude is the basis for right action. Jesus said we should first seek the kingdom of God and all other things would be given to us (Luke 12:31). The kingdom of God is the rule of God in our lives and in the lives of others. Kingdom values include the right relationships with people and the right behaviour towards them that constitute social justice. Social justice is a reflection of right relationships between people. If people are changed, the rule of God in their lives can flow into the structures of the society with which they interact. Jesus did not advocate the structural change of society, but this is likely to follow from the transformation of individual people. Social justice is the outworking of the change in individuals which results from that transformation. Acts of justice and compassion reflect the character of God and his desire for the wellbeing of individuals and communities. Christian people who do acts of justice and mercy can point people to the source of those values which they find in their God.

Seeking God's Kingdom may include campaigning for changes to the law or the activities of the State to protect the vulnerable, as well as encouraging private charitable activity. Many of the greatest social reformers have been motivated by the Christian faith. These include William Wilberforce, Florence Nightingale, the Earl of Shaftesbury, William Carey, John Howard, Charles Dickens, William Morris, George Cadbury, Tang Guo'an,[253] John Malcolm Ludlow, James Kier Hardie, Henry Scott Holland[254] and Elizabeth Fry.

In our own time, Christians have been active in many causes for social justice, notably the Jubilee 2000 campaign to relieve Third World debt, fair trade initiatives, campaigns against human trafficking, slavery, bonded labour and the caste system in India, and projects to relieve poverty, suffering, ill-health and illiteracy and to fight corruption, hunger, HIV and environmental degradation.

PART 3:

POLICY ISSUES

11
HUMAN LIFE

11.1   THE QUESTIONS OF HUMAN LIFE

Respect for human life is a given value in most societies, but it can mean different things to different people. The key issues cluster around the questions as to what constitutes a human life and what it means for something or someone to be alive, both at the beginning and at the end of life. When does human life begin? Are unborn babies human or are they less valuable than babies who are born? What rights does a mother have over an unborn baby? Who can represent the unborn child? When, if ever, is it in a person's best interests to die? And who can take that decision and in what circumstances? In this chapter we explore these issues in the light of Christian thinking.

11.2   THE CHRISTIAN VIEW OF LIFE

For Christians and for many others, life is a gift which should never be taken away by the choice of a human being. This applies equally to decisions about an unborn child as to those about a person's own life or the life of a person for whom they are responsible. From the Christian perspective, God gives human beings freedom of choice in many areas, but this freedom does not extend to an arbitrary power to end the lives of others or their own lives. The prohibition against the taking of life extends to suicide since decisions in relation to life affect not only the person whose life is in question, but also others near to them, and also influence the value attached to life in society generally.

The World Medical Association's First Declaration of Geneva of 1948, intended to update the Hippocratic Oath, which already forbade inducing an abortion, stated "I will maintain the utmost respect for human life, from the time of its conception...."[255] For the Christian, the Bible is clear. In Psalm 51 David refers to his existence "from the time my mother conceived me" (verse 5, NIV) and in Matthew 1:20, Joseph is told by the angel Gabriel with regard to Mary and the identity of Jesus Christ, that "... what is conceived in her is from the Holy Spirit" (NIV). The Gospel of Luke tells us that John the Baptist, who prepared the way for Jesus' coming was full of the Holy Spirit from his mother's womb (Luke 1:15 and 44 ESV).

11.3   PERSONHOOD THEORY AND PRO-CHOICE

Personhood theory maintains a distinction between a human being (which includes an unborn child) and a human person (which excludes an unborn child on the grounds that it is not sentient and cannot reason or do anything useful). Personhood theory therefore maintains that killing a human being who is not (yet) a person is acceptable.[256] This reasoning is flawed if, once conception has occurred, the genetic information required for the person to exist is complete. Personhood theory is inconsistent with the secular philosophical belief in determinism. This holds that human personality and the decisions that flow from it are pre-determined by genetics, environment, and natural forces.[257] If a large part of a human being's life is already pre-determined in the genes present in the womb, how can the foetus fail to be just as much of a person as the rest of us?

11.4   THE HISTORY OF ABORTION

The law in relation to abortion was clear when the Offences Against the Person Act 1861 specifically outlawed abortion, making it a crime to procure a miscarriage except when there was a danger to the life of the mother. In the 20th century hard cases, such as the rape of women, led to a relaxation of the law. The "danger to life" became a "danger to physical health", and then a risk to "mental" health. This culminated in the Abortion Act 1967, which has been so widely interpreted in practice as to permit abortion on demand. Since that Act was passed, over seven million unborn children have lost their lives. 189,931 abortions took place in 2011, 7.7% more than in 2001 (176,364).[258] The public are largely unaware of the scale of the destruction. A poll undertaken by *ComRes* in November 2010 revealed that only 3% of the population realised the scale on which abortions were taking place.[259] Abortion is permitted up to 24 weeks, when the child is substantially developed and capable of surviving outside the womb, and up to birth in the case of disabled children. The most common period when abortions are carried out is three to nine weeks,[260] when the unborn child has eyes and ears, a heartbeat, moves, and pumps its own blood around its body. Brainwaves are detectable from 40 days' gestation and the baby will recoil from the unpleasant and then painful touch of a medical instrument in the mouth area from just five weeks after conception and in other areas of the face, hands and feet from six to nine weeks' development.[261] Despite the widespread availability of abortion, there are still circumstances where abortion is an unlawful killing, for instance aborting a child because it has the "wrong" sex, or the abortion of a healthy child outside the time limit of 24 weeks.

Dr John R. Ling has pointed out that abortion is the result of failed relationships and that it reflects selfishness on the part of adults in that the seeming interests of the mother and the father are put first. Further, he explains that the ease of abortion has blunted our compassion for the weak and vulnerable, particularly the disabled, since prospective parents are advised to abort children who may turn out to have certain physical or mental conditions. John Ling also points out the drop in adoptions. In 1968 there were 27,000 adoptions, but in 1992 there were only 8,000.[262] This reduces the obvious (and in the Christian view, best) option for infertile couples wishing to care for a family.

11.5   PUBLIC HEALTH AND ABORTION

One of the current justifications for abortion is the ground of "public health". Hillary Clinton, testifying before the Foreign Affairs Committee of the US House of Representatives, has said: "…we are now an Administration that will protect the rights of women, including their rights to reproductive health care…." She added that, "reproductive health includes access to abortion that…should be safe, legal and rare."[263]

The proposition that a woman has an absolute right to abort an unwanted unborn child generally rests on one of two assumptions. One is that the unborn child belongs to a sub-species having a sub-human status (for instance based on personhood theory or viewing a foetus much as slaves were in the past), so that it can appear permissible to dispose of him or her. The other is that the unborn child is part of the mother's body with which she can do as she wills. In either case the conclusion is that a mother has absolute rights over the unborn child so that it is only the mother's wishes, and not the health, well-being or rights of the child, that are to be taken into account. Neither of these positions is consistent with the facts as they are observed. If the unborn child is sentient, the unborn child must be a separate human being, since the child is not a member of another species. Nor is it an integral part of the body of the mother because it is only a temporary resident. The body of the child must belong to the child and not to the woman.

There is an implication in the word "safe" in the words of Hillary Clinton quoted above that, if the "right" to abortion is not given, the mother will be unsafe. Whether the woman will be unsafe will depend upon (i) whether the woman will choose an abortion and (ii) if she does so, whether the abortion will be unsafe. These are matters over which policy and law makers have no control. Even if it were known that an unsafe choice would be made in a particular case, this does not permit a person (a doctor) to kill another human being (the unborn child) because the alternative is that another person may do so in a way which involves health risks for the mother.

11.6   FOETAL PAIN AND WOMEN'S MENTAL DISORDER

Over the last few years, there has emerged a body of evidence that unborn children are capable of feeling pain and suffering. Abby Johnson's book *Unplanned* is a recent example of anecdotal evidence (the first chapter can be read online).[264] More scientific evidence of the sentience and human behaviour of the unborn child can be seen in the work of Professors K.J.S. Anand[265] and Campbell.[266] If this research is correct, abortion procedures have involved barbaric cruelty that few human beings would wish to see inflicted upon animals.

An artist, Emma Beck, aged 30, committed suicide in grief at the abortion of her twins. Her suicide note said: "I see now I would have been a good mum. I want to be with my babies: they need me, no one else does."[267] A *British Journal of Psychiatry* paper has shown that women who have had abortions are likely to have rates of mental disorder 30% higher than other women[268] (though this has recently been disputed by a study made by the Academy of Royal Medical Colleges), not to mention the fourfold increase in rates of substance abuse, the danger of physical complications and the risks posed to future pregnancies.[269] These findings are consistent with a natural moral order that regards abortion as the killing of a person. The guidance of the Royal College of Obstetricians and Gynaecologists published findings that there was no psychological impact of abortion, but they were formulated by a group of eighteen people of whom eleven made their living from abortions and there were two representatives of large scale abortion providers.[270]

11.7   INVOLUNTARY EUTHANASIA

The justification for involuntary euthanasia is that the right of a person to life is diminished because the quality of their life is impaired. This argument has concerned those who advocate the interests of disabled persons. They fear that, if similar criteria were applied to disabled people, others could determine that the quality of life of disabled people was not sufficient to justify the resources expended on them.

In many cases it will be clear whether a person is being killed against their wishes, but in some cases the issues and the interpretation of the facts will not be as straightforward. Whilst abortion is a clear-cut issue for most Christians, it being only permissible in the cases where the life of the mother is at risk,[271] issues at the end of life can be more complex. Medical treatments are costly and their availability may be limited. Further, there can be a point in a person's life when it may not be the best course to continue treatment, for instance when a very elderly person is near death and further medical intervention would be intrusive, distressing and futile.

If it is right that in some circumstances treatment may have to be withdrawn, a key issue is what constitutes treatment. Christian principles indicate that it is right that a person, even in what is called "a persistent vegetative state" (PVS) (such as a long term coma), should continue to receive nutrition and hydration. The provision of food and water can be regarded as a basic human duty stemming from biblical principles. It is sometimes impossible to know exactly what functions of the brain or of perception are still active and a patient with no hope of recovery may regain consciousness after several years. A patient who is thought to be unconscious and to have no hope of survival may in fact be conscious, responsive and can live for years to come.[272] The withdrawal of food and water from a patient who was moving and making non-verbal noises was authorised in the case of *Frenchay NHS Trust v. S.*[273]

The withdrawal of food and water (together with sedation) designed to ease the transition to death for patients predicted to die "imminently" is a feature of what is called "The Liverpool Care Pathway" (LCP).[274] Patients have now resorted to giving formal instructions that the LCP must not be applied to them. It has been reported that the LCP is used for 130,000 patients each year. It is possible that most patients on the LCP are dying in any event. But it is wrong to remove what is called "nutrition and hydration" (food and water) since that act can be the principal cause of death. There may be no scientific basis for predicting death. Even if there were, mistakes could still be made, so doctors should not cause death to occur by prescribing the LCP based upon their prognosis. In many cases, the cause of death of a person on the LCP may be the original illness. However, if a person dies some days after the LCP has begun, the removal of food and water may have caused the death rather than hastened it. Defenders of the LCP acknowledge the requirement to consult with relatives and the need for better training for those administering the LCP to ensure that the patient does not suffer. But these do not affect the fundamental issue which is that the LCP can be the cause of death. On the other hand, it is right to relieve the suffering of those who are dying. Palliative care, for instance the administration of pain relieving drugs, should not be withheld because it may sometimes have a side effect of hastening death.

The provision of nutrition and hydration is right because it is a Christian duty to provide food and water, as the Good Samaritan did in the story Jesus told. It follows that not to provide food and water (as opposed to medical treatment) to a patient should be unlawful killing. When the House of Lords (at the time the highest court in the land) ordered that food and water could be withdrawn from Anthony Bland, a Hillsborough victim in a persistent vegetative state in 1993, he was dehydrated and starved to death over a nine-day period. John Ling quotes Melanie Phillips who observed: "If it [nutrition] is treatment, then what precisely is the ailment for which food is the remedy?" In the case of "M" in the High Court on 28th September 2011,[275] Mr Justice Baker declined to authorise the removal of food and water from a patient in a conscious state. The decision was on the basis that the patient enjoyed a quality of life (albeit limited) and also on the grounds of the principle of the preservation of life. A report published in May 2011 found that doctors needed to prescribe water to elderly patients to prevent them from being neglected.[276] A concern is that once the principle of the removal of food and water is accepted, this could then be extended to patients with dementia.

11.8   ASSISTED SUICIDE AND VOLUNTARY EUTHANASIA

Assisted suicide and voluntary euthanasia present different issues to those surrounding involuntary euthanasia. They raise the issues as to whether a life belongs entirely to the person living it and whether other people who may be affected by the death have interests that should be protected. Even in the absence of a belief in a God, there may be a sense that life is, in some sense, given or sacred. For the Christian, suicide and voluntary euthanasia are wrong because no one has the right to take a life, including their own, since it is given by God. Those wishing to die may express a temporary desire to do so, perhaps because of difficult circumstances or depression. Were they to live, they may be relieved that their wishes to die were not carried out. The prophet Elijah in the Old Testament was so depressed about the failure of his mission that he wished to die, and depression is a debilitating illness that can prompt thoughts of suicide.

For those responsible for facilitating assisted suicide, there are practical as well as moral difficulties. If a person of sound mind expresses a desire to die, but then mentally deteriorates so that it is no longer clear whether that wish continues, should the wish be given effect? Decisions of this nature, even if made without inappropriate influence or pressure, affect a wide range of people — family, friends, relatives and perhaps those yet unborn. The Apostle Paul wrote in Romans 14:7 (NIV): "For none of us lives to himself alone, and none of us dies to himself alone." The other people affected by a suicide would include, for instance, the friends and relatives of the person committing suicide, and the medical profession whose right to freedom of conscience should be upheld. Even if these people do agree, then they may be doing so without a complete understanding of the consequences for them or for others. Elderly relatives anxious not to be a financial burden might believe it is right for them to agree to euthanasia or may be influenced unduly into doing so by societal or family pressures. 35% of those requesting suicide in Oregon said that feeling a burden to their family or caregivers was a reason for their choice.

Dr Ling has examined what he calls the false principles of euthanasia: that a person has total freedom or autonomy to kill himself or herself; that a doctor can, or has the right to, decide whether a life is not worth living; that there is a fundamental difference between voluntary and involuntary euthanasia; and that euthanasia is compassionate.[277] Laws that allow voluntary euthanasia can easily be used to facilitate involuntary euthanasia. As recorded by Dr Ling, the *Remmelink Report* of 1991, which reviewed euthanasia in the Netherlands (where euthanasia was effectively legalised in 1984 following a ruling by the Dutch Medical Association (KNMG)), found that there must have been 10,558 cases where doctors had acted or refrained from acting with the intention to shorten life and that, of these, 5,450 patients must have been killed without their consent. According to Care Not Killing, a close reading of the statistics in the detailed report published in the New England Journal of Medicine[278] reveals that one in ten deaths in the Netherlands in 2005 resulted from some form of suicide or euthanasia, comprising continuous deep sedation until death (8.2%), voluntary euthanasia (1.7%) and non-voluntary euthanasia (0.4%).[279] In 2005, 20% of cases of assisted suicide or euthanasia went unreported, despite a legal requirement to do so.[280] A report commissioned by the Dutch government recorded that in 2001, in 900 of the estimated 3,500 cases of euthanasia, it was administered without consent. It is also noteworthy that in the Netherlands, the development of palliative care has been neglected, affecting the whole of that society, and the terminally ill in particular.[281] The examination of the euthanasia law in the Netherlands published in *The Lancet* on 11th July 2012 reveals that the rate of euthanasia in the Netherlands has increased by 73% in the last eight years (1,815 reported deaths in 2003, 3,136 in 2010 and 35% in the last two years). As of March 2012 mobile euthanasia units in the Netherlands planned to administer euthanasia to people with chronic depression, disabilities, dementia, and loneliness.

One of the reasons for the pressure in favour of assisted suicide is the concentration upon the feelings of the person who wishes to die and the prominence given to the alleviation of suffering, both mental and physical, over any other absolute principles. Suffering must always be alleviated where practicable, but not at any price. A context for the acceptance of assisted suicide may be the adoption of a secular utilitarianism that elevates human autonomy and the experience of the person affected, without regard to the wider implications for others and the principles that take more general considerations into account. There is currently a campaign for the legalisation of assisted suicide for terminally ill adults who are mentally competent. One of the concerns is that once the principle is accepted, it would then be extended to others (perhaps as a result of a human rights challenge), since the arguments in favour, principally those relating to the autonomy of the patient and the relief of suffering, apply equally to others.

The present state of the law in the UK in relation to "mercy killing" is unsatisfactory. The law in relation to murder remains unchanged, despite repeated attempts in Parliament to legalise assisted suicide in 2002, 2003, 2005, 2006 and 2009. However, the Director of Public Prosecutions was required by the House of Lords to issue a new offence-specific prosecution policy for assisted suicide. This was the result of the ruling in a legal case in which the House of Lords acceded to Debbie Purdy's request for a clarification of the law in relation to the circumstances in which a prosecution would be brought against a person assisting a suicide.[282] The policy requires an enquiry into the motives of those committing acts assisting suicide. The determination of the suspect's motives (whether they acted out of compassion) plays a part in the "public interest" of the decision of the Director of Public Prosecutions as to whether the perpetrator should be prosecuted. This policy presents difficulties, apart from the principle that it permits a killing to go unpunished. It gives undue prominence to the motive, which at best is difficult to determine and is sometimes unfathomable. Here it is important to understand the distinction between, on the one hand, the intention to do an act (in law is referred to as "*mens rea*") which is rightly important in all serious crimes and, on the other hand, the motive for an act. The absence of an intention to kill will in most cases rightly absolve a person of the crime of murder. In the case of assisted suicide, the nature of the motive for the killing (where there is already an intention to kill) can absolve the person where there is thought to be a good reason for the killing. In these cases the State is sanctioning murder where it has reason to believe that it knows why a person has intentionally killed another person and it has determined that the motive for the killing is justifiable. Further, it is in principle wrong to give discretion to a public authority as to whether the law should be enforced (see Chapter 8). The Bill of Rights 1689 denied the Crown and its servants the power to suspend the execution of laws without the consent of Parliament,[283] which suggests that the DPP was required by the then House of Lords (now the Supreme Court) to act unconstitutionally in issuing the policy.

Most European countries take a different approach to that taken in the UK. The Council of Europe has passed a motion that "euthanasia in the sense of an intentional killing by an act or omission of a dependent human being for his or her alleged benefit must always be prohibited". The compassionate way to approach the care of people in the last stages of life is to relieve their suffering by effective palliative care. Treatments of this nature may carry a risk that they shorten life, but this double effect does not constitute euthanasia. And any adult person has the right to refuse medical treatment, and may do so on the grounds that it will diminish the quality of the remainder of their life.

11.9   UTILITARIAN EMBRYOS

Issues relating to embryos pose the question as whether the embryo has any intrinsic human quality, and therefore dignity, apart from its use for other purposes. If the embryo is merely a collection of cells, then a utilitarian view would be that it may be used for any purposes that could confer a benefit upon others. (Utilitarian thinking focuses on the rightness of the end to be achieved, rather than on the means by which it is achieved.) It may be hard to question this perspective, unless the view is taken that the embryo has a purpose to its existence that is of value in itself. Christian thinking provides a framework for the intrinsic value of every human being at every stage of existence based on their creation in the image of God. Those who regard the expression of Christian principles in law as a minority view may reflect that the UK, in contrast to many States in Europe, has failed to sign the European Convention on Human Rights and Biomedicine 1997, which prohibits embryos being created merely for research.[284] The UK has also chosen not to sign the Additional Protocol to the European Convention on Human Rights and Biomedicine of 1998, which prohibits human reproductive cloning,[285] because the UK permits the cloning of embryos for research. The Charter of Fundamental Rights of the European Union of 2000 also prohibits human reproductive cloning, but it has no legal effect in the UK, due to a protocol attached to the Treaty of Lisbon.[286]

11.10   EMBRYONIC STEM CELL RESEARCH

The utilitarian thinking mentioned above guides current policies in relation to the use of embryonic stem cells for research. The interests of a patient whose suffering may be alleviated by a treatment derived from the use of embryos are given priority regardless of the means by which the treatment is achieved. It follows from the Christian view of the nature of embryonic life that many activities currently authorised by UK law are a wrong use of scientific knowledge. Human embryo research, including cloning to produce embryos for research, and the use of human embryos as a source of stem-cell treatment fall within this category. As Dr Ling points out, the primary objection to the production of embryos for research and treatment (which includes therapeutic and reproductive cloning) is that they result in the exploitation and deliberate destruction of human embryos.

Christian activists draw attention to the fact that adult stem cell research has to date been more effective in finding a practical use in treatments than embryonic stem cell research. After ten years, embryonic stem cell research has killed a large number of embryonic human lives (over two million), but so far has achieved modest results. Research using stem cells from adult sources or from umbilical cord blood or from the patient's own body — research that kills no-one — has produced over 70 effective treatments.[287] British scientists at Cambridge University have recently generated brain tissue from human skin.[288] However, the fundamental issue is not one of effectiveness, but one of ethics, which is whether it is right to use human embryos for the purposes of research or treatment and to destroy them. Even if the view is taken that the embryo is not a human being, but merely a collection of cells, there is also an argument that embryo research is wrong because it trespasses upon the process by which life is created.

Most people would reject any suggestions that medical experiments should be permitted on certain classes or types of people, for instance the young or the mentally ill, who are not able to give consent. For those who believe that life is conferred by God at conception, the use of embryos for research has a similar character, even if the effects on the donor's conscious experience are less obvious. The central issue that needs to be debated, in this issue as in abortion, is whether embryos are human beings or whether, until some moment in time, they represent a kind of sub-species (like an animal) that may be used and discarded in order to benefit "full" human beings. And the point at which the embryo becomes a human being would need to be a logical point in time, accessible to reasoned analysis, which is consistent with the world as we experience and observe it.

11.11 SAVIOUR SIBLINGS

Ethical issues arise in relation to those who are called "saviour siblings". This is where an embryo is selected free of genetic defects and of the same tissue type as that of an elder sibling needing treatment, so that doctors can use the tissue of the child brought into being in this way to treat the sick elder sibling. Apart from the issues surrounding the killing and discarding of unused embryos, there is a concern as to the welfare of the new child. In a case in the English courts, Josephine Quintavalle challenged a decision of the Human Fertilisation and Embryo Authority to license the selection of an embryo that did not suffer from the same disorder as its elder, sick brother and that would have sufficiently similar human leukocyte antigens (HLA) to its brother to make future stem cell treatments possible.[289] In arguing that HLA-typing was not permitted by the Human Fertilisation and Embryology Act 1990, Quintavalle put the case that the tissue typing was not for the benefit of the child being produced. The House of Lords held in 2005 that the activity was permitted because it fell within the definition of "activities in the course of providing treatment services". In this case the treatment was not for the benefit of the person represented by the embryo, but for another person. The central point that could not be addressed directly in the case is whether it is right to bring a person into existence to serve the interests of another person.

Whilst it is easy to understand the need to treat a particular sick child, Christian principles and the laws that flow from them exist for the protection of individuals. Hard cases, as the lawyers say, make bad law. The principle that a person can be created for the use of another person could be said to enshrine slavery at birth and deprive that person of the dignity, identity and freedom that have been given to each one of us by the Creator. The book by Jodi Picoult, *My Sister's Keeper*, and the film that is based on it, explore these issues.[290] In human terms, it is also easy to see how this can result in psychological dysfunction.

Animal-human hybrids are also now permitted for research purposes, although research projects involving them were abandoned because they did not attract the necessary funding, perhaps because of doubts as their usefulness to medical science.[291]

11.12 SURROGACY

Surrogacy raises a number of moral issues. Currently, under English law, surrogacy is not supposed to be permitted for gain, but is allowed in other circumstances.[292] The issue of gain was thought to be decisive during the passing of the latest Human Fertilisation and Embryology Act (2008) when the nature of the families created should have been the principal issue. Surrogacy destroys the link between the natural (biological) parents and the new (social) parents. It deprives the child of the right to know and be cared for by its biological parents and can therefore leave the child psychologically confused. Adoption can raise similar issues. However, whereas adoption is designed to provide an existing child with the love and security that it would otherwise lack, surrogacy introduces confusion by its very nature, particularly since the relationship between the donors and the mother (who may be unknown to each other) is entirely artificial. It also allows same-sex parents to adopt, or with anticipated new biotechnology to produce children.[293] The Human Fertilisation and Embryology Authority consulted upon proposals to create genetically modified babies with three or four "parents" (the consultation closed in December 2012). In the Christian view, these arrangements are not consistent with the God given family structure for the best interests of children.

11.13   THE PUBLIC DEBATE ABOUT LIFE ISSUES

The public debate about issues of life has understandably been operating to some extent on an instinctive level, since beliefs are deeply held. But it should also be a rational debate, since moral arguments are not irrational. Evan Harris, the former Liberal Democratic MP, in responding to a Reith Lecture on morality in politics acknowledges this when he said: "I do a lot of public policy on abortion and gay rights and assisted dying and embryos…I bring morality — the principle of non-discrimination, the principle of not harming someone unless there's evidence that your policy creates harm."[294] There can be a tendency to confine morality to a narrow perspective that is consistent with a particular world view or agenda. For some people, a principle of non-discrimination trumps all other considerations, such as the principle of the sanctity of life. It is difficult to define what is "good" and what is "harm" without an underlying framework of beliefs about the nature of mankind, about mankind's relationship to creation and to a creator (if there is one) and, following on from this, what constitutes a flourishing human life.

There are widely differing assumptions that underlie the moral thinking of those with opposing views in relation to issues about life. These can inhibit a rational dialogue and the resulting misunderstandings permeate the public debate. The debate needs to acknowledge the difficulty in finding a commonly understood context and the need to understand different worldviews. Otherwise there is a danger that each side of the debate will be proclaiming its position without explaining it in a way that helps the undecided person to understand and consider the issues involved. Christians would say that their account is logical, consistent and open to reasoned analysis. However, they should acknowledge that their analysis is most easily explained in the context of metaphysical beliefs about the character of human life and the nature of human relationships.

For them, these beliefs constitute a rational account of the world in which we live, but not everyone will share these beliefs. There are other grounds, apart from Christian belief, for valuing human life and these should also inform the debate. Those grounds could include, for instance, a belief in our common humanity, the importance of human compassion and the wisdom and experience of humanity down the ages. Christians do not have a monopoly upon moral values and moral reasoning.

In an article about the use of embryonic stem cells and assisted dying, Professor Neil Scolding explores the thinking behind the disrespect for life at its beginning and at its end.[295] He concludes that it is the fear of suffering that outweighs other considerations. Embryos can be experimented on and destroyed in order to produce cures for debilitating diseases. In relation to assisted dying, the suffering of individuals is used as a justification that the person affected or others should have the power to end their lives. Yet, as Professor Scolding points out, there has not been a time in history when there has been less suffering. It is just that we are not prepared to accept it any more. The reason lies perhaps in the assumption that this life is the only one we have and that there is no hope in a world to come. Therefore we must make this life as comfortable as possible. For the Christian, suffering is part of a temporary transition into a greater reality. St. Paul put it like this: "I consider that our present sufferings are not worth comparing with the glory that will be revealed in us" (Romans 8:18, NIV).

Issues in relation to questions of life and death are important because they deal with the application of one of the most fundamental moral principles, which in many ways is still reflected in our laws: the prohibition against unlawful killing.

If the Christian account of these issues is true and reflects a fundamental natural law, few issues in society are more serious and should be more pressing.

12
CRIME AND PUNISHMENT

12.1 THE HUMAN CONDITION

Christian thinking requires that crime and punishment recognise not only the imperfection of human beings, but also their capacity for good. It also needs to recognise the dynamic and addictive power of evil. For Christians, there is an active power of evil in the world. God said to Cain: "Sin is crouching at your door; it desires to have you, but you must master it" (Genesis 4:7 NIV). In human terms, the power of evil can operate through the mechanism of autonomy. Kant recognised that all natural talent could be put to both good and evil purposes and thought that only a "good will" could be taken to be good without qualification.[296] All human beings are naturally imperfect. Left to themselves, without moral guidance, without the restraint of law and without the recognition of God's ultimate judgment, people can be drawn into wrong choices. These choices may appear to be of their own making, but the results of those choices have a momentum of their own and can make it increasingly difficult to make the right choices and to act upon them. Tom Wright has drawn attention to the work of E.A. Maguire, which has shown how regions of the brain are developed by activity, for instance, the London cab driver's increased memory because of his or her mastery of "the knowledge".[297] Acknowledging the power of damaging thought patterns, the Apostle Paul urged his readers to think upon good things (Philippians 4:8).

Recent work has explored the role of mirror neurons which create structures in the brain that cause habits to become ingrained. Choices develop into patterns of behaviour and patterns of behaviour develop into addictions. The mechanisms by which this occurs may be variously described as physiological, psychological or spiritual. We know that some of our instinctive wants and desires, even if they are firmly entrenched, are not necessarily good. The fact that behaviour feels "natural" to a person does not mean that it is good. Some objective standards are required, though some people may find difficult the suggestion that what they feel to be their natural inclinations are wrong.

12.2 THE RESPONSE TO WRONGDOING

In Christian thinking, the State has an authority delegated from God to punish evil and encourage good. This is for the benefit of the offender, who should be brought to realise his wrongdoing and change course, and for the protection of society. Some thinkers have identified a weakness in contractual theories of the State, such as the social contract mentioned in Chapter 2. They point out that a rational person would never consent to his own punishment, since the agreement he has with the State is for his self-preservation.

In some cases the wrong done to people by others (rather than choices they themselves make) results in psychological (and some Christians would add spiritual) damage. This damage can make wrong choices hard to resist. Most people have difficulty in understanding the motivation of those who commit terrible crimes, such as the abduction and murder of young children. A Christian perspective can point to a dimension of an active evil force. This may have taken root and grown as a result of the abuse of the criminal himself at a younger age. Rejection by those who should care for a child can lead to rebellion and a desire to hurt. An absence in early life of the love, support, encouragement and guidance that should be provided by families can have profound effects. It is not surprising that the majority of young offenders come from broken homes. Christian thinking is that criminals must take personal responsibility for their actions, rather than excusing them, but that compassion can help others to understand the forces that have shaped the offenders' lives. This understanding can help offenders to overcome the challenges they face and lead better lives.

12.3   THE BASIS OF PUNISHMENT

Given the power of evil and the extent of human weakness, laws are needed to restrain evil through enforcement and deterrence in order to protect society. Also, people have been given the ability, through their consciences, to understand the difference between right and wrong. In Christian thinking, a change of heart in relation to wrongdoing, which Christians call "repentance" is an essential ingredient of a right relationship with God. In some cases this can also restore the relationship with those affected by the wrongdoing. Punishment should therefore seek to ensure that the offender understands that what he has done is wrong and is given the opportunity, while paying the debt that society requires in terms of punishment, to follow a changed life.

The severity of the punishment for a crime is likely to reflect a number of factors. These include the seriousness of the crime, the importance society attaches to it, the culpability of the criminal and whether the crime is in a pattern of behaviour or is a single occurrence. For the Christian, the severity of the punishment can also be informed by the moral laws and guidance derived from Christian teaching. Punishment involves a combination of retribution, deterrence and rehabilitation. The element of deterrence should provide a disincentive to others and to the offender who might consider committing the crime in the future. Deterrence is essentially utilitarian. The 19th century utilitarian philosopher Jeremy Bentham thought that it would be possible to change human behaviour by controlling pleasure and pain. This stark analysis recognises that imperfect human beings require disincentives to wrong behaviour. But this is not the only motivation for good behaviour. A change in outlook and attitude based upon some kind of moral framework is also required. The rehabilitation of criminals should aim to change the offender's behaviour in the long term and fit the person for a normal and productive role in society. A change in behaviour will follow from a change in the offender's attitude to what he has done and his view of what he can become in the future.

Later in this chapter we look further at the practical means by which these changes may be achieved.

The rationale for retribution may be alien to some. Giles Fraser, a past Canon of St Paul's Cathedral, has taken the view that the concept of retribution is not consistent with Christian thinking since Jesus taught forgiveness and mercy.[298] The concept of retribution has been seen by some philosophers as a way of restoring equality by depriving a person of the unfair advantage obtained by acting against the rules of society. For example, if I park in a disabled bay when I am not entitled to, or if I destroy property or intentionally injure a person for my own gain, I am gaining an unfair advantage. A parking fine may be adequate punishment for parking in a disabled bay that balances the benefit I have obtained by not observing the regulations. In the case of the intentional injury, the argument would be that I cannot put the situation right by making a payment in recompense, since I am still benefiting from my crime (perhaps by deriving satisfaction from it) and a further counterbalance to my behaviour is necessary.

According to the Apostle Paul, civil government was instituted by God to punish evil. This indicates that there is a moral purpose to the punishment. A serious punishment is an indication to society that the crime is serious. It is a statement by society of the values which it expects citizens to uphold. A realisation of the seriousness of a crime is necessary both for the offender and for others who may be inclined to commit a similar crime. This is different from mere deterrence, since the punishment has an educative purpose for the offender as well as for others. The Apostle Paul said that the law (referring in this case to the Jewish law) was a "schoolmaster" enabling people to distinguish right and wrong and helping them to see their need for faith (see Galatians 3:24 KJV), and the purpose of punishment to reform the individual is a strong theme in Christian thinking.

There is a difference between the personal response to wrongdoing and the response of the State acting on behalf of all citizens. While, at a personal level, we should forgive and show mercy to those who have harmed us, there must be boundaries around the mercy which the State is entitled to display. The State must act objectively by administering justice impartially in the interests of all citizens. There may be arguments for reducing the sentence of an offender who admits guilt, but there should be transparent, impartial and fair standards by which this is done.

12.4   THE CHALLENGES OF RESTORATIVE JUSTICE

Restorative justice describes a variety of theories and practice in relation to punishment which seek the restoration of the relationship between the criminal and society and, in some cases, between the criminal and victims of crime. Restorative justice emphasises that crime is against people and that it breaks down relationships, and so justice is seen as the process of restoring those relationships. Some of the early work on restorative justice has come out of Christian thinking. These can bring about a change in attitude on the part of the offender to the crime he has committed. While the aim of restoring relationships is right, critics of restorative justice have been concerned that it can put a premature emphasis on forgiveness and that it can by-pass some of the steps which in fact lead to a genuine restoration of relationships. There has been a perception that some versions of restorative justice can encourage a reduction in the severity of the punishment in exchange for vague intentions of goodwill on the part of the criminal which may not result in a change in behaviour. The concern is that, if there is a relaxation in punishment, this will both diminish the criminal's sense of responsibility for the crime and reduce the deterrent effect of the punishment.

Restorative justice can be helpful in providing comfort to victims of crime as well as helping victims to understand the social factors that may have contributed to an offender's behaviour. This understanding may help the victim to forgive the offender. For a victim who is a Christian, the relationship with God (who has forgiven so much) can help this to happen. Restorative justice can also bring in a wider community of people who may be able to support both victim and offender. However, there are obvious dangers in the suggestion that the community or the victim should be able to influence the severity of the punishment. This would undermine the rule of law, which should apply equally to all offenders, whether or not they behave well in the restorative process. It could even, if carried to extremes, allow scope for personal vengeance on the part of the victims or their families. Although it is good to recognise the concerns of victims and the value of reconciliation, the nature and severity of the punishment should be determined objectively and not by the victim.

12.5   PERSONAL RESPONSIBILITY

According to the socially conservative writer Christopher Hitchens, there is an undue concentration on the rights of the offender and a readiness to absolve criminals from blame because of social conditions. As he put it: "The new system refuses to believe that there are people who are so morally unrestrained that they are prepared to do wicked acts."[299]

A Christian approach to crime is to be realistic about the capacity of human beings to do evil and recognises that an offender needs to realise the true nature of the criminal acts and take personal responsibility for them. The causes of crime need to be understood and addressed but, however compelling the mitigating circumstances, it is necessary that offenders are made aware that they are responsible for their own actions. This is the nature of the human condition and it is not compassionate to suggest otherwise. Where people have offended, they need to accept responsibility. Otherwise they cannot move forward to a more fulfilling existence because they are trapped in a web of victimhood from which it is hard to escape. Taking responsibility is part of the dignity of what it means to be human. If we absolve offenders of responsibility, then we imply that they have no freedom of will and that others should take responsibility for them. This is to treat people as less than human. It is a dangerous path to tread and one which, if taken to extremes in other contexts, can lead to oppression and totalitarianism.

There need be no conflict between the aims of restorative justice and the other purposes of punishment which are the assertion by society of its values, the necessity of deterrence and the personal renewal of the offender. For the individual and for society, a change of heart is vital. A repentant criminal is more likely to be a rehabilitated one. Irrespective of the issues surrounding the severity of the punishment, schemes of restorative justice that enable a criminal to see the effect of wrongdoing and identify with victims of crime should be encouraged. However, repentance can never be guaranteed and it can easily be simulated, so the severity of the punishment should not be relaxed just because there is a system of restorative justice in place that encourages a change of heart, however desirable that change of attitude may be.

12.6 AGE APPROPRIATE PUNISHMENT

It is also important that punishment is appropriate to the age of the offender. While it is essential that young offenders are apprehended and punished, young offenders particularly need to be taught and encouraged, as well as punished, by appropriate intervention at the right age. The County Durham Youth Offending Service, recognising that a young person receiving a criminal record for a low-level offence limits his or her employment prospects, has introduced a system of "Pre-Reprimand Disposals" ("PRD"). This includes advice and support, addressing educational and welfare needs, as well as restorative justice. The results in the period May 2008 to November 2010 have been a fifty per cent reduction in re-offending following a PRD, and eighty per cent of those given a PRD engaged in twenty-five hours of education, training or employment at the end of the PRD. Restorative justice schemes are legislated for as a first option for youth justice in Northern Ireland.

12.7 A UTILITARIAN APPROACH

Professor Lawrence Sherman's work at Cambridge University is an example of a utilitarian approach to sentencing which aims at reducing what he calls the "total harm to society."[300] In practice, this is likely to lead to far fewer people going to prison. It suggests a policy of sentencing based upon the likely outcome for the individual offender, rather than the severity of the crime. Thus as he says, "Someone who is convicted of violent robbery or rape at 12 has a lifetime risk of killing somebody that is far in excess of somebody who is not charged with a serious offence until 18 or 19." Helpful though this analysis is (and practical in the light of the overcrowded prisons), sentencing must also reflect a measure of justice for the individual and how society views the crime. For example, it might be statistically proven that those convicted of particular crimes who are in a particular age group or who participate in a restorative justice programme are on average less likely than other groups to commit a further crime. However, this would not justify a sentencing policy based upon that likely outcome, since this would be unfair to offenders in other groups and the policy would still apply to the minority in the favoured groups who did go on to commit further crimes. This would undermine the principle of impartial justice. There is also the possibility that a sentencing policy based on likely outcomes might be wrongly applied, even in its own terms, because of inadequate information.

12.8 RESPONSIBILITY AND RENEWAL

For an offender, part of the process of renewal may involve the healing of psychological hurts suffered at the hands of others. In Christian thinking, only an all powerful and loving God can fill the gaps left by human dereliction. And the process of renewal may not be completed on earth, but only in the world to come, when all believers will shed their burdens of earthly sin. Pascal summed up our need to rely upon the help only God can give: "An ordeal which has been so protracted, so unremitting, so unchanging should certainly convince us of our powerlessness to reach the good by our own efforts."[301] Opportunities for those in prison to respond freely to the Christian good news of personal salvation are important for the welfare of the prisoners and for the health of society. Christian churches and charities give practical help and offer friendship to ex-offenders seeking to lead a new life in what are inevitably challenging circumstances.

Once an offender accepts responsibility for the crime, he or she is then in a position to regret it, to turn around and to resolve to be different. Acceptance of responsibility is a necessary part of the change of attitude which Christians call repentance. The restoration of a relationship with the Creator in the form of a personal faith in God can be the first step to a changed life. Christian programmes of rehabilitation for offenders have been successful in helping ex-prisoners and in giving them the emotional and practical support they so badly need in order to lead a different life. Byron R. Johnson has analysed the effect of Christian programmes of restorative justice in the US prisons.[302] He emphasises the need for ex-prisoners to connect with civil society and that this requires cognitive changes which a conversion to the Christian faith can bring about: "Essentially Sampson and Lamb, as well as other life course theorists, argue that having ties to social institutions (marriage, family, employment, etc.) significantly influences behaviour over the course of a lifetime..... In recent years several scholars have acknowledged that changes in the individual must take place before that person is ready to develop ties and bond to social institutions. In other words, the individual must change if the bond is to form.... These researchers suggest that religion can be viewed not only as a catalyst for new definitions but also a cognitive blueprint for how one is to proceed as a changed individual."[303]

The current punishment system in the UK has not generally been successful in the rehabilitation of offenders. According to

Nick Herbert MP, speaking in April 2012, half of all offences are committed by those who have already been through the courts.[304] Criminal behaviour can be reinforced in prison. Drug abuse, the cause of so much crime, is often easier in prison than outside. More effective drug rehabilitation programmes, combined with appropriate enforcement against drug abuse in prisons, are required.

Criminal behaviour can be powerfully addictive. There is a moral and psychological dimension in crime which needs to be addressed in rehabilitation. Destructive habits can more easily be broken where there is a change of attitude and a determination to lead a different life. An appreciation of the moral implications of crime can enable this to be achieved. Faith based programmes of restorative justice recognise that, where crimes have been committed, a moral wrong has been done and that relationships between people have broken down. These programmes recognise that for a criminal to recognise the hurt caused to others, for him to be sorry for it and to be willing to change can be an important part of the rehabilitation process. The offender is brought face-to-face with a victim of crime, but not the victim of the offender's crime. The offender can hear at first hand the impact of a similar crime and, as a result, can relate to the victim as a person. These programmes can also bring psychological release for some victims who have been traumatised by the offence (particularly if it has been violent), and who volunteer to share their experiences with offenders.

Restorative justice programmes cannot guarantee that any particular individual will come to a realisation of the nature and effect of the crime that he has committed and wish to change. Each person has free will and can reject the opportunity. But it is important that offenders have that opportunity. The justice system must continue to reflect the traditional principles of punishment, such as deterrence. But repentance is important, because only a change of heart brings hope and renewal for individuals and for society. A restorative justice process can encourage an offender to recognise his responsibility, to change course and to embrace a new life, and it is a valuable addition to the justice system.

It should be the aim of a justice system that those leaving prison are better adapted to living a life free from crime than when they entered prison. Prison should, while still being punishment, give the hope and the means of a better life thereafter. The concern is that in many cases this outcome is far from the current state of affairs where criminal behaviour can be reinforced in prison. Prison should teach basic literacy and mathematics skills where these are lacking and give the opportunity for training for future employment. Employment in prison should be encouraged. Employers should pay fairly, though the majority of the pay to prisoners should go to the State, particularly in the light of the significant expenses of prison.

The government has recognised the importance of rehabilitation for short-term prisoners (those in prison for less than one year) by announcing a scheme for them to have mentors when they leave prison. Longer term prisoners who are released already have probation arrangements. The requirement for ex-prisoners to have personal advice and support illustrates the human need for relationships as well as rules.

12.9 RESPECT FOR THE LAW AND ENFORCEMENT

Respect for the law and its enforcement are essential for a civilised society. Peter Hitchens, who approached issues of crime from a traditional perspective in his *Brief History of Crime*,[305] chronicled a series of statistics and anecdotes supporting the view that in many parts of society in the UK, respect for the law, and effective enforcement of it, has broken down. He was concerned about the increases in reported crime and saw an inability of the police to investigate crimes and bring offenders to justice. He recorded that reported crime was at the end of the century fifty times what it was in the 1920s. Some of this increase may be due to the fact that the number of potential offences has increased so the numbers may not fairly reflect an increase in lawless behaviour. There is also a difference between actual and reported crime, though some would say that people are less willing now than in the past to report a number of crimes. This could be because people perceive low rates of detection and believe that the police attach more importance to victim support than to detection and enforcement. One in four incidents ignored by the Metropolitan Police should have been recorded as a crime, according to a study published by HM Constabulary[306] and 12% of all cases handled by the police in 2011 were resolved by an informal ticking off compared with one in two hundred in 2008.[307] If these figures are correct, it seems implausible to suggest that the increase in crime figures can be attributed to the number of offences on the statute book and to differences in the reporting of crimes. There are also differences in the response to crime. If the UK today imprisoned the same ratio of people for serious offences as it did in 1954, there would be 300,000 people in prison, not 80,000.[309] Hitchens cited that in 1999, seven thousand people were let off with a caution for burglary and that one offender was so undeterred by the law that he had been arrested 186 times before he was seventeen. Fiona Pilkington killed herself and her disabled daughter after many years of harassment by local youths and after 33 appeals to the police who did not respond, allegedly because of lack of resources.[310] The coroner observed that there were a dozen laws which could have been enforced to deal with the behaviour.

If children are deprived of discipline based upon a moral framework, it is not surprising that they lack self-restraint at home or at school. Family breakdown, absent fathers and the lack of male role models are significant factors. Hitchens cited the increase in social provision, which has enabled people to be dependent upon the State rather than self reliant, though the experience of countries with low social provision, such as South Africa, and other European countries with high levels of social provision, do not suggest that the level of social provision is a determining factor. In addition to stable families and discipline at the appropriate age, there also needs to be effective law enforcement. Hitchens perceived the police as a heavily armed elite and a "motorised bureaucracy" appearing as a paramilitary force at football matches and demonstrations, but generally out of touch with ordinary citizens. This may be unfair, but over the past decades the police have retreated from the streets and the housing estates.

Philip Johnston has observed that, despite legislation such as the Crime and Disorder Act 1998 and the possibility of child safety orders, local child curfews, parenting orders, reparation orders, action plan orders, referral orders, detention and training orders, spot fines, drug treatment and supervision orders, drink banning orders and family intervention orders, lawless behaviour continues. Respect for authority has been eroded.[311] It appears that young people who are out of control and who reject authority are not disciplined by their parents, cannot be disciplined by their communities and are not dealt with effectively by the police. The police are not familiar as a matter of routine with those youths who may be liable to cause trouble on their watch. While individual police officers may be conscientious, hardworking and courageous, the police force as a whole does not do the job which the public expects of it.

A combination of the legal and regulatory environment in which the police operate, the priorities set by police management and the culture of police forces restricts police officers from carrying out what the public regard as their primary functions which are to prevent and detect crime and to bring offenders to justice. A report by Her Majesty's Inspectorate of Constabulary found that training for officers in six forces featured only one module out of 190 focussing on crime prevention and no evidence that this knowledge was being applied on the ground.

Training "focused more on how to use powers legally, than how to use them to be more effective crime-fighters."[312] The police are set targets for arrests which do not take into account whether or not those arrested are released without charge. There are 'crime management units' which classify crimes in ways that are constructive for the police.[313] David Gilbertson, a former Assistant Inspector of Constabulary was concerned about the misuse of resources by the police: "The cuts, in my view, are a side issue. The police waste resources in vast quantities. The key is deployment, coupled with intelligent, visible and brave leadership by senior officers who have a strategic vision."[314] As of 2011 the average proportion of time spent by police on the beat was 14% and only 12% of officers were ready to respond to 999 calls at any one time.[315] Her Majesty's Inspectorate of Constabulary found in that year that more police officers are at work on a Monday morning than on a Friday evening when trouble is most likely to occur. This may reflect the amount of bureaucratic work which the police have to do, poor leadership and management, perverse incentives or a combination of these. Some community liaison activities of the police may be unproductive. Bernard Hogan Howe, the Metropolitan Police Commissioner has commented: "I think in the past the police service has got trapped into some partnership working which is not always about fighting crime."[316]

Despite the heroic sacrifices that individual officers are sometimes called upon to make, distrust of the police is widespread. The lack of trust is because, in a number of instances, the police have proved to be untrustworthy. Deborah Orr, writing in the Guardian in March 2012, epitomises this: "The Metropolitan Police, in particular, seem to be in thrall to a culture of paranoid victimhood, in which the only people really worth protecting are themselves."[317] The behaviour of the police in the Hillsborough disaster, the relationship of police officers with the News of the World, the Tomlinson affair, and the resignation of Andrew Mitchell, a government minister, after false statements made by the police, have contributed to the erosion of public trust in the police.

The failure of the police to tackle systematic child abuse in the north of England shocked the public in September 2012. The Times quotes an example: "Police went to a house outside of which a father was demanding the release of his daughter, who was inside with a group of British Pakistani adults. Officers found the girl (aged 14) drugged under a bed. The father and his daughter were arrested for racial harassment and assault respectively. Police left, leaving three men at the house with two more girls."[318] In most (if not all) the cases, the police did not recognise that sexual intercourse with a girl under the age of consent is illegal. They disregarded the law in relation to the age of consent and also presumably chose to regard the sexual relations as consensual. Lord McColl, speaking in the House of Lords in May 2012, remarked that: "It is a matter of pride that in 1807 and 1833 Britain took the lead in combating slavery. We no longer do so. That Britain is the number one destination for sex trafficking in Europe and that we should have lost 301 rescued child victims of trafficking between 2007 and 2010 beggars belief."[319]

The use of the police to restrict freedom of expression and to enforce what many would regard as an unnecessary and oppressive agenda in relation to the expression of religious belief (as discussed in Chapters 7 and 15) also undermines the respect in which the police are held in the eyes of many people. Respect for law enforcers, as well as for the processes of the law, is important. The Rev. Roland Parsons has highlighted this: "I am aware that Christians, unfortunately, increasingly regard the police as their potential enemy due to the misuse of the Public Order Act 1986 by various militant groups in our society. The police often support these militant groups in their hatred against Christians and Christian values."[320]

There needs to be a perception that the law will be effective and that criminals will be caught and convicted. Otherwise the law will not act as a deterrent. Changes to legal procedures over past decades, which followed cases where the police tampered with evidence, have made it harder to convict criminals who may be able to rely upon technicalities to escape conviction. If criminals perceive that there is a small risk of detection or conviction, the nature of the punishment as a deterrent is less relevant. The police and law enforcement agencies may have some work to do in restoring public confidence in their effectiveness.

Government has been aware for some time that the police need to be more responsive to local needs. The introduction of elected Police and Crime Commissioners was designed to address this. The Commissioners have replaced the Police Authorities in their role of determining strategy, setting budgets and overseeing the work of police forces. This should improve the accountability of the police, but it will be important that people take an active interest in the elections (the turnout for the first elections was low) and that the elections respond to local concerns and are not driven by party politics. However, though this increased accountability may prove to be helpful, it should not be necessary to ensure that the police do the job which the public expect.

There have been some calls for changes to the law to reflect a fairer balance between the rights of criminals and the rights of victims. Some cases have involved the exercise of force by victims defending themselves and their property. The law of ancient Israel (in Exodus 22:2-3), although formulated for a different time and place, gives an indication of some of the considerations involved. Under the Old Testament law, if an intruder breaks in at night and is killed by a house owner, then the killing is not murder, but the normal rules of self-defence apply if the intruder breaks in during the day. This reflects the likelihood that, at night, the intentions of the intruder may not be clear. He may or may not be armed. He may wish to attack the householder or his family, or he may not. And in the dark the householder cannot know what danger he represents. Lord

Judge, The Lord Chief Justice reflected this in September 2012 when he said that frightened people could not be expected to remain calm when confronted with intruders and that burglary was an offence against the person as well as against property.[321]

12.10 LAW AND A SAFE SOCIETY

Laws and their effective enforcement are important. These reflect the values of a society and its determination to see those values reflected in practice. But laws and their enforcement do not in themselves ensure a safe society where general standards of behaviour and respect for authority have deteriorated. Changes in attitude on the part of individuals and society are also necessary. Individuals need to exercise self-restraint in accordance with a set of values. Society must be clear about what it believes to be wrong behaviour. The boundaries between lawful and criminal behaviour must be clear. The law must be enforced decisively and impartially. Offenders should understand from their punishment what is wrong and should be given encouragement to lead a renewed life.

The Christian outlook on crime and punishment combines realism with hope: realism about the imperfection of human nature and the need to restrain evil; and hope in the recognition that each person has the capacity for change and can, if they are willing, be helped by the grace of God to do so.

13
EDUCATION

13.1 MORAL EDUCATION

Recognising the imperfection of human beings, Christian teaching has emphasised the importance of moral education for the good of the individual and of society. Goodness (as opposed to good behaviour) cannot be enforced, but it can be modelled, taught and encouraged. For the Christian, temptation is an ever present reality and must be resisted. Those who do not identify with a metaphysical perspective on the existence of evil may nevertheless be able to acknowledge a value in Christian teaching and recognise that it offers a framework of ethical values and support for individuals. In Christian thinking, a dynamic and destructive force of evil can affect the human personality. Once wrong courses are chosen, this force can then reinforce wrong desires. Cicero recognised this when he said: "Hold off from sensuality for, if you have given yourself up to it, you will find yourself unable to think of anything else",[322] and he warns that human beings can be beguiled by pleasure.[323] Kant recognised the danger of the "seduction of the inclinations", stating that: "If the freedom of man were not kept in bounds by objective rules, the result would be the completest savage disorder." Addiction, whether physical (for instance to alcohol or drugs) or psychological (for instance to pornography) are examples of this.

The mechanism by which habits of behaviour become ingrained may be described in neurological, psychological or spiritual terms. But, on any explanation, human beings at all stages of their lives, and particularly as they are growing up, need guidance and encouragement to do what is right. Children who choose or are led into courses of behaviour, for instance drug or alcohol use or sexual habits, create patterns for the future that can be hard to erase. This perception is consistent with an understanding of child abuse which can damage people in the long term. Many Christians are concerned about the encouragement of sexual freedom in children and teenagers whose neurological development is insufficiently progressed for them to make mature choices. In Christian thinking the young need to be protected both from others and from themselves.

There is evidence that moral standards in the UK are in decline. According to a January 2012 study by the University of Essex, Britons are now less honest than they were ten years ago. Ten years ago 70% would not justify unfaithfulness in marriage; now half would do so. Two out of three people would not condemn lying if it was in their own interests. Around half thought falsifying a job application could sometimes be justified. Only a third of those under 25 said it could never be justified, compared with three quarters of those over 65.

13.2   THE FAMILY AND EDUCATION

For Christians, the primary place where moral values and self-reliance should be taught is the family. Christian thinking emphasises the duty of parents to teach their children (Deuteronomy 4:9) and of children to learn from their parents (Proverbs 1:8). Hannah More, the Christian writer and philanthropist of the 18th century, said that virtues are the product of "secret habits of self-control" and that they require both training and personal effort.[324] Katherine Birbalsingh echoes this approach: "For a child to learn how to be good, his parents must punish him when he does something wrong and reward him when he does something right. His parents must also spend enough time with him in order to set a good example so that he can copy their actions, learn that he cannot do whatever he likes, and see that every action has a consequence. Eventually, through constant repetition, the child will learn a moral code that will become instinctive as he grows older. As

Aristotle says, 'Excellence is not an act; it is a habit.' It is a habit that is learnt in childhood, when choice is managed by the control of the parents."[325]

Commenting in the context of the riots and looting of August 2011, David Lammy, Tottenham's Labour MP identified the need for family structures to underpin the education of values: "In areas like mine, we know that fifty-nine percent of black Caribbean children are looked after by a lone parent. There is none of the basic starting presumption of two adults who want to start a family, raise children together, love them, nourish them and lead them to full independence. The parents are not married and the child has come, frankly, out of casual sex; the father isn't present, and isn't expected to be. There aren't the networks of extended families to make up for it. We are seeing huge consequences of the lack of male role models in young men's lives…. There are virtually no male teachers in primary schools."[326]

13.3   CHILD CENTRED APPROACHES

Clashford Sterling, a youth worker who runs the football club at Broadwater Farm Community Centre in Tottenham, highlighted the change in climate in relation to the disciplining of children: "Parents are fearful about how they chastise their children. There's been an erosion of authority for a long time, parents move very gingerly not to upset their own kids. Bad behaviour and criminality has been glamorised on the streets. Teachers are scared to punish children. The modern child isn't frightened of their parents. They don't care if the police lock them up."[327] In the same report in *The Guardian*, a parent called Chris (who did not want to give her surname), said she felt under pressure not to discipline her children: "Responsibility has been taken away from parents. People here will call social services if they hear you disciplining your children. Children hear about Childline at school. It's all very well trying to be liberal, but parents need to be given back their right to parent."[328]

Some children suffer from neglect, but there is also a concern with the child-centred parenting of some children from prosperous backgrounds, as highlighted by Alice Thompson: "These children don't lack self-esteem, but have a huge sense of entitlement and no respect for others; they have never learnt to take control of their lives."[329] The Programme for International Assessment (PISA) of pupils ranks them by ability in different areas by country. In 2009 the US and the UK came 28th and 30th respectively for mathematics but pupils thought they were better at a subject than they actually were.

13.4   THE BURDEN FOR TEACHERS

A report by the Prince's Teaching Institute highlighted that currently schools are being forced to mop up social problems, which undermines their ability to teach academic subjects. Teachers have a difficult and, no doubt in some cases, impossible task if discipline has collapsed in the home and parents do not endorse disciplinary action taken by schools. As Estelle Morris, a one-time head teacher and former Secretary of State for Education put it: "There's a lot of talk about teachers having lost their authority to maintain discipline. I'm not persuaded that the legal position is any different from what it has always been, but what has most changed — and what can most undermine a teacher's authority — is a lack of support from parents. This, more than anything, can make it difficult to maintain discipline and set standards."[330]   Children need structure, discipline and challenges (which can involve competition), physical exercise and a group with which they can identify (for instance a team). They cannot be expected to organise their own learning until they have reached a sufficient level of maturity.

Inadequate parenting and discipline together with other social causes have contributed to the disaffected culture of many young people. In some schools, a number of children appear not to want to learn and teachers have inadequate sanctions to prevent disruption. In some cases, much of a teacher's time and energy are spent on "crowd control". Sir Michael Wilshaw has said that teachers in the best schools in deprived areas act as surrogate parents, helping with homework, giving advice, taking them to bus stops and providing meals in place of families who cannot, or will not, support their children.[331] This was even recognised by the Deputy Prime minister who said that: "We expect our teachers to be social workers, child psychologists, nutritionists, child protection officers."[332]

13.5   OBJECTIVE WISDOM

Christianity teaches that there is wisdom derived from objective knowledge and that this can be taught. Traditional Christian education does not favour the child centred educational theory, though there must be good communication and interaction between the teachers and the pupils. For instance, learning can be checked and reinforced by asking children to express in their own words what they have been taught.

Educational methods should recognise that learning, particularly in the early stages, is about understanding systems of knowledge and thought formulated by others, not by the pupils themselves. The rules of written language are not a matter of the child's subjective opinion, but are constructed around objective rules such as spelling and grammar, the learning of which enables children to understand new words and sentences for themselves and to learn other languages. A child-centred theory still pervades some teaching today, as is explained by Miriam Gross's pamphlet published by the Centre for Policy Studies. The ideology of autonomy and choice, derived from social liberalism, has been transferred into educational theory. Children have been taught in small groups around tables and have been invited to discover things for themselves, often without the necessary foundation of basic knowledge which enables them to make sense of it. Knowledge of the facts is the basis of understanding and of forming a rational opinion. Children do not learn well from each other or where they are expected to acquire habits of grammar and vocabulary without formal teaching. The weaknesses in liberal educational theories are now widely recognised and it would be helpful for there to be an investigation into how such ideas pervaded the educational establishment for so long. A Government source is reported as saying: "For too long, left-wing training colleges [for teachers] have imbued teachers with useless teaching theories that don't work and actively damage children's education."[333]

Notwithstanding the deficiencies of some liberal teaching methods, interaction with teachers is required and pupils learn from the enthusiasm of individual teachers. Learning is a process of assimilation and understanding, in addition to the learning of rules, important though this is. Teachers need to be able to assess whether the pupils have understood what they have been teaching and to respond to particular needs. Individual children may learn in different ways. While, for instance, most children should be taught to read with a system of phonics (and not with the 'whole word recognition' method) since this has been found to be the most effective, some children may also benefit from different systems.

79% of pupils achieved the required level in English and mathematics in 2012, up from 75% in 2011. This was 81% in London despite the number of children there for whom English is not a first language. Surveys indicate that between 1840 and 1865, before the introduction of State education, 80% to 90% of the population could read and write. In recent decades a significant number of children have left state primary schools functionally illiterate, despite the cost of schooling of (currently) at least £6,000 a year per pupil. Other countries spend less. Japan spends $4,000, France $6,000 and the USA $8,000.[334] It seems that many children in foreign countries, for instance Zulu children in South Africa, can spell better in English than many children in the UK.

The nature of the teaching and the school environment can be more important than the background of the children. James Bartholomew gives the example of a school in Whitechapel, one of the poorest areas in the country, where two thirds of the pupils qualify for free school meals and the majority come from families where little or no English is spoken at home.[335] The children at this school are taught by the phonics system and all the children can read fluently at the age of seven. There have been targeted programmes to help slow learners catch up, but these might not have been necessary to the same extent if the teaching methods had been adequate.

It would be wrong to attribute low educational standards only to misguided teaching methods or to poor schools. Order in the classroom, free from the disruption by a minority of pupils (which is very challenging for teachers to deal with) is also a major factor. Katherine Birbalsingh has highlighted the "low level disruption" of lessons. She attributes this partly to the teaching method by which teachers roam the class, hoping to be facilitators of learning, while a general level of noise and inattentiveness pervades the classroom.[336] She notes that in one school half the class can barely hear the teacher because there is too much noise.[337] She comments that where there is bad behaviour by pupils, teachers can be made to feel inadequate for not engaging them. She comments on the chaotic families where detentions are not a punishment for families who would prefer the children to be away from home for longer. She is concerned that there are no adequate means of discipline.[338]

There is an important link between misbehaviour and inadequate learning outcomes, particularly a failure to read and write. If pupils have not learnt enough to understand what is being taught and keep up with a class, teachers will find it difficult to motivate them to participate in the class. It is frustrating and dispiriting for children who cannot read and write adequately to continue their education and as a result they may try to disrupt the class. Mixed ability classes can frustrate the able pupils, who are not stretched, and leave the less advanced behind who, when they are not engaged, may then distract the other pupils. In some schools where pupils have been left behind and are disruptive, there can be a culture of failure. Here a lack of willingness on the part of pupils to learn is matched by a defeatist attitude on the part of teachers. Where pupils are not willing to learn, teachers may regard themselves as relieved from the considerable efforts required on their part to enable the pupils to reach higher standards.

Recent suggestions have included keeping pupils at primary school level until they have mastered the basics and the aim that all children should achieve a basic qualification in maths and English before leaving school.

13.6   OUTSTANDING TEACHERS

Outstanding teachers and schools can sometimes overcome the difficulties. The *Evening Standard* featured five "superheads" who have transformed challenging schools. They did so by instilling traditional standards of discipline.[339] As Colin Hall put it: "I introduced a school uniform, a clear code of conduct and measures to regulate behaviour. It was no longer acceptable for students to be rude or to say what they wanted when they wanted. I put the teachers back in charge in the classroom and made the students realise there was a time and a place for everything. Some say we civilised the children, but I prefer to say we made them more sophisticated. We also switched from mixed-ability classes to setting and banding and introduced personalised learning plans. I am passionate about helping children achieve their utmost." Sir Michael Wilshaw reflected that in providing structure and discipline "I tell my teachers that we are surrogate parents who must set standards that don't necessarily exist in their homes." His motto is that "Structure liberates children, especially those from deprived homes."

Martin Tissot mentioned an example: "One of our year eleven pupils comes from a tragic home with an alcoholic mother and an absent father. Today she is a girl transformed and on track for university." Jo Schuter summed it up when she said: "I am an advocate of tough love."

13.7 FREEDOM TO TEACH

The approaches outlined above reflect a traditional Christian view of education. The discipline given by parents and, while children are at school, by teachers, provides the right context for learning and enables children to flourish as individuals. However, once structure and discipline have been established, the State or even the school should not be too prescriptive about the way education is delivered. In fact, the State's prescription has often been a failure. Katharine Birbalsingh describes the philosophy behind teacher training: "One must remember that one isn't a teacher in a State school classroom. Instead one is a 'facilitator of learning'. One doesn't teach knowledge one teaches skills. So standing up in front of the class and actually teaching is frowned upon. Far better to set the children up in groups...."[340] These methods are hugely inefficient. Further, as she says: "The philosophy that underpins State education is that we are in the business of pursuing equality, not excellence."

The State provides prescriptive patterns for lessons that can inhibit originality and enthusiasm. Failure to comply with these models can result in low gradings by the State inspection authority, Ofsted. Birbalsingh highlights that Ofsted, in its 2011 report *Excellence in Education* (the author of which does not know the difference between grammar and stylistic devices) encourages teachers not to teach a knowledge based curriculum. But she points out that Ofsted, in assessing the results of schools in tests, penalises teachers for doing what they have been instructed to do, since the teaching methods that Ofsted advocates are ineffective.[341] She contrasts this with the freedom given to teachers in the private sector and, while the analogy may not be entirely appropriate given the disparity in resources between the private and the public sector, she concludes that, "The public school boys who run Britain aren't doing so because they were all considered to be the same at school: they run Britain because their teachers had the freedom to choose and, perhaps in the end, that is what it is to be a good teacher."

Teachers need clear powers to deal with disruption and physical violence. They should know that they will not be prosecuted unless their actions are grossly disproportionate and they should be allowed latitude to deal with challenging situations. Teachers who fear civil actions, criminal prosecution or disciplinary action unless they comply with a detailed code (as at present) may fail to intervene when they should, or will call the police to deal with the situation.

13.8   REWARDING ACHIEVEMENT AND RAISING STANDARDS

Rewarding achievement is necessary to encourage the pursuit of excellence. Rewards for all are not rewards at all and confer no particular benefit. On the other hand, whilst some pupils will be academically gifted, many will not be, but will have other gifts that need to be encouraged by recognising them. It is important that the educational system allows for both excellence and a diversity of gifting, where both are equally and objectively valued.

The current exam system, which reflects a "one size fits all approach" and fails to distinguish adequately between different abilities, is in need of repair. Bagehot records that "In 1994 twenty-one per cent of GCSEs taken at Westminster [private school] secured the top grade, A*. By 2004 the share of A* grades was fifty-nine per cent, and in 2009 hit eighty-two per cent (at which point Westminster switched to different exams)."[342] The reforms of the exam system announced in 2012 and modified in February 2013 may help to address this issue. The 2010 OECD Programme for International Student Assessment (PISA) ranked Britain 25th in the world after China (1), Estonia (13) and Poland (15).[343] The new exams should be set by reference to the best international standards.

For most people, state schools are the only viable choice. In the years of the last Labour government the attainment gap between state schools and independent schools at A-level doubled. In 2010, A-level candidates at independent schools were three times as likely to gain all 'A' grades as state school candidates, and most of the other good results were obtained from the 164 remaining grammar schools. The Free Schools programme, new styles of leadership in state schools and more effective teaching methods at all levels may be able to address the gap. An over-concentration on immediate results can be a mistake. It may take some time to change the culture of a school and may require the replacement of whole leadership teams, and not just the head teacher, to improve standards of discipline and teaching, together with a change of attitude on the part of both parents and pupils.

There is a concern that results in some GCSE exams imperfectly reflect achievement in education, since pupils can be specifically trained to achieve results. There is a similar concern that the targets set for State primary schools both distort the nature of teaching and deliver misleading results. The tests at Key Stages 1 and 2 may not be an effective measure of learning where children are taught to pass the test. If this is so, the solution is not to ignore or downplay the importance of tests or exams, since this can easily be a cover for underachievement, but to improve the test and exam systems. Even where the targets are achieved, some children can be left out. The target of 75% of children achieving Level 4 or 5 at Key Stage 2 can leave 25% of children unable to read and write satisfactorily.

13.9   MORAL EDUCATION

David Cameron has said that we "need to ask deeper questions about what causes this irresponsibility. About why some parents are not teaching their children the difference between right and wrong."[344] In this he was highlighting the role of the family in teaching morals.

The American psychologist Jonathan Haidt has argued that there is a weak causal relationship between moral reasoning and moral behaviour, but a strong relationship between moral emotions and moral behaviour. Psychopaths are often very intelligent, but do not experience the right kind of moral emotions. Guilt, sadness, shame, and empathy are among the most powerful of the moral emotions. They appear early in life — shame being in evidence before the end of the first year of life, guilt by around thirty-six months and empathy at around one year, but fully developed between eighteen and twenty-four months. Good character, where emotional intelligence is formed and exercised, develops under the examples and influence of parents, peer groups and other social interaction. Empathy is central to constructive moral emotions, and a child deprived of empathy is less likely to be able to show this to others.

In Christian education, virtues may be taught by example as well as by instruction. Jesus walked and talked with a group of disciples. Teachers and mentors can model good behaviour and introduce their pupils to great art and literature, which can teach through living stories. Emotions are an important motivating force behind moral behaviour and they can be false, good or bad, or unreasonable. Understanding emotions is a part of the study of literature and drama. Knowing the right responses and feeling them is the subject of moral education, and moral education requires a framework of moral values. Emotions may be stimulated by the arts, but individuals need to be able to make judgements about them.

Children need to be taught the advantages of self-discipline and the deferral of gratification. The Stanford marshmallow experiment, in which children were given a sweet and were told that they would get another in twenty minutes if they did not eat it, revealed a correlation between later achievement and the ability to restrain an appetite. Christianity provides a framework and a purpose for self-discipline. Social scientists such as Max Weber have associated the Christian Protestant work ethic with economic success. Self-discipline can impact a range of social challenges such as debt, obesity, public order and education. Given their stage of neurological and emotional development, children cannot be expected to discover moral rules for themselves (and it may also be optimistic to expect adults to do so). Aristotle identified twelve moral virtues which included courage, temperance, generosity, magnanimity, patience, truthfulness and modesty. The traditional Christian cardinal virtues are prudence, justice, temperance and fortitude together with the spiritual virtues of faith, hope and charity. The Apostle Paul identified the fruit of the Spirit as love, joy, peace, patience, kindness, goodness, faithfulness, gentleness and self-control (Galatians 5:22 NIV).

According to Richard T. McClelland, efforts to correct the immoral behaviour of corporate executives by requiring them to attend courses in business ethics is largely a waste of time and energy. The values learnt in childhood and in the culture of organisations and society are likely to be more important. Moral education is best started at an early age and there needs to be a coherent framework of values underpinning it. The public scandals in relation to phone hacking in 2011 illustrated the power of moral emotions, but moral emotions can be changeable where there are no generally accepted standards of behaviour. Relatively little attention was paid to the issue when the issue concerned celebrities, some of whom were paid six-figure sums in compensation. Although the issue in relation to celebrities may have been different because they choose the public limelight, the public mood changed dramatically once it was revealed that the victims included a murdered schoolgirl and the families of soldiers killed in Afghanistan.

13.10   SEX EDUCATION

The issue of sex education raises the question as to what is the purpose of different kinds of education. Is it just to give information or should there be guidance as well? Currently much information in relation to sexual activities is provided without a context as to what those activities can mean. Here the details of the activities and the lack of information about the context imply approval of the activities. Pupils might ask themselves why schools would give information about the practice of sexual relationships if they did not expect that information to be acted upon. Even where information is accompanied by appropriate guidance, the provision of the information may nevertheless itself increase the likelihood that the sexual activities described in the education will be practised. An example is the NHS endorsed Sexual Health and Education Programme, *Respect Yourself,* used in Warwickshire secondary schools for children of thirteen years and above, which covers a variety of sexual experimentation.

According to the latest neuroscience, the teen brain is unfinished and only reaches full maturity with the integration of cognition and emotion into the twenties. It is unwise to think that children can be given information about how to conduct sexual relationships in ways that do not lead to pregnancy, together with statements about the physical risks they run, without recognising that the provision of the information can give rise to temptation that young people do not yet have the emotional capacity to resist.

Explaining the physical risks of pregnancy and sexually-transmitted infections ("STIs") has not prevented young people in the UK from becoming sexually active and promiscuous, nor has it reduced the teenage pregnancy or conception rates. Gonorrhoea may become incurable since, according to the Health Protection Agency, some strains have now developed resistance to antibiotics. The UK is still the "teenage pregnancy capital of Europe" with 38.3 conceptions for every 1,000 girls under 18.[345] The most recent statistics available indicate that a quarter of 16 to

24 year-olds had two or more sexual partners during the previous year.[346] Additionally, rates of STIs continue to increase.[347]

A philosophy of radical autonomy underlies much sex education. This is exemplified by an illustrated booklet aimed at boys from 13 to 16 designed for use in schools and produced by the Family Planning Association with funding from the Department of Health. It suggests that boys may be "sexually interested in other men, or even men and women. It's not a problem; your body is yours to share with whomever you choose".[348] The booklet advocates criminal activity, since the children may be under the age of consent. Abstinence is discouraged. The Sex Education Forum (based within the National Children's Bureau) produced a booklet entitled *Just Say No! to Abstinence.*[349] The International Planned Parenthood Federation opposes families based on traditional marriage since "many families are neither safe, particularly for young girls nor models of gender equality".[350]

The introduction of compulsory sex and relationships education in primary schools was proposed by the Labour government before it left office but, as of 2012, there is a review taking place. Compulsory sex education would result in more schools using inappropriate material. Current government guidance is inadequate to protect children from explicit materials. Primary school children in some schools are currently being shown graphic pictorial material of a couple having sexual relations and are given information about a range of same-sex sexual practices which many Christians would regard as unnatural. This type of sex education is now being extended to more than a fifth of UK primary schools. If sex education is made compulsory in primary schools, governors and teachers may not be able to resist the use of material of this nature.

Parents currently have a statutory right to withdraw children from sex education, except those parts that are included in the statutory National Curriculum in science. But they may encounter resistance from teachers, or they may be reluctant to be regarded as uncooperative by the school. As Ofsted reported in 2010, parents are not adequately consulted on sex education. It should be compulsory for schools to inform parents fully of the nature of the materials to be used and to provide an easy means for parents to withdraw children from the relevant classes. In Christian thinking, the family is the best place to teach the facts of life. Abstinence in relation to sexual behaviour should be taught and self-control in relation to any untimely or inappropriate desires should be advocated. In fact, the reverse is now the case. One sex education pack states in its introduction that aims such as stopping children from having sex, dissuading children from having sex before marriage and promoting marriage are not achievable, that they are inappropriate for schools and often more to do with propaganda than education.

President Clinton described in his 1995 "State of the Union" address "an epidemic of teen pregnancies and births where there is no marriage" as "our most serious social problem". The policy in the US and the UK has been to use sex education to reduce teenage pregnancies. This has been ineffective because, as discussed above, it gives information about sexual practices to teenagers and therefore encourages those practices. In addition, the welfare system has encouraged teen pregnancy (this is explored further in Chapter 14). It has been said that teenage girls may have been taught *how* not to get pregnant but they have not been taught *why* not to do so. The welfare benefits might not be so attractive if prospective teenage mothers were to appreciate the huge challenges of lone parenting at such a young age.

The effects of the current policies and the state of society were highlighted in a conference of the World Congress of Families in 2011, where the Reverend Chuks Anierobi reported that in Croydon schools, sixty-five per cent of exclusions were for children raping other children, that oral sex is happening in primary schools and that some teachers assume that if a child does not wish to have a sexual relationship with the opposite sex, they must be homosexual.

There have been attempts to change the climate of opinion. Nadine Dorries MP sought to introduce a Bill to require schools to include in their sex education for girls aged from 13 to 16 the benefits of abstinence. The Bill did not have government support and was dropped. Andrew Copson, chief executive of the British Humanist Association was reported in *The Guardian* as calling it a "dangerously unrealistic proposition for our young people" and saying that "We will all certainly need to remain on our guard against such foolish proposals in the future."[351]

Christian teaching has emphasised that character can only be changed by a change of heart, and that a right relationship with the creator God can both bring about and sustain that change. For Christians, the responsibility for moral education should be primarily that of parents, not of State institutions, though parents may choose to delegate some of this responsibility to schools or other bodies such as churches. Moral behaviour should not just be taught as an academic subject, but needs to be learnt through the operation of natural and God-given relationships with parents and friends. This is consistent with Augustine's view that faith comes at the beginning of rational thinking about morality, and the teaching in the book of Proverbs that the fear of God is the beginning of wisdom.

13.11   SEX AND HEALTH EDUCATION

The relationship between education about health and the promotion of types of sexual activity is highlighted by the governmental grants given to the Terence Higgins Trust, a charity. Until recently, the NHS endorsed and directed children to *The Bottom Line* on the charity's website. In addition to describing some of the health risks associated with a variety of same-sex sexual practices, this contained graphic illustrations as to how they should be undertaken. If grants are given by governmental authorities to promote "safe" same-sex activity, this will involve advertising that activity. It might be reasonable to conclude that government authorities believe that the types of homosexual activity that were advertised on the website are good for the health and welfare of teenagers whose physical and neurological development is incomplete.

A homosexual lifestyle can be harmful to health. The US Food and Drug Administration reported that: "Men who have had sex with men since 1977 have an HIV prevalence…60 times higher than the general population, 800 times higher than first-time blood donors and 8000 times higher than repeat blood donors."[352] Sexually-transmitted diseases occur amongst gay men at a rate five to ten times higher than the average, according to research in the US by Marshall Kirk and Hunter Madsen.[353] The homosexual population comprises about 2.5 per cent of the total population of the UK, but has disproportionately high rates of sexual diseases. *Pink News* records that, out of the 6,600 new HIV diagnoses in 2010, over 3,000 were MSM (men who have sex with men). One in eleven MSM in London is estimated to be HIV positive. The sociologist Patricia Morgan has noted that in the US MSM are forty-four times as likely as heterosexual men to receive a diagnosis of HIV infection and forty-six times as likely to contract syphilis (a significant part of this risk being associated with predominantly homosexual sexual activities).[354]

It might be argued, that at least in relation to adults, if same sex activity is going to occur in any event, then people should be advised about how to reduce the risk of infection. There is some sense in this but, if the sexual practices are harmful to health, the risks must be clearly communicated. It would seem to be responsible for the burden of the health advice sanctioned by public authorities to counsel abstinence from the relevant practices.

13.12   THE TEACHING OF HISTORY

Democratic freedoms are part of our historical heritage. Christian belief has been central in the introduction and protection of those freedoms. Downplaying this heritage is not accurate history. Bishop Michael Nazir-Ali highlighted this in hoping that the new Education Secretary ensures that schools teach the true historical perspective that British national life is founded upon Christian teachings: "The struggle, stemming from the Evangelical Revival in the eighteenth century, against the slave-trade and then slavery itself, was explicitly Bible-based.... [This] struggle went hand-in-hand with the battle to improve the working conditions of men, women and children in the mills, mines and factories of early industrial Britain. ...So many of the precious freedoms that we value today, the fair treatment of workers and the care of those in need arise from the values given to us by the Judaeo-Christian tradition."[355] History reflects both successes and failures and contains the material necessary for us to understand the past and the way it has formed the present.

The practice of teaching themes, rather than narrative, to younger children can be premature since it is difficult for pupils to understand or interpret events in history without a secure narrative base. Teaching in terms of themes can also allow the teaching to include political interpretations about subjects based upon a selective arrangement of historical facts. Thus the subject of slavery might focus on the appalling conditions of slave ships, but without teaching that the slave trade was abolished following a movement led by Christians and that the abolition was enforced on the seas by the British navy at a time when other countries were content to let the slave trade continue.

There can also be an over emphasis on empathy with individuals in different times when pupils are asked to imagine what people in different times felt, without always examining from the historical records what they actually thought or wrote. True empathy with the feelings of those in the past may be impossible, given the different times we live in. It can invite false comparisons between the lives of past times and lives lived today and can be a cloak for the propagation of political views. The focus should rather be on a more objective search for truth, which may include the perceptions of past times by those living at that time.

A survey commented upon by Niall Ferguson found that only 34% of first year history undergraduates at one leading British University knew who was the monarch at the time of the Spanish Armada, 31% did not know the location of the

Boer War and 16% did not know who commanded the British forces at Waterloo.[356] In a similar poll of English children aged between eleven and eighteen, 17% thought Oliver Cromwell fought at the battle of Hastings.[357] Robert Tombs, professor of Modern French History at Cambridge, has contributed to a paper published by Politeia that outlines a revised curriculum for the teaching of history. His view is that "the present system, both at GCSE and at A-level, is too fragmented, too complex and too specialised, and unsuitable for most school children. Many state schools no longer teach it at all, even at GCSE level. Many schools repeat the same material at successive stages to improve examination outcomes: notoriously, it is possible to study the Third Reich three times, to the neglect, inevitably, of vast swathes of English, European, and world history, including everything before 1870." Tombs proposes "a simpler and broader curriculum covering the whole of English and British history, with examinations testing knowledge and understanding rather than (often spurious) methodology."[358] The report of the All Parliamentary Group on History and Archives in December 2012 favoured a chronological approach with an emphasis on key events and figures in a five year course. Chris Skidmore MP, the vice chairman of the committee favoured a focus on British History, the development of democracy and political freedoms.

It is impossible to understand the present state of the United Kingdom today without knowledge of the past, for example in relation to Anglo Irish relations or the challenges facing the Eurozone and the European Union. Though we are not in a position to pass judgment upon those acting in different times, the teaching of history can afford some scope for moral reasoning about the behaviour of people and their governments. Simon Jenkins has commented: "The Hundred Years War is a monument to the maxim that British government usually goes potty whenever it crosses the Channel. Henry VIII wisely turned his back on Europe by rejecting the supremacy of Rome in 1534 and privatising the wealth of the monasteries."[359]

One could add that the abiding theme of British foreign policy from the 1500s to 1945 was to preserve the peace and, within the limits of the times, to maintain freedom by protecting our independence and preventing any one power from dominating Europe. To this end, England fought the Spanish in the 1580s and the United Kingdom fought the French on numerous occasions from the 1700s to the 1800s and the Germans twice in the twentieth century. Simon Jenkins contrasts the "necessary wars" of Elizabeth I, Pitt, Lloyd George and Churchill with the wars of choice of Edward III, Walpole, Palmerston and Blair. Niall Ferguson has remarked that the Europe which would have been dominated by Germany in the First World War, had Britain not intervened, bears a resemblance to what is now proposed for the Eurozone. In encouraging banking and fiscal union in the Eurozone, which is likely to lead to political union under the leadership of Germany, the current British government is reversing British foreign policy over some 400 years. It may be doing so because it fears a European banking crisis, and the economic disruption that this would bring, more than it fears the expansion of German influence. Here the collapse of Credit Anstalt in 1931, which presaged a deepening of the depression, continues to cast a long shadow.

British history should be taught in the context of world history. Since 1500 European nations have interacted with different continents. Britain has influenced, and been influenced by, India, Africa and North America. British culture and society have been shaped by its multi-cultural Empire. Traditions of the rule of law and democracy survive in varying degrees in Britain's ex-colonies. This represents a common heritage which is also good for all people everywhere.

13.13 TEACHING SCIENCE

While there needs to be a common curriculum for exams, there can be dangers to free speech if the content of teaching is prescribed too closely by government. Some leading scientists want to ban all teaching about the theory of intelligent design of the universe, thus restricting teaching to the theory of evolution by chance. One commentator reflected that, if this were to be enforced by law, why not outlaw other scientific theories? Does atomic theory need protection against quantum theory or the big bang against steady state theory? All scientific theory should be open to debate and discussion in the light of the available evidence, and education policy should reflect this. The Department of Education has said that funding may be withdrawn from free schools that teach theories which are contrary to established scientific and/or historical evidence and explanations. Arguments in favour of intelligent design may be treated as falling within this category.

In this area Government policy could be on the wrong side of the most recent science. Evolution entirely by chance mutation is improbable because mutations are imperfections from the original and because the fossil record reveals insufficient evidence of gradual transformations from one species to another. Simon Conway Morris, Professor of Evolutionary Palaeobiology at Cambridge University, has discerned that the same design of organism has emerged in different species. His research indicates that the camera eye has similar features in species which evolutionary science holds have evolved along different paths which he calls "convergence".[360] Conway Morris believes that advanced cognition has evolved independently at least three times (apes, crows and octopus) and more likely three more times (dolphins, elephants and parrots and maybe bees).[361] If the evolution of species has taken place, it seems that this was not by chance and that there must be a self-organising principle in life forms. As Conway Morris puts it: "A good part of organic systems rely upon self-organisation. You know that things click together. They do that, from our perspective, almost effortlessly: yet there is no general theory to explain how that happens."[362]

Conway Morris says that he is not going back to 'vitalism', though there are similarities between this theory and his thinking. The 18th century scientist Lamarck identified what he called "Le pouvoir de la vie" (the life force) or "la force qui tend sans cesse à composer l'organisation" (the force that perpetually tends to make order), which is consistent with an intelligent designer of the universe. Proponents of vitalism in the 20th century pointed to the parallel development of species and the similar structural results in the development of animals having no common descent.[363] Vitalism emphasises the distinction between living organisms and non-living. Movement, reproduction, and growth by living things are different from the processes of the inorganic world. Living matter cannot be created from non-living matter. Vitalism holds that the behavioural and physiological development of plants and animals are designed to achieve the continuation of the life form. For instance, chickens grow, and then discard, a horny tip to their bills which enables them to escape from their shells and reptiles develop a temporary 'egg tooth'.

Conway Morris has posed the question: "If evolution is not a random process, what then? First it means that if you were able to wind back the spool of life back to its start and to run it again, the outcome – intelligent life – would be the same. Second, it suggests that there may be another principle at work, possibly even something that could be described by a general theory of biology. And thirdly, it suggests that alien life is both likely and likely to be surprisingly familiar."[364] The theory of evolution by chance alone seems to be inconsistent with Conway Morris's research.

13.14 SHARED VALUES

Since the United Kingdom is a multi-faith society, education needs to provide an understanding of the beliefs and traditions of the different faith communities. This has largely been achieved already in mainstream schools. In a number of schools in the UK, particularly in the inner cities, the vast majority of pupils are from ethnic minority backgrounds with faith traditions which are not Christian. But this should not be a reason for the marginalisation of the part played by Christian values in the history of the United Kingdom. Christianity is still legally the principal religion which should be taught in state schools. Section 375(3) of the Education Act 1996 provides that "every agreed syllabus shall reflect the fact that the religious traditions in Great Britain are in the main Christian whilst taking into account the teaching and practices of the other principal religions represented in Great Britain". Paragraph 3(2) of Schedule 20 of the School Standards and Framework Act 1996 provides that the collective act of worship shall be "wholly or mainly" Christian in character.

The cohesion of society depends upon a shared set of values and these can be communicated through an understanding of history, which can warn against the dangers of neglecting those values. The historian David Starkey has said that the "only way we are going to survive as a multi-cultural society is if we re-address the story of English history". David Cameron has spoken of the need for common values: "A genuinely liberal country… believes in certain values and actively promotes them. It says to its citizens: 'This is what defines us as a society. To belong here is to believe these things…'."[365]

Some Muslim communities are poorly integrated and parallel societies can develop reflecting the Islamic teaching of "sacred space" under which Muslims have a duty to occupy and keep territory for their religion and the values they espouse. Muslim schools separate Muslim pupils from the rest of society and private Muslim schools teach the National Curriculum of Saudi Arabia. Some books teach Sharia law with explicit descriptions of its punishments of amputation for certain crimes.[366] Christianity values freedom of speech for adults, but the State should not permit children to be taught that actions which would constitute crimes in the UK are good. A survey revealed that thirty-six per cent of young British Muslims believe that those who leave Islam should be killed in accordance with the dictates of Sharia law.[367] The government must ensure that children in the UK are not taught to approve of criminal activities and the inspection of schools should reflect this policy. Currently, Ofsted has delegated the inspection of many Muslim schools to an organisation controlled by the Association of Muslim Schools.[368]

13.15   PREPARATION FOR LIFE

Education must also prepare children for the world in which they need to survive and prosper, for their own benefit and for that of society. Studies reveal that employers increasingly put off employing young people directly from school. The Chartered Institute of Personnel Development found a strong perception among companies that school leavers lacked basic workplace skills, such as good communication "which may explain why fewer young people are being hired."[369] Marcus Wareing, the celebrity chef who runs a two Michelin star restaurant, has said that the young workers whom he has encountered are lazy and clueless, with an exaggerated sense of entitlement. He found that they were more interested in how many hours they had to work or how many holidays they took than learning how to cook.[370] Many companies, such as Pret A Manger, are believed to prefer to employ foreigners because they are prepared to work harder for less money.

Education should instil the moral values and the right attitudes for the challenging employment market, as well as the right skills. Even for those who have these, the employment environment is very difficult. Employers are cautious about taking on new employees and reluctant to create apprenticeships. Employment laws protect old jobs at the expense of new ones and the young are left behind. Education must give each school leaver the best possible start in life and, though the education reforms being instituted by the Coalition government are helpful, there remains much to be done.

14

THE FAMILY

14.1 THE VALUE OF THE FAMILY

In Christian thought, the family is the fundamental building block of society and lifelong marriage between a natural man and a natural woman is the central and essential part of it. Currently in the UK 9% of married parents split before their child's fifth birthday, compared with 35% of unmarried parents. Sexual ethics are not merely personal, but affect a wide range of those impacted by relationships. The breakdown of relationships has far-reaching consequences, particularly for children, and those consequences are visited upon society. It is estimated that half of all children born today will not be living with both parents on their sixteenth birthday. The Centre for Social Justice calculated that broken families cost the taxpayer £24 billion in a year.[371] The Relationships Foundation calculates the cost as £41.74 billion[372] and Guy Brandon in a Jubilee Centre paper, calculating additional costs including absenteeism, domestic violence, and educational underachievement has estimated that £100 billion a year would be a "reasonable starting point". This figure of £100 billion, when a range of factors such as crime and lost production were taken into account, was endorsed by Ian Duncan Smith (as Secretary of State for Work and Pensions) on 4th November 2010.[373] In addition, marriage rates have halved in the last 40 years and the number of lone parent families has increased by an average of 26,000 a year from the early 1980s to 2010.[374] According to the Christian Institute, one in five British children live with a single mother or father, which is 35% higher than in Germany and 50% higher than in France.

Christianity teaches that the biological natural family is the God-given structure for bringing up children. This appears to be borne out by evidence in that, according to research by the Centre for Social Justice in their study *Breakdown Britain*, children who are not brought up by both parents are 75% more likely to fail at school, 70% more likely to be a drug addict, 50% more likely to have an alcohol problem, 40% more likely to have serious debt problems and 35% more likely to experience unemployment or welfare dependency.[375] It said that the type of person (for instance in relation to class and economic well-being) who marries is less likely to bring up children having these problems, whether they marry or not. It is argued that it is not marriage but socio-economic status that makes the difference. In other words, it is acknowledged that there is a correlation between marriage and good outcomes for children but this does not imply that one is a cause of the other. However, research by the Centre for Social Justice, as well as common sense and anecdotal experience, suggests that the support, role modelling and guidance from two natural parents who stay together are preferable to the less stable arrangements of cohabitation and single parenthood, irrespective of socio-economic factors. Research by the Institute of Fiscal Studies found a lesser effect of marriage in higher socio-economic groups, but the central thesis that marriage is good for society remains a strong one. Married couples stay together longer than unmarried ones. According to research by the Bristol Community Family Trust and the Centre for Social Justice, divorce accounts for only 20% of family break-ups and 14% of the cost of family breakdown among families with children under five.[376]

Permanent marriage is more likely to lead to flourishing families and children, however challenging living out this ideal may be for individuals. Marriage and family life teach humility and the ability to adapt to the lifestyle of others, and flawed men and women need the framework of a rule, together with strong incentives to support it, in order to persevere with marriage relationships in unpromising circumstances.

14.2 MARRIAGE AND THE NATURAL ORDER

In Christian thinking the concept of marriage is based upon a God given model. For individuals this involves a promise to God and to the other person. In making and keeping these promises they should be supported by the community in which they live, the members of which may be affected by the success or otherwise of the marriage venture. Whilst the promises to God are only relevant to those who believe in God, marriage is also part of the natural order. This is why it has generally been recognised in civil society over a long period of time and all over the world, whatever the belief system of the society. That there are proven benefits to individuals and to society in the institution of marriage supports this proposition.

It follows from the promises implicit in marriage that there should be consequences of breaking those promises. The teaching of Jesus can be construed as being contrary to the idea of "no-fault" divorce. Jesus said "What God has joined together, let no one separate" (Matthew 19:6, NIV). Whilst there can be evidential difficulties in establishing the causes of marriage breakdown, there could nevertheless be a principle in law that the marriage contract cannot be broken without adverse consequences for the person doing so. That this area is profoundly challenging for individuals must be acknowledged. Sexual instincts are strong and, to the individual experiencing them, may appear natural and harmless, but they can so easily be misdirected and damaging. People can be challenged by what seems to be an unbearable tension between desire and obligation. It is because the temptations are so powerful (and often do not feel wrong), but the consequences can be so damaging for families, that Christians are perceived to have a disproportionate concern with sexual misbehaviour.

The objective standards of behaviour required of individuals should be reflected in a legal framework for the protection of those who may be affected by the breakdown of a marriage. However, while laws need to discourage behaviour that is harmful, Christians also emphasise the importance of opportunities for forgiveness and reconciliation. Ideals must be upheld, but compassion is required for those who are unable to live up to those ideals.

Christians recognise that they owe to duties to God as well as to other people and can look for God's help to fulfil their duties. The perception that there is a duty to God can provide a greater incentive to fulfil the obligations of marriage (and the means to do so) than the sense of obligations owed to other people (who themselves may have also broken their promises). Perhaps surprisingly, King David, having committed adultery with Bathsheba and contrived the killing of her husband in battle, says contritely to God "Against you, you only, have I sinned and done what is evil in your sight" (Psalm 51:4 NIV). For Christians, there is a duty in marriage to God, who can forgive shortcomings and restore the relationship with him.

14.3   FAMILY POLICY AND THE STATE

Some governments have seen families as a threat to the power of the State. The Bolshevik State introduced "no-fault" divorce. Some totalitarian governments have seen the education of children by families, rather than by the State, as a challenge to the ability of the State to indoctrinate children. On the other hand, General Franco's Spain encouraged traditional families as part of a hierarchy in which the State was nevertheless very powerful. Some elements in the current Chinese government have been receptive to Christian courses designed to strengthen marriage and there are reports that in one province *The Marriage Course* based on material by a London church could be compulsory.

Patricia Morgan, in her books on family policy — most recently *Family Policy, Family Changes: Sweden, Italy and Britain Compared*,[377] and *The War between the State and the Family*,[378] — has traced the thinking that has resulted in the UK governments' policies in relation to the natural family and their effects over the last half century. Some secular thinkers believe that people's living arrangements arise spontaneously and come in all shapes and sizes. This is akin to a free market, where people have no duties or obligations, but do as they please. A Christian perspective is that autonomy without guidance can reflect the worst of human nature. Some thinkers see the family as positively oppressive. Patricia Morgan quotes Carol Smart writing in 1984: "The idea of abolishing marriage may sound as attractive as the classical communist call to abolish the family, but such demands are probably as unpopular as they are unrealistic. It would be far more effective to undermine the social and legal need and support for the marriage contract. This could be achieved by withdrawing the privileges which are currently extended to married heterosexual couples."[379]

This withdrawal of privileges for married heterosexual couples advised by Carol Smart has happened in the UK over the last forty years. Government and business communications now refer only to "partners". "Family" no longer refers to a natural family of biological parents and children, but to any collection of adults and children living together, whatever the commitment (or lack of it) they have to the unit. The State supports these units, but on its own terms and in some respects deprives the parents of their authority to do what they believe to be right for their children. The State allows underage sex in practice, it encourages contraception and it permits abortions without parental consent. School nurses cannot generally administer medicine (e.g. paracetamol) without parental consent, but school nurses employed by a health authority may issue contraceptive pills and devices. David Paton, Professor of Economics at Nottingham University, has concluded that the Government policy of offering confidential advice to teenagers without consulting parents has not reduced pregnancies but increased them.[380] No advice is given on abstinence, marriage or fidelity.

Yet parents are held responsible for the behaviour of their children. The Children Act 2004 limits parents' right to smack children. Children's rights campaigners favour an outright ban on what they call "hitting" and favour a children's commissioner having the right of access to every home. This is a continuing discussion prompted more recently by the Labour MP, David Lammy, who said in January 2012 that working class parents should be able to discipline their children without fear of prosecution.

14.4   NEW FORMS OF FAMILY

The new forms of family, particularly lone parents, are not economically viable and so the State has to support them. As Patricia Morgan put it: "If an earning family member leaves the family setting, or does not stay with a pregnant wife or girlfriend, then in general, the State will substitute for that earner. Increasingly, the State will act as both breadwinner for a lone parent with children and as a child carer. There are few financial incentives to household formation for those on lower incomes."[381] Further, the tax and benefit system favours couples living apart. As Morgan recorded, "In 2004/5, a couple with two children where the mother was earning £10,000 and the father £25,000 per year would be twenty-two per cent better off if the mother claimed as a lone parent, rather than a couple (£6,017 could be claimed in tax credits if the couple lived separately compared with £544 when their incomes are combined into one household income)." Morgan noted that the Housing Act 1985 prioritised the needs of lone parents, either pregnant or with dependent children and that, contemporaneous with this policy, the proportion of births outside marriage has increased from 10 per cent in 1975 to 44 per cent in 2003 (having been 1 per cent in the mid-seventeenth century). In Germany, Holland and Italy married people get tax relief for children. One in five British children live with a single parent which is 35% higher than in Germany and 50% higher than in France.

The child benefit reforms of 2012-13, which withdraw benefit where one of the parents is earning more than £60,000, do not recognise that parenting is a shared undertaking and discriminate against one earner families. It has been suggested that tax relief could be given for child care costs, but this will benefit working parents and discriminate against families where one parent stays at home to look after children. The City commentator Allister Heath has pointed to the anomaly of a person earning £50,000 and paying 40 per cent tax and recovering child benefit. He has suggested that benefits for children should be given in the form of tax relief for each child which could be transferable to either parent. This would avoid discrimination against one earner families. For those not earning, a similar system could be applied to the universal credit.

There appears to be academic bias against the traditional family which is likely to have influenced generations of students. (Lord) Anthony Giddens is a professor whose textbook *Sociology*[382] is now in its 6th edition. He describes the traditional family of the 1950s: "men were still emotionally removed from their wives and often observed a strong sexual double standard, seeking sexual adventures for themselves but setting a strict code for their spouse." In the "Thinking Critically" box on the same page he poses the question: "If the traditional family, as described above, is a "myth", why do so many people still believe in it? What social consequences might follow from people's belief in and commitment to this mythical family form?"

14.5 MARRIAGE, DIVORCE AND THE STATE

Governments should support traditional marriage as a matter of public policy. In Christian thinking, marriage is part of the created order and that order applies both to Christians and to non-Christians. In history and in societies today marriage is part of the arrangements for society that are framed by laws. For

Christians, laws in relation to divorce should therefore reflect a moral order designed to encourage behaviour that is good for people as individuals and good for society as a whole. Divorce can have a profound effect upon children.

Given that governments regulate the marriage contract, the civil marriage contract should not be capable of being broken at will and in practice without just cause. It follows that the breakdown of a marriage should not automatically result in one spouse being able to claim half the other spouse's wealth, whenever that wealth was acquired. The principle that marriage is a contract would entail specifying the grounds on which a party is entitled to break the contract, by analogy with the concept of repudiation in the law of contract. In practice it may be impossible in many cases for the court to come to a conclusion on the facts as to whether those facts justify a repudiation of the contract. It may also be necessary to introduce concepts such as "contributory fault" and "provocation". However difficult these matters are to deal with in law, and however painful the process may be for individuals, a process which is able to take conduct into account would be more just than the current law. This effectively combines "no-fault" divorce, where either party can at will allege the breakdown of the marriage, or act as if it has occurred, with the possibility of making a claim for a large share of the other party's assets, irrespective of conduct.

In addition to taking conduct into account, it should be possible (as the Centre for Social Justice has suggested) to construct a set of rules governing the distribution of assets following divorce, rather than assuming that in every case all the assets of the parties are to be shared equally or almost equally. These rules could take into account the requirement to support any children of the marriage, the amount of the assets acquired during the period of marriage, the length of the marriage, the ages of the couple and their ability to support themselves in the future. The current law under which a young person married for a short period is entitled to half, or nearly half, of the parties' joint assets is unjust. Rules could also be made specifying how spousal maintenance is to be calculated. Maintenance could be provided for a defined period taking into account the length of the marriage, the ability of the parties to support themselves, the opportunities foregone by marriage or child care and other relevant factors. Despite opposition from some groups (including The Law Society), absent fathers are to be given a legal right to spend time with their children under changes to access laws announced by the government in November 2012 which recognise the role that both parents play in a child's life. In the past, it has been impracticable to enforce many access orders for fathers. Now mothers who prevent access will face penalties, including the imposition of home curfews. No system of regulating matters of divorce and separation will be entirely just in each case, but the challenge is to find a framework that best reflects principles of fairness and which protects the welfare of children.

The State can encourage stable families by discouraging divorce. The state school education curriculum could specifically promote marriage as a public good rather than merely a lifestyle choice. Governments can recognise the value of marriage in the tax system. Married couples should be encouraged, supported and helped to stay together in their own interests. A transferable tax allowance could be introduced for married couples, recognising that a family based on married parents represents a stable economic unit which benefits the society. Individuals who are emotionally vulnerable and hurting may be unable to see clearly what is best for them in the long term and may not understand fully the consequences of their actions. Counselling and cooling-off periods before lawyers are engaged may help, as well as the reintroduction of the idea of recognising "fault" in divorce, as mentioned above. The Centre for Social Justice has recommended a wide range of practical measures such as pre-divorce counselling and mediation designed to reduce the incidence of divorce and the damage it causes. Harry Benson's programme called "*Let's Stick Together*", which has been adopted by the charity Care for the Family, provides practical support for couples, particularly the disadvantaged, who are facing the challenges of parenthood.

14.6   PERSONAL MATTERS

Christianity teaches that other routes to sexual fulfilment apart from marriage are both wrong for the individual and damaging to others affected by them. The difficulty is that this constitutes the intersection of people's personal desires and experiences (which may be painful) with outcomes for others close to them and for society as a whole. For the Christian, human weakness in relationships is part of our humanity. The right response to the failure of relationships is generosity of spirit, forgiveness and the encouragement of a change of heart where appropriate. Ideals of faithfulness and enduring marriage should be encouraged. Those who are unable, for reasons that others may not fully understand, to attain those ideals are the casualties of the human condition. We should expect that that there will be failures, and we should endeavour to understand the temptations and difficulties that people face. But society and the law should not normalise the failure to live up to the ideals. If it does so, it fails to provide the needed encouragement to those who, in difficult circumstances, nevertheless struggle to do what is right.

14.7   THE RIGHT OF CHILDREN TO NATURAL PARENTS

For Christians, traditional natural marriage is the place where children should be brought up. In this belief, Christians adhere to a view that has been current for some thousands of years. Professor Julian Rivers has suggested the formulation of the human right of a child to joint bio-parental nurture, which is to be brought up with care, affection, education and guidance by its biological parents. The application of this right would not be absolute, but it would be applied proportionately and it would not be a right that could be released by the child itself. The right would be similar in type to the rights contained in the United Nations Declaration of the Rights of the Child of 1959 in that it would form a basis for examining family policy and legislation. The implications of the right would be profound. It would follow that it would generally be wrong to create a child unless the conditions for bringing the child up by its natural biological parents existed. Surrogacy and same sex parenting conflict with this right. The right would require a stable legal structure for both natural biological parents to be committed to each other and the child, which is found in traditional marriage between a natural born woman and a natural born man. It would also suggest that the child's wishes should be taken into account in divorce proceedings. The right could not prevent a party to a marriage deserting a spouse and a child, but it might suggest that the State should not approve divorce in these circumstances without visiting appropriate consequences upon the deserting party for the protection of the interests of the child. The right would also require rights of access to the child for both biological parents following separation. This could be extended to grandparents who can also often in practice be excluded by the parent with custody. It would also inhibit the removal of a child from its parents by the State unless the parents were proven to have committed an offence, or the child was in imminent physical danger (see Chapter 8).

A University of Connecticut study (published in *Personality and Psychology Review*) has found (from 36 studies involving 10,000 participants) that children who believe that they have been rejected by their parents, particularly by their fathers, tend to respond with negative personality traits which persist into adulthood, including aggression, anxiety, insecurity and hostility.[383]

14.8   SAME-SEX PARENTING

Many Christians believe that homosexual activities are dysfunctional, perhaps the result of gender confusion or unbalanced parenting. They also rely upon what they regard as the revealed truth of the Bible. Others may focus on the natural order which Christians see as the way in which the created world is designed to operate. Although there are those who profess the Christian faith and approve of same-sex relations, the mainstream of Christian thought views homosexual practices as not being part of God's plan for human beings and not in the interests of individuals or of society.

In the ancient world, even though homosexual relations were tolerated, they were not thought to be an appropriate environment for the raising of children. The fact that this form of "family" is now endorsed as a public "good" by the leadership of all three main political parties emphasises the contrast between current secular thought and belief in most societies down the ages. Since the introduction of same-sex parenting is such a fundamental change of culture and an experiment that affects the well-being of children, there should have been a commission of enquiry to weigh the evidence in relation to it. This could have explored the value and the health implications of the homosexual lifestyle, the permanence of same-sex relationships in the context of providing a stable home for children, and the long-term psychological effects of a child having two same-sex parents. Dr. Dean Byrd, a specialist in relation to same-sex attraction (Professor of Clinical Medicine of the University of Utah, past president and psychologist of NARTH and president of the Thrasher Research Fund) commented on the research that has been done in relation to parenting in different types of families (albeit that there is little scientifically valid research into same-sex parenting) as follows: "The extensive research spanning decades yields an overwhelming abundance of data supporting the importance of both mothers and fathers to the healthy development of children.   Recent evidence is likewise not only supportive, but compellingly demonstrates that a society concerned with optimal child development is most benefited by traditional marriage and married, dual-gender parenting."[384]

The issue of homosexual adoption should be debated in terms of the public good and the wellbeing of children. It should not be addressed from the perspective of alleged discrimination against those seeking to adopt. The debate should be about the public good, focussing on the interests of the child, rather than about so-called human rights of prospective same-sex parents. Same-sex parenting necessarily and intentionally deprives a child of the care of its biological parents. An examination could also address the outcomes for homosexual parents. Do they stay together and provide the same stability as a married couple? What are the psychological and mental health outcomes for children brought up by homosexual couples? Are the children more or less likely to become homosexual themselves and does this matter? Children raised by same sex parents may be more prone to promiscuity, sexual experimentation and crossing gender lines, and this should be investigated. Researchers Judith Stacey and Timothy Biblarz found that lesbian mothers had a feminising effect on their sons and a masculinising effect on their daughters,[385] while Professor Steven Nock has criticised the research methodology of studies involving same-sex parents that are favourable to the practice, saying "not a single one of the studies was conducted according to generally accepted standards of scientific research."[386]

Irrespective of any belief which policy makers may or may not have in God or in a created order, they should address themselves to the question as to what empirical evidence exists for overturning the collective wisdom of many civilisations over thousands of years. The practical difficulty of same-sex parenting arrangements can be illustrated by a case where a lesbian couple tried to exclude a homosexual sperm donor from parenting visiting rights in relation to a child born to one of the lesbians through IVF,[387] and by a case where a lesbian couple disputed the visiting rights of a homosexual friend who fathered a boy.[388]

Charles Howard QC, acting for the lesbian couple, said that "conflict had raged around this little boy since birth."

While there may be helpful research and debate over the outcome of different choices, Christianity teaches that some choices, which include same-sex parenting, are by their nature always wrong because they are contrary to a natural order in the world. This view is not confined to Christians or others subscribing to a monotheistic faith. Many people perceive a natural biological order even if they do not believe in a creator God. The view that some choices are always wrong, whatever the alternatives, avoids the confusion that can arise when it is argued that a child should be raised by loving homosexual parents rather than an uncaring children's home. Both alternatives are wrong, though for different reasons, and the lesser of two evils, even if it were one (and many would say that same-sex parenting would be worse than a children's home), would not be a "good" only because it appears to be better than another wrong outcome. To take this view and to call the lesser of two evils good (assuming that it is the lesser of two evils) would be analogous to saying that it is right to rob one person because the alternative is robbing two people. The better alternative to homosexual adoption is to find two parents of the opposite sex or to improve the children's home. Adherence to biblical standards of behaviour means that Christians in public life should not promote or facilitate adoption orders for homosexual couples in the same way they should not order or facilitate abortions unless the life of the mother is at risk.

14.9   SAME-SEX AND OTHER FORMS OF "MARRIAGE"

To give legal sanction to a ceremony of marriage between same-sex couples is wrong because it changes the nature of an institution founded upon the natural order. It undermines the institution of marriage, since this will be deemed to include same sex unions. Some have raised the etymological argument that, ever since the term marriage has been used, it has been used to denote the union of a man and a woman and that the meaning of the word cannot be changed by the State. The meaning of words may change over time by common usage, but it is not within the power of a government to change the meaning of language, even though the State has the right to confer all the benefits of marriage on same sex couples, and has already done so by instituting civil partnerships. The Archbishop of York, Dr John Sentamu, has questioned whether the State has the right to instigate same sex marriage: "Marriage is the relationship between a man and a woman. I don't think it is the role of the State to define what marriage is. It is set in tradition and history and you can't just [change it] overnight, no matter how powerful you are. We've seen dictators do it in different contexts...."[389]

Integral to marriage is sexual union which is a natural process between a man and a woman. Same-sex sexual practices do not have the same rationale, so adultery is not a ground for the dissolution of a civil partnership as it is for marriage. The sexual nature of marriage is integral to its definition. Brothers and sisters cannot marry because it is not lawful for them to have sexual relations. The Marriage (Same Sex Couples) Bill proposed by the government provides that the definitions of adultery and non-consummation for the purposes of marriage will not be changed in the new law for same-sex marriage. No sexual relations with a person of the same sex would therefore be a ground for divorce for same-sex couples unless there was adultery with a person of the opposite sex, which is unlikely. Marriage is by its nature monogamous and the concept of adultery is a necessary consequence of monogamy. Under the government's proposals this would not be the case in same-sex marriage. A Christian perception would be that this anomaly would not arise if same-sex activity were a part of the natural order in the same way that heterosexual relations are. It also illustrates the difficulty of attempting to apply the concept of marriage to same-sex unions. A civil union between same-sex couples may be endorsed by the State but it is wrong to call it marriage, since it lacks the essential characteristics of a marriage. To call a same-sex union "marriage" is to change the meaning of the word. Governments do not have the authority to do this.

Same-sex marriage also reinforces a legal right to parent on the part of same-sex couples and at least one biological parent will therefore be irrelevant. If and when same-sex marriage becomes law, there would be no grounds for distinguishing its consequences, particularly for children, from the outcomes for traditional marriage, so it will be difficult to evaluate.

There are also concerns about the freedom of speech of those who believe that same-sex marriage is wrong, particularly for those who are employed by the State or those who perform public functions. Teachers may be required to teach that same-sex marriage is right and many will be unable to do so as a matter of conscience. The current state of the law in relation to issues of conscience (discussed in paragraph 7.5) indicates that the UK state will be uncompromising in excluding those who take this course. Some MPs have called for a belief in traditional marriage to be a protected characteristic giving rise to a duty of non-discrimination.

The question as to whether the State should encourage a particular kind of behaviour should be a question of what the public good is, and not a question of discrimination against those who see themselves relatively disadvantaged by a restriction. The laws of the UK do not allow marriage between members of the same family and they do not permit bigamy. The laws of the State properly regulate marriage relationships and govern who can and cannot lawfully marry and adopt children. The UK state recognises polygamous marriages conducted abroad in the benefits system and in the law of succession to assets on death. This is inconsistent with the rest of the law. If something is wrong, it is wrong everywhere. The UK does not have jurisdiction over most activities which take place in other countries and so cannot (and should not) govern the affairs of those countries. However, where a contractual relationship (and a marriage relationship can be regarded in the same light) is unlawful in the UK as a matter of principle (rather than as a matter of formality or process), it should not be recognised in the UK, even though it has been entered into in another country where it is lawful.

14.10   THE DUTIES OF PARENTS

Traditional Christian teaching has always emphasised the need for firm, loving discipline to give children the psychological security of clear boundaries and also to train them for the challenges of the future: "Train up a child in the way he should go and when he is old he will not depart from it" (Proverbs 22:6 KJV). Dr Aric Sigman, author of *The Spoilt Generation*[390] reflected: "There seems to be a confusion between being a parent and being a friend. People want to endear themselves to their children. In our liberal age, it's thought much better to have a *laissez-faire* attitude to children doing what they want than to be authoritarian. But this is a highly destructive trend."   There is concern that the police investigate those who shout at or attempt to discipline unruly children when the parents of the children complain to the police. Some people may excuse the anti-social behaviour of children on the grounds of economic or social deprivation. It is easy to see how a lack of parenting leads to children finding security in gangs and being led into criminal behaviour. Parents and those in authority over children need to have the authority to discipline children and should be supported in doing so.

The natural social order is undermined by a lack of respect and parents (particularly from under-privileged backgrounds) find it harder to raise children, so there is a tendency for the State to intervene. The slogan "Every child matters", enshrined in the Adoption and Children Act 2002 and the Children Act 2004, poses the question: "Matters to whom?"   Christian teaching is that every child does indeed matter to God and that God has entrusted the care of children to their natural parents and not to the State. Where the parents have been convicted of a criminal offence against the child, such as violence or depriving a child of food, they should be punished. If a child's parents cannot look after the child, the child's closest relatives should have the opportunity to care for the child. If there are no relatives willing to care for the child then, only as a last resort, should the child be given to foster parents or an institution. However (as discussed in Chapter 8), there is no justification for the State to take children away from their parents on a permanent basis when the parents have not been convicted of any offence against the child. While social workers and the courts have these wide ranging powers, it is noteworthy that in some cases, such as that of Baby P, social workers have failed to stop crimes being committed even when the physical dangers to the child should have been obvious to an observer.

Parents are sometimes deprived of their right to take decisions in relation to their children on the grounds of "health and safety". In 2010 Mark McCullough was threatened with a child protection order by Lincolnshire County Council when he let his seven-year-old daughter walk the 20 yards to where the school bus picks her up and because he was alleged not to have dressed her warmly enough.[391] A public authority should not have any right to assume the duties of a parent to protect and decide for a child unless the parent is committing a criminal offence, for instance by physically harming the child.

14.11 TRANSGENDER ISSUES

Secular thought based upon human autonomy that is freed of the constraints of traditional or Christian norms has resulted in unnatural results for individuals. Gender has become a matter of choice, not biology, which is another example of radical autonomy. Those who have a psychological condition (which may or may not be treatable) resulting in their feeling as though they belong to the opposite sex can now have the condition treated by a surgical operation designed to make them resemble more closely the sex they feel they represent. While these psychological conditions may in some cases be associated with neurological changes in the brain, it is not clear that the changes are irreversible. The Christian position is that the essential genetic characteristics are given at birth (though in very rare cases this may not be clear) and that it is not possible to change sex. If the condition of gender confusion is a psychological condition, it is wrong to effect irreversible physical changes to the bodies of the individuals in this condition and to confirm the flawed, and perhaps temporary, choice of a change of gender.

The new gender identity of transgender people and the rights based on that identity are now recognised in law, and disclosure of their gender origins is limited. The Gender Recognition Act 2004 creates a criminal offence of disclosing the true biological gender of a person who has obtained a gender recognition certificate. The law has created a fictional new gender and, subject to some limited exceptions, it is a criminal offence to tell the truth about it. The law requires deception and misrepresentation which, as a matter of conscience for Christians and others, may require them to break the law. Practical issues abound. It is not possible for a woman to object to a transgender man with female physical attributes using the same toilets. Sport, however, is less accommodating than the law in the UK and is able to reflect the biological reality. Since those born as men have a built-in physical advantage in a women's competition, the World Long Drive Championship and the Ladies Professional Golf Association have adopted a female-at-birth policy. Few "sex changes" are aesthetically convincing, but images in the media can confuse. Chloe Sevigny, a woman, played a transsexual in Sky Atlantic's drama *Hit and Miss* in 2012, but was obliged to wear prosthetic male genitals.[392]

The Christian position on this issue may appear to lack compassion. But it is compassionate to face up to and deal with difficult desires rather than trying to solve the issue by physical changes. The fact that a woman who has been legally designated as a man can now give birth, with the attendant psychological confusion that this is likely to cause for the child, illustrates the issues that can arise from gender reassignment.

14.12   A FAMILY DAY

The Bible provides for a day of rest from work when families can be together.   Christians in the "Keep Sunday Special" movement headed by the Jubilee Centre in Cambridge fought a losing battle to maintain one day free of shopping and the inevitable demands it places upon those working in stores and related operations. According to the Relationships Foundation, more than 2.5 million families are affected by a parent working regularly at the weekend.[393]

14.13   CONCLUSION – CHRISTIAN VALUES AND THE NATURAL ORDER

Christian understanding of the importance of the natural family is informed by Christian belief. This recognises a created natural order designed by a rational creator. Many people of faiths other than Christianity, or of none, can relate to the centrality, both economically and socially, of stable natural biological families. Following changes in the attitudes of society over the last fifty years, a number of opinions informed by this perspective are now perceived as controversial. If there is a natural order, then humankind is not autonomous and cannot redesign family forms. The Christian perception is that changes which conflict with natural law damage those who are affected by them. More research is required to provide evidence for this conclusion, with which some may disagree or which, for others, may only be theoretical. Much money has been expended on research to find the Higgs boson particle which is necessary to explain the theoretical model of standard physics, but the reinvention of the family is of more immediate importance and relevance to the health of society.

15
FREEDOM OF EXPRESSION

15.1 FREEDOM OF EXPRESSION

A mechanic was warned he faced prosecution for promoting an engine spray named "Start Ya Bastard". Nick Palmer was told by the police that the advertisement for the Australian product, painted on the back of his van, could cause offence. As he said, "I was staggered — I never dreamt anyone could be offended, but they said if it wasn't covered up it would be a public order offence and action would be taken against me."[394] Hampshire police said: "If a complaint were to be received it could be regarded as an offence". While we may question the use of the law on this occasion and the characterisation of the alleged offence as one of public order, this incident highlights the question as to what circumstances justify the State in restricting freedom of speech.

Websites allow anonymous abuse and allegations to be directed at individuals, including children. Celebrities have sought privacy orders in relation to allegations about their private lives. Journalists are concerned about the use of libel laws and the threat of their use by wealthy corporations and individuals to silence those who wish to raise a matter of public interest. And there is often a debate about what that "public interest" is.

People have been arrested for a variety of offensive remarks. In March, student Liam Stacey was arrested for tweeting remarks about the footballer Fabrice Muamba and Paul Chambers was arrested for saying (clearly as a joke, though in bad taste) that he wanted to bomb Doncaster airport because it had closed.[395] Carolyn Still, the chief executive of a football league club, was arrested during an away match after making a remark (no doubt impolite) to a police officer for allegedly using "threatening words or behaviour,"[396] though it is mysterious that a trained police officer could feel threatened by mere words.

15.2 CHRISTIANS RESTRICTED

A Christian couple running a hotel were arrested after an allegation that they offended a Muslim when talking about her faith (their business failed as a result)[397] and two people protesting silently against abortion have been prevented from holding up placards showing the clinical results of abortion.

On 20th July 2011, Bill Edwards was arrested under Section 5 of the Public Order Act 1986 for using words "likely to cause harassment, alarm and distress".   He had preached a message from the Bible that sexual acts outside marriage are wrong. He was detained for six hours. False accusations may have been made, but the accuser did not suffer any consequences. It is a common feature of a police state that, where speech constitutes a crime, false accusations can easily be made and people denounced. Sometime later the case was dropped.[398]   Street preacher Mike Overd was arrested, charged but cleared by a magistrates court for referring to homosexuality as a sin[399] and the case of another street preacher Dale McAlpine, arrested in similar circumstances, was highlighted in a US State Department report on Restrictions on Religious Freedoms.[400]   Harry Hammond was convicted of a public order offence when he was attacked by gay rights campaigners for showing a sign which read: "Jesus is Lord. Stop immorality, stop homosexuality, stop lesbianism".

Margaret Forrester, a mental health worker, was suspended after giving colleagues a leaflet warning of the physical and psychological damage some women suffer as a result of abortion. Concerns have been raised that the NHS spends funds on Buddhist faith healing, while Christians who offer to pray for patients are disciplined.   Caroline Petrie, a nurse, was suspended by North Somerset Primary Care Trust for offering to pray with a patient. Duke Amachree was dismissed by Wandsworth Council after 18 years as a homelessness prevention officer for mentioning his faith to a client. And Olive Jones, a teacher, was dismissed for speaking of her belief in miracles and offering to pray for ill children.[401]

15.3   A CHRISTIAN PRINCIPLE

Free speech is a Christian principle required for the Christian faith to be explained. The Apostle Peter in the book of Acts (4:20 NIV) said: "For we cannot but speak the things which we have seen and heard." Free speech has long been defended in this country as an expression of the equality and dignity given to all people and as safeguard of political freedom. No human system of government is infallible and no one should be immune from criticism. Leaving aside issues of public decency (discussed below), in principle expressions of belief or opinion should not be restricted unless they constitute an incitement to commit a criminal offence or are harmful to children, such as obscene material.

There is another reason, apart from the fallibility of all people, why freedom of speech should be protected. Those who passionately believe in a particular cause may believe it so strongly that they are unable to contemplate the possibility of their being wrong. If they believe that they are right, they may also believe that they have the right to restrict the freedom of others to express a contrary view. The reason they are wrong in this, however, is not only because their belief may be wrong — Christian thought emphasises the fallibility and imperfections of human beings — but also because God has intentionally given humankind the freedom to explore for themselves what is truth and falsehood. So, even if our opinions or beliefs are wrong, we should have the right to express them, and we should be able to do so even if others are offended by them. It was wrong for a housing association employee to lose his management position and to have his salary cut for posting on a social networking site his opposition to same sex marriage.[402] The executives of the housing association thought it worthwhile to defend the demotion of the employee in the High Court (presumably at some expense to the organisation), though they lost the case. The ability of organisations to restrict freedom of speech by taking cases to court (even if they lose) can have a chilling effect on freedom of speech, since few individuals relish being at the centre of a court case.

In Christian thinking, human beings do not have autonomy in relation to certain matters, for instance the autonomy to end their own lives or to end the life of another person without legal justification. But they have been given the right to decide the truth about the world they live in, the values they should live by and their eternal destiny. For some people, the freedom to search for truth is so important that they will risk their lives to defend it. They may do so because they recognise that the gift of freedom is not just for themselves, but for subsequent generations. They may realise that there are values that transcend this world and perhaps even perceive a life to come. Antipathy to a belief in God may explain why some extreme secularist activists have been enthusiastic about restricting freedom of expression and speech. Conversely, the belief that there is a realm beyond the material world explains why Christian belief can help to sustain these freedoms.

Parts of the Racial and Religious Hatred Bill (now the Racial and Religious Hatred Act 2006) which would have criminalised expressions of belief that offend others were narrowly defeated, and there were repeated attempts by the Labour government before the 2010 election to remove from the Act Lord Waddington's clause protecting free speech. Under the Public Order Act 1986 it is a criminal offence to say "insulting" words likely to cause alarm, harassment or distress. There need be no intention to do so, nor need there be any evidence that alarm, harassment or distress has actually occurred. On 12th December 2012 the House of Lords voted to remove the word "insulting" from the Act, and on 14th January 2013 it was announced that the government would accept the amendment.

The effect of the current law is that it can be a criminal act to cause offence to a person because that person disagrees with the content of a belief, rather than the manner in which that belief is expressed. An attempt to criticise a person's views by an attack upon their personal qualities was characterised by Roman debaters as an *argumentum ad hominem* and is a logical fallacy. In the case of the Public Order Act an expression of belief may be unlawful, not because of the character of the person who expresses it, but because of the reaction of the person who hears it. In each case the focus is upon a person, in this case the hearer, not upon the nature of the views expressed or the objective manner in which they are expressed. To focus on the reaction of the hearer is as illogical as the *argumentum ad hominem* where an argument about a person's opinion is directed not at the opinion itself but against the personality of the person expressing it. Under the current law, a statement may be unlawful because of the reaction of the hearers, who may or may not be rational or reasonable in their reaction, irrespective of the nature of the communication (which may be entirely reasonable) or the intentions of the person making it (which may be directed towards the public good).

The current law has allowed abuse in a private argument to be criminalised. The footballer John Terry was charged with, but acquitted of, racial abuse for remarks to another player on the football field. It appears that it was not relevant that Anton Ferdinand, the person whom Terry was alleged to have abused, shook hands with Terry after the game and did not know all of what Terry said until he saw the incident on YouTube some time after the match. If Anton Ferdinand did not hear the relevant remarks, it seems unlikely that fans could have heard it so as to have caused a disturbance. In a public order offence the criterion should at least be whether the words or actions were likely to cause a disturbance of public order on the basis of a reasonable reaction by the actual hearers to the words in question. Terry's conduct was shocking but it should only have been the subject of disciplinary action by the Football Association and not a matter for the criminal law.

There is also a concern with Section 127 of the Communications Act 2003. The case of DPP v Collins[403] makes it clear that it is an offence to send a message by means of a public electronic network which is offensive to the people to whom the message relates even if those people never see and are intended never to see the message. Thus a person who sends a communication which contains a grossly offensive message about a particular person or group commits a criminal offence even if there is no prospect of anybody being offended by it (whether reasonably or unreasonably) because it is sent only to a person who shares the opinions of the sender. Whether the message is grossly offensive is to be decided by the Court on the basis of the standards of society. This offends the principle of freedom of speech. The legislation can be used by the State to criminalise private communications, even when there can be no possible effect upon public order.

The excessive scope of the law which allows the State to criminalise freedom of speech was recognised by the Director of Public Prosecutions in December 2012. He admitted that thousands of people could be accused of crimes as a result of messages posted on Twitter or Facebook and issued guidelines that only the most extreme instances would be prosecuted. The guidelines are welcome, though the law still restricts freedom of speech where there is no violence or even intention to stir up hatred. And it should be the operation of an objective law, and not the discretionary decision of a law enforcement officer, that protects freedom of speech.

15.4 ARE THERE LIMITS TO FREE SPEECH?

There are limited types of expression that should be restricted in particular circumstances. Threats of violence should be prohibited. Three Muslim men were found guilty of distributing written material intended to stir up hatred on the grounds of sexual orientation by advocating the death sentence for homosexuals in accordance with Islamic law.[404] If there was an incitement to violence for people to take the law into their own hands, then this should have been a criminal offence. If, on the other hand, the men were advocating a change in the law (however unpleasant) without advocating violence, then there should have been no offence. In this case the material showed a person hanging from a noose and it quoted Islamic texts. It implied that the law should be changed and said that "the death sentence is the only way this immoral crime can be erased from corrupting society". In making this statement, albeit with assumptions that few would share, the writers may not have been advocating private violence, which would have been against the law. Instead, they may have been campaigning that the State adopt their interpretation of an extreme utilitarian philosophy espoused by totalitarian regimes which, contrary to Christian principle, holds that it is permissible to eliminate people whom the State views as undesirable. This was wrong and highly distasteful but, if there was no threat of violence, there should not have been a criminal conviction.

Current libel laws provide a redress for those whose reputations (which may include their economic interests) have been damaged by statements made without justification. There is a defence of fair comment on a matter of public interest. Opinions are divided upon whether the private lives of individuals, who may be private people, celebrities or political figures, are a matter of genuine public interest. The government has proposed new libel laws in a draft Defamation Bill that would provide some defences to those exercising their freedom of speech if the statements were substantially true or were honestly (and reasonably) held opinions. However, there are concerns that this would not leave newspapers with a strong enough defence where the journalism resulted in false statements which were nevertheless responsibly made in the public interest, known as the "Reynolds defence" after the Irish politician Albert Reynolds. There are also concerns with Lord Leveson's proposals which could prevent journalists handling personal information unless this is necessary for publication, rather than being able to do so with a view to publication. If implemented, the proposals could discourage journalists from gathering information where they do not yet know whether there is a story worthy of publication.

Reflecting again on Nick Palmer's advertisement, we can ask ourselves what limits, if any, there should be to free expression. If people want to use coarse language in an advertisement, is there any reason why they should not do so? Should there be any constraint on expression on the grounds of public decency? Should there be any right not to be offended and, if so, by what? An advertisement in poor taste may give offence. It may be right to limit some expressions in advertisements in public places because they use language that is offensive to all and sundry (though language regularly used in television programmes is frequently more offensive than that in Nick Palmer's advertisement). It is important that the rules in relation to what is acceptable are clearly laid down and understood. Otherwise, as in the case of Nick Palmer's advertisement, the matter becomes one of discretion for the authorities, who can be inconsistent and may lack impartiality.

People will always have the capacity to be offended by statements or expressions of beliefs with which they strongly disagree, or that engage their consciences, but such expressions should still be allowed in the marketplace of ideas. It is not the train of thought or a belief that should be restricted but only, in certain cases, the manner of its expression. There should be no right to legal redress when a person is offended by an idea with which he or she disagrees, however disagreeable the idea. The ability of the State to ban the expression of ideas because of their content, rather than the manner in which they are expressed allows it to silence dissent.

However, the way an idea is expressed may be in such bad taste, or the manner of its transmission may be so obscene, that it is right to restrain it. Thus the statue of Christ with prominent private parts sponsored by a public authority in Gateshead should not have been allowed, not because it was offensive to Christians who hold a particular belief about Jesus as the Son of God, but because it should have been regarded as contrary to public decency. Similarly, if people generally felt that the words used in "Start Ya Bastard" were grossly offensive (which they did not), there would have been a case for restricting their expression. The way in which the sentiments in the advertisement were expressed could have been changed. The message about the product (that it can encourage even the most stubborn engines to start) could have then been conveyed in a more appropriate way. In these cases the police should respond according to criteria laid down in law and apply those criteria impartially.

Governments should not restrict press freedom, but the laws must be adequate to ensure that those who are wronged by the press, for instance by a wrong accusation or an unjustified invasion of privacy, have speedy remedies in terms of an injunction (where appropriate), a public apology and damages, which should also be sufficiently serious to deter wrongdoing. The appointment of a State regulator of the press with statutory powers, advocated as a result of the Leveson Report, could lead to political interference which would undermine democratic politics.

15.5   THE CHALLENGES OF THE INTERNET

Pornography and violence in online or other media does not express a rational opinion or belief, nor can it normally be regarded as artistic. But while pornography does not express a belief or an opinion, it does something to the people who access it. The long-term neurological effects of pornography have been studied. The creation of neural pathways by mirror neurons and the release of dopamine by the brain (associated with addictions as well as other bodily needs) generate increasingly extreme expectations which are associated with a lack of self-confidence, social isolation, depression and difficulties in bonding.[405] Pornography can teach people the false lesson that sex is available where it is not associated with relationships and where it has no emotional correlation. The problems are intensified for teenagers whose brains have not developed sufficiently for them to integrate their sexual experiences with the appropriate emotional responses. An NSPCC survey found that the highest proportion of sexual abuse experienced by teens (66%) was perpetrated by people under 18.[406]

There is evidence in the case of the murder of Joanna Yeates, the Bristol landscape architect, in December 2010 by Vincent Tabak that Tabak, in other respects a normal and balanced individual who was able to hold down a prestigious professional job, was accessing material online which foreshadowed Jo's murder. A teenager who raped a five year old girl while babysitting was spared imprisonment by the judge who said that the boy was corrupted by online pornography for which the judge blamed society. He said that he was satisfied that the boy had been sexualised by exposure to pornography.[407] Darren Jackson, a porn obsessed man who spent his days watching obscene violent internet videos raped and strangled a grandmother in her home.[408] It is estimated that there are 200,000 internet sites where illegal child pornography is viewable and that 23% of all internet searches are for pornography.[409]

Access to pornography on the web can be restricted by the "active choice" of the user so that parents may subscribe to a service which blocks adult content and there is currently a debate about whether it should be necessary for all persons to have to opt in, rather than opt out of pornographic sites.[410] The current *Safety Net* campaign calls for internet service providers (ISPs) to apply network pornography filters, giving adults the choice as to whether to opt in. According to *Safety Net*, one in three 10 year olds have watched pornography on line, the single largest group of viewers of pornography are children aged 12 to 17 and four in five 14 to 16 year olds regularly access explicit photographs and footage on their home computers. Baroness Howe's Online Safety Bill would require ISPs to operate pornography filters, with the ability for adults to opt in. It had its second reading in the House of Lords on 9th November 2012. The Bill received widespread support, although some members were concerned about the definition of pornography or that it might give parents a false sense of security. Neither of these objections is compelling. It remains to be seen whether the Bill will attract sufficient government support to become law. Other measures should be considered. Even for adults, violent and child pornography could be banned. ISPs knowingly hosting material which is likely to encourage criminal activity, such as child abuse or violence, could be criminally liable.

The criminal law contains a number of provisions (for instance in the Malicious Communications Act 1988, the Communications Act 2003 and the Protection from Harassment Act 1997) which make it a criminal offence to send malicious and grossly offensive communications. But these do not work if those sending the messages cannot be traced. Sean Duffy did not know any of his victims yet caused Natasha MacBryde, aged fifteen, to commit suicide because of the abuse that he posted on the internet, including via YouTube. A principle upon which the libel law is based is that the identity of the person making the statement is clear. Except in rare cases where it would be unsafe for the person making the statement, or where a whistle-blower would be victimised, a person should know the identity of anyone making allegations against them and should have the opportunity to answer them. And before a matter is raised publicly, it should be raised privately between the individuals involved, allowing the possibility of forgiveness and reconciliation. This is a principle that Christians draw from the words of Jesus in the Gospel of Matthew: "If your brother sins against you, go and show him his fault, just between the two of you. If he listens to you, you have won your brother over. But if he will not listen, take one or two others along, so that 'every matter may be established by the testimony of two or three witnesses'. If he refuses to listen to them, tell it to the church...."[411]

Where anonymous malicious communications have been received via email (and email addresses may not reveal the identity of the sender), it should be considered whether there could be a legal mechanism to address these. For example, the individuals affected could be able to contact the ISPs (perhaps via an impartial ombudsman) so that the ISPs would then have an immediate legal duty to close down communications from the sender. This might be helpful, but an anonymous sender can change email addresses at will and can escape detection and control by stealing bona fide email addresses and routing messages via other countries. There are mechanisms by which individuals can screen out unwanted messages containing, for example, certain offensive words in the same way as companies eliminate "spam" messages, and a range of these could become standard for people to opt to use as a matter of course.

15.6   RESTRICTIONS ON FREE SPEECH OUTSIDE THE LAW

There should be no restrictions on free speech imposed by the forces of the State acting outside the framework of the law. Discretionary action outside the law is a characteristic of police states. An example is the Cross Government Action Plan on Hate Crime published by the last government. A "hate incident" was defined as a "non-crime incident which is perceived by the victim or any other person to be motivated by hostility or prejudice based upon a person's race or perceived race" and the same applies to religion and transgender. Thus any person could perceive and define the hate incident. Even if an objective rather than a subjective test were applied, the word "hostility" is vague and the word "prejudice" could be applied to any sincerely held moral or religious belief with which someone disagrees. The Action Plan contains an aspiration "to create a duty on all public bodies to report hate incidents". Threats to a person were already covered by existing legislation, so the actions intended to be covered by the Action Plan were lawful expressions of opinion. The use of the police to investigate non-criminal free speech is contrary to the liberty of a free society and a waste of scarce police resources. Further, since it erodes the respect which the public should have for the police as enforcers of the law, it could contribute to a lack of cooperation with the police.

15.7   A FOUNDATION OF DEMOCRACY

Freedom of expression is a foundation of a democratic society. Unless people are free to express opinions and to circulate facts about the activities of government, the value of the right to vote in an election is diminished, because people do not have the information that enables them to know what they are voting for. Hence the expression "free and fair elections" includes the right not just to vote, but to receive and publish the knowledge necessary to make an informed choice. Freedom of speech has therefore long been a fundamental condition of democratic politics.

Public decency, the protection of minors and, where the relevant expressions are an incitement to crime, the prevention of crime and the interests of national security may justify appropriate restrictions to free speech and freedom of information. Those in possession of confidential information (where there is a justification for that confidentiality) have a duty not to disclose the information. There should be an exception to this duty of confidentiality where disclosure is necessary to expose criminal activity or public malpractice. Thus the disclosure of the information relating to the MPs' expenses was justified, but the disclosure of all the "Wikileaks" information was not, since the disclosure of the confidential information could have endangered lives. In principle, any restrictions to free speech and freedom of information should be limited and, in relation to freedom of speech, they should be defined by law and should not be within the discretion of law enforcement officers.

Crimes which are based upon the offence that they cause to others are morally wrong. They give legal justification to resentment. They encourage self esteem and fuel personal insecurity. The crimes provide a disincentive to greatness of spirit and forgiveness. They discourage intellectual curiosity and free debate. Instead of encouraging people to engage with and understand those with whom they disagree, these crimes enable people to become blinkered, since their prejudices cannot be disturbed. We should be open to others and endeavour to understand them. We should not take offence if others express opinions with which we disagree, even if they are expressed in an unpleasant way. Christians can view offensive remarks in the light of a wider perspective, since they should derive their significance and security from their relationship with God and not from the opinions of others.

PART 4:

SOCIETY AND THE MARKETS

16
THE VALUE OF COMMUNITY

16.1 COMMON CITIZENSHIP

Christian thinking provides a framework for the values of a society, but it shares many of those values with those whose thinking derives from a secular framework of belief. Community values can flourish in other belief systems and none, though Christianity can make a valuable contribution to building civic society. Non-religious organisations, such as the Citizenship Foundation, seek to help young people understand and participate in political life and the processes of civil society. As the Foundation puts it, they want "young people to leave school or college with the political and economic literacy, and the social and moral awareness, that will enable them to thrive in adult society."[412] This is an aim with which people of different backgrounds and beliefs can identify. Intercultural understanding in a diverse ethnic country is an important goal for all community groups. Christian commitment is cross cultural and multi-ethnic. The common identity of Christian believers provides a powerful bond between people of different cultural and ethnic backgrounds.

16.2 CHRISTIANS IN THE COMMUNITY

Christianity has long emphasised the value of community, both the community of believers and the service of the wider community. This service of the community encompasses activities which may involve structural change (such as seeking a change to unjust laws) and remedial charity to address particular needs. As Jim Wallis described it,[413] Christians must not only haul people out of the river but they must also go upstream to find out why they are falling in and try to prevent it. Both activities can be the good works that Jesus commanded his followers to do and can express compassion for others, particularly the less advantaged.

16.3   COHESION AND IDENTITY

Shared values and identity of interest are necessary for social cohesion. While the law is a framework for this, it is not the only factor. As Leslie Stephen wrote in the nineteenth century: "Society is the work of law in some proportion but in a much greater proportion it is the work of very different agents — love of companionship, curiosity, the desire of all sorts of advantages which are to be derived from mutual assistance founded upon mutual good will."[414] Francis Fukuyama examined different types of societies in terms of their cohesion and argued that the trust and quality of relationships in a society play a large part in creating the structures required for economic success. He singled out Germany as a high trust society, where representatives of labour sit on company boards and there is a high degree of institutionalised reciprocity. On the other hand, social cohesion, whilst being a good in itself, can be used to support wrong ends, and he cited the "small unit cohesion" as "one of the reasons for the extraordinary fighting prowess of the Reichswehr and Wehrmacht".[415]

Commonly accepted values are essential to the operation of an ordered society and to the exercise of democratic freedoms. Those values are grounded in communities. There has been a concern that there are parts of the UK where this does not apply. In some inner cities, for instance Birmingham, it has been reported that there have been police "no go" areas where ethnic minorities can operate with little or no contact with civic and legal structures of a Western State and where, for instance, the Taliban flag was reported to have flown for a period of months. A lack of community cohesion presents a challenge for Christians and secular liberals alike. Freedom of belief and expression are essential, but the standards of law and the operation of State must be universal. An agreement on democratic values, such as the impartial rule of law, freedom of belief and freedom of expression, should be shared by all members of society.

Education in citizenship and the values of a democratic society is important. This is common ground in secular and Christian thought. Those acquiring British nationality should affirm and provide evidence of their understanding and belief in these values. It is reasonable for there to be some restrictions on immigration on the part of those who choose a location in the country in order to escape the requirements of civil society or to form a community which does not subscribe to the values underpinning society. Restrictions on immigration are required in relation to the country as a whole and those who settle should be encouraged to integrate in society. However, it is at the level of local communities, not the country as a whole, that immigration makes a difference. It could be considered how the interests of the community in the place in which immigrants plan to live can be taken into account. Immigration from countries within the EU cannot be controlled and this is one of the reasons against a supranational organisation having the jurisdiction that the EU now exercises.

Communities together form a country and, although there may be diversity of belief within communities and between them, it is essential that all the people in a country owe a common loyalty to the State in which they permanently live. For particular families and individuals, a sense of identity of interest with the country, its people and its values may take a generation to achieve. If it does not happen in the longer term, the country may be vulnerable to internal unrest as well as to destabilisation from abroad. Christian belief has always been a powerful unifying force between different ethnic communities. Although active Christian believers may be a minority in the UK, a common agreement on certain Christian values can provide cohesion in society. Edmund Burke highlighted the importance of the small units in society: "To be attached to the subdivision, to love the little platoon we belong to in society, is the first principle (the gem as it were) of public affections. It is the first link in the series by which we proceed toward a love to our country and to mankind."[416] People commonly admire the concept of Burke's "little platoons" but, rising above any ethnic, cultural or faith diversity, those little platoons need to be members of the same army.

16.4   GOVERNMENT AND COMMUNITY

Libertarians argue that healthy communities can more easily be built when the government withdraws to its core functions of defence, public safety, infrastructure and public education but does these well and does not encroach upon the responsibilities of parents and communities. It is consistent with Christian thinking that in the long term the role of government in the UK should be reduced, not simply to lessen the burden of national debt, but also to encourage personal responsibility. Unless government has a reduced role, people may assume that Government will take care of every problem. Government needs to encourage personal responsibility through welfare and taxation policies and support the involvement of charities, including churches and Christian bodies in their communities.

James Odgers, the founder of Besom, a Christian charity with a network of centres across the country that recycles and provides household goods to the disadvantaged and refurbishes their homes for them, has remarked on the inability of the State, despite its huge growth, to provide the kind of help that is needed: "At Besoms across the land we meet with social workers every day who tell us that there is already neither the time nor resources available to stem the tide of domestic abuse and violence, still less to assist the ever larger underclass towards a more worthwhile and meaningful existence." He points out that A. J. P. Taylor wrote in his English History 1914-1945, that: "Until August 1914, a sensible law-abiding Englishman could pass through life and hardly notice the existence of the State, beyond the post office and the policeman." As he remarks, about 7 million people now work for the public services, a further 6 million are dependent upon welfare payments and about 12 million people are drawing State pensions. The difficulty with State provision is that it can remove responsibility and discourage initiative, and therefore hope, on the part of those most in need. Their conditions are not likely to improve if they are passive. Christian charity can be based upon a personal relationship where the individual receiving the benefit is the primary focus. Christians believe that people need practical help, but also that there are values for living and there is hope and that these can give a framework for life and a purpose for living. While the functionaries of the State may not be uncaring, Christians acting for a charity should be able to engage with people, express personal compassion and encourage personal growth in a way that may not be appropriate for a State employee.

16.5   THE BIG SOCIETY AND PHILANTHROPY

An aspiration of the Coalition government's "Big Society" was to encourage community initiative and action. However, the government did not articulate clearly what the "Big Society" was to achieve in terms of the vision and values that it promotes or what success would look like. To some extent, these were beyond the control of government, and rightly so, since people were being invited to participate and would do what they chose to do. But a vision of the kind of society that would be created might have encouraged people to get involved. If an idea is being promoted by government, government should know what it would like to see achieved. For instance, if the aim is social justice, what does this mean? If the aim is social cohesion, what values will underpin this cohesion? In practical terms, what is expected of whom and by whom? In the absence of answers to these questions, the public was confused and unenthusiastic.

A sense of shared purpose is vital. Until government withdraws from the areas where it has overstepped the boundaries of good government, for instance in arbitrary policing of matters which are not criminal offences and in its interference with the rights of parents (as mentioned in previous chapters), it may be difficult to motivate some people to serve their communities. Before helping to perform what might otherwise be regarded as the functions of government, people need to sense that there is an identity of interest between them and the State. Individuals may perceive that, if they perform hitherto publicly provided functions, this may free up resources for government to pursue agendas which infringe their freedom, or which waste resources (such as on the propaganda mentioned in Chapter 6). To assist the State in these circumstances may be unattractive. The "Big Society" agenda is not likely to succeed if those who might support it are alienated from the policies of government. People may not support public authorities that do not permit them to exercise democratic freedoms. Christians may be unenthusiastic about assisting a State that restricts their freedom of speech, that makes certain positions in the public sector untenable for them and that deems them unfit to be foster carers because of their Christian beliefs (as in the Johns' case mentioned in Chapter 7). It is even possible that some Christians might take the view that it would be morally wrong to support certain authorities in the same way that it would be wrong to collaborate with an unjust regime.

A practical difficulty with the "Big Society" is that, where the State performs functions which were previously charitable, changes to society are required to transfer responsibilities to communities and these changes may take some time to achieve. In the short term, cuts in government spending can result in the withdrawal of funds from charities that are the institutions the government aims to encourage. Another aspect is that most people are members of a number of complex and overlapping communities, many of which are not united by their geography. Local communities are no longer hierarchical where it is expected that the wealthy have paternalistic duties. The very rich often have no fixed abode, dividing their time between different residences throughout the world with little sense of belonging in any location.

Although government policy may encourage civic virtue, a change in the outlook of individuals is required for philanthropy to increase. Giving in the UK was 1.15% of GDP in 2006, half that of the US. The philanthropy of the nineteenth century was motivated largely by Christian belief — schools, hospitals, and homes for orphans were established — and in the UK there is currently not the culture of philanthropy among the wealthy that exists in the US.

16.6   THE MARKET AND COMMUNITY

In addition to the increased influence of the State, the operation of the market has served to loosen the traditional bonds of society. Some of these bonds were built upon deference to class and few would mourn their passing. In the last half century changes in culture, family, law and public education have contributed to a decrease in respect for the established order and for authority, particularly among the less advantaged. Adherence to standards of behaviour out of a respect for hierarchy needs to be replaced by common values which all can embrace. Principles are acted out in community. The community can both encourage responsible behaviour and provide the context in which it is acted out. Here Christian thinking, notably that of Michael Schluter and the Jubilee Centre, together with their non-faith based organisation, The Relationships Foundation, can be valuable. Drawing upon biblical principles and appreciating that stable relationships are crucial elements in the wellbeing of individuals and of society, they have looked at ways of strengthening long-term relationships in a number of areas of public policy. These include policies in relation to health, housing and prisons. Inevitably, there is a tension between the encouragement of long-term relationships and the operation of the free market, which encourages geographical mobility and can replace loyalty to community with material considerations.

16.7   THE CHRISTIAN CONTRIBUTION

Archbishop Temple said that the church is an organisation which exists for the benefit of non-members. Christians are called to serve the community as a whole and not just those who share their faith. In this they will be aspiring to demonstrate the character of God shown in Jesus Christ. Where local communities already exist, Christian activity can help to strengthen them. This is the context for the continuation of the Anglican parish system and the wider Christian church's involvement with communities. Where new housing developments are being built, Christians can help to establish communities by providing services and space for people to meet and work together. The local church often has facilities that can be made available. Churches are now used for nursery schools, mother and toddler groups, exercise groups and a host of other activities, including community shops. The charity Christians Against Poverty (often based in churches) gives free debt counselling to those in need of it, bringing hope to those in despair over the burden of debt, and many churches run a variety of activities to help people in need in the community. Christian charities house and feed the homeless and provide resources, such as furniture and electrical appliances, to those in need. The importance attached by Christians to the values of civil society is shared by non-Christian groups also serving in the community. The Christian principle of service to others can be a unifying factor to bind people of different background together as they give and receive from each other.

17

COMPANIES AND MARKETS

17.1 THE USE OF MONEY

Money is necessary. It enables the division of labour. As Professor Philip Wood puts it: "Money is a public utility. It is the commons. As a means of exchange, money is essential to modern societies. One could not in practice otherwise buy a loaf of bread. As a store of value, it enables us to control the future by saving now for future income and diversifying....It was Dostoevsky who observed that 'Money is coined liberty'. Liberty is a product of the rule of law."[417] The freedom inherent in the common law of Anglo Saxon jurisdictions permits behaviour which is not expressly denied by the law and has allowed commercial activity trade to flourish. Historically, through developing case law, it has adapted to the requirements of commerce while upholding freedom of contract.

Some have argued that the common law is ill adapted to the complexities of modern commerce and that it has failed to regulate the activities of complex markets. This is somewhat unfair since the common law preserves principles of honesty essential to transparent and efficient markets. In the common law, dishonest conduct which disadvantages others can attract criminal and civil penalties, and systems of statutory regulation can be built upon the foundations established in the common law. But neither the common law nor statutory regulation can ensure ethically good behaviour, though codes of practice can be helpful.

Aquinas believed that in a just transaction there should be equal advantage to both parties and the Old Testament prophets frequently inveighed against the exploitation of the poor by the rich. While the prophets did not attempt the structural reform of economic systems, they required individuals to act fairly, honestly and with mercy. They also emphasised the personal dangers of riches in the effect that an excess of wealth can have on people's moral wellbeing and their happiness. In the Book of Proverbs, there is advice about the need to act wisely in borrowing and in lending and taking security. Wisdom in spending money efficiently is a theme in the Book of Proverbs where the wise and virtuous wife profits from her business to provide for her household. All resources that human beings have are gifts from God, and should be used for good purposes. Christian virtues are not inconsistent with commerce. While we may not agree with the 20th century historian R. H. Tawney's thesis about the Protestant faith being the cause of the rise of capitalism, we may conclude with the German social scientist Max Weber that the conscientious work ethic was suited to capitalism and gave it moral justification. In Christian thinking wealth should be put to good purposes. As Aristotle observed, money is never a good in itself but must be used for something.

Jesus recognised that there was a world of commerce. He frequently used concepts such as debt, payment and wages in his parables and teachings. He taught about the pearl of great price, the talents, the lost coin, the workers in the vineyard, the dishonest steward and the rich fool. He taught (in Luke 16:19) that we should use worldly wealth and opportunities for heavenly purposes and that we cannot serve both God and money. Capitalism favours those who, through inheritance, opportunity, luck or sheer ability (and in many cases a combination of these) already own resources, while those without them cannot prosper in the same way. In the parable of the talents Jesus taught that we need to account to God for the use we make of what we have been given both in material wealth and in personal qualities and opportunities. The book of Deuteronomy warns against taking personal credit for the creation of wealth by saying: "My power and the might of my hand has gained me this wealth" (Deuteronomy 8:17-18 NKJV). Good stewardship is a recurrent theme in Christian thinking. We do not own what we have and, as the Apostle Paul said in his letter to Timothy, "... we brought nothing into this world and it is certain we can carry nothing out" (1 Timothy 6:7 KJV). The 18th century preacher

John Wesley said that Christians should earn as much as they can, save as much as they can and give as much as they can, highlighting the importance of the stewardship of resources. Money spent inefficiently or wasted is not in God's plan. This critique underlies Christian concerns about many of today's economic structures. The concern is that economic structures encourage the misuse of resources and that they incentivise and reward the wrong kind of behaviour.

17.2 THE ALLOCATION OF RESOURCES

Christians will differ over the mechanisms required to achieve a just allocation of resources, and some of the questions surrounding this issue are discussed in Chapter 10. It may be easier to agree on the fundamental ends to be achieved than on the measures required to achieve them in an imperfect world. For Christians, the ends are that God's gifts of material resources should be used wisely to enable individuals and societies to flourish as God intends them to. This flourishing does not require the amassing of large amounts of personal wealth. There is little indication that those in possession of great wealth lead happier or more fulfilled lives as a result. Those who have riches have a responsibility to use their wealth wisely and for the benefit of others. The Christian perspective is that they did not earn it all themselves, but were given talents and opportunities by God that they were able to use.

Transient though the material things of life are, even the manufacture of inessential luxuries can bring benefits. There may be great skill and artistic craftsmanship in their manufacture and their distribution brings prosperity to those who produce them. *The Fable of the Bees* written by Bernard Mandeville in 1714 makes this point and it is drawn out in the philosophy of Adam Smith who held that purely selfish choices can contribute to the common good by enabling the creation of employment and wealth for the benefit of all.

17.3 THE FREE MARKET

Whilst free markets tend to achieve greater efficiency than other systems of distribution, they are imperfect even in their own terms. The restraints provided by the rule of law are required to moderate the misuse of power that dominant market positions can bring and the misallocation of resources that can result. Markets reflect the flawed nature of human beings which are magnified where they act together. Markets operate imperfectly, even in their own terms, for a variety of functional reasons. Transactions are often not transparent, so people act on imperfect or misleading market information. There is still a lack of transparency in relation to a range of transactions, for instance derivatives, which affect the decisions of traders and the stability of the markets. There is insufficient knowledge as to the liabilities and contingent liabilities of companies, particularly banks and other financial institutions. Companies achieve dominant positions in markets and abuse them, for instance by temporarily pricing competitors out of the market. There are barriers to entry for new companies entering a market and these include over-regulation which larger companies can deal with more easily than small companies. (This may explain why it is those running the bigger companies who tend to favour membership of the European Union.) In many cases there are practical difficulties for customers to gain the best prices, for instance in the complexity of energy tariffs or even supermarket pricing. The human beings who operate the markets are often irrational. They are prone to misjudgement, they can act upon sentiment or herd instinct and they cannot predict the future. Further, the perception of these imperfections, and the reactions to them, can amplify them as participants in the market endeavour to compensate for their effect.

In Christian thinking, free markets reflect the free will given to mankind, but the operation of the market also needs to reflect the responsibilities that such freedom requires. There is only one earth, for us and for succeeding generations, so the control of land development by the state and regulations to prevent pollution are essential. Natural monopolies, for instance in public utilities such as water, need to be controlled by governments or regulated appropriately. Privatisation of public utilities, although favoured by many Western governments as a means of bringing greater efficiency in the operation of public utilities, is not necessarily the optimum solution. Dr. William T. Muhairwe, in his book *Making Public Enterprises Work*, tells the story of how, by inspirational leadership and sound management techniques, he turned Uganda's National Water and Sewerage Corporation from an inefficient, unresponsive and loss making public body into an efficient and profitable organisation.[418]

Elements of capitalism — the free movement of goods, trade and competition which can spur scientific discovery, creativity and innovation — are necessary for societies to flourish economically, although profit should not be an end in itself. These elements of capitalism are based upon the freedom of individuals to engage in these activities, and there is an association with Christian concepts of political freedom. Although there have been examples of economic freedoms being combined with political repression, for instance in Franco's Spain and (to some extent) in today's China, in the long term economic freedom may prompt moves to democratic freedom.

It is easy to critique the effect of economic structures, but less easy to propose alternativeness without endangering fundamental freedoms, or giving too much power to the State, which can easily be misused. The free market may be the least inefficient way to distribute goods but, like all human systems, it can cause damage to individuals and communities, and can create inequalities. It needs to be moderated by the individuals and organisations populating it or by governments. Failure of self restraint leads to regulation by government, and in this respect the operation of the free market is similar to other areas of human activity. The freer moral culture of the 1960s and 1970s was followed by a freer economic climate which, though it encouraged enterprise and creativity, also led to excesses of speculation, remuneration and debt unknown in the earlier periods. Freedom is a gift from God but, if restraint is not exercised, its exercise can damage both individuals and society. The Book of Revelation contains indictments of the excesses of commerce. The Reformation theologian Martin Luther criticised bankers who, as he saw it then, left the risk with others, while profiting themselves. The free market offers freedom of choice, but where this choice is constrained by unfair trading practices, the freedom is limited. A concentration upon the accumulation of wealth, rather than its use for the benefit of others, contributes to deprivation and hardship for the less advantaged.

17.4   THE PURPOSE OF COMMERCE

The functioning of a capitalist society involves the making of profit by companies and individuals. Economic thinking characterises this in utilitarian terms, for instance in terms of inputs and outputs. Even people can be regarded as commodities, as is witnessed by the now near universal use of the term "human resources" rather than "personnel". When values are espoused by companies, it is usually to promote the success of the business by creating a climate of goodwill amongst customers and staff rather than to advance purposes for the wider public benefit.

Companies, like organs of government, act in some ways like human persons. Their actions affect those around them. They have legal personality, they make contracts and they have purposes which are defined by law and their constitutions and by the characteristics of the people who populate them. There are inevitably conflicts between the interests of the various parties affected by the business of a company. These parties are the executive management of a company, its shareholders, its employees, its customers and the communities whose environment and livelihood the business of the company affects. The constitution of a company is designed to regulate the relationship between the executive and the shareholders. The law also governs this relationship and the relationships of the company with other parties. Employees will have individual contract arrangements and may also have collective agreements with the company, for instance in the form of union agreements. The customers are in theory free to buy the products and can exert some influence. The inhabitants of the places where the business is situated have little power or influence, except as customers (if they are such) and through their influence on local planning matters. Later in this chapter we look at different structures for reconciling these interests. But we can ask ourselves first whether it is possible to answer the question: what is the purpose of the commerce in which companies are engaged?

Simply the making of money should not generally be the purpose of any company, though investment vehicles are necessary to achieve returns for savers. If it were thought that profit were the sole purpose of commerce, there would be no need for the constraints of morality or the law, since any activity that made money would be acceptable. Although profit is an aim of those working for a company, the company itself is doing something else. A manufacturing or services company is serving its customers by producing a product or providing a service. An investment bank advises on and facilitates transactions. Investment banks also trade currency or securities for their own account. Critics say that they do this simply to make money and that there is little social or macroeconomic purpose in this kind of trading, and that it is also liable to contribute to instability in markets. They would point to the fact that only a small proportion of foreign currency transactions are entered into for the purposes of trading in goods or services. Others would say that the ability to trade sets the right price for financial assets and that this is necessary for an efficient market.

The activity of a business can be examined to see if it produces a good for society. If it causes harm, its activities may need to be restricted or curtailed. This is the heart of the debate about the structure and activities of the banking industry. The question arises as to whether there can be a corporate purpose beyond making a profit and the particular business activity in which the company is engaged. James Featherby, in his book *Of Markets and Men*,[419] has made the case for businesses to use section 172 of the Companies Act 2006 to introduce social purposes into their corporate objectives. Success could be defined as achieving a measured contribution to the welfare of its employees, its customers, its suppliers and the public interest. There have been some moves in this direction. Featherby cites the example of Unilever which has undertaken to reduce the environmental footprint of its supply chain and to source agricultural materials sustainably.

This leads us to examine what principles should underlie the purposes of a business and commerce and we turn next to the Christian theory of relationism.

17.5   THE IMPORTANCE OF RELATIONSHIPS

Michael Schluter, a Christian thinker and founder of the Relationships Foundation, has posed the challenge to move from an economic system where the end is business profit and personal gain, to a focus on good and right relationships. He has proposed a number of steps to achieve this aim. These include a priority for a shared family day off from work (for most employees); the strengthening of family balance sheets; encouraging extended family networks in voluntary and commercial activities; encouraging more personal engagement by the providers of capital to business, and entrusting welfare to local communities. These ideas rightly emphasise that economic activity is a means to human flourishing, not an end in itself. For Schluter, that purpose centres around the concept of good relationships. For him, the principle of relationship is a central theme to be drawn from the model of society given in the Bible. To achieve the goals he proposes, there will need to be a change in the thinking of the opinion formers and the business community, together with changes in legislation. It can be debated how practicable it is to expect business practices to change, given the motivation of many people in business and the necessity for businesses to take difficult, and possibly non-relational, decisions in order to survive in an increasingly challenging business climate.

Many Victorian business people were known for their large-scale philanthropy, but the business environment was not necessarily a more moral place than it is now, as is evidenced by Anthony Trollope's *The Way We Live Now* which was inspired by the financial scandals of the 1870s. Changes to the legislative framework can provide a framework to facilitate relational networks to grow. As Michael Schluter suggests, the Sunday trading laws could be changed; there could be new legal structures for family associations for welfare, insurance and consumption purposes; and encouragement could be given (perhaps by tax incentives) to those who relocate near elderly relatives and look after them.[420]

17.6 CORPORATE RESPONSIBILITY AND THE RUGGIE PRINCIPLES

Some have looked to the concept of corporate social responsibility as the way to mitigate the effects of capitalism upon society. This can mean that companies undertake ancillary and charitable activities which are unconnected with their core business. These initiatives are not central to the strategy of companies which operate their businesses to make a profit. Nevertheless, profit should not be an end in itself, but merely a necessary condition of a successful business. Many businesses, particularly those in finance, have concentrated upon short-term financial advantage and there have been insufficient incentives for other perspectives to prevail. The difficulty with corporate social responsibility initiatives is that they can be espoused without affecting the way in which companies operate in terms of their business practices. A wider conception of the public good as part of the mission of a company is required. This might, for instance, prevent a supermarket opening a second store in a town where the effect would be to put local shops out of business. It might discourage a company from despoiling an area of natural beauty to increase profitability even when it is permitted by law to do so. Or it might result in a company only dealing with suppliers in developing countries which provide good conditions of work and fair pay to its employees.

Chris Blackhurst posed a number of questions[421] to the assembled company of business leaders at Davos in 2011 relating to the morality of business practices that are worth repeating here:

- How many of you have ordered your people to delay paying suppliers and renegotiated your terms of payment, telling suppliers they will lose their business unless they accede?

- How many of you employ teams of accountants and lawyers, and erect complex financial and ownership structures, to avoid paying the tax the politicians with you in Davos claim they so desperately require?

- How many of you have ever taken up inducements from a foreign national or regional government to open a factory there and then, once those subsidies have run their course, closed it?

- How many of you have traded with regimes that have poor records on human rights?

- How many of you have sanctioned a payment overseas to someone to secure a deal which, if it was made in your country, would be considered illegal?

- How many of you have switched production to countries where labour is cheap and the workers are employed in conditions that would be regarded elsewhere as sweat-shops?

- How many of you have been shown an idea by a budding entrepreneur and passed it off as your own?

- How many of you have told your staff to find a way of copying someone else's innovation or product — and avoid the expense and risk they incurred in developing it?

- How many of you have told your lawyers to drag out a legal action for as long as possible and not to settle, in the hope that the litigant, who has a solid case, will give up because he or she cannot afford to pursue it?

- How many of you have lobbied against changes to the law and regulations which are intended to benefit society as a whole, but made your cost of doing business slightly more expensive?

- How many of you have appointed directors who, despite the love you declare for hearing opposing views in the thin air of Davos, you know will not challenge you in the distinctly less heady atmosphere of your boardroom?

The Relationships Foundation has published guidelines for companies which address many of these issues, which could be embodied in a code of conduct. The guidelines describe the value of relationships of trust between the company and its customers, between managers and employees and between the different departments in a company. They also highlight the importance of generosity to the local community, care of the environment, fair advertising and fair dealing with suppliers.

Companies should recognise that the right to operate in a country is a concession and this needs to be associated with duties to the wider community and the payment of appropriate taxes. They should pay tax proportionate to the value of the business they conduct. Since companies structure their businesses to avoid tax, effective legislation and its enforcement is required. Companies operating in the UK should not be allowed to reduce taxation on their UK activities by transfer pricing or by borrowing from companies in lower tax jurisdictions to enable profit to be booked in those jurisdictions (rather than in the UK where more tax would be paid).

There has been progress to encourage companies operating in the developing world to respect human rights. In 2005 Professor John Ruggie was appointed the Special Representative of the Secretary General of the United Nations. In June 2011 the UN Human Rights Council unanimously endorsed the Guiding Principles prepared by Ruggie and established a working group whose first report was issued in April 2012. The Ruggie principles do not redefine human rights. These have been defined by the International Bill of Human Rights, the International Labour Organisation and the Geneva Conventions. The Ruggie principles provide a framework for states and businesses to ensure that the parties over which they have jurisdiction and the parties with whom they do business respect human rights. Thus states have a duty to protect against human rights abuses within their jurisdiction, including abuses perpetrated by businesses. States must prevent, investigate, punish and redress abuse through legislation and the judicial system. Business enterprises should both avoid infringing human rights themselves and take steps to ensure that those with whom they do business are not abusing human rights. Guiding Principle 13 requires businesses to: "seek to prevent or mitigate adverse human rights impacts that are directly linked to their operations, products or services by their business relationships, even if they have not contributed to those impacts." Businesses will therefore have to investigate their supply chains, lenders will have to know about the practices of their borrowers and corporate investors should be aware of the activities of the companies in which they invest. The subscription by a company to the Ruggie Principles might in the future be sufficient to establish a legal duty of care to persons whose human rights have been abused as result of a failure to comply with the principles. This duty of care in law could then form the basis of a legal action in negligence. The OECD Guidelines for Multinational Enterprises requires the establishment of 'National Contact Points' to receive complaints and mediate disputes and Chapter IV covers human rights.

Some national laws, such as laws against bribery, have extra territorial effect. The laws of many countries, including the UK, make bribery in a foreign company a criminal offence. The Alien Torts Act of the US can allow a person injured by the operations of a US company in an overseas jurisdiction to take legal action in the US.

Self-restraint and a clear vision of moral behaviour, as well as the constraints of the law, are required to encourage and require corporations to operate responsibly. Profit is required as a necessary condition to the survival of companies, but it should not be the principal reason for their existence. The dilemmas in practice may be challenging. Companies need to respond to shareholders who, as investors, are concerned with profits and the success of their investment in terms of value. But companies can advertise (and some already do) that they will, for the public benefit, take or refrain from taking action that might otherwise have resulted in a profit. They can explain these matters to the public and to shareholders who can then buy their products or invest in their shares accordingly.

17.7 THE ROLE OF SHAREHOLDERS

The size of many companies today means that their owners (the shareholders) may have little control over them, though some institutional investors in the UK are beginning to assert more influence. Apart from the limited power of organised labour and encouragements to exercise corporate social responsibility, companies may not perceive much incentive to respond to wider community interests. An example of this was the take-over of Cadburys by Kraft where a promise made before the take-over to keep the factory in Keynsham was broken. Shareholders can buy and sell shares, but have few powers to hold the directors of a company to account for their conduct of the business.

Companies could sign up to a code of business practice and shareholders could decide to invest accordingly. Companies can already state their adherence to the Ruggie principles on human rights mentioned above. The code of business practice could be written into the contracts of employment of directors and management. Directors could then be held to account by shareholders for ensuring that the activities of their companies adhered to the code. Transparency is important and in some cases the only means of obtaining information about departures from the code might be from employees of the business. Legal protection from dismissal and compensation could be made available to "whistle blowers" who uncover transactions which breach the code.

A common difficulty is that directors and senior management who are dismissed, even for good reason, leave the company with large compensation packages. The law could be changed so that any contractual term which is liable to give rise to compensation above a stated amount, and any decision to pay that compensation without a legal judgment requiring it to be paid, would need the approval of shareholders in general meeting.

17.8   THE FRAMEWORK OF THE LAW

While good regulation in terms of both the formulation of rules and their enforcement is essential, there are inevitably limits to their effectiveness. Free market thinkers may be suspicious of regulation and much regulation may be poorly formulated. However, advocates of unbridled capitalism would do well to remember that they can only prosper by the operation of the rule of law and the intervention of the State in upholding the law (for instance in enforcing contracts).

The market reflects the collective activity of imperfect human beings, inevitably seeking their self-interest, though moderated by law, social restraint and personal morality. Companies cannot operate without governments which provide a framework of law. The structures (for instance concepts of legal personality) and the legal framework that enable companies to trade have been created by governments to further those ends and they are man made. The legal personality given to limited companies enabling them to enter into contracts and the limited liability given to the individuals who invest in them exist because policy makers have determined that this is the most efficient way to promote wealth. While the limited liability profit orientated company may have been the most productive commercial entity devised so far, it is an artificial structure rather than part of a natural order. It follows that it has no right to exist apart from its usefulness to society and that the rules surrounding it should respond the needs of society. James Featherby points out that "there is no such thing as limited liability. There is only liability allocation. Liabilities do not magically evaporate when a business becomes insolvent. They are left to be borne by others."[422] Limited liability is a privilege conferred by the State that is taken for granted in too many instances. However, modifying limited liability in a globalised trading environment would require multinational agreement, given the need for countries to attract investment and the ability of companies to transfer their businesses intra-group and relocate their domiciles. This "social dumping" or "race-to-the-bottom" scenario continues to present major challenges in regulation and taxation.

Despite the plethora of companies legislation over past decades, a fundamental principle of company law, understood and preserved by previous generations, has been undermined in the UK. It was a principle that the shareholders of a company should not benefit from a company otherwise than through the distribution of profits by way of lawful dividends. It followed that there was an immutable rule that a company could not assist, by way of guarantee or otherwise, the purchase of its own shares. This was to ensure the distinction between the assets and interests of shareholders and the assets and interests of the company. There could therefore be no transfer of value from the company to the shareholders except to the extent that profits were made by the company and the proceeds realised and distributed to the shareholders. This rule of company law has been so modified in the case of private companies that it is now in practice meaningless. The change in the law has allowed purchasers to buy companies facilitated by debts secured upon a charge on the assets of the company which they are purchasing. The new owners can benefit from the assets owned by the company, even if it is making a loss. The owners realise the profit if the company prospers, but the company that has provided the security for the debt (used to purchase the shares of the company) bears the burden of the charge on its assets if the owner's investment fails. This allows and encourages excessive debt. It is potentially a fraud on the trade creditors of the company whose receivables are unsecured — that is, unlike the debt used to acquire the shares, not guaranteed by a charge on the company's assets. The guarantee of the debt, which has been incurred for the benefit of the owners, can put the livelihood of the company and the interests of the employees in jeopardy.

Transactions in business should be based upon honest relationships and an appreciation by each party of the legitimate aspirations of the other parties involved. Until the passing of the Criminal Law Act of 1967, there was in the UK a law against what was called champerty and maintenance which prevented trading in the right to bring legal actions. The principle here was that a person should only bring a legal action where he had a genuine interest in the subject matter of the action. This principle could have been applied in the case of the credit default swaps (CDSs). Under a CDS a financial institution guarantees the liability of other companies in return for a fee but it has no commercial interest in the underlying transaction other than the receipt of a fee for giving the guarantee. The principle could also have been applied in the case of trading in collateralised securities (bundles of loans secured on property assets) and derivatives that are the product of hedging transactions. During the years before the 2007 crash, the value or liability in these transactions was transferred to parties quite remote from the underlying transaction who had no knowledge of the other parties to it and little understanding of the risks involved. Those who originated the loans were able to persuade borrowers to borrow imprudently and to induce purchasers to acquire the loans without appreciating the risks. The transactions were characterised by a lack of relationship and knowledge of the other parties involved. This kind of trading has the potential to create significant financial instability.

By analogy with the rule against champerty and maintenance, there could be restrictions on trading in financial instruments where the purchaser does not have a commercial interest in the underlying transaction. It would still be possible for the companies owning portfolios of these transactions to be bought and sold, and it would have to be assumed that a buyer of a company would undertake appropriate due diligence. The principle of restrictions on trading in derivatives has already been recognised in US law. The Dodd-Frank Wall Street Reform and Consumer Protection Act of 2010 provides that securitisers of certain collateral mortgage and debt obligations (that is, companies who package and sell them), are required to retain not less than 5 per cent of the credit risk. The Dodd-Frank Act currently applies to a specified range of securities but the range could be extended. In the absence of a prohibition on trading in derivatives, the percentage of the credit risk to be retained by the originator or securitiser could be increased to, say, 30 per cent or 50 per cent.

17.9   WHAT CAN LAWS DO?

A pessimistic perception of the imperfect nature of humankind might suggest that, until different morals prevail generally, corporate behaviour will not change and that, even then, there will be those who wish to ignore the prevailing moral customs in the pursuit of profit. Laws, however imperfect, can nevertheless provide restraints on undesirable behaviour and incentives for good behaviour. The legal framework for financing companies could recognise that limited liability is a privilege granted by the State that benefits investors at the expense of creditors. In practice the executives of a business, however negligent, also benefit from limited liability, since they are rarely, if ever, held to account for the failure of their businesses. One possibility would be for this limited liability to be withdrawn from executives, perhaps to the extent of the amount of a number of past years' remuneration if their companies become insolvent.

A restriction of the privilege of limited liability to the extent of their remuneration might also be considered in the case of directors who failed to take reasonable account of the interests of their wider stakeholders. Alternatively, it might be thought possible to have incentives in the taxation regime to encourage companies to take the interests of the wider community into account. These possibilities would suffer from the difficulty in defining the kind of behaviour which would give rise to the restriction of limited liability or the taxation benefit. And further government bureaucracy would be required to administer compliance with the requirements. Board representation of community and other wider interests is another possibility, although it would probably be necessary for those representing the parties with a financial stake in the business to have the final say in decisions.

There are detailed laws and accounting standards designed to ensure that companies present true and fair accounts so that shareholders and buyers and sellers of shares can be properly informed. There can be a conflict of interest where a firm of accountants provides both audit services and other services, for example in relation to taxation. The flow of an accounting firm's non-audit work from a company may depend upon the goodwill of the directors of that company. The concern is that the quality of the audit work could be adversely affected by the need to secure the work on the other services. Firms of auditors have signed off accounts of companies which collapsed thereafter. Reform would involve prohibiting any firm from carrying out audit services where it, or an associated company, carries out non-audit work for a company within the same group. In addition, the term of office of an auditor could be limited to, say, five years to ensure that more than one firm examines a company's affairs over the longer term.

17.10 THE LIMITS AND BENEFITS OF REGULATION

Good laws and good structures, although necessary to restrain damaging behaviour and desirable as a framework, cannot ensure good practice. Regulation has its limits in human imperfection and failure. Those operating in commercial and financial markets understand them better than the regulators and can outflank them by avoiding or evading the effects of the rules. The terms of reference of the regulators, and an example would be those of the Financial Services Authority and the Bank of England in the first decade of this century, may be inadequate to deal with what transpires to be the most important issues. Regulators may not do their jobs effectively. Before the Gulf oil spill The Mineral Management Service of the US government is said to have allowed oil companies to short change the government on lease payments and to have accepted gifts from industry. Regulation might even have encouraged complacency and corporate recklessness to the extent that people assumed that the companies with whom they were dealing were acting properly because they were subject to regulation. The US Securities and Exchange Commission failed to spot frauds at Enron and WorldCom, gave Bernie Madoff a clean bill of health, and allowed Wall Street investment banks an excessive amount of leverage while other regulators ignored myriad signs of fraud and recklessness in the sub-prime market. The limits of regulation might suggest that the renewal of individuals is more important than the reform of structures.

John Denham, the shadow business secretary from 2010 to 2011, highlighted the importance of individuals taking responsibility in the context of a moral framework: "If you look at the things that have ripped off consumers, whether it is the payment protection insurance, credit card scams, insurance referrals — they all have in common [the fact that] people at the top of the company knew they were wrong and no one thought they had a responsibility to do anything about it." He suggested that a change of culture is necessary and that a change in law could contribute to this: "It is a change of culture. But usually changing culture can mean you change the way you form laws as well."[423] He suggested that, rather than having specific detailed laws, it was necessary for the law to provide for "a set of principles that underpin the way you should be treated."

Having acknowledged the limits of regulation, there are benefits in having clear and objective general rules. These rules should have the characteristics of laws and be easily understood and enforced, rather than being over dependent upon action by investigative and discretionary regulators. For example, it would be possible to discourage borrowing and encourage other types of finance. The incentives for companies to borrow could be reduced by treating debt and equity equally for tax purposes, thereby abolishing tax relief on interest payments. Borrowing for mortgages could be regulated using a maximum loan to value ratio. There could be restrictions on credit default swaps or guarantees of the obligations of another company for the purposes of fees. Guarantees would be permitted in the case of genuine corporate interest, for instance to further the business of a trading subsidiary. Or, as suggested above, the transactions themselves could be permitted but trading in them restricted, so that companies entering into the arrangements would be bound to retain some of the risk associated with them.

There are challenges in seeking to regulate commercial transactions. For example, it might be thought possible (in theory at least) to distinguish between transactions which are for a valid commercial purpose, for instance where an exporting company hedges a foreign exchange risk, and those transactions entered into simply to make money by trading. Some might suggest a tax on "non-commercial" transactions to discourage that type of transaction. However, on this basis all savings transactions could be regarded as non-commercial. To protect genuine savers, it could then be suggested that the tax could be avoided where an investment was held over a longer term. But some might observe that this would be unfair in circumstances where an investor had a good reason to dispose of the investments, for instance to pay for an unforeseen emergency. And it is possible that financial engineers would find a way (for instance through derivative contracts) of avoiding the effect of the relevant rules. Others might point out that rules of this nature could distort the market for investments and savings so the market would not reflect a true view of supply and demand. Regulation should be rule based, so that it can be clearly understood and it should be specific so that it does not hit unintended targets, but this is difficult to achieve in practice. Rules need to be carefully formulated but it should be recognised that they will almost inevitably be imperfect both in their definition and their enforcement.

Although impartial regulation requires clear rules, a too narrow approach to the formulation of the rules can be ineffective and even counter-productive. During the credit boom years, the Bank of England Monetary Policy Committee largely succeeded in achieving its target for retail price inflation. It achieved this due to the under-pricing of goods from Asia, while other asset inflation increased and borrowing ballooned as a result of low interest rates. A holistic approach needs to be taken when formulating the basis for regulation.

17.11 IDEAS AND BEHAVIOUR

Individual behaviour influences the structures and operation of societies and economies for good and for evil. Ideas in the shape of secular ideologies, for instance Marxism, capitalism and liberalism, or in the form of religious belief such as Christianity, influence people. The people influenced by the ideas can then change the structures of society and government, perhaps through collective action as part of a democratic process, or through power exercised by an elite. The operation of the changed structures may then give rise to new ideas which, through the exercise of the will of a person or a group, in turn change society and political structures. At the same time, the operation of the structures can influence or reinforce the effect of the decisions of individuals.

The appetite for over-consumption by society was the force behind the excessive personal and State borrowing in Western economies from 2000 to 2007. However, the structure of "fiat" money (not based upon any assets such as gold in a central bank) and the low interest rates of the central banks facilitated the over-consumption and reinforced the appetite for it. At the 2010 Davos summit, a Middle Eastern leader posed the question that, if a person crashes an expensive sports car, should we blame the makers of the car, the driver or the State for failing to impose or enforce a speed limit?

17.12   THE EFFECTS OF GOVERNMENT POLICY

The policies of governments and central banks can have a significant effect upon corporate and personal financial decisions. Without a clear and accepted framework of personal restraint, if structures allow over indulgence, it is likely that this will take place. For example, the creation of money supply by unlimited credit supported by low interest rates gave rise to over borrowing. The reaction of the US government to the mini-recession of 2001 was (as highlighted by the financial publisher and commentator Bill Bonner) to turn the fiscal balance of the US Government upside down, to add $2 trillion to the national debt in 48 months and to lower interest rates below the rate of inflation. Banks (and, in the US, the government through its guarantees of mortgages) then lent into the asset boom. In many cases those buying the resulting financial products failed to understand the instruments they were acquiring. Here government policy could have restrained the over indulgence but failed to do so. The result of government negligence and the foolishness of institutions and individuals has been a misuse of resources, and the effects may take decades to unwind.

17.13   OVER-CONSUMPTION

Over-consumption is wrong, not just because it leads to debt and imbalances in the world economy and the depletion of scarce resources, but also because it leads to relational imbalances. Over-consumption is associated with a focus on material goods to the exclusion of other values. This can lead to overwork in what can be unsatisfying and unfulfilling jobs, diverting people from family and relationships and those things that contribute to a flourishing life. The focus on individual wellbeing can draw people away from a vision of the collective good of their communities. Money is only the means to an end and human beings need to have an idea of what that purpose is. The Christian vision is for all of people's true needs to be met — materially, in food, shelter and housing; socially, in communities in which people care for each other; culturally, by way of provision of opportunities to appreciate God's creation and human creative endeavour; and spiritually so people have the opportunity to learn about their creator and have an experience of knowing God. A focus on wealth as such is not a useful guide to what it means for a person or a society to flourish. Christians also point to the dangers of idolatry, which is putting the love of a created thing before respect for the creator. This is particularly important in relation to material possessions, since this idolatry can create disharmony and dysfunctionality in systems as well as in people.

17.14   SCARCE RESOURCES

There are challenges in relation to the depletion of scarce resources and competition for them. As Chandran Nair has pointed out,[424] our current economic models do not account for the costs of resources beyond the costs of their extraction or for environmental damage and degradation. Productivity is measured by the output per person in relation to the economic inputs without taking into account other long-term costs. Further, he has suggested (in a speech in 2011) that economic policies should be directed at employing the maximum number of people and using the minimum amount of resources. Whilst many governments interfere with freedoms of belief and conscience, they often fail to intervene to protect the physical resources entrusted to their countries for the sake of succeeding generations. We explore these issues at greater length in Chapter 20.

17.15   STRUCTURAL EVIL AND THE FUTURE OF CAPITALISM

The Bible recognises, particularly in the Book of Revelation, the ability of individuals to create structures of evil. Babylon in Revelation is a symbol of a decadent world system — "the merchants of the earth grew rich from her excessive luxuries" (Revelation 18:3 NIV). Although structural evil exists, it does not follow that reforming the structures will eradicate the evils. What is important is the reformation and renewal of the individuals populating the systems. Adam Smith, the free market economist, assumed a moral framework that included generosity and compassion as well as prudence, industry and justice. Max Weber, writing in 1930, pictures capitalism, cast adrift from its Protestant Christian foundations, by quoting Goethe: "Specialists without spirit, sensualists without heart;

this nullity imagines that it has attained a level of civilisation never before attained."[425]

The structures and practice of capitalism are an expression of free will. Capitalism should be guided by moral values and the integrity of those who operate it. Capitalism needs to be regulated by the nation state and it should also be supplemented by charitable activities. But because of free will, capitalism carries within it, if not the seeds of its inevitable destruction, at least the potential for crises which destroy wealth, institutions and livelihoods. The economist Nouriel Roubini pessimistically reflected: "Karl Marx, it seems, was partially right in arguing that globalisation, financial intermediation run amok, and redistribution of income and wealth from labour to capital could lead capitalism to self-destruct."

So far, better technology and increased wealth has not, as Chandran Nair has pointed out, led to a more efficient use of resources, which he would define as including the consumption of fewer resources for each monetary unit of output. The crises that have followed the misallocation of resources due to excessive debt and over-consumption are inevitable. Just as forest fires can be necessary to the re-growth of healthy habitat and allow a diversity of species to flourish, so the natural laws of economics are necessary to regulate excessive consumption fuelled by unsustainable debt. Attempts by government to change the rules of the game, for instance by creating additional money by quantitative easing (see paragraph 18.13 below) or keeping interest rates artificially low (which impoverishes savers) may enable uneconomic businesses to survive for longer, but are likely to be ineffective in the long term and may only prolong the crises.

A degree of economic growth is helpful for the redistribution of resources from richer to poorer countries. The incidence of economic crises may not mean that there are necessarily limits to economic growth, just that growth must be of the right type and not the result of over-consumption facilitated by debt. However, we should not rely upon growth continuing at the rates to which we have become accustomed. Much of the economic growth of the last two centuries has been due to the relative lack of scarcity of natural resources and the ease of their extraction, together with the efficiencies achieved by advances in technology. The first tractors may have increased production by ten to one hundred times.[426] These are unlikely to be repeated to the same extent in the coming years. Recent technological improvements have only been incremental. There was little global economic growth before the last two hundred and fifty years.[427]

While theories of the limits to growth may be over pessimistic, new models of the free market requiring less may be required. Tim Jackson's *Prosperity without Growth* suggests a model which operates on the basis of stable economic output, higher investment, lower consumption and increased public spending.[428] But public spending is in most cases inefficient and industries have to compete in a globalised market. A transfer of resources from the private to the public sector can also reduce the incentives to innovation. Having said this, State involvement in venture capital can be successful. Professor William Janeway, a US economist, has argued that private venture capital investments have been generally unsuccessful and that most of the big technological breakthroughs have been the result of state funded research, not private enterprise.[429] In the UK successful companies started life in the 1970s as investments of the Labour government's National Enterprise Board before being sold into the private venture capital market when the Conservatives came to power. State sponsored enterprises are capable of being efficiently run, and some are. Not all the utilities in the UK may be best run by the private sector (in the light of their efficiency and the costs of their services), and there are dangers for strategic security of supply if utilities are controlled by foreign companies.

17.16 CONCLUSION

The weaknesses in the capitalist system need to be mitigated, accepting that they reflect the ineradicable imperfection of the human condition. There is scope for companies to adopt wider purposes and respond to broader constituencies and interests, including the communities in which they operate and environmental concerns. The powers of shareholders to control the executives of a company can be enhanced. Business practices adopted by companies can better reflect an ethos based upon fair dealing and transparent relationships. Regulation may inevitably be flawed but laws and company structures can prohibit or discourage specific unethical business practices and certain types of destabilising transactions.

The cumulative effect of commercial and trading structures may be imperfect, but companies and individuals can endeavour to operate honestly within them. Christianity recognises that there can be structural evil beyond the immediate control of individuals, but that individuals are called to do right in an imperfect world despite their own limitations and the constraints of the structures that they inhabit.

18

DEBT

18.1 DEBT AND THE BIBLE

An example of long-term structural evil that has been caused by individual and collective wrongdoing is the issue of debt, both public and private. The Old Testament laws suggest some guidance. The laws against usury, defined in the book of Exodus as the lending of money with interest, were given by God for his chosen people, the Israelites, at a particular time in history. We should not apply all the civil laws of the Old Testament to societies today. Nevertheless we can learn from these laws about the unchanging character of God and his purposes for human communities. Theologians modified the prohibition on interest by defining usury as the unequal sharing of risk and the Fifth Lateran Council of 1512 allowed loans by *montes pietatis*, institutions sponsored by local government which made loans at low rates of interest on the security of goods deposited. The concern with the unequal sharing of risk was that the lender receives back all his money, plus a return on his investment (the interest), without a risk in terms of the success of the business, and this was seen as unjust.

The Christian economist Paul Mills has, with the Jubilee Centre, for many years emphasised the Christian teaching that God's order intends people to be free of debt and that debt is slavery: "The rich rule over the poor, and the borrower is servant to the lender" (Proverbs 22:7 NIV). The Old Testament laws provided for the periodic cancellation of debt and the return of leased land to its original owner at the Jubilee every forty-nine years. Mills' Christian understanding is that debt enslaves people for the purposes of gain. He believes that it encourages both arrogance and speculation, while shifting hidden costs to third parties through the mechanism of limited liability, inflation and government bailouts — in short, that it is structurally and necessarily unjust. The thinking is that the creditor can be indifferent to the success of the business in which he is investing since he receives a fixed return on the loan, providing he is repaid.

While this indifference is true of some lending, it does not apply to all. For example, lenders to project companies in limited recourse financings (where the equity shares and subordinated debt rarely amounts to more than 10% of the capital required for the project) have an important stake in the success of the project and examine the risks in great detail. The lenders' return is at risk if the project fails because their repayment is dependent upon the revenues flowing from a successful project. In the rare instances that the lenders are guaranteed a return even if the project fails, the lenders do not have the same incentive to examine the risks of the project.

18.2   UNCERTAINTY AND INSTABILITY

In practice, for lenders lending with inadequate security (in the form of a charge over the assets of the lender) or no security, which applies to a significant proportion of recent lending, the prospect of repayment is less than certain. The modelling of bad debts used by the major banks before the credit crunch was based upon false assumptions. The then recent lending history, even of the previous 20 years, was not an accurate guide to the future. As the Apostle James noted, "Why, you do not even know what will happen tomorrow" (James 4:14, NIV). The banking system has resulted in the unequal sharing of risk because of the uncertainty of repayment. The current high interest rates on credit cards are unfair in that each borrower pays a high interest rate to cover the risk of others defaulting. Interest rates charged by banks would be lower if the banks did not have to rebuild their capital following the losses caused by defaulting creditors or poor investment decisions. To the extent that banks calculate their provisions for bad debts inaccurately, the losses can destabilise the whole banking system with potentially disastrous results, in some cases leaving the taxpayer with the ultimate liability.

There is a permanent potential instability in the whole banking system in that banks borrow short from their depositors and lend long, and in a crisis may not have enough liquidity to meet their short-term liabilities. The reason for this is that they can profit from the yield curve where higher interest rates are paid on longer term lending. Conversely, as explained by Bill Gross,[430] a flatter yield curve, where longer term rates are little higher than short term rates is likely to reduce lending. In 2012 the yield curve was relatively flat since Ben Bernanke, the Chairman of the US Federal Reserve, signalled that the US Federal Reserve would freeze rates for two years. The fractional reserve system, where only a portion of bank deposits are represented by liquid assets, has led to a huge expansion of credit. Where a bank is unable to borrow to finance its short term liabilities, for instance where other banks lose faith in its long term viability, the bank may be technically insolvent even though its unrealised assets exceed its liabilities.

18.3   STEALING FROM THE FUTURE

For individuals, and this applies to governments as well, debt allows the consumption in the present out of wealth that has not yet been earned and that should be allocated to the future. Money has been borrowed and the wealth of tomorrow is already spent. In Spain, for instance, house building that should be providing employment tomorrow has already happened. The generations of tomorrow will pay for consumption by others in the past that they will never enjoy themselves.

Unless there is a good, perhaps certain, prospect of excess wealth in the future with which to repay, borrowing is unwise.

In many cases borrowing is prompted by greed, which overcomes a rational analysis. Paul Mills has pointed out that "a good case can be made for believing that we have a financial system dedicated to inflation, because a debt-based system cannot survive if prices fall for a sustained period (as occurred during the Great Depression). Central banks will now seemingly do anything to stop prices from falling in order to prevent the real value of debts from rising."[431] This presents a particular challenge to the less competitive countries in the Eurozone such as Greece, where prices need to fall in order for the economy to compete with the more successful economies of the northern part of the Eurozone.

18.4   BAILING OUT BANKS

The Austrian school of economists would argue that there should be no central bank supporting commercial banks, setting interest rates and able to increase the money supply artificially. They would also argue that for the government to bail out commercial banks creates a moral hazard that encourages excessive lending. They point to the low interest rates set by the US Federal Reserve in the early 2000s (in effect negative since they were less than the rate of inflation) which encouraged irresponsible lending. They argue that there should be a stable monetary supply and that interest rates should reflect the supply and demand in the market for credit and should not be dependent upon the policy of central banks. They would say that any bank bailout, by transferring money from the State to certain players in the private sector, at some point impoverishes others since either the money is borrowed and paid out of future taxes, or the value of the money is inflated away which defrauds the holders of the currency.

The experience of Japan over the last twenty years indicates that State interference can prolong rather than shorten a recession. The realisation of liabilities and insolvency are postponed. This prevents new businesses from growing. And the burden of taxation resulting from the State support of financial institutions and spending inhibits economic activity. On the other hand, the temporary rise in unemployment, the hardship of those who lose their wealth when their deposits at a bank are lost and the resulting disruption to economic activity indicate the need for a limited role for government in averting sudden and unexpected crises and securing an orderly transition to the new state of affairs. However, the State should not interfere with market mechanisms for too long, since this will lead to greater distortion and imbalances in the market and result in the misallocation of resources.

In relation to the bailouts of banks by government, there is no reason why shareholders and bondholders should be treated any differently from investors in other types of business when a bank becomes insolvent. Insolvencies may happen for a variety of reasons and there may be times when liquidity dries up and otherwise solvent banks may be unable to obtain short-term funding. In these circumstances the central bank may lend to banks on a temporary basis. But if the bank's liabilities exceed its assets, or there is such uncertainty about its liabilities that it is unable to obtain the capital funding it needs and is unable to meet its liabilities, then it should be allowed to go into insolvent administration. There is a market for investments in banks. It may be necessary for a central bank to provide temporary finance but, if a bank cannot raise finance in the long term, it should be allowed to become insolvent and its equity investors and bondholders should bear the consequences without any special protection.

The position should be different for depositors, including businesses as well as individuals. They rely upon a solvent banking system for their commercial transactions and they expect government to regulate banks sufficiently to protect them. Unlike investors, they do not benefit from the profits made by banks. In 1993, Paul Mills suggested that banks should share losses, as well as profits, with depositors, thus avoiding the need for a blanket government guarantee.[432] The difficulty with this proposition is that businesses and individuals just want a safe home for their money and a banking service. They do not expect to become investors in a business that they do not understand. However, since even depositors should have some duty to investigate the credit-worthiness of the bank they are using, and may benefit from higher interest rates where the bank is less risk averse, they should in some circumstances suffer a discount on the recovery of their deposits if their bank becomes insolvent. For example, where depositors have benefited from above market interest rates, it may be unjust for them to retain that benefit when the bank becomes insolvent, particularly where the interest rates are associated with the circumstances which led to the insolvency. The discount on the recovery of their deposits could be equivalent to (or even a multiple of) the interest above the market rate over the period of the deposits. Currently, depositors in the UK are only guaranteed by law amounts up to £85,000, which is inadequate, particularly for businesses. However, in practice the government is expected to protect all depositors in UK banks, however prone to risk-taking they may be, since to adhere to the statutory scheme would cause widespread financial disruption. This fails to distinguish between the prudent depositors and those who take excessive risk.

18.5 BANKING REFORM

Reform of the banking sector is required and is planned. Mervyn King, the Governor of the Bank of England until July 2013, quoted in an interview with Charles Moore,[433] recognised that, "We allowed a [banking] system to build up which contained the seeds of its own destruction", and that, "We've not yet solved the 'too big to fail' or, as I prefer to call it, the 'too important to fail' problem." He pointed out that: "Hedge funds were allowed to fail, 3,000 of them have gone, but banks weren't." The City commentator, Matthew Lynn, suggested that banks split themselves into their retail (depositor based) and investment divisions. If a retail bank becomes insolvent, the consequences of insolvent liquidation can be too severe for the government to allow it to occur and bailouts (at least to protect depositors) may be required. But it is the investment banks that take many of the big risks. Investment banking could therefore be separated from retail banking and the investment banks reconstituted as partnerships as most of the merchant banks were thirty years ago. In the credit crunch it was the banks which turned to the State for support, not the hedge funds and private equity houses. Partnerships operate on the basis that the long term wealth of the staff, and particularly the senior managers, are bound up with its future. If the decisions that they take fail, they bear the consequences. The risks they take are with their own money and, if the enterprise becomes insolvent, they will probably lose their jobs. It follows that the remuneration of senior managers at State owned banks should reflect the security that State ownership brings.

The proposals in the Banking Reform Bill, which are derived from the Independent Commission on Banking (ICB) chaired by Sir John Vickers, are that the capital of the retail banks will be ring-fenced from their investment banking activities. Some, for instance, Lord Lawson in the House of Lords Economic Committee on October 18th 2011, have criticised the ICB proposals on the grounds that ways will be found to avoid or evade the restrictions. And there is a concern that the retail banks may still be allowed to undertake some risky transactions, such as interest rate swaps. There is also the concern that, unless the entities conducting retail banking and investment banking are economically independent with different management teams and different shareholders, there will be conflicts of interest. This means that the business interests of one of the entities will influence the decisions of the other to the detriment of the other, because they are part of the same economic group even though the capital assets of the two entities are separate.

Whilst investment banking generally involves greater risks than retail banking, some banks (such as Northern Rock) failed because of poor retail lending decisions. Effective rules on free capital and gearing, the ratio of loans to deposits and capital and to realisable assets, are therefore required. The ICB report requires higher levels of capital for retail banks. It also suggests that individual depositors should rank higher than senior creditors, and this should apply even if the creditors are secured by charges over the business.

Entities undertaking investment banking activities should not benefit from an implicit State guarantee of their solvency because of their integration with entities undertaking retail banking activities. The removal of the guarantee may result in higher funding costs and reduced profitability for the investment bank activities. Some commentators have suggested that the removal of the State guarantee might even divert resources from investment banking to retail banking which would become comparatively more profitable, thus increasing support for commercial businesses since the retail banks would have greater resources for lending.

Retail banks need to have adequate capital. Currently the Basel II rules (the Basel III rules are yet to come into effect) on capital adequacy require the capital ratios to be assessed on a risk adjusted basis. This means that some financial assets are deemed to be risk free and no capital need be held against those assets. European Union sovereign debt falls into this category. This does not reflect either reality or the markets, where some sovereign debt is discounted to reflect the risk of default.

18.6   FUNDING AND REWARDING ENTERPRISE

Mervyn King (in the interview referred to above) highlights the moral dimension and contrasts banks whose sole aim appears to be to make money, with the manufacturing and service industries that he visits. These firms pay lower rewards than the financial services companies, but have "an incredibly successful record. They care deeply about their workforce, about their customers and, above all, are proud of their products." He points out that "most jobs have the property that employees can choose to do them well or badly, so employers need to think about the long-term welfare of the staff, not just pay today."[434] The pursuit of short-term profit is neither sensible, nor consistent with common morality or Christian teaching. Good relationships within a business promote efficiency and productivity. The London Business School's research on employee centred management indicates that trust is essential. It concludes that the main determinant of trust and the engagement of employees in the business is a good first line manager and that other aspects of working conditions are comparatively insignificant.

Enterprise and economic activity require finance. Entrepreneurs require investors. But debt may not be the best way to fund businesses. In the 1950s debt was far less common as a means of funding businesses than it is today. But there are limitations in the company structure. Although the shareholders and directors of a private company may be the same people, the law in relation to limited companies does not allow shareholders (in their capacity as shareholders) to give directions on the conduct of the business to the directors, and in practice the standard models of constitutional documents of a limited company permit the directors of the company a large degree of autonomy. Shareholders have the power to remove directors in a general meeting and in public companies they have the right to approve specified major transactions, and they can of course sell their shares.

The Victorians had a business model of limited partnership. This is still used in venture capital businesses today, having been revived in the 1980s as a result of a change in the taxation guidelines. In this structure a general partner conducts the business and the limited partners invest in it. A condition of the investment is that the limited partners set the parameters of the business (as set out in a limited partnership agreement), but take no part in the day to day management and the liability of the investors is limited to their investment on this basis.

Limited liability partnerships, where the partners may take part in the business without losing their limited liability, became available in 2001 and these are commonly used for professional partnerships. However, they cannot give floating charges over their assets which are a standard requirement of banks lending to companies. A model of limited partnership where investors would be permitted to participate in the business without losing their limited liability, and which has the ability to give floating charges, could encourage a greater involvement in the business on the part of investors than does a limited company.

18.7   EQUITY INVESTORS

Equity investors take the risk of the failure of the companies they invest in. However, most personal investments in companies are too small for an equity shareholder to have any influence over the matters which shareholders could collectively control, for instance, the pay and remuneration of directors. The requirement that investors take risk in a business should be balanced by their ability to influence the business. Large public companies need funding on a scale that inevitably involves a significant number of individuals or institutions and in this situation the connection between ownership and the conduct of the business is likely to be more tenuous. The Association of British Insurers (representing institutional shareholders such as pension funds) was thought to be largely ineffective in influencing boardroom decisions, but there were some significant shareholder revolts in relation to executive pay during 2012.

A possible model for companies which could increase the influence of shareholders is a structure similar to that which is mandatory in the UK for charities. Charities have a wholly non-executive board of trustees that is responsible to its members (if it has members) and to the Charity Commission representing the public interest. The trustees are responsible for all decisions relating to the selection and appointment of the senior executives and their remuneration and for the strategic direction and key decisions affecting the business. The trustees are not compromised by sitting on the same board as the executive and they are not (or should not be) selected by the executive directors. There would also need to be shareholder representation on a non-executive board and the shareholders would need to have the right easily to remove its members if they failed to protect their interests. To a limited extent, an audit and remuneration committee of a major company is capable of reflecting this idea, but the non-executive directors sitting on these committees are often selected by, and beholden to, the executive board. There may also be too few retired executives eager to take on the responsibilities (and assume the potential legal liabilities) of a non-executive appointment. If the costs of remuneration of the non-executives are to remain reasonable, there would need to be suitable balance between potential liability and reward.

Other changes could be made to increase the influence of shareholders and their involvement in the business. For instance, the remuneration of directors and senior executives could require a resolution in a general meeting and the remuneration packages could be simplified and explained transparently. The classes of transaction requiring the approval of shareholders of a public company could be expanded. The long term commitment of shareholders to the businesses in which they invest could be increased by reductions in capital gains tax dependent upon the length of time the shares have been held. It might also be necessary to re-examine the effectiveness of shareholders benefiting from the tax free band by disposal and reacquisition in different tax years. Take-overs of companies, which have rarely benefited the businesses of companies or their employees, could require a two thirds or three quarters majority of registered shareholders (whether or not voting) in favour of the transaction. Increased votes could be given to shareholders who have held shares on a long term basis. Take-overs could also be discouraged by higher rates of capital gains tax on a sale of shares associated with a change of control.

18.8   THE BURDEN OF DEBT

Edmund Burke spoke of the contract between the generations. Although debt can be used to improve infrastructure for the benefit of succeeding generations, the burden of public debt placed by one generation upon a later one breaks this contract. Until the middle of the last century it was normal for governments to borrow to meet unforeseen liabilities, typically those arising from wars, such as the Napoleonic wars and the First and the Second World Wars. With the wisdom of foresight it would have been good to accumulate a fund to meet these liabilities. The example of Joseph in the Bible is instructive. Guided by God, he ordered savings of grain to be made in seven fruitful years and this saw Egypt and surrounding peoples through seven years of famine. During the period from 1997 to 2007, Brazil, Chile, Russia and China increased their central bank reserves from 4 per cent to 27 per cent of GDP and as a result are now able to use those reserves as required in the current downturn. Chile, under the guidance of Finance Minister Andrés Velasco, set aside revenues from sales of copper and was able to draw on these to stimulate spending and cut taxes. Some years ago Paul Mills suggested a national investment fund, in which each citizen would have a share. He noted in the year 2000: "The current healthy state of the public finances offers a further opportunity to establish such a fund",[435] when the receipts from privatisation and North Sea oil were available. It would have been wise for UK governments to have taken his advice. Norway set aside a national fund from the proceeds of North Sea oil, the income from which continues to assure its prosperity.

The Keynesian solution of government savings in the prosperous years to spend in the lean years reflects the principle of Joseph's stewardship of Egypt's resources in the biblical account. But money should not be spent unless it is first saved. The policy of borrowing more to increase government spending in a downturn when no money has been saved is not sustainable. In a downturn of the economy the calls on government spending will increase due to reduced tax revenues and increased claims on welfare benefits. It is therefore essential that spending is reduced and that there is a credible plan to eliminate the deficit and begin to repay public debt.

Uncontrolled borrowing in a downturn is unsustainable because lenders will perceive an increased currency risk, or even a risk of default, and require higher rates of interest which will increase the debt yet further. The perception of default risk (realised with a 50 per cent write down of Greek government bonds) increased the cost of Greek debt to the point where debt became uneconomic to obtain and a European bailout became necessary. Without a degree of austerity (which may be unsustainable) only growth in the economy or devaluation of the currency can enable a large debt burden to be repaid. In the case of Eurozone countries with large debt burdens, devaluation is not possible and growth is challenging when the debtor economies are uncompetitive because productivity is low and real wages are high compared with other countries in the currency union.

Over the decade to 2011, UK government debt increased from £312 billion to £920 billion or from 31.5 per cent to 60 per cent of GDP.[436] As of the beginning of 2013, investors in UK government debt still have confidence that this debt will be repaid and the value of the currency has not depreciated to the extent where higher rates of interest are required. This confidence is based upon a perception that the government has a credible plan to reduce the debt. This plan could be called into question if there is a further deterioration in the economy and it is perceived that tax revenues will fall further and the benefits bill will rise. This serves to illustrate the folly of borrowing and the dependence upon others that can result from it.

18.9   THE IMMORALITY OF PUBLIC DEBT

When money has been borrowed for unforeseen liabilities it should be repaid as soon as possible, so that those who benefited from the spending should bear the cost of repayment. There is no justification for permanent Government borrowing, still less in times of prosperity. Borrowing for current expenditure is stealing from the future. A case can be made for borrowing to invest, but only where it is demonstrable that a specific investment will yield measurable returns. The use by some politicians of the term "investment" as a proxy for general government spending is misleading. In the UK at the present time the interest burden on the public debt is set to become as large as the defence budget and the overseas aid budget put together.

Taxes from today's taxpayers need to be raised to pay the interest alone on money that was spent years, indeed decades ago, on other people. People have been bribed, not with their own money, but with money that belongs to other people. The money spent does not belong to the generation spending it because it has been borrowed from future generations. People have accepted benefits, retirement, healthcare, employment (or payment in lieu) that have not been paid for by anyone — yet. These social benefits provided by the State have meant that families have not needed to save for a "rainy day", since the State has taken care of the relevant needs. The difficulty is that the State has not saved either, but has itself borrowed and is asking the taxpayers in future years to pay the bill. Total UK debt (including government debt, corporate debt and household debt) has risen since the credit crunch and amounted to 507% of GDP at the beginning of 2012.[437]

Governments that have borrowed are committed to taxing future generations, unless they default on their debts or inflate their debt away (which impoverishes others). We should include in government borrowing any unfunded future obligations (for instance, pension liabilities) that arise out of benefits currently enjoyed (such as the services of currently employed public servants). As Dambisa Moyo pointed out, countries that borrow excessively are mispricing current benefits, and misallocating resources as a result.[438] As she said, if a company does not fund its pension liabilities, the true cost of labour has not been taken into account in the pricing of its goods. As a result, wrong strategic choices have been made by companies, and individuals have favoured jobs with longer-term benefits though these have not been paid for. And, as she put it, "cheques that were written thirty years ago are, today, impossible to cash, in essence leaving government and some corporate defined-benefit pension schemes little more than Ponzi schemes."[439]

18.10 THE EFFECTS OF THE DEBT CRISIS

Debt is the temporary transfer of wealth from one person to another. The person who borrows has the temporary use of the money. The lender has the right to repayment and believes that he has an asset but he may not value this objectively. European banks currently hold debt which may never be repaid, but which is still fully valued in their books. The de-leveraging of both the public and the private debt that must now take place will cause colossal damage. Countries planning to repay debt can raise taxes and cut spending. Or they can default, in which case they will be unable to borrow more, leading to further hardship. Or, if they control their currencies, they can print money to inflate away their debt, defrauding their creditors and those holding their currency. What they cannot do is borrow more without adverse consequences at some point sooner or later.

Some people have doubted the ability of the US to repay its debts. In 2011 Christopher Caldwell posed a question (in somewhat extreme language) in the name of those who want to see the deficit reduced: "Under what assumptions can the US, with its [****] education system, its increasingly work-shy labour force, its corrupt and sybaritic elites and its unshakable sense of entitlement, conceivably pay down a debt that already stands at $40,000 for every man, woman and child in the country?"[440] As Bill Bonner has pointed out, in the future the Federal Reserve may have to pay a historically more normal, and higher, interest rate on its government debt than it does at present.[441] It would need to offer a real return (after inflation) in the range of 3 to 5 per cent. Since inflation is at 2 per cent, the range would be 5 to 7 per cent. At 5 per cent the annual interest bill would be $750 billion, which is between a quarter and a third of all tax revenues. It is possible that investors might doubt the ability of the government to repay its borrowings and consequently require higher interest rates, leading to a spiral of default or to inflationary money creation, either of which would deter future lenders. There is only a limited amount of income in an economy that can be used to repay debts without causing the economy to contract significantly.

Inflation is a particularly unjust way of transferring wealth from savers (who rely upon the stable value of money) to debtors (who benefit from the reduction in value of their debt). Inflation, where too much money chases too few goods, is normally a function of the amount of money in circulation and the velocity of circulation. The triggers for inflation include additional government spending from money created by quantitative easing (effectively the creation of money by a central bank) and leapfrogging wage inflation. Inflation can also be caused when, as a result of government money creation schemes, which could include quantitative easing, people lose faith in the value of money and liquidate their financial assets to spend upon physical assets. John Maudlin and Jonathan Tepper, in their book *Endgame*, cited the research by Professor Peter Bernholz of the University of Basel that examines the historical episodes of inflation and hyper-inflation. His conclusion is that public budget deficits of forty per cent or more are likely to lead to inflation or hyper-inflation. Maudlin and Tepper conclude that, "Interestingly, the only country in the world that currently fits the bill for hyperinflation is the United Kingdom, where one hundred per cent of the budget deficit was monetized by the central bank."[442] For a government to allow substantial inflation is an infringement of the principle in Proverbs 20:10 which prohibits false measures. A rapid change in the value of a currency means that the value of money diminishes and is likely to be uncertain. In these circumstances people will be defrauded.

The dangers of debt have been highlighted by many traditions of thought. Nassin Nicholas Taleb (the author of *The Black Swan*) gave a historical perspective and warned against the transfer of debt to future generations: "The Bible, the Koran, early Christianity, the Romans — everyone learned the perils of debt. What happened to that wisdom? Business schools. If you are facing uncertainty, it's a bad idea to have private debt. But I think it's criminal to transfer private debt into public debt because you're taxing the unborn. A debt bubble is almost impossible to survive and we've known that since the Babylonians. This is why Mediterranean cultures banned debt. What happened to all that collective wisdom? Three thousand years."[443] Greece and Ireland have been bailed out by the European Central Bank which bought their government bonds once they became unsaleable in the market, and loans from a Eurozone stability fund have been made to Spain to rescue its banks. But, as the then German President Christian Wulff questioned in 2011, as even Germany's public debt reached 83 per cent of GDP, "Who will rescue the rescuers?"

18.11   TRANSPARENCY AND RELATIONSHIPS IN LENDING AND BORROWING

One of the challenges in an era of increasing financial complexity has been transparency. Lehman Brothers did not disclose liabilities by the use of Repos 105 and 108. These were sale and repurchase agreements that were recorded as outright sales because they were over collateralised, so the obligation to repurchase was not recorded as a liability. Although the transactions may have been correctly recorded in accordance with the applicable accounting rules, the relevant accounts did not fairly reflect the company's state of affairs. Rules, and even adherence to them, do not ensure transparency and honesty, since rules may not be perfect and they can be avoided or misused.

Lending and borrowing inevitably involve risk for both the borrower and the lender. The ability of each to judge this risk depends upon the quality of the relationship between lender and the borrower and the knowledge each has of the other. Lenders should owe a duty not to lend to irresponsible borrowers and borrowers should owe a duty not to borrow more than can be repaid. Until relatively recent times, most banks had a personal knowledge of their borrowers which enabled them to assess the risks of lending. Later mass borrowing, coupled with the securitisation of debts, and their disposal to those who had no knowledge of the financial position of the borrowers, increased the risks for both lenders and borrowers. The transfer of risks via credit default swaps further separates the borrowers from the effective lenders or their guarantors. In October 2008 the total amount of outstanding derivatives, hedge fund transactions and credit default swaps in the US economy amounted to $1,444 trillion. Only one per cent of this would exceed $10 trillion, a fifth of the world GDP of $50 trillion. In the case of a credit default swap, once the credit event has occurred, the loss is transferred from one party to another. The results of credit events and defaults may be unpredictable for institutions and national economies, particularly since there is imperfect knowledge in the market as to which institutions are at risk of insolvency.

Lending and borrowing on a massive international scale have also unbalanced world trade. Since the middle of the last century banks have operated on an international basis. Before the credit crunch of 2007-2009, Charles Dumas and Diana Choyleva foretold the consequences of over production by China and other Asian countries as they lent to Western economies to enable those countries to over consume their goods.[444] As we have seen, medieval theologians defined usury as the unequal sharing of risk. In this case both the borrowers in the West and the lenders in the East are exposed to excessive risk.

18.12   STEWARDSHIP

The Christian principle of good stewardship suggests that government should endeavour to spend money as efficiently as private individuals. Keynesian theory advocates State spending to stimulate depressed economies. But this presents challenges.

The Harvard economist Robert Barro has calculated that each dollar of public spending has a net cost of a reduction of $1.50 in private spending. A study by the European Bank concluded that for every one percent increase in the proportion of a country's GDP spent by the public sector, GDP can be expected to fall by 0.13 per cent. Thus spending by the State may be inherently inefficient, though some State spending is necessary. The government of Japan borrowed and spent for twenty years to stimulate the economy — some would say on unnecessary infrastructure projects — and it did not work to lift the economy. But the excessive borrowing of the Japanese government (largely from its own people) has made their savings in government bonds potentially fragile if it is perceived that the Government cannot repay. If taxes are raised to pay for the increasing debt burden, the Japanese people will suffer.

18.13   PRINTING MONEY

Recently, governments across the world have engaged through their central banks in the policy of quantitative easing (QE). This is the purchase by a central bank, which is one organ of government, of the debt issued by another government body, the treasury. This means that the money is created, unless the treasury repays the central bank (and it would be necessary for the government to raise taxes to do so), or the bank later sells the debt into the market (and receives payment from the buyers) as the treasury would normally do if it were borrowing money. The created money increases the total money in circulation. When quantitative easing started it was thought that, while economic activity remains depressed, this increase in money supply would have little effect on prices. It was believed that in a recession a decline of lending and a decrease in the velocity of money in circulation as a result of fewer transactions would offset the effect of the increase in money supply. A concern is that the decline in lending may not be permanent. Further, the additional money in circulation affects different parts of the economy in different ways. It is likely that it has already had some effect by raising the price of commodities and food, which hits the poor hardest.

Money creation can in the long term to lead to a decline in the value of money, which is inflation, since the quantity of money increases without a similar increase in economic activity. By the time inflation becomes apparent, which may be some time after the money creation, it may be difficult and costly to stop other drivers of inflation. These may take the form of wage and benefits increases and/or higher import costs as a result of a currency devaluation prompted by a loss of faith in the currency.

Inflation breaks the contract between the generations. The value of money declines over time thus eroding savings. Serious inflation causes mispricing and the misallocation of resources since those who carry out the transactions before its effects are evident benefit at the expense of those who do so when its effects are clearer. Some economists have seen in the past a link between inflation and employment, but other economists have concluded that this was because inflation lowered real wages thus enabling more people to be employed. If there is inflation, this may be curbed by fiscal measures (higher taxes) or central bank policy (higher interest rates) but this would be likely to cause a further recession.

A long or indefinite delay by the central bank in selling the debt that it has acquired to the market could undermine the currency by making the increase in money supply appear permanent, as would any cancellation of the debt by the treasury. Commentators have highlighted the risk of a currency crisis, rather than inflation, as being the most immediate likely result of continued QE. The result would be higher import costs and lower standards of living. If there were a currency crisis, an attempt at that point on the part of the central bank to sell the debt could lead to a collapse in the government debt market, higher interest rates and a decline in economic activity.

John Stepek commented in 2011 on the effect of quantitative

easing in the US: "Ordinary voters in America see quantitative easing as a bailout for Wall Street. And it's hard to argue with them. Quantitative easing has driven up the cost of living by pushing up commodity prices, but has done nothing to improve the employment market, or boost the price of their house, unlike in the UK, where low [interest] rates have more popular support, because they're the only thing propping up housing."[445] Nassim Taleb takes the view that: "Quantitative easing is a transfer of wealth from the poor to the rich. It floods banks with money which they use to pay themselves bonuses". He is pessimistic about the future: "Every single person who has tried QE, or a form of printing money, has effectively lost the argument. Turkey had it, Brazil had it, Argentina had it, Italy had it when they debased the lira. Even Weimar Germany claimed that QE made the government rich. There's always an argument to print money."[446]

Quantitative easing depresses prices in the gilts (government debt) market and, in distorting this market, reduces the value of savings and pensions. The National Association of Pension Funds has warned that QE (which was £325bn as at June 2012 and £375bn as at November 2012) could cost pension funds £270bn by driving down long term interest rates and increasing the cost of pensions. According to Liam Halligan,[447] the UK's base money supply has increased from 7% of GDP by an additional 15% of GDP. He records that since 2009 the government has bought more than half of the £475bn of debt issued while £100bn has been bought by government owned banks or other institutions encouraged by the government to buy the debt.

Quantitative easing creates a false market in government debt which cannot last for ever. It may (and, some would say, inevitably will at some stage) cause disillusionment in the government debt markets which could result in higher interest rates being required to sell the debt. Tim Price, discussing QE,[448] referred to Murray Rothbard's 1963 study, *America's Great Depression*: "In his view, the more government tries to intervene to delay the free market's adjustment of a credit boom, the longer and the more gruelling the depression. Unfortunately government depression policy 'has always aggravated the very evils it has loudly sought to cure'. "

As noted above, there may have been some inflation of commodity prices (as of 2012) as a result of QE. However, if global economic activity recovers, the effect of quantitative easing may become more obvious. As Liam Halligan put it: "What happens to inflation when that massive increase in base money is lent out?"[449] The money creation would then lead to a rise in prices, since the additional money in circulation created by QE has not been matched by a proportionate increase in economic activity. Inflation will then increase further as a result of a decline in the value of the currency which increases the cost of imports and causes commodity prices to rise further.

Inflation may be controlled (at some cost) by fiscal and central bank measures. Although hyper-inflation may be unlikely, it is possible. Money creation on the scale necessary to cause hyper-inflation, as in Germany in the 1920s, happens because the alternatives seem non-existent or unpalatable. The President of the German central bank in 1923, Von Havenstein, may have calculated that raising additional taxes was not an option since the economy was depressed and this would lead to social unrest. Ruined by war, the country had no reserves left. Borrowing money was impossible, since other countries would not lend at affordable rates. Money creation to pay civil servants, the police and the army and to enable private businesses to continue may therefore have seemed the least unattractive option to avoid anarchy and revolution. And, as prices rose, more money had to be printed. The eventual result was a worthless currency (4 billion marks to the dollar), and the wiping out of wealth in old marks (as well as debt). When people lose faith in the value of money, commerce can collapse. As Bill Bonner observed, "People starved in the winter of the great inflation of the early 1920s, even though farmers had a record harvest. Why? Because farmers didn't want to sell. They kept their produce in their barns until the money problems resolved themselves."[450]

The parallels with today have been noticed. Jens Weidmann, the head of Germany's Bundesbank, said in September 2012 that QE (in this case debt purchases by the European Central Bank) reminded him of the scene in Goethe's *Faust* when Mephistopheles persuades the emperor to issue large amounts of paper money. This worked briefly before the state collapsed in rampant inflation and anarchy.[451]

18.14 EUROZONE DEBT

The Eurozone crisis has highlighted the dependency created by debt. Greece is beholden to its lenders. The normal relationships between nations have been distorted. At the end of the First World War Keynes advocated that the US cancel the debt owed by the allies. The British government asked the US to accept the reparations obligations owed to the UK by Germany in payment of the UK's debt to the US. The US government declined, leaving the consequences of the German default with the UK while it had to repay the US. There was no aid to help Germany recover and the continent suffered the consequences. The dire economic circumstances in Germany were a contributory cause of the Second World War. In the US excess liquidity caused the Wall Street crash and the Great Depression. The lessons were learnt by the end of the Second World War, when Germany was forgiven much and given aid to recover. The challenge for Germany is to remember the past. Greece can become competitive by leaving the Eurozone and reverting to a devalued Drachma, and Germany can help in this process. Or, if Greece does not abandon the Euro, it will need assistance to rebalance the economy and achieve greater productivity. In debt there is a dependency of the debtor upon the creditor, but this is to some extent mutual since debtors can damage their creditors by default.

18.15 SOME CONCLUSIONS

A concern with the dangers of debt is not a specifically Christian one. But Christian principles in relation to justice, the use of wealth, the imperfection of mankind and human inability to foresee the future, as well as biblical teaching on debt, can illuminate the current predicament and help to envision a better future. In the meantime, the consequences of personal and public debt will have to be borne. One or more of the three solutions of repayment, inflation and default will inevitably reduce real incomes and living standards.

Much commercial activity has been funded by debt and over-consumption on an unsustainable basis. In the short and medium term there could be fewer economically viable jobs. Economic growth will be necessary to create more employment. With increasing competition and ever scarcer financial resources in a global economy, the incentives required to encourage entrepreneurial endeavour and investment could exacerbate inequality and this may be regarded as unjust. Popular unrest arising from a sense of injustice may prejudice perceptions of the country and further weaken the economy.

The single currency union of the Eurozone may break up, damaging trade with the UK. The austerity required by Germany on the part of the southern Eurozone countries may be a price which the people of those countries will not pay. The austerity measures have caused a severe contraction in the Greek economy and there appears to be little immediate prospect of the situation improving. Unless the Greek economy grows, it will not be able to repay its debts. The creditor countries could write off the debts, but this would not address the uncompetitive nature of the Greek economy within the Eurozone. It is possible that Greek wages and costs could be cut, but this is unlikely to happen to a sufficient extent before the resulting social unrest becomes unsustainable. Leaving the Eurozone would be traumatic in the short term, but it could offer the best hope of recovery in the long term. If Greece were to leave the Eurozone, it would fix the exchange rate between the new Drachma and the

Euro and offer to repay its debts in Drachmas which its central bank could then print. The exchange rate for the new currency would be very low and the country might not be able to import to meet its food and energy needs. It is likely that it would not be able to borrow, except at very high rates of interest. It could suffer severe internal disorder. However, in the long term it would be able to export more easily, its tourist industry would be competitive (as it was some decades ago) and there could be economic growth.

A default by a Eurozone country would result in losses for European banks holding its government debt or liable for guarantees in the form of credit default swaps. This could further weaken the financial system and the ability of UK banks to lend which would cause a further contraction of the UK economy. Merryn Somerset Webb has made the point that there may never be enough growth in the UK economy to repay the government debt in real terms.[452] If this is the case, even austerity measures will not enable repayment to be made and austerity could lead to further declines in economic activity. Since the UK can always print money to repay debt, technical default is unlikely. The result of printing money will be inflation and/or currency decline, higher debt costs and lower standards of living.

Little can now be done to alleviate the inevitable onset of austerity and the adjustment to lower living standards for some years to come. It is possible that one or more of the world's financial systems will collapse. Those with resources have a responsibility to share them in charitable giving and an opportunity to build community relationships. Helping people to live within their means and deal with debt problems is the mission of the charities Christians Against Poverty (CAP) and Credit Action inspired by Christians. Other charities, many of them Christian, provide practical help and resources for those unable to deal with the challenges of the economic environment. The economic and social strains could be greater than those experienced in the two World Wars and the depression of the 1930s. Christian values form a basis for social solidarity and cohesion which can help the country to weather the unavoidable storms.

PART 5:

GLOBAL ISSUES

19
NATIONALITY AND
GLOBALISATION

19.1 THE IMPORTANCE OF NATIONS

Nations are recognised in the Bible as forming the basis for a common identity. They are part of God's order for the world (see Deuteronomy 32:8) and God's plans for guidance and for salvation were enacted through one nation, Israel. The common identity of the people of Israel was characterised by a shared belief in God and a distinct heritage of ancestry, history, culture, language and destiny which gave them a unity and a loyalty to each other. The social contract, the notional compact between the rulers and the people, can only operate if the people share sufficient common aspirations and values so that they are able to consent to be governed together in a way that reflects those aspirations and values.

The nation of Israel was chosen by God in Old Testament times to exemplify the operation of God's moral law for the benefit of other nations: "For this is your wisdom and your understanding in the sight of the peoples who will hear all these statutes, and say, 'Surely this great nation is a wise and understanding people.' For what great nation is there that has God so near to it, as the Lord our God is to us, for whatever reason we may call upon Him. And what great nation is there that has such statutes and righteous judgments as are in all this law that I set before you this day?" (Deuteronomy 4:6-8 NKJV).

Moses asked permission to travel through Edom, thus recognising territorial boundaries (see Numbers 20:17). The Apostle Paul told the Athenians that God "From one man... made every nation of men, that they should inhabit the whole earth; and he determined the times set for them and the exact places where they should live" (Acts 17:26, NIV). Christian thinkers Paul Mills and Michael Schluter have pointed out that a diversity of distinct national identities, cultures and languages, generally associated with nation states, are part of God's design in the providential restraint of evil. The course of history gives weight to this perception. There have been few multinational democracies, Switzerland being a notable exception to the general rule. Most multinational entities, such as Napoleon's Europe, Hitler's Europe, the Soviet Union or Tito's Yugoslavia, have been autocratic. The US, where people have originally come from many different ethnic and cultural backgrounds, places great importance upon a common US nationality. The Bible records that God confused language, so that people could not understand one another when they decided to make a name for themselves by building a massive tower — the Tower of Babel (from where we get the verb "to babble"). The differing nationalities, languages and cultures can therefore be seen both as a reflection of mankind's imperfection and as a response to it — for the protection of mankind. Too great a concentration of power can be dangerous to liberty which is an essential element in people being able to flourish. Having said this, human beings can and should transcend nationality in many contexts. We are not defined by nationality, but by our humanity. Socrates, when people enquired of him what his nationality was, did not say Corinth or Athens, but the universe.

Differences between nations in culture, geography, infrastructure, history, public traditions and governmental and other institutions remain. Nations are defined by their inheritance. This is the shared perception among their people of a link with a common past and an experience of a common identity linked to a particular land. The cultural distinctiveness of a nation cannot easily be erased, though some totalitarian regimes have sought to do so, and the variety of cultures embodied in different nations enriches human existence.

Globalisation, particularly when this is associated with the free market, loosens the restraints on trade, but without necessarily affecting any of the underlying differences between the countries. Differences in economic performance, for instance between Germany and Greece, will persist despite free trade and the sharing of some governmental functions. Indeed, by erasing some of the boundaries between countries which serve to protect them, a process of globalisation can exaggerate differences in the types of economic activity in which countries engage. Global free trade policies incentivise countries to specialise in particular types of economic activity, rather than diversify. This makes them more vulnerable when those activities encounter economic difficulties.

19.2   COUNTRIES, NATIONS, STATES AND SCOTTISH INDEPENDENCE

The inexact correlations between ethnic groups, national cultures and political states, together with the multiple identities of many of the people populating them, mean that we should be cautious in applying to all states principles which best apply to ethnically and culturally uniform nation states. Nations exist without states and vice versa.

Many people in Scotland would see themselves as primarily Scottish, others would see themselves as British or having two equal identities. The proposal for Scottish independence illustrates the ingredients of sovereignty which are required for an independent country. There are three principal pillars to political independence as a state. These are first, the armed forces and defence, secondly the system of law making and the enforcement of law and order, and thirdly the possession of a separate currency. It is doubtful whether an independent Scotland could ever be responsible for its own defence, but this could be overcome were it to agree to become a member of NATO, and it could also enter into bilateral treaties with Scandinavian countries. In relation to law making, as a member of the European Union (assuming that it would not have to apply to be a member) it would not be responsible for a large proportion of its laws, but this is true of the UK as a whole.

An independent Scotland would probably not be able to sustain a currency of its own. It would have to choose either the pound sterling or the Euro, though sterling may not be a possibility. The opt-out from the Euro enjoyed by the UK would not apply to an independent Scotland under the current treaties and the other Eurozone countries may not agree to an opt-out. Membership of a currency union involves a loss of sovereignty, since there is no domestic political control over the currency. It can give rise to serious difficulties, as is apparent in the case of Greece, Italy, Spain and Ireland.

19.3 GLOBALISATION

Globalisation has both dangers and benefits. The benefits include the new opportunities for trade, communication and understanding. New markets can benefit producers while access to technology, such as mobile telephones, radio and television, can improve educational standards and enhance the quality of life. However, globalisation in the form of free trade can favour richer nations, many of which were protectionist when their own industries were being built up. Ha-Joon Chang described how global free trade has impoverished developing countries and prevented them from building up local capacity. He records that in the 1960s and 1970s when developing countries were pursuing policies of protectionism and State intervention, per capita income grew by three per cent annually, whereas since the 1980s, after they implemented neo-liberal policies, they grew at 1.7 per cent per annum.[453]

In recent decades, globalisation has allowed some of the less desirable features of capitalism to dominate. These include greater inequalities in pay, the increased power of large chains of shops, often at the expense of small scale producers and local shops, and the production of cheap goods and food in developing countries where only "sweat shop" wages are paid. Some years ago Philip Allott presciently described it thus: "What is being globalised, all over the world, is the offer of this extraordinary poisoned chalice."

Arguments in favour of the globalisation of trade are based upon the pragmatic grounds that it creates jobs in developing countries and it enables goods to be produced more cheaply, which benefits consumers in richer countries. It is argued that, in the long term, the developing countries will achieve higher standards of living and better conditions. Larger and richer middle classes have emerged in some developing countries, though the distribution of wealth in these countries has become more unequal. Given the imperfection of the human condition, freedom of choice in the context of global free trade brings both benefits and challenges. Christian teaching is that freedom must be tempered with responsibility and charity, though the effects of endeavouring to implement these in a complex and unpredictable world may be uncertain. Fair trade initiatives which seek better conditions for workers in developing countries are to be applauded, whatever their inevitable imperfections.

19.4   FINANCIAL GLOBALISATION

Countries have the ability to borrow and over borrow in the global capital markets. The globalisation of financial markets has allowed a vast, although temporary, transfer of resources from Asia to the US and some European countries. Asians have saved and Asian governments (particularly China) and Asian institutions have lent to finance western consumption. This imbalance was documented by Charles Dumas and Diana Choylesa whose 2006 book *The Bill from the China Shop* was subtitled "How Asia's saving glut threatens the world economy".[454] In the last two decades capital has been transferred from less developed countries to the most developed countries (as countries such as China buy American debt). In the future, if the debts are repaid, capital will drain away from developed countries. Investors, seeing the poor performance of the developed markets weighed down by debt, will seek better returns elsewhere. Globalisation in terms of free trade in goods and capital increases economic activity but can create damaging imbalances.

The sale of securitised sub-prime "assets" by financial institutions in the US to banks in Europe, who were very distant from the original borrowers, was made possible because of globalised financial institutions. Globalisation has magnified the imperfections of the free market and allowed local mistakes to be exported so as to contaminate institutions on a worldwide scale. Given the imperfection of human nature, thicker hedges of national jurisdiction are required to provide a protection against such infection.

Globalisation of the ownership of companies has weakened the ability of governments to retain the commercial benefits from, and to tax, the companies operating in their jurisdictions. The Dutch takeover of ICI resulted in several UK factories being closed. Intellectual property can leave the jurisdiction. Before the takeover of Boots, the group paid £89 million in UK tax in its final year as a quoted company on The London Stock Exchange. It now pays only £9 million, since it is based in Zug, Switzerland.[455]

19.5 TRANSNATIONAL ORGANISATIONS

Responding to the global challenges and to the difficulty of controlling companies that operate on a global scale, some people would promote transnational legislation, even world government, as the only solution. While international cooperation in the form of treaties can be the best way of addressing individual issues, there is a danger in the transfer of power to transnational organisations. This is undesirable for the reasons discussed earlier in relation to limited government and accountability. Transnational government is not wrong because it produces the wrong result, though many would argue that this is the effect in particular cases. It is dangerous because it loosens, and in some cases destroys, the accountability structures between the governed and the governing. This is one of the principal arguments against the European Union.

Resistance to ecclesiastical transnational jurisdiction has long been a theme in Protestant discourse. In relation to transnational institutions, the answer to the question of accountability: "*Quis custodiet ipsos custodes?*" may (in human terms) be no one. Some transnational legislation is promoted by the transnational organisations themselves. These organisations have no democratic basis because they are incapable of responding to an electorate that has the necessary cohesion and common identity. And they can also provide a framework for secretive associations of people seeking to influence democratically elected political leaders.

Once obligations, even treaty obligations, have been entered into, they cannot easily be repudiated even if the circumstances have changed. The UN Convention on Refugees and Asylum, though worthy in its aims in requiring States to offer asylum, was (as Roger Scruton has pointed out) entered into before the era of mass global mobility on economic grounds. A loss of control of the UK over its borders, and over those who form the people who will operate its democracy, is capable of changing the basis of that democracy if those permitted to enter the country do not share its underlying values. Some may approve this, but the mechanism of an international institution, rather than democratic consent, to achieve change infringes the freedom of people to make choices.

A permanent transfer of the powers of a national government to unelected and unaccountable institutions, which may have institutional agendas different to those of the country ceding the powers, prevents the free choice of legislation. Where this also results in the transfer of assets (which, some would say, is the effect of the European Union common fisheries laws) or in the compulsory payment of taxes to transnational institutions, this freedom can be seriously impaired. If transnational cooperation is required on particular issues, this should be achieved through sovereign states acting in a manner which reflects the interests of their people. Governments may need to cooperate on particular issues, but this can be done without a transfer of power to transnational institutions.

Currency unions without an integrated economy and political union which enables the transfer of funds from the richer parts of the union to the poorer ones, leads to imbalances which have been seen in the Eurozone with serious effects. Italy lost 30 to 40 per cent of labour competitiveness in the 1990s which turned its trade surplus into a structural trade deficit. It cannot remedy this by devaluation of its currency. Wages cannot decline by the degree necessary to make Italy competitive and so unemployment, particularly youth unemployment (at 36 per cent in 2012), has risen. This is occurring despite fiscal rectitude not achieved in the UK. Italy has had a positive government balance for some years.

Governments also need to be cautious about even the temporary transfer of authority to overseas institutions. The inability of the UK government to overrule the judgments of the European Court of Human Rights (the European Court) was highlighted by Lord Mackay, a former Lord Chancellor, in relation to the issue of voting rights for prisoners. He was right in saying that the UK government should obey the law, but it is not clear that rulings of the European Court bind the English Courts since this precedence was only stated by the European Court in 2005 and was not in the Convention. The Prime Minister said that votes for prisoners made him feel physically sick, although some might say that there are better candidates for such a reaction. There is no right in the European Convention for prisoners to vote. The right was invented by judges over whom the UK has no control. Similar concerns arise in the case of a decision by the European Court that dangerous prisoners given indeterminate sentences in the UK may be entitled to claim compensation for a breach of human rights.[456] Foreign offenders have escaped deportation from the UK on the grounds of their "right to a family life", it being assumed that this takes precedence over the right of the State to remove a foreign person who is guilty of a violent crime. If the UK and other European countries are bound by the decisions of the European Court this, by interpreting the European Convention on Human Rights, creates new law. The decisions of the European Court cannot be changed by Parliament, or by any other European country, even if acting together, and the judges of the European Court cannot be removed by governments or a democratic institution.

19.6 GLOBAL COOPERATION

The challenges facing the world in the current financial crisis have been exacerbated by globalisation and transnational institutions, such as the common currency in the Eurozone. The single currency enabled borrowing and over-consumption by uncompetitive economies. There have been imbalances between the economies running surpluses and those running deficits in trade and in government balance sheets. There were unsustainable booms in property and construction resulting in over capacity in the less competitive countries. These countries suffered a higher rate of inflation than other countries in the Eurozone and became uncompetitive. They did not have the ability to devalue a national currency to regain competitiveness. Commentators, historians and public figures warned that a single currency was unsustainable without a fiscal or political union which, if it were achieved, would be undemocratic.

International cooperation must be based upon honesty. This was not the case in relation to the European Union Lisbon Treaty signed in 2007. This replaced the proposed 2004 constitution which was not likely to achieve the necessary consent of member states in referenda. A number of European politicians spoke of the need for the treaty to be unreadable so that it would not be understood. Valery Giscard D'Estaing said that: "Public opinion will be led to adopt, without knowing it, proposals that we dare not present to them directly."[457]

Cooperation between independent countries underpinned by democratic institutions is clearly necessary. International treaties are necessary for a wide range of issues where the actions of one country can affect those of another. These include the international laws in relation to the sea and the air and to issues relating to the environment and trade. In trade, for instance, countries acting by themselves in what they perceive to be their best interests can easily turn to "beggar my neighbour" policies, such as excessive protectionism. Free trade (at least between developed countries) is generally beneficial and works when it is mutual, and this is most easily achieved by international agreement. But the cooperation which is necessary in international affairs can be achieved without the permanent transfer of power to international institutions. Lack of consent by a population to the exercise of power by international institutions can lead to unrest, as seen in Greece and Spain during 2012. Particularly in troubled times, countries need to ensure that their actions retain the legitimacy which accompanies the democratic institutions of a nation state.

20
THE ENVIRONMENT

20.1 THE CREATOR AND THE CREATION

Christian teaching on the environment has much in common with the spirit of the age, although the foundation is different. For the Christian, the earth and all the creatures in it have been given by God (Psalm 24:1-2). Mankind has been given both the duty and the ability to look after it and all the animals that inhabit it and enjoy it. Mankind is given "dominion" over the earth (Genesis 1:28 and Psalm 8:6) but the duties to God, to our neighbour and to following generations mean that we should exercise this wisely.

There is a relationship between all animals and human beings because they were made by the same creator from the same raw materials. The created order was pronounced by God to be "good" before the arrival of man and so it has a value independent of human needs and desires. After the destruction of Noah's flood, God promised to preserve the environment so that all living creatures could "be fruitful and multiply" (Genesis 9:7 NKJV). God himself through Christ chose to live as a human being upon earth, and the existence of the material world reveals that there is a Creator who sustains it. Psalm 18 says that the creation praises the Lord. The Apostle Paul reflected: "For since the creation of the world God's invisible qualities — his eternal power and divine nature — have been clearly seen, being understood from what has been made…" (Romans 1:20 NIV). In preserving nature, we are therefore honouring God and reflecting his character of love for what he has made. Albert Schweitzer put it like this: "The ethic of reverence for life is the ethic of love widened into universality."[458]

There is, nevertheless, much in the natural order which Christians may struggle to understand. The processes of nature can seem brutal and arbitrary. Nature is indeed "red in tooth and claw" and the forces of nature can wreak terrible destruction. Christians differ in the extent to which they are able to attribute all the suffering in the world to the dislocation brought into the world by the disobedience of the first man or of mankind in general. And some people have difficulty in believing in a loving God in the light of human suffering. Nevertheless for Christians, despite that suffering, the intervention of God in human lives as recorded in the Bible and the possibility of rescue from the effects of our wrongdoing through the death and resurrection of Jesus Christ show God's love for humankind.

20.2   CARE FOR THE ENVIRONMENT

God's covenant with Abraham was to him "and [his]... descendants forever" (Genesis 13:15 NKJV). Christians do not know when Jesus will return and, in the meantime, future generations will be living on the earth. The physical environment affects people. Industrial and agricultural land development can contribute to resource depletion, pollution, waste, species reduction and extinction, deforestation, erosion and economic misdistribution, which affect the wellbeing of millions.

Markets and prices do not reflect the long-term costs and loss of benefits associated with the environment and do not allocate resources to protect the environment. If human beings were to attribute the correct value to the environment in all their dealings, then there would be less need for intervention by governments. The duty to care for the environment and its animals is part of a larger range of duties to live responsibly in a way that reflects God's wider purposes. Human beings, but also animals — intentionally created by God — have a purpose to their existence and a reason to flourish. In evaluating whether the destruction of a particular environmental habitat or creature is justified, a balance needs to be struck between the competing requirements, based not upon the operation of the market, but upon what it means for the world and the creatures in it to function within the framework of the purposes for which they were created.

There can be a tendency to utilitarianism which seeks to justify care for the environment on the grounds that it benefits people. Environmental projects are justified on the grounds that they have proven benefits in these terms. Though it is helpful to explain the interconnectedness of ecological systems and that their preservation can benefit human beings, for Christians this is an incomplete analysis. The Christian approach is to recognise that the created world exists as a reflection of the grandeur of God and that it has a value in itself irrespective of any calculations as to its value for human beings. In any event, the benefits to human beings of a particular policy may be impossible to evaluate because we cannot predict the exact effects of particular measures. Christian thinking recognises that human beings may not always be able to determine for themselves what will benefit them. It also recognises the complexity of creation which in some respects may be unfathomable. Thus it is right to preserve a species even if scientists have determined that in human terms it serves no purpose.

20.3 FLAWED MARKET SYSTEMS

Humankind and human structures are imperfect. The operation of market systems, and the self-interest and self-preservation that are an integral part of them, result in companies and individuals ignoring environmental issues. So it is necessary for charities and governments to take active steps to protect the environment. As a result of our lack of knowledge, understanding and foresight, we may take wrong measures at the wrong time and some measures might even be counterproductive. This is inevitable — in environmental policies there will be flawed judgements and people with their own agendas can confuse the issues. Some individuals and organisations, both charities and commercial companies, have personal or economic interests in environmental protection and in presenting a particular picture of reality. But these interests should not cloud the principle that human beings have a God given duty to care for the environment and that the operation of free markets requires some intervention, however imperfect this might be.

20.4 THE DESTRUCTION OF THE ENVIRONMENT AND PROTECTING HABITATS

It is difficult to avoid the conclusion that the environment continues to be destroyed and degraded in order to enhance the profitability of companies and to enrich people beyond the limits necessary for them to lead flourishing lives. Reflecting upon the paradise of nature encountered by the American settlers when they arrived in the seventeenth century, we can ask ourselves whether the wholesale destruction of the North American environment was necessary for survival or flourishing of the human beings or whether it was the result of human greed. The American historian, Henry Steele Commager, describes the devastation: "from Maine to Oregon he [the settler] left forests in ruins; instead of cultivating, he mined the soil; he killed off bison and pigeon, polluted streams, wasted coal, oil and gas. His habits of waste he transmitted to a generation that could no longer afford them."[459] The destruction of the rain forests (although the rate of destruction is now being reduced) and the likely virtual extinction of a large number of species indicate that humankind has got the balance wrong. A report by Paven Sukhdev, head of the UN's investigation into how to stop the destruction of the natural world, estimates that the global destruction of forests costs US$ 2 to 5 trillion a year.

Most development damages the environment to some extent, but habitats and species should be protected wherever possible.

Christian charities like A Rocha, active in nature reserves in many countries, preserve habitat and species and are seeking to care for God's creation. Where rises in CO_2 or changes in ocean temperature (whatever their relationship to climate change) are proven to degrade habitat, for instance the degradation of ocean reefs, then measures need to be taken to safeguard them. Pollution and contamination are clearly not in God's plan, though there have been some improvements in recent times. For instance, pollution in London is said to be now at its lowest since about the year 1600 and the Ford Anglia car of the 1960s produced two hundred times the pollutants of a modern Ford Fiesta.

20.5 OVER-CONSUMPTION AND SUSTAINABLE DEVELOPMENT

The issues surrounding sustainable development reflect concerns arising from the Christian principle of the stewardship of resources. The earth's resources are not infinite. Although Christianity teaches that, following the second coming of Jesus Christ, there will be a new created order, Christians do not know when this will be. In the meantime, we have a duty to care for the existing creation. Human activity has the capacity to destroy ecosystems on a small and a large scale, and this highlights the interdependency of people and their activities across the planet. Over-consumption, particularly by Western countries, represents what some would call the theft of resources by the rich from the poor.

In his book *Consumptionomics*, Chandran Nair sets out the dangers of Western individualism as applied to our care of the environment.[460] Here he echoes Christian thinkers such as Abraham Kuyper, who reminds us that human rights to property (which must include natural resources) are not absolute. God's word tells us that "...absolute property belongs only to God; all of our property is on loan from him; our management is only stewardship...."[461] This has consequences for the extraction of water and natural resources. Chandran Nair cites forecasts that demand for food, water, energy, transport and healthcare will double or treble by 2050. Older readers may remember the films *Jean de Florette* and *Manon des Sources*, in which a dispute over water rights caused tragedy and bitter division down the generations. This type of conflict is echoed in the competition between landowners, regions and countries for the extraction of water from aquifers, many of which, such as those in the Mid West of the United States and the Middle East (Jordan and Saudi Arabia) are old sources of water that are not being renewed. Chandran Nair has stated that some three quarters of the world's ocean fisheries have either been fished out or are being fished beyond their capacity to regenerate. His argument is that the right to extract natural resources must be subject to regulation that can (no doubt imperfectly) construct a price beyond that of abstraction and that reflects the value of resources lost to future generations, as well as the collateral damage to communities and to the environment. The approach is utilitarian and this may not reflect fully the value of ecological systems. Nevertheless, in a world where transactions are valued by markets, it is sensible to ascribe a more realistic value to the resources consumed. Chandran Nair puts it in three principles:

1. Resources are constrained: economic activity must be subservient to maintaining the vitality of resources.
2. Resource use must be equitable for current and future generations: collective welfare must take priority over individual rights.
3. Resources must be re-priced and productivity efforts should be focussed on reducing use of resources and not of people.[462] (The current theory of labour productivity needs to be replaced with an emphasis on using fewer resources, while employing more people.)

20.6   CLIMATE CHANGE

The debate over climate change, its causes and likely effects can evoke strongly held views. There is a danger that opinions can become entrenched as both the current orthodoxy and opposing opinions are dismissed without adequate examination. Some of what follows is conjecture or matters for further investigation and discussion. It is important that issues which are open to argument are debated. This book is written without specialist scientific knowledge and it is not intended to suggest with any degree of certainty that one view is right and another wrong. The arguments that climate change is man made are well rehearsed and are not repeated here. The contrary suggestions are included in this chapter to stimulate debate among those who are better informed.

It appears that, at least until recently, there has been some long-term climate change. Average global land temperatures have risen by about one degree since the 1950s. Parts of the world are suffering droughts and others floods to a greater extent than in the past. July Arctic ice from 1979 to 2012 has declined at a rate of 7.1% per decade. On the other hand, forecasters at the Meteorological Office have predicted that by 2017 global average temperatures will not have changed significantly for twenty years. They will remain .28C to .59C above the long term average (from 1971-2000), an average change of .43C, only slightly higher than the .40C rise recorded in 1998. The year 2012 was cooler than the average for the last decade.

The principal questions are (i) whether climate change has been caused by increases in CO_2, and (ii) if it has been, whether the increases in CO_2 are man made or are the result of other processes.

Those who have concluded that climate change is man made need to base their conclusions upon predictions. These predictions are based upon assumptions as to the past. Some people are sceptical about our knowledge of the distant past and assumptions about its uniformity with today. Some Christians might view extreme confidence about the accuracy of future predictions as trespassing upon the unknowable providence of God.

Climate change has occurred in the past. In Britain the Roman warm period was probably warmer than today. Tacitus records that vineyards were planted by the Romans in Britain. The medieval warm period may have had temperatures similar to those of the late 20th century warm period, and thirty-eight vineyards can be identified in the 11th century Domesday Book. The historian monk Bede writing in about 730AD records that there were "no lack of vines" in Ireland.

While it is essential to protect the environment and preserve habitat and species, and the existence of some climate change has not been doubted, some people doubt that a rise in CO_2 has caused climate change or that the rise in CO_2 has been caused by human activity. Lord Turnbull (the Permanent Secretary to the Department of the Environment, to the Treasury and Cabinet Secretary during the years 1994 to 2005) takes the view that there is no scientific consensus on the relationship between CO_2 emissions and a rise in temperatures and that many scientists argue that other variables, such as the sun, cosmic rays, oceans and clouds have been underplayed. As he says, CO_2 concentrations in the atmosphere have risen steadily since about 1940, but the rise in temperature started in the 1880s.

Professor R. M. Carter of James Cook University cites research that indicates that, if there were a connection between CO_2 and warming, the increase from 280ppm in pre-industrial times to 380ppm today should already have produced 75 per cent of the theoretical warming which would be caused by a doubling to 560ppm.[463] He refers to research about extensive glaciation which occurred between 444 and 353 million years ago when atmospheric carbon dioxide was up to 17 times what it is today. He argues that the current rise in CO_2 may be more due to the medieval warm period than to modern industrial output. While there may be some correlation between rising temperatures and increases in CO_2, that correlation is not conclusive of cause and effect. Carter suggests that research in relation to ice cores indicates that there is a delay of some eight hundred years in the rise of CO_2 after a rise in temperature. If this is correct, the current rise in CO_2 has been caused by rising temperatures, and not the reverse.

Complications inevitably attend the creation and use of climate modelling, particularly in relation to increases in CO_2 in the atmosphere and its effects. There is only one earth and so we cannot do control experiments. Our knowledge is incomplete and, even if we had all the relevant knowledge, we do not have the computing know how and capacity to run the necessary models. Each model uses equations that seek to describe the effect of given phenomena and then they have to be applied together on parts and then the whole of the earth. Reliable models can only use data from about 1860 because it represents pre-industrial conditions, and temperature measurements exist from that time. Feedback, both positive and negative, is difficult to take account of. For instance, desertification feeds plankton in the ocean. This takes up carbon dioxide from the atmosphere and also emits dimethyl sulphate, which helps in turn to create more reflective clouds, thus cooling the atmosphere. These processes are now being incorporated in the most sophisticated models but their findings are not yet included in the IPCC reports (this is expected by 2014).

There can be a tendency to exaggerate or misuse evidence. Sir John Beddington, the government's scientific adviser, in a report entitled *International Dimensions of Climate Change*, has indicated that the government should use natural disasters to advance carbon reduction programmes, though the Meteorological Office takes the view that individual events cannot be connected with climate change.

It is possible that climate change is irreversible by human effort, and this could suggest the powerlessness of human beings in the face of natural forces. In the past, a sense of the limitations of human effort could evoke a dependence upon God. The challenges of climate change are serious and some humility may be overdue.

20.7 THE COSTS OF CARBON REDUCTION

Governments need to facilitate a balanced debate about the costs of the measures planned to reduce carbon emissions. It has been calculated that if some thirty per cent of the UK electricity were renewable in 2020, this would require an annual subsidy of £6 billion or more on the basis of a subsidy of five pence per unit. The Renewable Energy Foundation shows that 7,000 turbines are to be built onshore by 2020 and estimates that the total subsidy paid on all renewable energy by 2030 will be £130bn.[464] The operators of the larger schemes and beneficiaries of the subsidies appear to be predominantly overseas companies. The UK government has said that the renewables industry will create jobs. This may be correct, but the additional jobs could be more than offset by the negative effects of increased costs in other areas as a result of higher energy payments. The additional costs could make businesses uneconomic and increase unemployment.

Potential gas supplies particularly from shale, where the US is a net exporter, have proved greater than expected. The costs of gas, even when carbon capture is taken into account, may make it a more attractive option than renewable resources, though it is not yet clear how economic extraction will be. The volumes of shale gas in the UK could be significant, though there may be environmental difficulties associated with its extraction. The find near Blackpool is of approximately 200 trillion cubic feet. Even the celebrated environmentalist James Lovelock now believes that shale gas should be used while better solutions than the current inefficient renewable programmes are found.[465] As of December 2012, the government has given shale gas a high priority in its energy policy.

Wind farms affect the visual environment (which can include heritage sites), create noise and destroy habitat for wildlife. Matt Ridley reminds us that they also require an element called neodymium whose production leaves toxic radioactive tailings and that the structures may only work for 25 years.[466] The cost of the power generated by wind farms is up to three times that of gas fired stations and nine times where the wind farm is offshore. Wind farms can only operate intermittently and the necessary back-up power facilities are wasteful of fuel and inefficiently used.

The production of power from biomass can potentially take land that would otherwise be used for food out of production. It can even result in wood being harvested from unsustainable sources in developing countries to be used in power plants, while coal and gas deposits are left in the ground. Waste to energy projects (the incineration of household waste to produce heat and power) enhance the environment by reducing the need for landfill, though the emissions need to be carefully dealt with. And nuclear power presents safety and other long-term challenges, involving the disposal of radioactive waste with a half-life of generations.

There are no easy answers to the issues of energy generation. Responsible governments may need to make difficult choices, since no mix of solutions is entirely satisfactory. There is a concern that decisions may be taken for reasons of ideology. There needs to be a full assessment of the effect of policies on the environment. The costs of their implementation and the impact of the increased costs on consumers and industry (which may be less competitive as a result) need to be understood. The lack of an obvious optimum solution to the challenges of energy should not come as a surprise in the imperfect world in which we live.

20.8   ONLY LIFE TENANTS

Whatever view is taken about climate change and energy policy, we all have a duty to care for the environment. Professor Stephen Hopper, the former director of the Royal Botanic Gardens, has said that a fifth of the earth's plant species are in danger of extinction. He said: "We're at a crossroads. We have half the wild vegetation on the planet that was around 200-300 years ago."[467] He emphasised the need for governments and people to act: "It's really important for us to decide, as a global community, do we want to care for what remains and get into the business of repairing and restoring diversity? Or will we continue on the path of ever more incursions into wild places?"

A Christian perspective on conservation can bring hope that the earth can be renewed, together with confidence that those who contribute to conserving the natural environment are working with the grain of God's purposes for his created order. As Dr Simon Stuart, a scientist with the International Union for the Conservation of Nature (IUCN), has put it: "Christian theology can provide the conservation movement not only with the basis for much needed hope, but it can provide the promise of the presence of the Creator God working with us in our seemingly weak and inadequate conservation efforts."[468]

Not everyone will acknowledge that the earth is God's earth, but we know that it certainly does not belong to us, since none of us are here for long. We are tenants of our space on earth, passing through for a brief time, and we owe it to succeeding generations, if not to our creator, to preserve and hand on what we have been given.

21
INTERNATIONAL DEVELOPMENT AND AID

21.1   THE CHALLENGES OF AID

Charity is a Christian duty.   It is part of the injunction to act justly, love mercy and walk humbly with God (Micah 6:8).   International aid organised by individuals or charities can be regarded as an expression of this duty.   Aid provided by governments can be regarded as an extension of charitable activity and can be guided by the same principles.   Christian principles require the good stewardship of resources.   Individual donors and taxpayers should require that the funds they provide for international aid are used effectively.

Government aid can often become entwined with other government aims, such as trade or diplomatic purposes. Developing countries can be persuaded to purchase plant or capital equipment on concessionary terms which can then be accounted for as aid.   Large scale government planned development can endanger human rights.   Britain is Ethiopia's largest bilateral donor and plans to give £1.3 billion between 2010 and 2015.   However, the current programme in Ethiopia to move families from fertile agricultural land to "villages" without adequate facilities is reminiscent of the forced collectivisation of farms in the Soviet Union between the World Wars. Human Rights Watch found "widespread human rights violations, including forced displacement, arbitrary arrest and detention, beatings, rape and sexual violence."[469]

There are concerns about the effectiveness of international aid.   Ian Birrell has provided a critique of aid policy: "The sums spent on aid over the years are astronomical.   Haiti, for example, was given official assistance in today's sums of more than £6bn in the 50 years before that terrible earthquake last year — four times as much per capita as Europeans received under the post-war Marshall Plan. Additional cash came in private donations, with more charities working on the ground per head than any other place on earth.... For all the noble intentions, the torrent of Western aid all too often erodes rather than builds civil society. It encourages corruption, fosters dependency, undermines innovation, reduces local investment and even boosts military spending.... A report from Harvard Medical School found that when health-related aid was given to governments in sub-Saharan Africa they often reduced spending on health. Politicians let aid pay for schools and hospitals, allowing them to steal money or spend it on security. Then they win elections using bribery or violence rather than by providing decent public services and being accountable to voters."[470] Billions of dollars have been spent on aid to Kenya, yet its infrastructure has not improved. By contrast, Somaliland has been able to institute good governance without dependency on aid.

Some aid is stolen. A US government report found that insiders at a Kabul bank had stolen $1 billion from foreign donors, including the UK. It is estimated that up to 80% of the value of food aid given to Afghanistan is spent on "entrance fees" to local warlords.

21.2 THE PROBLEM OF WEAK STATES

Francis Fukuyama has analysed the problem of weak states and the courses open to western aid donors. Local institutions tend to be corrupt, but taking over their tasks can weaken them further.[471] He takes AIDS treatment as an example: "Working through the local government inevitably means that fewer AIDS victims will be treated. The public health infrastructure may be non-existent, incompetent, or highly corrupt; medicines will be stolen, records will not be kept and donor funds will end up in the hands of bureaucrats rather than going to the patients they are meant to serve. Taking over these functions directly, by contrast, means a far more efficient delivery of healthcare services. But when the external aid agency bypasses the local government, the local government's function is less one of service provision than of liaison and coordination with the foreign donor. This will never be sustainable, can degrade local capacity and increase dependence."[472]

The challenge is to build structures and institutions of good governance in developing countries which are efficient, responsive and not corrupt. Surveying the development of government in the history of the UK, some have said that this will inevitably take a long time, even centuries, to achieve. This is an incorrect parallel. There is no reason to suppose that the government of, say, Alfred the Great in Anglo Saxon times was uneducated, corrupt or inefficient or that it failed to respond to the needs of its people. The foundation of good governance is a moral code which is understood and adhered to by those in government. Education is essential. Principles of accountable, democratic government such as the separation of powers and free and fair elections, and the institutions that embody them, can be encouraged as a condition of aid. Western governments providing aid should praise examples of good governance and draw attention to where this is lacking. Oversensitivity to cultural differences can be misplaced. There are differences between countries and regions in tradition and cultural norms. These differences must be understood and respected where appropriate but, in relation to ethical issues, what is right is right everywhere.

21.3 SUSTAINABLE DEVELOPMENT AND BUILDING CAPACITY

The aim of aid should be sustainable development that enables the country to develop without permanent dependency upon aid. There are several ingredients to sustainable development and their interrelationship is complex.

A vital factor is the ability of people to build sustainable livelihoods. To achieve this in sub-Saharan Africa, agriculture is essential. Projects that provide irrigation and resources, as well as training, for local agriculture projects can make an important contribution. The way in which deserts in Israel have been transformed into productive agricultural land since the establishment of the state of Israel is an example of what can be achieved. Surpluses from agricultural production can raise living standards and enable economic growth. There is still much that can be done to enable people to be self-sustaining. Charities like Send a Cow can provide the resources and training necessary for people to become self-sufficient. Once this is achieved, people can make choices about education and can pay for other essential services.

Education is important, both for the quality of lives and for further economic development. A cadre of educated people is necessary for good governance and to provide the entrepreneurial skills required for economic development. Once a family has surplus income, it can pay for education. Some would see payment for education as providing the discipline necessary for education to be useful. There is a role for aid to help developing countries provide education, particularly basic numeracy and literacy skills. Education can encourage the educated to seek jobs abroad. Scholarships for students to study specific skills could be given on the basis of loans to them which could be written down for each year worked in the developing country, thus diminishing the drain of talent to developed countries.

Economic development is necessary for employment to be created. Building up local capacity in technical, financial and commercial skills is essential. Economic development beyond agricultural self-sufficiency also requires infrastructure — transport and utilities — as well as capital and entrepreneurial endeavour. Basic infrastructure, such as clean water and sanitation, was provided by public authorities in the development of Western countries in the 19th century. Where a developing country does not have the resources to provide this infrastructure, aid can be used to do so.

Other requirements for aid may include healthcare. Natural and other disasters require swift and efficient emergency relief. But aid projects should, wherever practicable, lead to self-sufficiency and not dependency. Some temporary camps set up after natural disasters remain for many years after the event that prompted them. Charities that encourage and facilitate small-scale affordable finance and credit unions enable individuals and local communities to take responsibility for developing local resources, though some micro-finance initiatives have been criticised for charging high interest rates or trapping people in debt.

Good governance is essential to underpin sustainable development. The rule of law provides individual justice and also permits confidence in economic transactions. Contracts should be entered into fairly and freely. Effective remedies for the innocent party must be available in the courts when contracts are breached. Corruption in public administration and the courts is morally wrong. It also causes the misallocation of resources and increases the cost of transactions. (This is the reverse effect of what R. H. Coase saw as the purpose of law from the point of view of the economist — the reduction in the costs of transactions.) Aid must not contribute to corruption, and incentives may need to be given for countries to operate the objective rule of law. The practice of Christian principles of government can contribute to the achievement of this objective.

21.4   PUBLIC PRIVATE PARTNERSHIPS

The World Bank has promoted models for public-private partnerships (PPP) in the developing world for the larger infrastructure projects that are required for sustainable economic development. Taking the water sector as an example, few waste or drinking water projects have been undertaken in the less developed countries, for instance in Sub-Saharan Africa. This is because these PPP models involve private finance, typically equity or sub-debt and senior bank lending. This funding requires political, legal and economic stability to reassure investors that they will receive a return on their investment and convince lenders that they will be repaid. The requirement for private finance in these PPP models, and the perception by funders of risks in the projects (which could stop the debt repayment or equity return), results in investors seeking high project rates of return on their investment. Some equity funders require in the region of a twenty per cent or more per annum return. The projects may be unaffordable because the returns that investors require make the projects uneconomic for the host country. Debt funders look for interest rates above the rates prevailing for projects in the developed world. Lower interest rates may be obtained in some cases where export credit agencies are involved, but the politics and the economics of the potential projects can still make them impracticable because they are perceived to be too risky. The PPP model may have been promoted partly for ideological reasons, despite the fact that it has not been capable of delivering many of the projects that are needed.

21.5   ALTERNATIVE MODELS

Alternative models for major infrastructure development are required. For example, there may be some types of projects that, once completed, can be gifted to the countries concerned without creating a long-term debt dependency. These are projects that in colonial times would have been undertaken by government, but which developing countries are now unable to afford or do not yet have the local capacity to organise. New infrastructure could be provided by way of grant from donor nations. There could be a procurement following international standards, under which a combined construction and operation and maintenance contract would be awarded. Funding by 'soft' loans (loans on concessionary terms), rather than a grant, might be appropriate in some cases. An element of loan might be helpful to reinforce the commitment of the host country to the project. But it would be important that any repayments of interest and capital are viable.

During the operation and maintenance phase of the contract (say, two or three years after project completion) local capacity to operate the facilities could be built up. The facilities would then be handed over to the host government at the end of that period. The handover would not take place until the relevant local governmental authority had satisfied the aid donors that it was going to have the technical skills and procedures required to operate the facilities, and that the undertaking would be free from corruption. There could be a requirement that a certain proportion of the materials and services required for construction and operation must be procured in the country of the project and that training be provided by the contractor so as to enhance the local economy and operational capacity.

The upgrading of existing infrastructure presents additional challenges to those involved in new infrastructure, since the state of the existing infrastructure may be uncertain until works are undertaken. But the same principles could be applied on the basis that the operation and maintenance part of the contract would apply to the existing infrastructure as well as any new infrastructure. In each case the assets would be publicly owned and maintained. The donors could assist in building up the capacity of the relevant public ministries to achieve this.

In these types of scheme there needs to be local buy-in. The communities in which the projects operate need to benefit from them, for instance by opportunities for employment. Local support should help to protect the assets, but projects can be damaged by individuals for short term gain. There are reports of pipework being stolen from water projects and sold, so effective security and law enforcement is necessary. It is also possible that individuals in the governments of certain countries would object to these types of scheme on the grounds that they would not give the scope for their personal gain that other models of government aid afford. However, if this were the only type of aid on offer, it may be hard to resist.

21.6   AID PARTNERSHIPS

An effective means of delivering aid for the smaller infrastructure schemes and for a wide range of other projects is for aid to be delivered by way of grants to charities undertaking projects in partnership with local organisations, such as local churches. This can achieve local 'ownership' of projects. Peter Grant, writing when he was International Director of Tearfund, a Christian development charity, has highlighted the vital role that can be played by local churches, as well as looking at the role of governments, international organisations and corporations, and the responsibility of individuals to be personally involved in relationships and projects. He observed that in many African countries, the church provides between forty and sixty per cent of the basic education and healthcare. Importantly, the recipients of help, for instance of AIDS treatment, receive personal care and compassion. He has pointed out that there are many villages in Africa where the church is the only local institution committed to remaining in the community after the international donors have gone.[473] In many countries churches represent the only widespread network capable of meeting welfare needs. But churches or local organisations may not always be the most effective partners for larger projects and each project needs to be looked at on a case by case basis.

An example of a charity working with local organisations is The Lawyers' Christian Fellowship CLEAR project, which works in partnership with local Christian lawyers' organisations in a number of African countries to deliver free legal representation and education about legal rights to the many who are too poor to afford legal representation. Some one hundred thousand people are helped in a single year.

Where government funded aid is delivered through a charity working with a local organisation, the choice of charity or scheme could be made by the donor government, but the charity would be solely responsible for the carrying out of the project. This should reduce the scope for government interference and corruption in the country in which the aid is being delivered. One possibility would be for additional gift aid tax relief to be given to those donating to charities on a government approved list so that the aid can be directed towards the countries in the Government's aid plan. In these cases, the gift aid tax relief currently shared between the donor and the charity could be given entirely to the donor, thus increasing the incentive to give.

There is a rationale for limiting the amount of giving which should qualify for tax relief, since the duty of citizens is to pay for the activities of the State as well as to support the charities that they select themselves. A suitable balance should be struck. This could be done, not by limiting the absolute amount that can qualify for tax relief, but by restricting this amount to a proportion, perhaps half or two thirds, of a person's income, however large the sum.

A concern with the delivery of aid through charities is that charities might spend increasing resources in publicity to obtain donations. Some charities already spend a disproportionate amount of their funds on administration, publicity and what they call "advocacy", which is raising awareness of the issues they are addressing and which also promotes the charity for fundraising purposes. This could to some extent be restricted by law (although this might be difficult to enforce in practice) or it could be regulated by requiring charities to advertise exactly on what they spend their money.

21.7   UNFAIR TRADE

In his book *Bad Samaritans* Ha-Joon Chang sets out the case that countries that are in the process of development, benefit from a degree of protection in order to establish their industries.[474] This applies to the countries of Western Europe and North America when they were developing their industries as well as to the recently developed countries of Asia and to the developing countries of Africa. It is in the economic interests of developed countries that the less developed countries remain as primary producers of food and raw materials. Free trade policies serve to preserve these roles, making development into more sophisticated activities difficult because initially these are usually uneconomic and a period of protection is required in order to establish them. There is an argument that developing countries need to establish their own protected trade blocs in order to redress this situation and enable their economies to develop.

The World Trade Organisation (WTO) continues to be ineffective in dealing with subsidies which benefit richer nations at the expense of underdeveloped ones. For example, the US benefits from subsidies to its cotton farmers ($3 billion in the 2008-2009 growing season, according to the International Cotton Advisory Committee) which distort the international market and make it difficult for African farmers to obtain a fair price. Despite WTO rulings calling for reform, the US failed to act, though it agreed to subsidise Brazilian farmers after a case brought by Brazil. Fair trade may be a better prescription than aid for the challenges facing developing countries.

Producers in developing countries are at a disadvantage in negotiating with multinational companies. There are a handful of companies negotiating and a very large number of producers selling perishable produce. This puts the buyers in a commanding position. Cooperatives of producers have had limited success and these may need to be organised, as trade unions were in their early years, at a national level, and also at an international level.

The EU and the US 'dump' (sell below fair value) excess produce in developing countries and developing countries need the ability to impose tariffs on these products without infringing international agreements, so as to protect their local producers.

21.8   AUDITING CHARITABLE AID

The motivation of compassion and responsibility which prompts overseas aid is praiseworthy, but the challenge is to help in a sustainable way for the long term without wasting resources, diminishing local responsibility or causing further problems. Aid will always be inefficient to some extent and this should not deter donors. However, there needs to be independent review, auditing and feedback by governments to their taxpayers, and by charities to their donors, on the outcome of their interventions.

Currently donors to charities have little idea of the effectiveness of the money they donate and taxpayers have limited knowledge about the results achieved by government aid.

Appeal literature is often emotive but uninformative about the finances of the charity and their relationship to the delivery of aid. Once money has been received, there is usually little feedback on the effectiveness of the expenditure made. Giving examples in appeal literature about what money *could* be spent on does not ensure that it is actually used for the purpose that is advertised. There is rarely adequate information about how much money is spent on delivering the aid and how much is spent on administration, fund raising and advocacy, though it can be difficult to separate administration from the costs of staff required to deliver the charitable aid. Advocacy of the cause which the charity seeks to represent, which may be justified to an extent, can overlap with fundraising. A charity is reported to have spent £1.1 million on charitable projects in 2010 but £500,000 on staff.[475] Ian Birrell reports that one charity was searching for a new head of communications at £75,000 per annum and that another spent £16,722 taking journalists to India and Nicaragua and said it was equivalent to £161,000 in fundraising.[476] There are concerns about the cost of the personnel involved in government aid. The UK's Department for International Development (DfID) paid almost £500 million to consultants in the year 2011-2012.[477]

Many charities, particularly the smaller ones, provide good value for money. In these charities skilled and dedicated staff work for salaries which are much less than they would receive for the equivalent jobs in the public and private sectors. However, donors need to know that the money they give is being well spent. The information sent to donors should show the income and the use of funds in a way which is helpful to the donors. Some charities already do this. But a more widespread culture of accountability is required on the part of the recipients of aid and government donors.

22
THE FOREIGN POLICY OF STATES

22.1 WHY FOREIGN POLICY IS VERY DIFFICULT

Issues of foreign policy commonly present a collision of facts, assumptions and values which can be hard to disentangle. There are differences between national interests, different world views and beliefs, different perceptions of entitlement to territory based upon history (or interpretations of it) as well as differences of opinion within countries. All of these exist in an unpredictable and imperfect world. It is not difficult to see why both controversy and uncertainty attend so many issues. Attempts to generalise should be undertaken with caution, and an approach to an issue from a particular standpoint may raise as many questions as it seeks to answer.

Human nature is flawed and perceptions of national interest, especially when intertwined with ideological belief, ethnic identity and cultural differences can result in seemingly unbridgeable gulfs of misunderstanding. Mistaken philosophies have been used to justify attempts to impose beliefs by force and there have been countless examples of countries endeavouring to extend their territories or influence by war or military action. The historical causes of the conflicts may be complex, but we can see examples of this in the 20th century in the case of Germany (in two World Wars), Japan (in the Second World War), Russia (in the Cold war) and China (in the Korean War). As we shall discuss in this chapter, the issues of conflict today present significant dangers.

Some conflicts, particularly rival claims to territory, may be impossible to resolve without compromise, because what appear to be the legitimate expectations of each side are irreconcilable. Each party may have to accept that in an imperfect world there might be no perfect justice but that peace can be achieved by each party giving up what it nevertheless believes belongs to it by right.

The relationship between the US and China illustrates the gulfs which can open up between different world views and perceptions of national interest. China cannot understand US support for Taiwan and regards attempts to promote democracy there as an attack upon its sovereignty. It sees itself threatened by a circle of US alliances in the region and by US military bases in nearby countries such as Pakistan, Afghanistan and Kyrgistan. It sees a large US military capability in the Pacific region and the ability of the US to mobilise economic sanctions against China, for instance arising from human rights issues in China or dissatisfaction with the level of the Chinese currency. The US, on the other hand, sees the continuing manipulation of the Chinese currency facilitating huge trade surpluses for China and the decline of US manufacturing. The US resents China's refusal to prevent North Korea acquiring nuclear weapons and Iran's attempts to do so. The US sees the deployment of Chinese cruise missiles as threatening its bases and ships in the Pacific. It is concerned about China's cyber-warfare and anti-satellite weapons and the expansion of its nuclear arsenal. And it is worried by China's disregard of intellectual property rights and its attempts to gain technology transfers from US companies in exchange for access to its markets.

22.2   MORALITY AND IDEALISM

Despite all the challenges in foreign affairs, morality in foreign policy and war is surprisingly resilient, as Christopher Coker has shown in his *War and Ethics in the 21st Century*.[478] These ethics may be based upon a neo Kantian perception of integrity, a perception that we should not as a nation act other than in the way in which we as individuals would like to act, and to be treated by others. Or they may be founded upon Christian beliefs and values. The Western world generally espouses democratic values underpinned by the rule of law. It would be inconsistent to abandon these values when engaged in conflict situations. It is possible to be dismissive about the sincerity of idealism in foreign policy. But an aspiration to selflessness, as much as the enduring condition of imperfection, is a true reflection of what it means to be human.

22.3   IDEALISM AND NATIONAL INTEREST

George W. Bush looked to bring idealism and self-interest together when he outlined the principles of his foreign policy thus: "We are led, by events and common sense, to one conclusion: the survival of liberty in our land increasingly depends on the success of liberty in other lands. The best hope for peace in our world is the expansion of freedom in all the world. America's vital interests and our deepest beliefs are now one. From the day of our founding, we have proclaimed that every man and woman on this earth has rights, and dignity and matchless value because they bear the image of the Maker of heaven and earth. Across the generations, we have proclaimed the imperative of self-government, because no one is fit to be a master and no one deserves to be a slave. Advancing these ideals is the mission that created our nation. It is the honourable achievement of our fathers. Now it is the urgent requirement of our nation's security and the calling of our time. So it is the policy of the United States to seek and support the growth of democratic movements and institutions in every nation and culture, with the ultimate aim of ending tyranny in our world."[479] Although some may have thought him naive, the above quotation underlines the requirement for the foreign policy of a nation to be rooted in its own philosophy and culture and to reflect its national interest, while also responding to the needs of the other countries that it influences.

Zbigniew Brzezinski, reflecting on the preservation of American influence in 2001, underlined the need for moral leadership which reflects the internal character of America: "American global leadership, and especially American authority, is thus bound to become dependent upon what actually transpires in America — on how America responds to a set of tangible and intangible challenges. The response to the tangible challenges will probably be of decisive importance in defining America's relationship to its economically powerful rivals, especially Europe and Japan. The response to the intangible ones will be even more decisively important in shaping America's broader capacity to exercise genuine global authority — that is, to transform its power into leadership that commands moral legitimacy."

From the Christian point of view, foreign policy should encourage in other States, for the best interests of their citizens, ideas and polices which are consistent with Christian thinking, though these have to be applied pragmatically. These include support for the rule of law, freedom of expression and democratic institutions. President Obama summed up the idealistic underpinning of US foreign policy in explaining his decision to intervene in Libya, when he said: "To brush aside America's responsibility as a leader and — more profoundly — our responsibilities to our fellow human beings under such circumstances would have been a betrayal of who we are…. Wherever people long to be free, they will find a friend in the United States."[480]

22.4   APPLYING THE IDEALS IN AN IMPERFECT WORLD

While fundamental ideas may be true for all people for all the time, their application at any particular time to a particular country will depend upon the state of political and cultural development of that country. Even if a policy is appropriate for a country, it should not generally be imposed from the outside, since nations have autonomy that must be respected. Christian teaching on free will indicates that nations should have a measure of autonomy, characterised as national sovereignty. Neither individuals nor peoples should be coerced, however meritorious the intention. The exercise of caution in any proposed intervention reflects Christian teaching on the innate imperfections of individuals and their political projects.

Human imperfection is concentrated and magnified in power structures. Individuals are prone to vanity, pride, selfishness and corruption. Those in political power have the means at their disposal to exercise it unjustly. The Bible recognises that people groups exist each with their particular culture. Separate nations are ordained by God and this disperses power. They also allow differing cultural and linguistic groups to require different responses from their governments.

Brzezinski, writing before 9/11 and the invasion of Iraq and the experiment in Afghanistan, reflected on the challenges of foreign policy in relation to the spreading of democracy: "Democracy may be the West's most important contribution to the world, but it is a vessel that has to be filled with content. The democratic process, the constitution system and the sovereignty of law, are all peerless guarantees for the preservation and enhancement of individual rights and of human potential. But democracy by itself does not provide the answers to the dilemmas of human existence and especially the definition of the good life. That role is played by culture and philosophy, which together generate the values that motivate and shape behaviour." In Iraq the institutions of civil society that should support a democratic State cannot be assumed by the holding of elections. Even "free and fair" elections are only part of good governance and these may be inadequate unless supported by the effective rule of good laws and a wide measure of consent.

For Christians, the truth of God's revealed law is true for all people for all time. The jurist Grotius, writing in the sixteenth and seventeenth centuries, believed that the legal principles derived from Christianity were reflected in an international law. However, these principles cannot easily be grafted on to cultures that have developed with different customs. Montesquieu acknowledged this when he said that "Laws should be so appropriate to the people for whom they are made that it is very unlikely that the laws of one nation can suit another." [481] Idealism as a motive is important, and perhaps even essential, but its outworking must be shaped by pragmatism that engages with the world as it is. Despite the conventions of international law (and its mechanisms of custom, treaties and courts), the governments of nation states, with laws adapted to their particular cultures and peoples, remain the principal source of legitimacy in world affairs. It was the task of national governments to address the initial stages of the banking crisis to prevent insolvency and a run on the banks, though international institutions such as the International Monetary Fund (IMF) had a later part to play.

In Christian thinking, any actions in the international sphere should also be shaped by an understanding of a divine order. Grotius rejected the idea of a universe the fundamental framework of which was a series of contracts or agreements. As Oliver O'Donovan puts it, Grotius saw instead a "universe in which the primal government of God has generated a range of governmental forms, from purely moral authority at one extreme to political structure at the other."[482] Once the idea of God is rejected, contract and power, rather than inherent human duties and rights, can become the dominant way of thinking. This is particularly dangerous in the international sphere since it leads to the subjugation of the weakest by the strongest without restraint.

22.5   IDEALISM AND *REAL POLITIK*

It might seem that there is only a stark choice between an amoral "*Real Politik*" on the one hand and idealistic naivety on the other. But ethical values need to be applied in the world as it exists, not as we would like it to be. Those responsible for foreign policy must be aware of the contexts in which they are acting and a robust scepticism about schemes of human perfection is necessary. Foreign policy involves engaging with the objects of diplomacy in a way which indicates an understanding of the beliefs and world view driving them. But what is true is true everywhere, what is right is right everywhere, even if freedom of choice must be respected and the scope for action is limited.

Realism about the motives of others is necessary. Some Western diplomats may not have appreciated early enough the uncompromising mission behind Iranian foreign policy

— its religious reasons for requiring the destruction of Israel — and that dissembling to achieve that aim may be regarded as a diplomatic necessity and justifiable under the Sharia Law doctrine of *takiyya* (allowable covering/disguise/deception). The inability of relatively moral governments to understand the nature of the threat posed by those with a different world view was a feature of the 20th century from Hitler's Europe to the genocide in the Balkans.

Eliza Manningham-Buller, the former MI5 Director, speaking on terrorism in the Reith lectures in August 2011, said that terrorism was a technique and not a state and that, consequently, terrorist acts should be regarded as crimes and not acts of war. Terrorist acts are crimes, but they are not *just* crimes. We should not underplay the ideological nature of the conflict. Eliza Manningham-Buller rightly advocated increased understanding of the causes of terrorism, saying that terrorism is a global problem which needs to be "solved through politics and economics, not through arms and intelligence", acknowledging that terrorism is more than only criminal behaviour. Tony Blair has said that it was "deeply naive" to blame the approach taken by the West and that we need to understand the ideology which lies behind the aims of the terrorists. While the West may have made mistakes in the way it has dealt with Islamic terrorism, this is realistic. Christopher Coker quotes Sayyed Fadallah, a leading Shiite cleric who supported suicide bombings because of their effectiveness: "The death of such persons is not a tragedy, nor does it indicate an 'agitated mental state'. Such a death is calculated; far from being a death of despair, it is a purposeful death in the service of a living cause."[483] The ideology of extreme Islamism which manifests itself in terrorism is powerful and is coherent, though it is deeply damaging to individuals and society. It therefore needs to be confronted and debated rather than being dismissed as deranged or merely criminal.

Realism about ideology needs to be accompanied by a belief in the ability of people to change affairs for the better. Some historians may tend to attribute important changes only to impersonal forces, but reflection upon the history of the twentieth century would suggest that individuals can exercise powerful influences for good as well as for evil. But there are great challenges. Hearts and minds must be changed, but they must first be reached. The decentralisation of some of the networks in which particular ideologies thrive makes them difficult to address. As Coker (writing in 2008) expressed it: "What makes Islam such a potent force is that through its network it has become deterritorialised, detribalised and diffused. The network society has arrived with a vengeance and it is beginning to shape the war on terror."[484] Speaking of Iraq, Coker refers to the armed factions as Hobbes' "worms in the intestines of the State" gnawing away at what remains of civil society.[485]

Engagement with those opposed to the State may require force to restrain them in some cases, but force should not be the first option. However challenging, the West must demonstrate with integrity its belief in freedom, natural justice (even for terrorists) and democracy. We may not agree with our opponents but we should endeavour to engage in discussion with them, even if the result is likely to be fruitless. As Winston Churchill said, "To jaw-jaw is always better than to war-war."

22.6   THE MIDDLE EAST

We can reflect upon the tension between idealism and pragmatism in US and British policy in relation to the Middle East. It may have been right for the UK to encourage Libya to give up weapons of mass destruction and in return to confer some recognition of the regime. But it was not right (if this happened) to nurture relations with the Gaddafi regime to the extent of freeing the Lockerbie bomber for the purpose of securing trade deals.

We can contrast this seemingly pragmatic approach with George W. Bush's policy of encouraging democratic movements in the Middle East which might have seemed idealistic. George W. Bush took the view that Islamic extremism thrives in undemocratic and economically underdeveloped States and that democracy was objectively right and good for the people of the countries concerned. He believed that it was also in the long term best interests of the US to make friends for the future in fostering democracy.

Despite the uncertainties in Egypt, the democratic movement in that country has not been anti-American, although some politicians wish to revisit the peace treaty with Israel. Elections to the People's Assembly and the presidency have provided the Islamic Brotherhood with increased power, though the effective influence of the military is uncertain. President Mohammed Morsi has shown different faces. At a pre-election event in Cairo he said "Sharia! There can be nothing but Sharia, Sharia, Sharia! There is no other good for this nation. I swear before god and I swear to all of you, regardless what is written in the constitution, Sharia law will be applied."[486] After his election victory, Morsi promised protection for the Christian community.

22.7 THE LIMITATIONS OF IDEALISM

The foreign policies of both President George W. Bush and President Barack Obama illustrate the value, but also the limitations, of idealism. The belief that democracy could be encouraged in the Middle East was admirable, but in an Iraq driven by sectarian rivalries and following an almost total breakdown of law and order and a lack of planning for the period following the invasion, its implementation proved extremely challenging.

President Obama began his Presidency by extending the hand of friendship not simply to the Muslim world in the Middle East in his Cairo address, but also to Iran, China and Russia. He recognised the need to curtail the overseas commitments of the US and, at the same time, hoped to reset relations with countries previously hostile to the US and also operate on a more cooperative basis with allies. However, whilst his standing in the eyes of the elites of the democratic world increased, his policy delivered very little and may have been perceived by some countries as a sign of weakness. Iran remained hostile and continued its nuclear programme with the assistance of North Korea, with whom (according to a study by the International Institute for Strategic Studies) it shared missile technology. China continued with its cyber attacks and Russia's policies remained unchanged. After about eighteen months, the President had to revise his strategy to a more assertive one, enhancing the relationship of the US with its allies in the Asia Pacific region, using its leverage with the Egyptian military to assist regime change in Egypt and intervening in Libya (albeit more tentatively than some would have liked).

22.8   THE TASK OF NATION BUILDING

Nation building, even if intervention is justified, is always challenging. Rory Stewart and Gerald Knaus have highlighted the need for a deep understanding of the country, its customs and institutions.[487] They are sceptical that Western concepts in relation to governance, gender, conflict resolution, civil society and public administration can be easily exported without their being adapted to the country concerned. According to them, it must be a priority to engage with the existing structures and to allow space for local leadership. Avoiding putting foreign troops on the ground will prevent this provoking a reaction and will make it easier to disengage. It will also be significantly cheaper. The costs of the UK's intervention in Libya were one twentieth of the annual cost of operations in Afghanistan.

22.9   PROSPERITY AND POWER

President Obama recognises the link between prosperity and power. He said in 2009: "Our prosperity provides a foundation for our power, it pays for our military, it underwrites our diplomacy". It seems unavoidable that America's economic problems, principally caused by the level of public and private debt, will curtail its influence. The Federal Government receives $2.2 trillion in tax revenue and spends about $3.6 trillion. Borrowing is nearly half of expenditure. A large part of the proposed cuts of $2.4 trillion will need to come out of defence spending. A former Pentagon official calculated that it cost $20 billion a year to supply air conditioning to US forces in Afghanistan and Iraq.

Similar constraints apply to the UK. The Commons Select Committee warned in 2011 that the cuts in the Strategic Defence and Security Review have left the UK's armed forces at full stretch in its current missions and unable to defend the country's interests in the world. Meanwhile, Russia and China are able to increase their defence spending. If the UK has decided to become only a minor European state in its power and influence, this change of policy needs to be stated and acted upon. The current mismatch of resources and aspirations may be dangerous, because it can give an ambiguous signal. There has to be a limit to the reduction in armed forces. The defence of a country is a primary duty of government and must be determined by the potential threats to the country and the role it seeks to play in the world. Other priorities should be secondary. It is inconsistent that the Government has determined that the UK needs aircraft carriers but that, following the decommissioning of the current vessels, no new carriers will be available until 2020. If carriers are required, then they should be retained and, if they are not required, there is no need to have them in 2020. Moreover, if only one carrier is ordered, the one carrier can only be at sea for between 150 and 200 days a year. If a carrier needs to be in operation, two are required so that one is in service throughout the year.

22.10   DECISIONS MAKE A DIFFERENCE

Individuals can change policy and policy can change history. Here history is instructive. As George Weigel (in a lecture at Baylor University in 2010) counsels, hard questions need to be asked about failures of the past and the lessons for the present. Could the allies have crafted a more sensible peace settlement after the First World War, thus making the rise of national socialism less likely? Would concerted international action in the 1930s have prevented the Second World War? Could or should the US have prevented the absorption of half of Europe into the Soviet Empire? Could or should the US have prevented the bloodbath in South East Asia that followed its withdrawal from Vietnam? Could President Carter have better anticipated the effects of the Iranian revolution and what difference would this have made?

The questions of today are no less exacting. What action should be taken to contain the nuclear threat posed by North Korea and the dangers of a nuclear armed Iran? If Iran were to obtain nuclear weapons, it is likely that there would be an arms race in the Middle East, as states such as Saudi Arabia would seek to arm themselves against the threat to their resources. A failure to prevent Iran from acquiring nuclear weapons could result in permanent instability, or in war, if Israel or the Gulf States seek to destroy a nuclear Iran before it exerts its power. Iran is not an Arab nation and its Shi'a Islamic faith is a challenge to the Sunni Islamic world. Unlike Israel, Saudi Arabia currently has no ability to threaten retaliation with nuclear weapons. It also has a significant Shi'a population that could be mobilised to undermine the Saudi regime. Doubts have been raised as to whether missile defences could overcome a combination of sustained salvos of conventionally armed and nuclear missiles. Missile defence systems may not be able to distinguish between nuclear and non nuclear warheads. Countries in Europe and the Middle East will need to recognise that the US is unlikely to wish to expose its own cities to the risk of attack in order to defend them. Containment and extended deterrence may be difficult, if not impossible. There is still a possibility that diplomacy may be effective before the middle of 2013 (when it is estimated that Iran will be able to manufacture a nuclear weapon). There is also a possibility (hopefully remote) that the success of the rebels in Syria against Iran's ally could prompt

Iran to make a pre-emptive strike. The military option to stop Iran developing nuclear weapons should not be dismissed, unpalatable though it may be.

It is possible that the current Syrian regime may wage war on Israel as a distraction from domestic issues. Or, if the Syrian state collapses, Hezbollah may secure access to weapons of great, if not mass, destruction. Despite the humanitarian horrors perpetrated by the current Syrian regime, to arm and encourage the rebel forces, as many countries are now doing, could result in even greater suffering for the people of Syria or catastrophe for the region. There were reports of 50,000 Christians having been driven from their homes in Homs as a result of persecution and violence by the Islamist rebels.

It is not clear what circumstances should give rise to a duty or a right on the part of a state to interfere in the internal affairs of another country. If a state does intervene, it must be confident that it has compelling grounds for doing so and that its actions will improve the condition of the people. Many would say that military intervention in another country is only justified under the auspices of the United Nations, although others would doubt that this is necessary to confer legitimacy upon the enterprise, since the United Nations only represents the interests of a collection of states, albeit acting together.

22.11 UNCERTAINTY RULES

We reflected in Chapter 4 that there are no predictive laws in history. The future of the Egyptian revolution could pose major challenges for Western powers and for Israel, or could result in beneficial changes for Egypt and for the whole region. Revolutions favour the most organised, not the most popular, parties and the Muslim Brotherhood has benefited in elections from the organised support which it has in the population. Risalat al-Ikhwan, the Muslim Brotherhood periodical in Britain had a headline "Our Mission: World Domination". Polls of the Egyptian population suggest that seventy-seven per cent want to see whipping and hands cut off for robbery. Eighty-four per cent favour the death penalty for a Muslim who changes his religion and eighty-two per cent favour stoning for adultery. There has been a transition to democracy but the high level of support for Islamic values could lead to greater hostility to Israel, which could further undermine the stability of the region. Much is in flux. Syria's regime may eventually collapse and give way to a possibly more democratic but almost certainly more Islamist government and/or the protracted civil war could continue.

Old rivalries remain. As we have noted, Iran is predominantly Shi'a (rather than Sunni) and the Gulf States have significant Shi'a minorities. Saudi Arabia and the Gulf states fear Iran and the political leverage it would enjoy from the possession of nuclear weapons. They would not be unhappy if Israel were to launch a successful attack to destroy or set back Iran's nuclear capability. Egypt may see the truce between Hamas and Fatah which it brokered as dividing Hamas and Iran. Iran could threaten NATO bases in Turkey, and Turkey appears to seek a more active role in the region. Iraq is currently heavily influenced by Iran but, following the withdrawal of the US forces, it may become more independent and seek to limit the power of Iran in the region. The factors which could influence future major events are manifold.

There can be a tendency to assume that there is a right answer in each situation and, if things go wrong, it follows that the wrong decisions must have been taken. Similarly, it can be assumed that the opponents of an oppressive regime are necessarily better than the regime they seek to displace and should be supported. This is to misunderstand the nature of evil in our imperfect world. Events may turn out well or badly, but it is often a mistake to believe that there is any kind of easy answer, or that it will necessarily be clear what will be the right response to unpredictable events. It is quite possible that the only choice may be between two equally unpalatable or even disastrous consequences. An example might be the invasion of Iraq. People have concluded from the resulting disorder and sectarian violence that the war was both unjustified and a failure.

But it may be too early to say what effect on the region the change of regime (and some element of democracy) will have in the longer term. It is possible that the alternative to the invasion might have been worse (particularly if one views the facts as they were perceived at the time without the benefit of hindsight) — a dictator with the capacity to destabilise the region, and not afraid to terrorise his own people.

Christians have no reason to believe that the world will be rescued from the consequences of the evil in it except by the second coming of Jesus Christ. Indeed Jesus, looking to the time before his return, predicted an increase in international tension, violence and destruction. This means that a government must do what is right but without assuming that the results of its actions will necessarily reflect the character or motivation of those actions. The actions may be good, but the results may or may not be. In the case of the Iraq invasion, if this was only authorised by the UK government and Parliament on the basis of information known to be false or misleading then the war was not justified, irrespective of whether the outcome was good. It was understandable that, called to make what appeared to be an historic choice of an alliance with the US or siding with Europe, a British Prime Minister should have wanted to choose the US. However, if the use of false or misleading information was the only way for the war to have been lawfully authorised, even if it were accepted that the war was good, the UK should not have joined the war. From a Christian point of view, it is important to do the right thing and to leave the consequences to the providence of God.

22.12 DIVINE INTERVENTION

There are examples in British history where Christians would say that God intervened for good in response to the prayers of his people, some of the most striking being in the Second World War. On May 27th 1940 the German High Command correctly recorded "The British Army is encircled, our troops are proceeding to its annihilation."[488] Meanwhile, at the request of King George VI, a National Day of Prayer was held on May 26th. The King, together with members of the cabinet, attended Westminster Abbey and millions prayed in churches all over the country. The storm over Flanders and the great calm that settled over the English Channel allowed the army to escape. *The Daily Telegraph* reported that the officers of high rank did not hesitate to attribute deliverance of the army to the day of prayer. Smaller miracles also occurred. The same article recorded the story of a chaplain on the beach at Dunkirk who, after being targeted with bombs and shot at with a machine gun as he lay on the beach, rose to find that the sand around was pitted with bullet holes and that his figure was outlined in the ground by bullet holes. Similarly, September 8th 1940 had been fixed some time before as another National Day of Prayer. This just preceded the height of the Battle of Britain on September 15th when the Luftwaffe launched their strongest force and were defeated. On September 17th Hitler decided to postpone the invasion. General Montgomery publicly acknowledged divine help. On November 11th 1940 he said to one hundred officers and men: Gentleman, I read the Bible every day and recommend you do the same.[489] In a message to be read to all troops in July 1943 following the landings in Sicily, he said: "We must not forget to give thanks to the Lord, Mighty in Battle, for giving us such a good beginning."

22.13   THE EVIL OF WAR AND THE "JUST WAR"

The conduct of foreign policy brings with it an encounter with numerous moral dilemmas. War is not good and, as Christian teacher Martyn Lloyd Jones reminds us: "The Bible does not isolate war as something unique — no, it is one manifestation of sin, and one of its consequences."[490] It is, however, sometimes necessary, and Christian "just war" theory provides a framework for examining the conditions which allow it. The war must have a just cause, it must be waged by a right authority, with a right intention, it must have a reasonable chance of success and it must be a last resort. It must also be conducted in a just way, distinguishing between legitimate and illegitimate targets and force must be minimised and proportional to the aim. The Geneva Convention on the treatment of prisoners of war and civilians can be seen as a development of this. This is an expression of the command of Jesus that we should love our enemies. To prevent a greater evil, we may have to harm their interests, but we do not have to hate them or take any more action than is necessary for the greater good to prevail.

If a society destroys what makes life worthwhile, then it will have undermined the prospects of a just and therefore long lasting peace. Augustine came to conclude that the true evil in war was not death (since we all have to die sometime) but: "the desire for harming, the cruelty of avenging, an unruly and implacable animosity, the rage of rebellion, the lust for domination and the like. These are the things to be blamed in war." For Augustine, peace was not only in the City of God, it was for this world as well, even though he lived in a world ravaged by war and died in the city of his birth besieged by the Vandals. As Christopher Coker concludes, war should only be waged for peace.[491] Coker quotes Augustine: "Be careful, therefore in warring", Augustine urged, "so that you may vanquish those whom you war against, and bring them the prosperity of peace."

22.14 ARMS SALES

Arms sales can be viewed from a similar perspective to that discussed above. Arms are about defence and about war. If they are necessary for a country's defence and are unlikely to be used for offensive war then it is right to sell them. Unless the pacifist position is taken, it seems illogical for a Christian to decline on principle to take part in any arms sales, since many sales will be justified for legitimate purposes. If, on the other hand, the arms are not necessary for defence, or are likely to be used for aggressive purposes or for intimidating or repressing internal dissidents, then the sales should not be made.

Trade with countries repressing human rights or torturing dissidents raises moral questions. No goods should be sold where it is clear that they are to be used for repression or the abuse of fundamental rights. But economic sanctions by only one exporting country would be unlikely to have any effect upon the country targeted by the sanctions and could harm the exporting country. Such a ban could do harm without doing any good. Each government can restrict its trade, though in a particular case it might not be advisable to do so. There is no point in banning trade unless the action (in the words of the just war theory) "has a reasonable chance of success", since it could harm innocent people. Concerted action by a number of States, rather than one State acting alone, is more likely to be successful. Sanctions targeted specifically against the ruling parties are sensible since they should not harm the general population. This reflects the just war theory distinction between combatants and non-combatants.

22.15   THE STATE OF ISRAEL

The issues surrounding the state of Israel present apparently insuperable challenges. The legal right of Israel to exist is founded in the San Remo Agreement of 1920, which was included in the Treaty of Sèvres and confirmed by the Council of the League of Nations on 24th July 1922 in its *Mandate for Palestine*.[492] The Mandate gave the administration for Palestine to Britain and confirmed in its preamble the Balfour Declaration of 1917, in which the British government undertook to establish "in Palestine…a national home for the Jewish people."[493] Article 6 of the Mandate required the Administration of Palestine to "encourage, in co-operation with the Jewish agency referred to in Article 4, close settlement by Jews, on the land, including State lands and waste lands not required for public purposes." Article 25 permitted Britain to withhold application of the Mandate to the lands to the East of the Jordan River. In accordance with this provision, 77 per cent of the Mandate lands were given to Abdullah creating the new country of Trans-Jordan or Jordan, as it was later named. All the land to the West side of the Jordan (which includes the territory now referred to as the "West bank" or "Palestine") was within the territory given to the Jewish people under the Mandate.

The West bank territory was occupied by Arab forces in 1948 when the surrounding Arab nations rejected the creation of the state of Israel (which was sanctioned by the United Nations) and tried to destroy it. The surrounding Arab states did not accept the partition of Palestine proposed by the United Nations. The West bank territory was annexed by Jordan during the 1950s. There has never been a sovereign Arab state of Palestine. Israel regarded the West bank territory as part of the original homeland under the Mandate and occupied it in 1967 during the Arab Israeli war. It is not clear whether the Palestinians acquired any prescriptive rights to the West bank by virtue of their occupation between 1948 and 1967, or that there should be a requirement under international law for Israel to surrender this territory.

Some have claimed that Palestine was part of the territories promised to the Arabs in 1915 by Sir Henry MacMahon. This was rejected by the British Government and by McMahon himself in a letter to The Times in 1937, though the syntactical ambiguity of McMahon's note to Sharif Husein of October 1915 did not survive its translation into Arabic. It is also claimed that the Mandate gave a right of self-determination to the Arabs living in Palestine, though the Mandate documents and treaties refer to the purpose of the Mandate as the creation of a national home for the Jewish people. The Fatah constitution calls for the "obliteration of Zionist economic and political, military and cultural existence" and the Hamas Charter calls for the elimination of Israel.

Although some in the Arab world wish the state of Israel to be destroyed, the Israeli state should behave justly to the Palestinians who have over many years established *de facto* rights of ownership over land in Palestine. They should not be arbitrarily evicted. If it is right that the territory belongs to Israel, Israel should behave with justice and compassion to all those living there. Whether this means that there should be a 'right of return' (which Israel rejects) for Palestinians evicted from their lands when the state of Israel was established is a difficult question. Israel would take the view that a right of return would destabilise the state of Israel. During 1947-48 both Jews and Palestinians were forced to leave their homes. There is an asymmetry in the way refugees from Israel and from other countries are regarded. In 1947-8 about three quarters of a million Arabs left Israel but an equal number of Jews were driven from other countries. Arab refugees from Israel, though settling in other Arab countries, never acquire citizenship there (as they would do in the US or the UK), but remain refugees down the generations.

For Christians, Israel was called by God to be an example nation to the other nations — to illustrate God's purposes and laws and to provide the physical place for God to intervene in human history, through the life, death and resurrection of Jesus Christ. Some would interpret the Bible as saying that, at his second coming, Jesus will return to Jerusalem (see Acts 1:11). A number of Christians see the existing state of Israel as the fulfilment of biblical prophecy and take the view that the surrender of East Jerusalem to a Palestinian state or the surrender of territory in the West bank would conflict with the purposes of God.

The issue of biblical prophecy in relation to the territory of Israel is controversial. Some may attach little importance to the prophecies, while others would regard them as a reliable guide to the present and to the future. In the book of Genesis (15:18), God promises a wide area of the Middle East to the descendants of Abraham, which might include other Semitic peoples, traditionally viewed as the descendants of Abraham. The promise to Abraham was repeated to Joshua before the conquest of Canaan (Joshua 1:4), though it has been suggested that this could be limited to the areas actually conquered. There are also a number of promises that, if the people of Israel disobey God's commands, they will be dispossessed of the land (see for example Deuteronomy 28:64 and 30:1). This has happened twice in history, first in the exile recorded in the Old Testament and again when the Romans destroyed Jerusalem and the Jewish state in 70AD. There are also promises of the restoration of Israel to the land which refer to a gathering of people from many nations and not just from those countries from which the people of Israel returned in Old Testament times. This appears to be consistent with the return to the land by Jews in recent times where Jews from a large number of countries have returned to settle in the state of Israel.

Some Christians interpret a number of references to Israel in the Old Testament as referring to all Christian believers. In support of this view, they would cite the letter to the Hebrews in the Bible (8:8-12). This passage quotes the book of Jeremiah (31:31-34) which makes promises to Israel and Judah but says that God will make the first covenant with the people of Israel obsolete by replacing it with the new covenant. This new covenant, through the death and resurrection of Jesus, offers salvation to people of every race for the benefit of all Christian believers. Others would say that the first (and now superseded) covenant referred to in the letter to the Hebrews refers only to the Mosaic laws and sacrificial system and that the other covenants with the people of Israel, particularly in relation to the land, endure to this day. (For Christians, the Mosaic laws have been largely superseded and one interpretation is that for Christians only nine of the ten commandments remain valid. Most Christians would say that they are not obliged to keep the Jewish Sabbath or Sunday as a holy day in the same way that Jewish law prescribes.)

Some have perceived a difficulty with the application of the promises of the Old Testament to an ethnic group of people in relation to the land of Israel in that the promises included all the tribes of Israel. Ten of the twelve tribes did not return to the land after the exile in the Old Testament and were dispersed among many nations. An answer to this difficulty is that there is a remnant of the people of Israel which represents all of them. There are promises in the Apostle Paul's letter to the Roman church in the New Testament that "all Israel will be saved"

(Romans 11:26 NIV). It is clear that in its context "all Israel" in this passage refers to those of the Jewish faith and not to gentile (non-Jewish) Christians as the inheritors of a new covenant.

Many Christians therefore see the promise of restoration of the people of Israel to the land as being (at least partially) fulfilled in the present day secular state of Israel. They point to the covenants made by God in the Old Testament which they say have not been superseded. They also draw attention to what they regard as miracles associated with the establishment of the state of Israel. The promises in the Old Testament of the restoration to the land are often associated with the return of people in Israel to God, which is taken by Christians to include the recognition of Jesus as the Messiah. This is not yet widespread, though the number of Jews believing in Jesus (Messianic Jews) is increasing. For other Christians, all the covenants to Israel as an ethnic people in relation to a specific territory have been superseded by the new covenant instituted by Jesus. They would read references to Israel in prophecies in the Old Testament as references to Christian believers, though this may not be consistent with the references to Israel in Chapter 11 of Paul's letter to the Romans.

There is a view that the British government failed to fulfil the undertakings in the Mandate to create a homeland for the Jewish people and this is referred to as a forsaken promise. The Mandate for Palestine given to the British was contested by a large Arab population which, in 1921, was more than 600,000 compared with a Jewish population of less than 80,000. There was pressure from the Palestine Arab Congress and the Supreme Muslim Council for Britain to withdraw from the Mandate and numerous disturbances in which Jews and Arabs were killed, and there was an Arab uprising and strike in 1936. Despite rising anti-Semitism in Europe, the British government restricted immigration by Jews to Palestine from 1930. In 1939, despite the Nazi persecution, it restricted Jewish immigration for the next five years to 75,000 after which it was to cease altogether, and forbade land sales to Jews in a large part of the territory of Palestine. A White Paper also proposed a Palestinian state within ten years and partition between Arabs and Jews in proportion to their populations. The restrictions on Jewish immigration, while Arab immigration was unrestricted, were in breach of the terms of the Mandate which required the British government to encourage settlement of Palestine by Jews as a homeland for them. In reneging on the terms of the Mandate, the White Paper said that the framers of the Mandate could not have intended a Jewish state against the will of the Arab population. After 1945, some 50,000 attempted Jewish immigrants to Palestine were detained in camps. It is also reported that, after the war, the British prevented the Jews from arming themselves against the expected Arab invasion and, before they left, failed to protect Jews from Arab attack. Further, the British government failed to take any action during the war to prevent the holocaust; it has been suggested that rail links to the concentration camps could have been destroyed. In March 1943, Archbishop Temple, speaking in the House of Lords, urged action to help the Jews. He cited the parable of the good Samaritan, who had no part in the injury but went out of his way to help. He concluded: "We at this moment have upon us a tremendous responsibility. We stand at the bar of history, of humanity and of God."[494]

Some Christians regard the failure to fulfil its undertakings in the Mandate to give the Jewish people a homeland and the failure to take any action to prevent the holocaust as advocated by Archbishop Temple as a reason for the rapid decline of British power after the war and the loss of its empire. They say that Britain failed to honour its promises and to protect the Jewish people and that, in the providence of God, consequences flowed from that failure.

Currently, neither Israel nor Hamas appear to want a two state solution. Israel withdrew from south Lebanon in 2000 and from Gaza in 2005 and in each case the areas became bases for terrorist attacks upon Israel. Israel will be unlikely to agree to a two state solution with Jerusalem as the capital of a Palestinian state. For Israel, Jerusalem has significance as a national and spiritual capital. Israel will be reluctant to evict settlers from East Jerusalem. Israel will also be concerned that a Palestinian East Jerusalem would become a base for terrorists in the same way as Gaza. If a US or European peace plan requires the transfer of East Jerusalem, it is almost bound to fail.

A Christian view would be that true peace in the Middle East will only be achieved when Arabs and Jews worship together the same God revealed in the Christian faith. Jews and Arabs join together in Christian congregations in Israel. For many Christians, the role of Israel in God's plans as prophesied in the Bible indicates that, in ways we cannot necessarily predict, the plans of Islamic extremists to eliminate the state of Israel will not succeed. However, a belief in the importance of Israel in God's purposes cannot excuse injustice on the part of the Israeli state. The ends do not justify the means. God's ends must be achieved by God's means. Despite provocation, for instance the sustained rocket attacks on Southern Israel from Gaza, some of the counter insurgency measures adopted by the Israeli security forces may have been disproportionate to the immediate threats. They are also likely to have increased resentment on the part of Palestinians and to have encouraged their support for extremist Islamic movements. Meanwhile, Christian believers are asked to pray for the peace of Jerusalem for the sake of God's purposes on earth (Psalms 122 and 127).

22.16   FORGIVENESS AND RECONCILIATION

Christian thinking has an important part to play in international peace and reconciliation. Humility and forgiveness can be essential to a peaceful resolution of international tensions. Individuals and countries naturally wish to defend their own actions. Where damage has been done, the tendency is to assume that we (as people or nations) are good and in the right and that it therefore follows that our opponents must be bad and in the wrong. The Christian perception is that this is to underestimate the imperfection of all people. As the Apostle Paul put it: "For all have sinned and fall short of the glory of God" (Romans 3:23 NKJV). We need to try to see ourselves, if not as God sees us, at least as others do. In our eyes others may be right or wrong, just or unjust, but there is a duty to understand the positions of those with whom we disagree. Even where there are irreconcilable differences with a nation or nations, we nevertheless need to take into account their genuine interests as well as our own.

Reconciliation requires generosity of spirit and can avert conflict. The German statesman Gustav Stresemann, shortly before he died in 1929, reflected, "I pledged myself to achieving a Franco-British-German accord... I gave and gave until my own followers turned against me. If they [the allies] could have granted me just one concession, I could have won my people. But they gave me nothing... That is my tragedy and their crime."[495] Hitler rose to power in 1933.

For peace to prevail, it is not necessary for there to be agreement. Jesus said that we should love our enemies, which means wanting their best interests to be protected. An example of reconciliation in our own times is the work of Canon Andrew White, the "Vicar of Baghdad". Following the sectarian murder of some 120 Christians in Iraq in 2010, Andrew White convened a meeting in Copenhagen in December of religious and community leaders — Shi'ite, Sunni and Christian. They saw each other as people, not as ideological foes. The Shi'a and the Sunni leaders were persuaded that the Christian community was good for Iraq — it includes doctors, teachers and other professionals — and that further departures by these people would weaken the country. Following the meeting, *fatwas* were issued requiring the killings to cease. As a result sectarian killings of Christians were dramatically reduced. Iraqis could identify with each other as fellow citizens and human beings without needing to agree on the issues that divided them.

In Christian thinking, there is right and wrong, justice and injustice, but the scope for remedying wrong and bringing in justice in the world may often be limited. Conflict will continue as long as there is imperfection in the world — in ourselves as well as others. Rival claims to land and conflicting interests may be irreconcilable, but parties need to live together. Not everyone can have all they want. To accept compromise is not to give up a cause, but it may be necessary to recognise that a desired end is not achievable, at least not without unacceptable costs in terms of human suffering. Good motives and pure intentions need to be balanced by realism about the limitations of the human condition. Nevertheless, situations may arise in foreign affairs where neither idealism nor pragmatic realism can protect people from the consequences of their own miscalculations or from their inability to predict the actions of others. Christians would say that in all circumstances the right must be done and the outcome left to the sovereignty of God.

PART 6:

LOOKING AHEAD

23

CHANGE AND HOPE FOR THE FUTURE

23.1 CHRISTIAN WISDOM AND THE STATE OF THE NATION

Christian political thinking is founded upon the assumption that it is possible to reflect the purposes of the Creator in human institutions. Individuals have been given the freedom and the moral responsibility to make choices, together with a vision of the good life, although this may only be achieved in a fragmentary manner on earth. What constitutes the good life for societies is accessible in part from our knowledge of the world as we encounter it, but specific guidance is given in the Bible and through the wisdom of Christian teaching. For Christians, the good life for individuals involves an acknowledgement of dependence upon God and his mercy in offering forgiveness and the restoration of a relationship with him.

It is not difficult to be pessimistic about the state of the nation. The UK is socially and economically dysfunctional. It has lost much of its industry over the past fifty years and squandered its natural and human resources. Its balance of payments current account deficit is ballooning and a balance of payments crisis is possible. The decline of UK manufacturing from the 1970s was offset by North Sea oil and gas, and by income from overseas companies. But the oil and gas are running out, and overseas companies may now own more of the UK economy than UK companies own overseas. The UK relies upon other countries for investment in manufacturing. The World Economic Forum rankings for the quality of infrastructure ranked the UK at number twenty-four.

The country relies upon a large public sector (which it cannot pay for) to employ many of its graduates, though a large proportion may end up unemployed or underemployed. A significant section of its potential workforce is unemployable and survives on welfare benefits, not having the necessary literacy or numeracy skills, or experience, or motivation for employment, while overseas workers fill the gaps. Though there have been some recent improvements, its past educational policies have not provided basic standards of literacy to a significant proportion of school leavers. Failures in education and welfare provision have been caused by, and have also been reinforced by, government social policies. These social policies have reflected values of relativism and autonomy that have undermined traditional family structures and social cohesion. Business in the City has not adhered to basic ethical standards. Parliament, the police and the media are discredited and distrusted.

The country is vastly over borrowed in terms of both government and personal debt. The international bond bubble may burst, leading to higher rates of interest at which point interest payments will absorb an even larger proportion of government spending. At the present rate of progress, it may take decades to reduce personal debt to the level it was in 1976. Bank of England policy maker Andrew Haldane said in December 2012 that, if we are fortunate, the cost of the crisis (he could have referred to the accumulated debt) will be paid for by our children but more likely by our grandchildren. The pound has lost 14% of its purchasing power since 2008, pay has declined by 5% in real terms since then, and consumer spending has declined by 8%. Negative real interest rates impoverish savers. The UK state's monetary creation (quantitative easing) policy can create asset bubbles and could lead to more general and higher inflation and/or a decline in the currency, either of which would lower standards of living. And the challenges facing the nation would be intensified were there to be disorder in Europe, or even the collapse of the European Union, as a result of policies implemented to preserve the single currency.

Christian wisdom and standards of behaviour in relation to

a range of social and economic issues could have averted many of the current difficulties facing the nation. Secularism and post modernism have not delivered. Just as the rise of Christian values in society and government, which was built upon a foundation of committed Christian faith, laid the foundations for the success of the nation in the Victorian era, so the departure from Christian faith and values has been a factor in the continuing decline of the UK.

This chapter explores some of these themes from a specifically Christian perspective. It suggests that Christian values can yet provide hope for the nation and looks at some of the changes in attitudes and culture that would be necessary for these values to take hold.

23.2 A POST-CHRISTIAN SOCIETY?

The evaporation of many Christian standards in society and in the laws of the UK over the last fifty years can be linked to a number of the issues facing the nation. These include the departure from a respect for marriage and natural families, the loss of discipline in the home and at school, inappropriate sexual education, the decline in personal responsibility and excessive materialism and consumerism.

There have also been a number of areas where Christian principles have been abandoned which affect the wellbeing of individuals, but where the consequences for society as a whole may be less obvious. These include issues relating to the beginning and end of life. In the case of abortion, the people primarily affected are the aborted children themselves and the mothers having the abortion. Other areas where Christian principles no longer apply include issues relating to gender, in particular the promotion of same-sex relationships. These affect those in the relevant relationships or those who may be encouraged to enter into them. Equality, non discrimination and diversity policies affect children given up to same-sex adoption as well as teachers and pupils. They also impact those seeking to perform public services such as adoption or fostering, as well as those providing commercial services. There are also laws and policies which, while contravening a fundamental moral law, as yet appear to affect relatively few people. For instance, experiments with life such as cloning are wrong in principle, even if in human terms it may not be easy to demonstrate a particular social harm.

Government policy encourages people to approve of LBGT (Lesbian, Bisexual, Gay and Transgender) identities and activities. This policy has relied on a particular interpretation of human rights which has been supported by influential lobby groups. The competition for influence continues. There has been no forensic analysis in terms of the common good, for instance in relation to the effect of the policies on children, and there is no logical firewall to the encouragement of other expressions of sexuality, for instance polygamy or incest.

While the costs of family breakdown can be attributed at least in part to the absence of government support for conventional marriage, it may seem odd to attribute any general malaise in society to policies in relation to issues such as the sanctity of life or gender. But if the only viable structure of moral order is that based upon a view of natural law underpinned by a belief in the Creator, then the lack of respect for this order is likely to lead to a lack of respect for any moral order, and this will affect all aspects of society. Rulers should not expect to generate willing obedience to standards and laws which derive their authority only from the intentions of individuals. There needs to be an objective moral authority and a coherent and logical framework of values to which a society can subscribe.

23.3   A SUPERNATURAL DIMENSION

Some Christians perceive the judgment of God on the United Kingdom at the current time in the breakdown of aspects of society in the UK. They say that it is possible to apply similar principles to those in the Old Testament where, on numerous occasions, a turning away from God's laws resulted in serious consequences for society. It is also possible to reach a similar conclusion on pragmatic grounds since, if God's guidance is in fact good, it would be reasonable to expect adverse consequences when straying from it. The Rev. Dr Clifford Hill in his magazine *Prophecy Today*, which ran from 1982 to 2005, predicted the current social and economic troubles. The book *Earthquake in the City* by Clifford Denton and Paul Slennet, was published in 1997 and records a message which Paul Slennet recounts as having received from God in 1989.[496] Non-Christians (and some Christians) may not relate to supernatural prediction (prophecy) and to the concept of God's judgment in this world, but many Christians would say that these are consistent with a view of God's dealings with people as recorded in the Bible.

Christian teachers such as David Pawson identify a large majority of prophecies in the Bible which have already happened and a small number which are yet to occur before the second coming of Jesus. Jesus said that there would be increasing instability in the world in the time before his return (see Luke 21:25-28 and Matthew 24:7-8). The political landscape of the 20th century was shaken by two world wars. Nuclear terror states are now a possibility. Social structures in Western states have been weakened. With the rise of militant Islam, religious conflict is widespread. Natural disasters such as earthquakes, droughts, floods and storms are increasing. And the economic crisis has yet to reach its conclusion, which could take the form of global currency collapse. In God's economy, a purpose of this instability may be to loosen people's attachment to the transient things of this world so that they may seek those things that are eternal (see Hebrews 12:27). If God exists and cares about humankind, it would be irrational not to call upon him in prayer.

23.4   THE IMPORTANCE OF PRAYER

If God is concerned with the health of a society for the wellbeing of its people, Christians have a particular role to play in seeking to uphold God's standards for the benefit of the nation and in praying for its government and politics. Christians will be familiar with the words in 2 Chronicles 7:14 (NIV): "If my people who are called by my name will humble themselves, and pray and seek my face, and turn from their wicked ways, then I will hear from heaven and heal their land." When Nehemiah heard of the broken down state of Jerusalem and the distress of its inhabitants, he wept. He then fasted and prayed for many days, confessing the sins of the Israelites on their behalf. Jesus said that whatever Christians (successfully) bind on earth shall first have been bound in heaven (Matthew 18:18), so Christians pray to God for guidance as to how his will is to be done on earth as it is in heaven.

National days of prayer were called by the King in times of crisis in the Second World War. Rick Perry, the governor of Texas, called on Christians to join him at the 71,000-seater Reliant Football Stadium for a prayer event: "with praying people asking God's forgiveness, wisdom and provision for our State and nation. There is hope for America. It lies in heaven, and we will find it on our knees."[497] The Anglican clergyman and theologian Simon Ponsonby, speaking at a Christian conference in August 2012 upon what he saw as the serious state of the nation, reflected that Jesus' teaching signified that some problems are so deep that they must be addressed by prayer and fasting. The belief is that God can act supernaturally as well as through the enabling he gives to individuals and through natural means.

23.5   A CHRISTIAN VOICE

If there is to be change in the values of society it is important that there is a recovery of an authentically Christian voice in the nation generally and that this is heard not merely among the Christian community. In Psalm 40:9 (NIV) the writer says: "I will proclaim righteousness in the great assembly." While many people in the nation, including those without a personal faith, can see the effects of falling away from standards which were acknowledged fifty years ago, it is the role of Christians to explain this in the context of Christian thought and belief. George Orwell wrote in June 1945, just before the publication of *Animal Farm*, that Christian thinkers were right to believe that "if our civilisation does not regenerate itself, it is likely to perish — and they may be right in adding that, in Europe at least, its moral code must be based on Christian principles."[498]

In the serious state in which the UK finds itself, a realisation of the mistakes of past public policies and the irresponsibility of personal behaviour can be likened to the realism required for repentance before God. An acknowledgement of the truth of the situation is an essential condition of regeneration. It may be that the nation has to experience prolonged hardship in order for it to be convinced of its past follies.

On a personal level, Christians are bound to make people aware that all individuals need to be rescued from the eternal consequences of our failings — by repentance and faith in Jesus Christ as Saviour. Moral laws are important for protection, but the good news of Jesus Christ is that each individual can be forgiven and renewed by a supernatural transaction with the Creator. And it is the state of people's hearts which, without the restraint of laws or social values, has contributed to the state of society today. A recovery of good laws and generally accepted values is important for the wellbeing of people and society but it is personal faith that can change people's desires.

23.6 LAWLESSNESS

Matthew Leeming recalled the effect of the Montreal police strike in 1969 when most downtown stores were looted, a sniper killed a police officer and a doctor killed a burglar.[499] By the end of the day, six banks had been robbed, a hundred shops looted, twelve fires had been set and three million dollars in property damage inflicted. As in the English riots of August

2011, once people perceive that law and order is not being enforced and they believe (wrongly as it turned out in the case of the English riots) that offenders will not be prosecuted, a Hobbesian state of nature can resume. Leeming put it starkly in his letter: "Human nature is utterly violent and wicked."

It is interesting to contrast the situation on the raft of the Medusa in 1816 with that down the Chilean mine in 2011. On the raft there was lawlessness leading to anarchy and cannibalism and only fifteen of the 147 people set adrift survived. Down the mine José Enriquez, one of the miners, led Christian prayers twice a day. Rules were established and adhered to. And (according to José Enriquez) twenty-two of the thirty-three miners who were rescued found a personal Christian faith. José was able to share the Bible with them for 17 days before the drill broke through, although he had no Bible with him. "How did you remember all those Bible verses?" he was asked afterwards. "Well, I knew the Bible from having been to church, Sunday school and Bible studies all my life, so it was not difficult."

There is a perception that public values have collapsed in many places. Peter Whittle reflected upon the August 2011 riots in Woolwich: "There is no sense of there being a public sphere at all, and certainly no sanctions against selfish or aggressive behaviour. Communal pressure is non-existent and with it has gone any sense of shame."[500] This can be partly attributed to the moral relativism favoured by many in the intellectual elite. In some communities the result has been an absence of effective moral discipline in the home, in the schools and on the streets. As Whittle puts it: "Authority, whether it be moral, social, familial or legal, has been chipped away at so relentlessly, that it has finally collapsed." This has been replaced by lawlessness on the part of some and fear on the part of the rest. Whittle gives the example that: "If faced with a group of gang members in a car playing music unbearably loudly next to them, I personally know of nobody — nobody from *Daily Telegraph* to *Guardian* readers — who would risk asking them to turn it down."

23.7 IDEAS AND CULTURE

The world of politics can be viewed in terms of structures, but those structures derive from ideas. Those ideas in turn come from formal education, from people's families and peer groups, from art and literature (for some) and from the current entertainment and news media. Ideas change people who in turn can change political structures. Equally, political structures, for instance government policies in education, promote ideas in people that in turn contribute to the structures. Revolutions happen when those inhabiting the structure (whether in or out of power) reject the received ideas and decide to change the structure. The process of the change of ideas and the resulting cultural and political change can be slow or can be rapid.

Many expressions of culture are morally neutral, though some may be thought to be aesthetically more valuable or more rewarding in terms of knowledge than others. Some people would say that art or music which is chaotic and disorderly is less likely to reflect the best of the human spirit than artistic creations which have an aesthetic structure, and they would view some of the art of the twentieth century as meaningless. Much popular culture describes a reality that is outside the everyday personal experience of those who consume it. People do not — perhaps fortunately in many cases — encounter in their normal lives the types of people, relationships and situations that they see in television series. However, these cultural experiences create impressions of what is good, normal or acceptable. These in turn affect how people think and behave and what they expect of their political institutions.

The following illustrates how the media are capable of presenting a misleading picture of the world we live in. The American film critic Michael Medved has commented: "A Martian gathering evidence about American society, simply by monitoring our television, would certainly assume that there were more gay people in America than there are evangelical Christians."[501] Moreover, as Michael L. Brown continues: "The

Martian would also conclude that gay people were, with rare or no exception, incredibly nice, family-orientated, creative and considerate, while evangelical Christians were all mean-spirited, judgmental, dull, greedy and hypocritical." [502]

The successful UK musical "Billy Elliot" champions the aspirations of a young dancer. It contains scenes where Billy Elliot's friend who is about eleven years old is enthusiastic about cross dressing and demonstrates this. His enthusiasm is celebrated in song and dance, although scenes of miners wearing tutus are clearly pastiche. The theme of individuality in the musical is generally admirable, but the effect is to influence people, including children, as to what is normal behaviour. We should question whether it is right for adults to make use of children in artistic productions to promote their unconventional values. The book of Judges in the Old Testament describes a collapsing society where people make up their own rules: "Every man did that which was right in his own eyes."[503]

23.8   CHANGES IN VALUES

Changes in the direction of more traditional publicly acknowledged morals and culture have happened in the past. There was a change from the licence of Georgian England to the moral and philanthropic values of mid-Victorian England. Herbert Schlossberg in his book *The Silent Revolution and the Making of Victorian England* acknowledges the role of Christian faith and values in this transformation.[504]

The media plays an important part in shaping public opinion and popular culture. However, it is possible that people may reject the influence of the media if they realise that it has an agenda or values which work against their best interests. The outcry against the journalistic methods of the *News of the World* was important, not so much because the crimes committed were the most serious in society — they were not — but because it illustrated the propensity of public opinion to act independently of the media and change the political landscape. The difficulties with MPs' expenses and then those surrounding the police and the media may make the public less willing in the future to accept the pronouncements of those in authority and more likely to examine the evidence for themselves. This ability to question received views is a fundamental basis of the evangelical Christian faith and of democratic politics. The composer Handel, berated by a bishop for his views on a theological topic, is reported to have replied: "I have read my Bible very well and will decide for myself."[505]

The outpouring of a cohesive community spirit, particularly in the volunteering, in the 2012 Olympics has been heart warming and illustrates the mutual goodwill which can exist. This goodwill is an ingredient for a flourishing society, but deeper changes in values are required. The popular music culture of the last fifty years which was celebrated at the opening and closing ceremonies, with its emphasis on personal fulfilment, contrasted with the virtues of personal discipline and sacrifice in the participants and altruism in the volunteering which contributed so much to the success of the games. While we may not agree with Peter Hitchens that pop music is "self-pitying, self-indulgent and self-righteous,"[506] it was not surprising that lyrics in the music at the opening and closing ceremonies reflected moral values that characterise our dysfunctional society.

23.9   CONSENT AND DEBATE

In the UK today, our laws reflect some of the accumulated traditions of our society, but they are also an instrument of government policy. Policy can reflect the agenda of an elite, enacted without the consent of those whom it affects. People might cite the participation of the UK in the political structures of the European Union or mass immigration as examples. The concessions made to Sharia law, such as the adoption of halal meals in schools and the recognition of Sharia law in arbitration tribunals, were not in the public domain before their introduction. Government that is not transparent is dishonest. Public policy should be debated fairly and democratically voted upon.

A belief in freedom of belief and expression is not shared by all religious communities and all sections of society. For some Muslims, the Muslim religion is right and can therefore be enforced. As the spokesman for the Salafist group Jam'a al-Islamiya, allied to the Muslim Brotherhood in Egypt put it: "Allah's words must rule and Islam must be in the hearts of citizens." According to the Rev. Patrick Sookhdeo, all schools of Islamic law prescribe the death penalty for Muslim adult males who choose to leave their religion. An example is the decision of the Iranian Supreme Court in the case of Christian Pastor Yousef Nadarkhani who was sentenced to death.

The limits to the law suggested by Christian thinking should inhibit totalitarianism, but in a democracy the free and fair debate of ideas and the giving of a fair hearing to contrary opinions, as John Stuart Mill advocated, is always required. As well as changing opinions, debate helps us to know the reasons for our beliefs which, in the absence of understanding, become mere prejudice. Fair debate requires transparency of information. The Freedom of Information Act 2000, though flawed in some ways, has done much in this regard. But there are other barriers to free and fair debate and we turn to these next.

In a democracy, laws should only be changed by mechanisms that involve consent. These mechanisms do not directly transmit the will of the people into the actions of government, but governments should respond to public opinion. If Christian values are to be respected and reflected in our politics, it will be because the people recognise that these values form the best and most coherent explanation of the moral world that we inhabit.

23.10   OBJECTIVE TRUTH

Some thinkers, such as Jacques Derrida and Michel Foucault, have founded their thinking upon the impossibility of objective truth and absolute values. They would hold that all knowledge is transitory and subject to endless challenge and revision. There is some truth in this in relation to the facts of history, where what are called "post-empiricist" theories of knowledge recognise that human understanding and communication is flawed and can easily be biased. As the historian Quentin Skinner has pointed out, concepts can shape facts and language itself carries a theory of explanation. However, in its extreme form, this kind of thinking means that all we are left with are the shifting sands of different opinions with no guide as to whether they are true or even debatable. Such thinking is difficult to deal with because (as the philosopher Roger Scruton has explained) no argument, however rational, that there is such a thing as truth can succeed. This makes all reasoning meaningless.

Unlike Christian faith, which can point to the reasons for faith and its meaning (whether in creation, in history or in the lives of believers), the belief that no truth exists is itself a leap of faith that is not borne out by the order of life on earth and the way human beings actually operate. Nor does it appear intelligible that we can be certain that there is no certainty. For the post-modern philosopher to say that we can know (for certain) that it is impossible to know anything for certain is logically incoherent. The sceptic can at best be uncertain as to whether there is such a thing as absolute truth.

The Christian perception is that what we can know is objectively true in that it describes reality but that, because we are imperfect human beings with a limited capacity to understand all things, our knowledge is finite. As the Apostle Paul says (in 1 Corinthians. 13:9 NKJV): "For we know in part ...." However, he also said that if what Christians believe about the resurrection of Jesus is not objectively true, they are to be pitied (1 Corinthians 15:19). We need the humility to recognise that there are limits to human understanding and knowledge. Truth is an absolute value and it is a unity, but we cannot understand all of it. The Christian perspective is that the Creator has given us enough understanding of our nature, of the world we inhabit and his nature for us to provide some answers to the question as to how we should live as individuals and to what we should aspire as members of a political society.

23.11   PERSONAL REACTIONS

There can be another difficulty in having a free and fair debate. A requirement that an individual should behave in a particular way in what they regard as their personal life tends to engage their emotions, sometimes in an extreme way. As we have seen, a degree of autonomy is necessary for individuals to act as moral beings and people should take responsibility for determining whether their actions are right.

For Christians, the lesson of the Garden of Eden is that the source of our imperfections and our capacity for evil is the desire to be independent of the moral order ordained by God. The prophet Isaiah, who diagnosed the corruption, oppression and injustice of the society of the day, saw the root of it all in the desire to act independently of God's standards: "All we like sheep have gone astray, we have turned, every one, to his own way."[507] Attempts to persuade people that a moral order exists, and that it makes demands upon them, can spark emotions that cloud rational debate. Any criticism of a person's behaviour or lifestyle or even their opinions may automatically be interpreted as a criticism or an irrational fear of them as individuals and consequently an affront to their dignity.

Those resisting the claims of objective values may maintain that there is an intellectual justification for their solipsism. Renford Bambrough reflected upon this: "Those who cry that morality is a matter of personal choice usually do so in opposition to what they rightly or wrongly regard as moral dogmatism or the misuse of authority. But if all morality were a matter of personal choice, then it would be a matter of personal choice whether it is proper to exercise authority in any particular case, or at all. The argument that the exercise of authority is morally repugnant because morality is a matter of personal choice is an incoherent amalgam of bad morality and bad epistemology...."[508]

Any truth statement about the nature of morality may have implications for behaviour. Christianity can be unattractive to people because it inhibits human autonomy and, if a person's conscience still operates, it can produce feelings of guilt that few people relish. Although rules are not the entire solution to the human predicament, they have been given for guidance, for protection and for the restraint of evil. For the Christian, individuals can have freedom from condemnation and guilt by accepting God's gift of forgiveness, which is given to those who recognise the lordship of Christ and his assumption of the burden of our sins. As Isaiah put it "…the Lord has laid on him the iniquity of us all" (Isaiah 53:6b, NIV). For those for whom personal autonomy is a guiding principle, this may not be an attractive message.

The emotional reaction against moral absolutes may explain, for instance, the concepts of homophobia and Islamophobia which are applied to those who take issue with the practice of homosexuality or the beliefs or practices of Islam. A logical criticism (which may or not be correct) is not the result of an irrational fear akin to the fear of a person of a different race. This is an example of the *ad hominem* logical fallacy, where the character of a person is attacked, in this case on the grounds that the person is said to harbour an irrational fear, rather than debating the content of their opinions.

Perhaps surprisingly for some, Christianity promotes tolerance. The position of the established church in England can help other faiths defend their freedom of belief. This might seem paradoxical, but there are two reasons for it. First, Christian theology puts a high value upon freedom of conscience and the free will of each individual to choose belief. Secondly, opposing opinions can easily irritate. Toleration of other beliefs, and a charitable disposition towards those who hold them, requires patience, humility and goodwill which are encouraged by the Christian faith.

23.12   THE NATURE OF THE DEBATE

It can be convenient not to debate the logic of the points at issue but simply to explain away an opponent's position entirely in language that reflects a particular way of thinking. This is a device sometimes used by politicians, but it alienates people, since it does not address the concerns of those who honestly hold a different point of view. Its effect is to create conflict and not understanding and to confuse or deceive those who are not aware of both sides of the argument.

There can, for instance, be a tendency to call those who oppose same sex marriage "bigots" or "homophobes" where the use of language imports judgment on the opinions expressed without the necessity to acknowledge or discuss them. This is the meaning of prejudice where there is a pre-judgment which all are expected to share without examination. It is also to assume motives on the part of those holding opinions without any evidence of those motives. This is unfair and likely to be offensive to those against whom the remarks are directed. There can also be a tendency to frame a debate only in terms that appear favourable to a particular point of view without acknowledging that there may be another perspective which needs to be addressed. So, for instance, in a discussion about same sex adoption, those in favour will frame the discussion in terms of the "rights" of homosexual people, rather than the wellbeing of the children involved.

People's emotions are engaged when it appears to them that their lifestyles are being challenged and there can be a tendency to interpret the criticism of a belief or behaviour as a personal attack. The Christian perspective is different. For Christians, as the Apostle Paul put it, all human beings have fallen short of the glory of God and there is no one righteous and in a position to pass judgment on another person. There is, nevertheless, good and bad in behaviour. The difference between the person and the behaviour needs to be understood and wrong actions need to be addressed in the appropriate way. Sadly, in relation to many issues today, it is impossible to criticise lifestyle without this being interpreted as a personal attack.

On the other hand, where injustice is being done, it may be appropriate for people to engage emotionally on behalf of the oppressed, although beliefs should be expressed calmly and with respect to those with opposing views. As Adam Smith put it: "The proper expression of just indignation composes many of the most admired passages both of ancient and modern eloquence."[509] The debate about abortion illustrates the way in which emotions can be engaged on both sides. "Pro-Choice" activists resent what they see as intrusion upon the autonomy of women bearing children and label anti-abortion campaigners as 'anti-choice'. "Pro-Life" campaigners regard abortion as the murder of human beings. Jesus himself, who did not sin in any way, exhibited righteous anger over injustice as well as sorrow and grief over suffering. Nevertheless, despite the emotions there should be a rational debate. Pro-Life campaigners need to explain why mothers do not have authority to end the lives of their unborn children and why those babies are as valuable as children who have been born. Pro-Choice campaigners need to explain why they treat living unborn children as a less valuable form of life than children who are born and why the positioning of a child in or outside the mother's body changes its essential characteristics. Or they need to justify the position that an unborn child is until birth a part of the mother's body over which the mother has absolute rights. These arguments and any others need to be debated calmly and rationally.

Where there is an absence of rational debate, perhaps because emotions are engaged too easily, weak reasoning may appear credible. The Christian approach must be to engage in reasoned discussion and persuasion, since rationality has been given by God for purposes such as these. At the same time, Christians also believe that knowledge of God and his laws is possible and that this is the foundation of truth. At the heart of any political theory is the creation of a polity conducive to flourishing lives. Good laws cannot make people good, but they create a framework for people to lead good lives, both as individuals and together in society. For the Christian, however good the laws and the structures of society are, the attitudes and behaviour of the people are as important, if not more so. People can be guided by laws and structures can provide incentives to right action, but behaviour is personal.

23.13   LESSONS OF THE RIOTS

The riots of August 2011 prompted much discussion. While the manifestations of the breakdown of society which the riots illustrated were manifold, they stemmed from a failure to reflect the wisdom of the Creator in political and social structures and the values of those who populate them. Family breakdown leading to rejection and rebellion, the absence of loving discipline in the home and the school, the all-pervasive effect of selfish materialism and greed, the absence of many moral values at every level of society and the lack of reverence for life all reflect a turning away from the patterns for living given by the Creator. The dynamic and self-perpetuating nature of imperfect structures and cultural influences mean that the individuals affected by them may be drawn into damaging behaviour by forces which they find hard to control or resist. Those who have fallen into those behaviour patterns are personally responsible for their actions, but human beings are morally weak and require loving discipline, guidance and training to enable them to make the right choices.

23.14   BACK TO ABSOLUTE VALUES

There needs to be a wholesale repudiation of the relativism in moral values which is prevalent in academic life and many of our schools and universities. Relativism is both intellectually incoherent and pragmatically damaging. Political leadership is required. Jeremy Rifkin summed up an intellectual basis of the autonomy which negates any settled moral values based upon objective wisdom: "We no longer feel ourselves to be guests in someone else's home and therefore make our behaviour conform to a set of pre-existing cosmic rules. It is our creation now. We make the rules. We establish the parameters of reality. We create the world and, because we do, we no longer feel beholden to outside forces. We no longer have to justify our behaviour, for we are the architects of the universe. We are responsible for nothing outside ourselves, for we are the kingdom, the power and the glory for ever and ever."[510] Relativism in relation to moral values or the sense that, though these values may exist, there is no logical basis for them, has undermined the confidence that comes from doing the right thing in challenging circumstances. As a society we need to affirm that there is objective truth. Christian thought provides a basis for this truth which works for the benefit of society.

Currently there is no clear basis for moral principles in British politics because there is no common understanding of where they come from. Politicians claiming unnecessarily expensive flat screen televisions on expenses do not command respect when they call for morality in the face of rioters looting flat screen televisions. If leaders do not have moral authority, they will struggle to inspire moral behaviour in others. Increased freedom of information about people's lives and the decline of deference over the last half century mean that those who govern can no longer apply double standards. Where wrong things have been done, they must be owned up to, not parried by self-justifying and self-serving responses. Respect for a number of British institutions, in particular Parliament, the police and the press, has declined as a result of recent scandals. Respect must now be earned.

The new vision for society must reflect a coherent outworking of what it means to be human. It must encompass an acceptance of the human capacity for both good and evil, the freedom to choose and, for each citizen, a moral obligation to take responsibility for actions which reflects accountability to fellow human beings and (for some) to the Creator God. Sarah Palin famously taunted Barack Obama (perhaps a little unfairly): "How's the hopey, changey thing going for ya?" A vision based on Christian values can survive setbacks, failures and hardship, as was shown in the Second World War. Christian values are eternal and are based upon the unchanging aspects of human nature and upon the designs of the Creator for humankind. Personal Christian belief can give hope to individuals and help them to rise above challenging circumstances and contribute to the common good.

The UK is suffering the serious effects of the poor choices of governments and individuals over many years, whether they have contributed to family breakdown, excessive consumerism or mountainous debt. A Christian perception is that when individuals and societies determine that their actions should be guided by the principles that God has given, God can help them build a healthier society, acting both within the natural processes of cause and effect and also supernaturally. There is much work to be done and the challenges are huge, but the message of the Christian faith is that God can be with us as we face them.

CONCLUSION

Philosophers teach us that we cannot offer a satisfactory explanation of something unless we use in the explanation concepts different from those that we use to describe the phenomenon in question. We cannot explain the goodness of something by saying that it has good qualities. Explanations need to be linked to other explanations and also to something which is ultimate. We need to explain moral qualities not just in terms of patterns and examples but by reference to a framework of general and necessarily transcendent values.

Explanations in terms of related matters are helpful but can take us only so far. We can explain Wagner's Ring Cycle by reference to the *leitmotifs* played out within it, but this does not tell us how, if at all, these are connected to something that can provide a more complete explanation. Love and power, the themes of the Ring Cycle do exist, but it is also relevant whether Wotan and the gods exist, and we know that they do not. The map of the world of Tolkien's *Lord of the Rings* has geographical features, but the places described are imaginary and have no connection to a higher reality.

The map of the moral landscape exists and has recognisable features that are rationally connected to each other. To describe a phenomenon in terms of its connections with other phenomena is not to explain it in the sense of accounting for its existence. To do so in relation to moral values, which most people believe do exist, we need something that is ultimate, that itself stands in need of no explanation. Otherwise, we would journey through a maze of linked explanations that ultimately have no meaning (because there is nothing to confer it), whilst our common sense suggests that these explanations are nevertheless a true description of the world we inhabit.

E. M. Forster reminded us to make connections. The connections between the elements of our physical world suggest a design and a designer. The logic and coherence of our moral world point to a similar conclusion. The structures of politics, economics and society reflect our God given human nature and the wisdom of the Creator can inform our individual choices and those we make as a society and a nation. Christians believe that there is a framework of values that derives from a God who has communicated with mankind. Human knowledge of ultimate reality is limited and human reason is flawed, but the Creator has endowed human beings with the ability to seek truth and to pursue it. Purely human systems of thought can convey partial truths but cannot deliver complete meaning or fulfilment. In Christian thinking, the wisdom of God can illuminate the past, inform the present and provide hope for the future. The Christian message is that there is a creator God, a rational order, an explanation of good and evil and the means for societies and individuals to seek what is objectively good. This is good news for all people, whatever systems of government they are subject to.

The standard of good that has been given by God provides the basis for divine justice under which all human beings, and particularly those with responsibility for others, are accountable. The revelation of God in the created order, and his interaction with mankind in coming to earth to live among us as recorded in the Bible, can give guidance both to individuals and to societies as to what constitutes a flourishing life and how this can be achieved. But the imperfection of the human condition has to be taken into account in any activity of government, however well meaning.

Systems of government cannot be redeemed or renewed except through the actions of the individuals populating them. For individuals, the acknowledgement of duties, as well as rights, provide a framework for right behaviour. For Christians, the source of those duties is our creator and he can bring personal renewal and, through people, renew society. Christian belief provides an escape from the closed systems of secular thought, where humankind is the measure of all things. It provides hope that human beings can rise above their limitations by participating in a divine plan founded upon the love of God and neighbour.

Not everyone will make the leap into personal Christian faith, with its challenges and consolations, but God's truth for society can reflect in this transitory world eternal values that are good for all humankind because they reflect the nature of the one who created us.

POSTSCRIPT

Individuals can have a personal relationship with God who can guide them, particularly in testing times. Field Marshal Viscount Alanbrooke recalled in his diary for VE day on May 8th 1945 the time he was offered the appointment of Chief of the Imperial General Staff during some of the darkest days of the Second World War: "I remember the night Winston offered me the job of C.I.G.S. in the large smoking room at Chequers, and when he went out I was so overcome that my natural impulse was, when left alone, to kneel and pray God for his assistance in my new task. I have often looked back during the last three and a half years to that prayer."[511] Prayer is communication with the Creator God and, for the Christian, access to God is only possible through belief in what God has done for us in Jesus Christ in dealing with our sin (which would otherwise separate us from God). In some ways prayer can be likened to a conversation. We bring our failings and our aspirations to God and we ask for his perspective on our lives, for his forgiveness and his strength to address the challenges we face.

Faith in God can help us see and understand things differently. John Dryden, in his *Religio Laici*, says that faith can inform reason and he sums up the character of the Christian God:

> "Revealed religion first informed thy sight
> And reason saw not till faith sprung the light
> Hence all thy natural worship takes the source
> 'Tis revelation what thou think'st discourse
> …
> The forfeit first, and then the fine impose,
> A mulct thy poverty could never pay
> Had not eternal wisdom found the way
> And with celestial wealth supplied thy store:
> His justice makes the fine, his mercy quits the score.
> See God descending in thy human frame,

Th' offended, suffering in th' offender's name;
All thy misdeeds to Him imputed see,
And all his righteousness devolved on thee".[512]

The Christian faith is intelligently pessimistic about human frailty and the ability of human beings to deal with the challenges of existence in an imperfect world. Christian belief makes sense of our human nature and helps us to deal with a world which is often confusing and uncertain. We need the guidance of unchanging values to run our lives, and we need the help of the Creator God (who in Jesus Christ has taken our human form) to overcome the challenges we face. Without God's help, we may struggle both to know what is right and to do it.

Personal belief in the Christian God involves an acceptance of the historical truths of the Christian faith and their significance. These truths are not symbolic but factual, though their meaning expresses deep truths about our human nature. We are all eternal beings with an eternal destiny and each one of us is called by God to understand his will. The good news (the gospel) of Jesus Christ is that, although we are personally responsible for our own actions where we have fallen short (we have sinned), we can be rescued from the consequences of our sin by belief and trust in Jesus Christ.

Christian faith involves personal submission to the rule of God in a believer's life. This requires a fear of God, a recognition of sin, and repentance which is a condition of forgiveness. Forgiveness is made possible by the death of Jesus who took the burden of our wrongdoings on the cross and by his resurrection to glory. The personal result is what Christians call salvation. This means being saved from the penalty of sin and given help to resist it. While a preoccupation with sin can appear negative, sin is the reverse of love. Love is expressed both by positive acts of kindness and by not sinning against people. The character of the life to come for those who ignore the good news of salvation is what Christians refer to as "hell", which is alienation from God and separation from the source of all goodness. Jesus taught that this would be a profoundly uncomfortable experience. Christian teachers characterise repentance, belief in Jesus as Lord and Saviour, baptism and receiving the Holy Spirit as the process by which people are to become Christians.

Only God in Jesus Christ has the power to forgive and redeem our imperfect state, to call us to live for him and, by his grace alone, to endeavour to live for others. The power of God working in individuals engenders both a purpose and a joy in our lives which Jesus described as "abundant" life. The abundant life that Jesus describes is not that of wealth, health and obvious happiness, and Jesus promised that in this world we would have trouble. But in all circumstances Jesus promised peace of a kind that the world cannot give, the peace which the Apostle Paul described as passing all human understanding.

Jesus said that he is "the way, the truth, and the life."[513] Christianity offers the way and the life because it offers the truth. That truth is based upon the revelation of God in history, as recorded in the Bible, and explains the reality of our life on earth and the world to come.

END NOTES

Chapter 1: Knowledge and Morality

1   Renford Bambrough, *Moral Scepticism and Moral Knowledge,* Routlege and Keegan Paul (1979), p.44

2   Rupert Sheldrake, *The Science Delusion: Freeing the Spirit of Enquiry,* Coronet (2012), Chapter 9

3   Philip Larkin, *Days: Collected Poems,* Faber & Faber (2003), p.98

4   Michael Brooks, New Scientist, 22nd January 2011

5   1 Corinthians 13:12, KJV

6   *The Guardian,* 1st February 2012

7   Job 42:3, NIV

8   Job 42:5, NIV

9   Alexis De Tocqueville, Democracy in America, Bantam Classics (2002), p.644

10   Renford Bambrough, *Reason, Truth and God,* Methuen (1969), p.110

11   Renford Bambrough, op. cit. p.115

12   T.S. Eliot, *The Four Quartets, The Dry Salvages: V,* Faber & Faber (1979), p.30

13   Renford Bambrough, op. cit. p.97

14   Alistair McIntyre, *After Virtue: A Study of Modern Theory,* Duckworth (2007)

15   Christopher Coker, *Ethics and War in the 21st Century,* Routlege (2008), p.12

16   Renford Bambrough, op. cit. p.125

17   Michel Houellebecq, *The Map and the Territory,* translated by Gavin Bowd, William Heinemann (2011)

18   Renford Bambrough, op. cit. p.44

19   Cicero, *The Republic,* Book Three, paras 29-31, Oxford World Classics, translated by Niall Rudd (1998), p.68

20   Mary Warnock, *Dishonest to God,* Continuum (2010)

21   Mary Warnock, op. cit.

22   Carl Schmitt, *Political Theology,* Cambridge (1985), p.36

23   Francis Fukuyama, *The Origins of Political Order,* Profile Books (2011), Chapter 18

24   Renford Bambrough, op. cit. p.123

25   Renford Bambrough, op. cit. p.112

26   Proverbs 29:18, KJV

27   Philip Allott, *Eunomia,* Oxford (1990), p.74, para 5:19

28   *Standpoint* magazine, September 2011

29   *Standpoint* magazine, September 2011

Chapter 2: Theories of Political Philosophy

30   Thomas Aquinas, *Selected Political Writings: On Princely Government,* translated by J.G. Dawson, edited by A. P. D'Entreves, Basil Blackwell, Oxford (1970), Chapter IV, p.21; see also Chapter III, p.15

31   *The Teachings of Epictetus,* translated by T.W. Rolleston, George Routledge
      & Sons (1898), p.3

32   Francis Fukuyama, *Trust: The Social Virtues and the Creation of Prosperity,*
      Simon & Schuster (1995)

33   Michael Schluter and David John Lee, *The R Option*, Relationships
      Foundation (2003)

34   Philip Allott, op. cit. para 4.8, p.55

35   *Pascal's Pensees,* Harvill Press (1962), para 667, p.319

36   *The British Church Newspaper,* 25th February 2011, p.6

37   *The British Church Newspaper* and see *The Irish Times,* 15th July 2011

38   *The British Church Newspaper,* 12th August 2011, p.5

39   Immanuel Kant, *Groundwork of the Metaphysics of Morals,* translated by H.J.
      Paton, Harper & Row, New York (1962), p.43 and op. cit. *Critique of Pure
      Practical Reason*, Chapter 111, p.115

40   Thomas Hobbes, *Leviathan*

41   Calvin, *Commentary on St. Paul's Epistle to the Romans.* The version quoted is
      not referenced but an accessible version is available, translated by John King,
      Forgotten Books (2007), p.359

42   Calvin, op. cit. p.360

43   Calvin, op. cit. p.360

44   Calvin, op. cit. p.358

45   John Coffey, *Politics, Religion and the British Revolutionaries,* Cambridge
      University Press (1997), p.162

46   Aristotle, *The Politics,* Book I, in *The Philosophy of Aristotle*, translated by J.L.
      Creed and A.E. Wardman, edited by Renford Bambrough, Mentor (1963),
      p.382

47   *Vindiciae, Contra Tyrannos*, edited by George Garnett, Cambridge
      University Press (1994), p.92

48   Samuel Rutherford, *Lex Rex,* quoted in John Coffey, op. cit. p.159

49   Roger Scruton, *The West and the Rest,* Continuum (2002), pp.12-13

50   Miroslav Volf, *Exclusion and Embrace,* Abingdon Press (1996)

51   See: Augustine, *City of God,* translated by Henry Bettenson, edited by David
      Knowles, Penguin Books (1972), Book XIX, Chapter 21, pp.881-882

52   Augustine, *City of God,* Book XIX, Chapter 24, op. cit. p.890

53   Jeremy Bentham, *Introduction to the Principles of Morals and Legislation,*
      included in *Utilitarianism and On Liberty,* edited by Mary Warnock,
      Blackwell Publishing (2003), p.18

54   Herbert Schlossberg, *The Silent Revolution and the Making of Victorian
      England,* Ohio State University (2000)

55   Herbert Schlossberg, op. cit. p.192

56   Gerard Manley Hopkins, *The Windhover, To Christ Our Lord,* written in
      1877 and 1879, *Poems* 1918

57   See Plato, *Gorgias* paragraphs 514A and 515D in *Plato, Gorgias and
      Aristotle, Rhetoric,* edited by Joe Sachs, Focus Philosophical Library (2009),
      pp.106 and 108

58   See Nick Spencer, "A Game of Consequences", *Standpoint* magazine, January/February 2011, available at: http://www.standpointmag.co.uk/counterpoints-janfeb-11-a-game-of-consequences-nick-spencer-baroness-warnock-church-and-state (accessed 30th May 2011)

59   Nick Spencer, op. cit.

60   Ecclesiastes 8:7, Good News Bible

61   Thomas Aquinas, *Summa Theologica,* Chapter V, Article 4, in Aquinas, *Selected Political Writings,* op. cit. p.117

62   David W. Hall, *Calvin in the Public Square,* P & R Publishing (2009), p.89

63   John Stuart Mill, *On Liberty* (1859), Oxford World Classics (1991), Chapter 1, p.14

64   William Temple, *Christianity and the State,* MacMillan (1929), p.80, quoted in: David Holloway, *A Nation Under God,* Kingsway (1987), p.90

65   Matthew 22:37, NKJV

66   Matthew 22:39, NKJV

67   Roger Scruton, op. cit. p.66

68   Edmund Burke, *Reflections on the Revolution in France,* Oxford University Press (1993)

69   Blond, Phillip, *The Ownership State,* ResPublica and NESTA (October 2009), at p.10, available at: http://www.nesta.org.uk/library/documents/The-ownership-state-FINAL.PDF (accessed 24th June 2011)

70   Christopher Coker, op. cit. p.12

71   Fareed Zakaria, *The Future of Freedom,* W. W. Norton & Company (2003)

72   Dambiso Moyo, *How the West Was Lost,* Allen Lane (2011), p.171

73   Thomas Aquinas, *On Princely Government,* Chapter VI, in Aquinas, *Selected Political Writings,* op. cit. p.35

74   *The Philosophy of Aristotle,* translated by J.C. Creed and A.E. Wardman, ed. Renford Bambrough, Mentor (1943), Book 1, para 5, p.289

75   Thomas Aquinas, *On Princely Government,* Chapter XIV, *Selected Political Writings,* op. cit. p.75

Chapter 3: Secular Thought

76   Rob Parsons, *Teenagers,* Hodders (2007), p.11

77   See the book review on *UK Parents' Lounge* at: http://www.ukparentslounge.com/index.php?pg=69&utwkstoryid=1049&title=Teenagers+-+What+Every+Parent+Has+To+Know&ind=17 (accessed 16th June 2011)

78   *The Daily Telegraph,* 25th January 2012

79   These phrases were also quoted in the blog *"Imitatio Christi"* on 29th September 2005 at: http://imitatiochristi.blogs.com/imitatio_christi/2005/09/volfs_exclusion.html (accessed 16th June 2011)

80   See in particular Adam Smith, *The Wealth of Nations,* Bantam Classics (2003)

81   Adam Smith, *The Theory of Modern Sentiments,* Prometheus Books (2000)

82   John Rawls, *A Theory of Justice,* Clarendon Press (1971); 2nd Revised edition, Oxford University Press (1999)

83   Alain de Botton, *Religion for Atheists,* Hamish Hamilton (2012)

84   Also quoted in chapter 13.I.B of Plantinga, Alvin, *Warranted Christian Belief,* available at the following link: http://www.ccel.org/ccel/plantinga/warrant3.vii.iii.i.ii.html (accessed 22nd June 2011)

85   The essay in which that sentence appears, *Ideology and Terror: A Novel Form of Government,* has been reproduced on the "Mr. Renaissance" website (see the fourth paragraph from the end at the following link): http://www.mrrena.com/misc/h_arendt.php (accessed 16th June 2011)

86   Miroslav Volf, op. cit.

87   Savitri Hensman, *The Best Path to Peace, The Guardian,* 15th January 2011, available at: http://www.guardian.co.uk/commentisfree/belief/2011/jan/15/rowan-williams-reconciliation-peace?INTCMP=SRCH (accessed 20th June 2011)

88   Callum Brown, *The Death of Christian Britain,* Routlege (2001)

89   *McFarlane v Relate Avon Ltd* [2010] EWCA Civ B1 (29th April 2010) available at: http://www.bailii.org/ew/cases/EWCA/Civ/2010/B1.html (accessed 20th June 2011)

90   Laurence Rees, *Auschwitz: The Nazis and the Final Solution,* BBC Books (2005), p.91

Chapter 4: Natural Law

91   Philip Allott, op. cit. para 5.23, p.75

92   Cicero, *De Re Publica,* translated by C.W. Keyes, Loeb Classical Library, Book III, xxii, p.211; see also Oxford World Classics, op. cit. pp.68-69

93   Cicero, *The Laws,* Book Two, 8, Oxford World Classics, p.124

94   Philip Allott, op. cit. para 5.40, p.82 and para 6.72, p.112

95   See Thomas Aquinas, *Summa Theologica, Prima Secundae,* Question 91, "The Natural Law", Art. 2, in Aquinas *Selected Political Writings,* op. cit. p.115; also available at: http://faculty.tcu.edu/rgalvin/readings/St.%20Thomas%20Aquinas%20%20Legal%20Naturalism.doc (accessed 14th June 2011)

96   See Thomas Aquinas, *Summa Theologica, Prima Secundae,* Question 95, Art. 2, in Aquinas, *Selected Political Writings,* op. cit. p.129; also available at: http://www.op.org/summa/a4/summa-I-IIq95a2.pdf (accessed 14th June 2011); the exact words used to translate Aquinas' texts vary between versions.

97   Aquinas, Summa Theologica, Question 93, Article 3 in Aquinas, *Selected Political Writings,* op. cit.

98   Gratian, Decretum *(The Treatise on Laws),* translated by Augustine Thompson, Catholic University Press of America (1993), Distinction One, Part 2, para C 7, p.6

99   C.S Lewis, *Mere Christianity,* Harper Collins; 50th Anniversary edition (Reissue) (2011)

100   Luke 6:31, NIV

101 Immanuel Kant, op. cit. para 52, p.88

102 Immanuel Kant, op. cit. para 54, p.90

103 Michel Houellebecq, *Atomised,* translated by Frank Wynne, Vintage Books (2001), p.37

104 Immanuel Kant, op. cit. para 17, pp.69-70. There are several slightly different translations of Kant's work, which is also known as *Fundamental Principles of the Metaphysic of Morals;* its First Section, *Transition from the Common Rational Knowledge of Morality to the Philosophical,* from which these quotations were taken, can be found at: http://www.sussex.ac.uk/library/etexts/philtxts/kant/pr_moral/fstsect.txt (accessed 15th June 2011)

105 *The Teachings of Epictetus,* op. cit. p.12

106 A.J. Ayer, *The Central Questions of Philosophy,* Weidenfeld and Nicolson (1973) pages 15-16

107 A.J. Ayer, op. cit. p.9

108 A.J. Ayer, op. cit. p.11

109 John Coffey, op. cit. (quoting from Samuel Rutherford, Lex Rex), p.153

110 Adam Smith, *The Theory of Modern Sentiments,* 1st edition, II, (ii) 3, quoted by D.D. Raphael in *The Impartial Spectator,* Clarendon Press, Oxford (2007), p.98

111 Quoted by Melanie Phillips, *Welcome to the Age of Irrationality, The Spectator,* 1st May 2010, p.20

112 A.J. Ayer, op. cit. p. 219

113 Renford Bambrough, op. cit. p.148

114 Christopher Coker, op. cit. p.21

115 See Nick Paumgarten, *Acts of God, The New Yorker,* 12th July 2010, available at: http://www.newyorker.com/talk/2010/07/12/100712ta_talk_paumgarten (accessed 14th June 2011)

116 Tolstoy, *War and Peace,* translated by Rosemary Edwards, Penguin Classics (1957), p.1427

117 See Carl G. Hempel, *The Function of General Laws in History* (1942), in Michael Martin & Lee C. McIntyre (eds.), *Readings in the Philosophy of Social Science,* pp.43-53, at p.44, available at: http://books.google.com/books?id=oUx60TFkLxoC&pg=PR2&dq=0-262-63151- 2&hl=de&sig=ACfU3U2o4EciGiuB9V1BryQ6cI5TFUiAoQ#v=onepage&q=0-262-63151-2&f=false (accessed 14th June 2011)

118 I.D. Jones, *The English Resolution,* London (1931) p. 106 quoted in: William Dray, *Laws and Explanation in History,* Oxford University Press (1957), p.138

119 Available at: http://www.spiritualityandpractice.com/films/films.php?id=7663 (accessed 15th June 2011)

120 *The Fountain Magazine,* Trinity College, Cambridge (Spring 2011)

121 Paul Bloom, *The Moral Life of Babies, The New York Times Magazine,* 5th May 2010, available at: http://www.nytimes.com/2010/05/09/magazine/09babies-t.html (accessed 15th June 2011)

122 See Philip Allott, op. cit. paras 6.80-6.85, pp.114-116

123 Roger Trigg, *Religion in Public Life: Must Faith Be Privatized?* Oxford, OUP (2007) at p.79, available to view online at: http://www.scribd.com/doc/30837784/5/Rights-and-Freedoms#page=81 (accessed 15th June 2011)

124 John Locke, *An Essay Concerning Human Understanding,* Book IV, Chapter (iii), section 18, available at: http://humanum.arts.cuhk.edu.hk/Philosophy/Locke/echu (accessed 15th June 2011)

125 John Locke, *Second Treatise on Civil Government,* Chapter ii, section 4, available at: http://jim.com/2ndtreat.htm#2CHAP (accessed 15th June 2011)

Chapter 5: God's Laws and Human Laws

126 John 10:10 (KJV): "I am come that they may have life and that they may have it more abundantly."

127 Cicero, *The Laws,* Book Two,11, Oxford World Classics, p.125

128 Annabel Brett (Translator and Editor), Cambridge Texts in the History of Political Thought, *Marsilius of Padua: The Defender of the Peace,* Discourse I, Chapter 5, Section 11, at pp.28-29, available to view at: http://www.scribd.com/doc/18003980/Padua-The-Defender-of-Peace-Cmbrdg-Txt-Hstr-Pltcl-Thgt (accessed 16th June 2011)

129 Philip S. Ross, *From the Finger of God,* Mentor (2010)

130 Christopher J.H. Wright, *Old Testament Ethics for the People of God,* IVP (1988). The five categories are criminal law, case law, family law, cultic law and compassionate (see pp. 288-301)

131 See *The Jubilee Manifesto,* edited by Michael Schluter and John Ashcroft

132 John Donne, *No Man is an Island,* available at: http://www.poemhunter.com/poem/no an-is-an-island (accessed 16th June 2011)

133 The story can be viewed at: http://www.thisislondon.co.uk/standard/article-23811226-the dispossessed-mother-of-11-lives-on-just-pound-7-a-dayper-child.do (accessed 16th June 2011)

134 Magna Carta, available at: the British Library's website: http://www.bl.uk/treasures/magnacarta/translation/mc_trans.html (accessed 3rd June 2011)

135 John Coffey, op. cit. p.169

Chapter 6: Limited Government, Personal Restraint and Welfare

136 David W. Hall, op. cit. p.85

137 See the second part of Michael Dewalt's post on the Calvin Quincentenary blog at pp.8-9: http://calvin500blog.wordpress.com/2009/03/09/calvin%E2%80%99s-principles-of-government-in-the-venues-of-church-and-state-part-2 (accessed 20th June 2011)

138 David Hall: *Celebrating Calvin,* available at: http://www.chapelbythelake.org/downloads/calvin_03.pdf (accessed 20th June 2011); David W. Hall, op. cit. p.86

139 David W. Hall, *The Reformation Roots of Social Contract,* Acton Institute (1997), available at: http://www.acton.org/pub/religion-liberty/volume-7-number-4/reformation-roots-social-contract (accessed 20th June 2011)

140 This quotation can also be found at the following link to David W. Hall's speech, *The Reformation Roots of Social Contract,* available at: http://www.phillysoc.org/reformat.htm (accessed 20th June 2011); see also David W. Hall, op. cit. p.179

141 John Stuart Mill, *On Liberty,* Chapter 1, *Utilitarianism and On Liberty,* edited by Mary Warnock, Blackwell Publishing (1962), p.90

142 Bede, *Ecclesiastical History of the English People,* translated by Leo Sherley-Price, Penguin Books (1990), p.77

143 Peter Hitchens, *Brief History of Crime,* Atlantic Books (2003), p.14

144 This quotation has been reproduced on the following website: http://homepage.eircom.net/~odyssey/Politics/Quotes/Peter_Hitchens.html#Intro (accessed 20th June 2011); see also Peter Hitchens, op. cit. p.6

145 Quoted in Ferguson, Niall, *To do 'God's work', bankers need morals, The Daily Telegraph,* 5th July 2010, at: http://www.telegraph.co.uk/finance/newsbysector/banksandfinance/7871781/To-do-Gods-work-bankers-need-morals.html (accessed 20th June 2011)

146 The original e-mail by Tourre to his girlfriend was partly in English, partly in French and contained vulgar language. A translated and expurgated version of this quotation can be seen in *The Daily Telegraph* article of 5th July 2010 above

147 *The Spectator,* 10th September 2011

148 *The Spectator,* 17th September 2011

149 Margaret Kennedy, *The Ladies of Lyndon* (1923), Virago Modern Classics (1981), p.215

150 Brendan O'Neill, *The Spectator,* 24th April 2010, p.22

151 See Alfred J. Freddoso, New English Translation of Thomas Aquinas' *Summa Theologiae (Summa Theologica),* Part 1, Question 96, Article 4, at p.5 at the following link: http://www.nd.edu/~afreddos/summa-translation/Part%201/st1-ques96.pdf. The source of this translation can be seen by opening the following links: http://www.nd.edu/~afreddos/creationhumannature.html and http://www.nd.edu/~afreddos/Summahome.html (all accessed 21st June 2011)

152 This quotation also appears in Roy Maynard, "Amsterdam unravelled", *World Magazine,* "Pilgrims' progress" issue 28th November 1998, available at: http://www.worldmag.com/articles/2477 (accessed 22nd June 2011)

153 *The British Church Newspaper,* 11th February 2011

154 *The British Church Newspaper,* 11th February 2011

155 *The British Church Newspaper,* 23rd September 2011

156 *The Sunday Times,* 15th December 2012

157 *The Metro,* February 22nd 2012, p.8

158 Heather Brooke, *The Silent State,* Windmill Books (2012), p.47

159 This is quoted on page 12 of the PowerPoint presentation entitled *Disquietude* of 10th July 2009: http://www.authorstream.com/Presentation/POETKnoxville-212358-Disquietude- Founding-Fathers-References-Spiritual-Inspirational-ppt-powerpoint (accessed 22nd June 2011)

160 Heather Brooke, op. cit. See pp.8-36

161 *The British Church Newspaper,* 28th January 2011, citing a report by the Manifesto Club, authored by Adrian Hart

162 Philip Johnston, *Bad Laws,* Constable (2010), p.190

163 Philip Johnston, op. cit. p.191

164 James Bartholomew, *The Welfare State We're In,* Politico's (2004)

165 *The Spectator,* 15th September 2012

166 *The Spectator,* 9th July 2011

167 Harriet Sergeant, *When Nothing Matters, The Spectator,* 13th August 2011

168 *Krona capitalism, The Spectator,* 9th July 2011, available at: http://www.spectator.co.uk/essays/all/7075543/krona-capitalism.thtml.

169 *The Spectator,* 7th May 2011

170 Philip Johnston, *The Daily Telegraph,* 18th September 2012

171 *Moneyweek,* 2nd September 2011

172 *The Spectator,* 15th September 2012

173 *The Daily Telegraph,* 31st December 2011

174 William T. Muhairwe, *Making Public Enterprises Work,* Fountain Publishers, Kampala (2009)

Chapter 7: Conscience, Rights and the Public Good

175 See: "Christian Loses Sunday Working appeal", *The Guardian,* 25th July 2005 at: http://www.guardian.co.uk/money/2005/jul/25/troubleatwork.religion

176 Cicero, *The Laws,* Book One, op. cit. p.117

177 See Article 9(2) at the website of the European Court of Human Rights: http://www.echr.coe.int/NR/rdonlyres/D5CC24A7-DC13-4318-B457-5C9014916D7A/0/ENG_CONV.pdf (accessed 22nd June 2011)

178 See: "Christian found guilty of 'malpractice' for sharing his faith", *Christian Concern & Christian Legal Centre,* June 14th 2012:http://www.christianconcern.com/our-concerns/religious-freedom/christian-gp-found-guilty-of-malpractice-for-sharing-his-faith

179 Ladele v Islington LBC, Court of Appeal [2009] EWCA Civ 1357

180 R. (on the application of Johns) v Derby City Council, QBD [2011] EWHC 375 (Admin)

181 The case of Peter and Hazelmary Bull where Judge Andrew Rutherford awarded Mr Hall and Mr Preddy £3,600 damages. See (inter alia) *The Daily Telegraph,* January 19th 2011, p.17

182 Michael L. Brown, *A Queer Thing Happened to America,* Equal Time Books (2011), p.535

183 A.V. Dicey (1904) 17 Harvard LR, 511, quoted by Ian Leigh in *Religious Liberty and Human Rights,* edited by Mark Hill, University of Wales Press (2002), p.133

184 *The Guardian,* 3rd March 2012

185 US Supreme Court: Christian Legal Society, Chapter of the University of California, Hastings College of Law v Martinez et al. See: http://www.supremecourt.gov/opinions/09pdf/08-1371.pdf

Chapter 8: Impartial Justice and the Separation of Powers

186 Plato, *The Laws,* translated by Trevor Saunders, Penguin (1970), p.284

187 David W. Hall, op. cit. p.89

188 Philip Johnston, op. cit.; see Chapter 3

189 Jamie Whyte, *City AM* newspaper, 9th May 2012, p.22

190 *The Daily Telegraph,* October 8th 2010, p.12

191 See the DownloadsEdge article, "Now police are ordered to protect 'Doggers' indulging in outdoor sex with strangers from hate crime", available at: http://www.downloadsedge.com/now-police-are-ordered-to-protect-doggers-indulging-in-outdoor-sex-with-strangers-from-hate-crime/2010/10/07 (accessed 23rd June 2011)

192 See *Ian Tomlinson death: Police officer comes forward to IPCC, The Guardian,* 8th April 2009, available at: http://www.guardian.co.uk/uk/2009/apr/08/tomlinson-death-inquiry-police-officer (accessed 23rd June 2011)

193 See Christopher Hope, *The Daily Telegraph, White Christian Britons being unfairly targeted for hate crimes by CPS, Civitas claims,* available at: http://www.telegraph.co.uk/news/uknews/law-and-order/7897125/White-Christian-Britons-being-unfairly-targeted-for-hate-crimes-by-CPS-Civitas-claims.html (accessed 23rd June 2011)

194 See paragraphs 2 and 3 of Mark Durie's blog on the OIC Fatwa on Domestic Violence and the Rights of Women in Islam, at: http://markdurie.blogspot.com/2011/05/oic-fatwa-on-domestic-violence-and.html (accessed 23rd June 2011)

195 For a version of the Bill, see the Parliament website: http://services.parliament.uk/bills/2010-11/arbitrationandmediationservicesequalityhl/documents.html (accessed 23rd June 2011).

196 Douglas Murray, *The Spectator,* 22nd October 2011, p.14

197 This is quoted in M.J.C. Vile, *Constitutionalism and the Separation of Powers* (2nd ed.) (Indianapolis, Liberty Fund, 1998), Chapter 4, which is available on the Online Library of Liberty at: http://oll.libertyfund.org/index.php?Itemid=287&id=462&option=com_content&task=view (accessed 24th June 2011)

198 John R. Bradley, *Aims of the Brotherhood, The Spectator,* 5th February 2011, available at: http://www.spectator.co.uk/essays/all/6666343/aims-of-the-brotherhood.thtml (accessed 24th June 2011)

199 Available at: the British Library's website: http://www.bl.uk/treasures/magnacarta/translation/mc_trans.html (accessed 3rd June 2011)

200 *The Sunday Telegraph,* 18th March 2012

201 *The Daily Telegraph,* 30th March 2012

202 *The Daily Telegraph,* 11th April 2012

203 *The Mail Online,* 22nd February 2011, available at: http://www.dailymail.co.uk/news/article-1359252/Family-torn-apart-15-minute-court-case-Judge-James-Orrell.html?printingPage=true

204 See: http://towardchange.wordpress.com/2012/09/26/the-president-of-the-family-division-is-a-lord-justice-wall/

205 Webster v Norfolk CC [2009] EWCA Civ 59

206 See this example of their literature: http://www.bathnes.gov.uk/
SiteCollectionDocuments/Health%20and%20Social%20Care/
Safeguarding%20Adults%20Inter-Agency%20Partnership%20Annual%20
Report%E2%80%A6.pdf (accessed 24th June 2011)

Chapter 9: Accountability and Democracy

207 Also known in modern translations as *The Devils:* http://zavierellis.blogspot.
com/2011/05/possessed-curated-by-john-stark.html or Demons: http://
en.wikipedia.org/wiki/The_Possessed_%28novel%29 (accessed 3rd June
2011)

208 Hannah Arendt, *The Origins of Totalitarianism,* 2nd edition, Harvest Books,
Harcourt Press (1968); see Chapter 9, Part II, the Perplexities of the Rights
of Man, p.290

209 Quoted in Patricia Sheridan, *Pirates, Kings and Reasons to Act: Moral
Motivation and the Role of Sanctions in Locke's Moral Theory,* Canadian
Journal of Philosophy, Volume 37, Number 1, March 2007, pp. 35-48, at p.
38: http://www.canadianjournalofphilosophy.com/PDFs/cjp37-1--035-048-
-Sheridan.pdf (accessed 24th June 2011)

210 John Myers, *Voices from the Edge of Eternity,* Whitaker House (1968), p.142

211 Alexis de Tocqueville, *Democracy in America,* Bantam Classics (2002), p.357

212 Plato: *The Laws,* translated by Trevor J. Saunders, Penguin Books (1970), p.277

213 Quoted on the House of Russell website: http://www.houseofrussell.com/
legalhistory/alh/docs/deTocq.html (accessed 24th June 2011)

214 Hannah Arendt, quoted on the *Got Fascism?* website: http://www.
gotfascism.org/other.html (accessed 24th June 2011)

215 Vishal Mangalwadi, *Truth and Transformation,* YWAM Publishing (2009),
p.109

216 Vishal Mangalwadi, *Truth and Social Reform,* Article 8328, The Network
for Strategic Missions, at p.1, available at: http://www.strategicnetwork.org/
index.php?loc=kb&view=v&id=8328&pagenum=1&lang=(accessed 24th
June 2011)

217 Marsilius of Padua, *Defensor Pacis (Defender of the Peace) (1324),* Discourse
I, Chapter 12, paragraph 5

218 See Marsilius of Padua, *Defensor Pacis,* Discourse I, Chapter XII, paragraphs
5 and 9, available at: http://cassian.memphis.edu/history/jmblythe/
MedRenF07/MarsiliusOfPadua%20government.htm (accessed 24th June
2011)

219 Marsilius of Padua, *Defensor Pacis,* Discourse I, Chapter 13, paragraph 3

220 Marsilius of Padua, *Defensor Pacis,* Discourse II, Chapter 9, paragraph 3

221 See John Calvin, *Harmony of the Law,* Volume 1, available online via the
Christian Classics Ethereal Library at: http://www.ccel.org/ccel/calvin/
calcom03.iv.xviii.iii.html?scrBook=Deut&scrCh=1&scrV=13#highlight
(accessed 6th June 2011)

222 *Vindiciae, Contra Tyrannos,* edited by George Garnett, Cambridge
University Press (1994), Editor's Introduction, p.xxv

223 *Vindiciae, Contra Tyrannos,* op. cit. p.21

224 John Coffey, op. cit. p.164

225 David W. Hall, op. cit. p.256

226 David W. Hall, op. cit. p.256. Both these quotations can also be found half-way down the following webpage: http://www.worldviewweekend.com/worldview-times/article_feedback.php?articleid=225&page=2 (accessed 24th June 2011)

227 Fareed Zakaria, *The Future of Freedom,* W.W. Norton & Company (2003)

228 Plato, *The Republic,* edited by Renford Bambrough, Everyman (1976), Introduction, p.ix

229 Quoted in *Moneyweek,* 14th September 2012, p.6

230 See: *The Weak Foundations of Arab Democracy,* 28th May 2011, available at: http://www.nytimes.com/2011/05/29/opinion/29kuran.html?_r=1&scp=1&sq=Timur%20Kuran%20Democracy&st=cse.

231 *The Spectator,* 26th November 2011

Chapter 10: Equality and Social Justice

232 David Bentley Hart, *Atheist Delusions, The Christian Revolution and Its Fashionable Enemies,* Yale University Press (2009), pp.177 and 179

233 *Evening Standard,* 1st May 2012, p.18

234 *The Daily Telegraph,* 12th December 2011, p.B3

235 This report is available in full at:http://www.instituteofhealthequity.org/projects/fair-society-healthy-lives-the-marmot-review

236 Christopher Caldwell, *The Spectator,* 15th January 2011, p.19, citing Michael Young's work of 1958

237 Quoted on the following web page: http://www.pbs.org/wgbh/amex/carnegie/filmmore/description.html (accessed 7th June 2011)

238 Phillip Blond, *The Ownership State,* ResPublica and NESTA, October 2009, at p.10, available at: http://www.nesta.org.uk/library/documents/The-ownership-state-FINAL.PDF (accessed 24th June 2011)

239 Martin Van De Weyer, reviewing Michael Lewis, *Boomerang: The Meltdown Tour, The Spectator,* 22nd October 2011, p.41

240 Bill Bonner, *Moneyweek,* 1st October 2010, p.50

241 *Economia* magazine, July 2012, page 58

242 Dennis Sewell, *The Spectator,* 13th September 2011, p.15

243 Merryn Somerset Webb, *Moneyweek,* 1st June 2012, p.26

244 Merryn Somerset Webb, op. cit., loc. cit.

245 Matthew Lynn, *Moneyweek,* March 2012

246 Anthony Hilton, *Evening Standard,* 10th November 2010, p.37

247 See section 149(1)(b), available at: http://www.legislation.gov.uk/ukpga/2010/15/section/149 (accessed 27th June 2011)

248 See, for example, the foreword to *Our Strategic Plan: Executive Summary 2009–2012,* at p. 3, available at: http://www.equalityhumanrights.com/uploaded_files/strategicplan2009-2012summary.pdf (accessed 27th June 2011)

249 See *ECJ gender ruling hits insurance costs, The Guardian,* 1st March 2011, available at: http://www.guardian.co.uk/money/2011/mar/01/ecj-gender-ruling-insurance-costs (accessed 7th June 2011)

250 See, for example, Gilbert Bagnani, *Divine Right and Roman Law, Phoenix,* Vol. 3, No. 2. (Autumn, 1949), at p.59, available at: http://www.scribd.com/doc/10498854/Divine-Right-and-Roman-Law (accessed 27th June 2011)

251 See Daniel Finkelstein's article in *The Times, Civic conservatism replies to compassionate conservatism,* 20th February 2008, available at: http://timesonline.typepad.com/comment/2008/02/civic-conservat.html (accessed 27th June 2011)

252 Quoted in Paul Bickley, *Building Jerusalem? Christianity and the Labour Party, Bible Society* (2010), at p. 30, available at: http://www.lulu.com/items/volume_68/9345000/9345824/3/print/Labour_FINAL.pdf (accessed 7th June 2011)

253 See the speech by Dr. Carol Hamrin of 9th October 2010 entitled "Lost Heritage: Chinese Christians as Early Reformers", available from the following website: http://www.comumn.org/scripts/detail.asp?i=75 at: http://www.comumn.org/temp/ChineseChristianReformers.doc (accessed 7th June 2011)

254 See the Google books online copy of: *Christian Social Reformers of the Nineteenth Century,* by Hugh Martin, James Granville Adderley, currently available at: http://books.google.co.uk/books?id=jznelvvxxquc&printsec=frontcover&dq=christian+social+reformers+of+the+nineteenth+century&hl=en&ei=1kkitu38no3pobmrkb0n&sa=x&oi=book_result&ct=result&resnum=1&ved=0cc4q6aewaa#v=onepage&q&f=false (accessed 27th June 2011)

Chapter 11: Human Life

255 Available on the website of the Medical Ethics Alliance, at: http://www.medethics-alliance.org/geneva-declaration (accessed 27th June 2011)

256 See http://news.christiansunite.com/Religion_News/religion03738.shtml and Christian Concern's *Abortion* pamphlet at pp. 6-7: http://www.christianconcern.com/sites/default/files/docs/Abortion_Pamphlet.pdf.

257 The 500th edition of Melvyn Bragg's *In Our Time* programme explored determinism, free will and the possibility of them being compatible with three professors of philosophy on Thursday, 10th March 2011 on BBC Radio 4: http://www.bbc.co.uk/iplayer/console/b00z5y9z/In_Our_Time_Free_Will (accessed 10th March 2011 and 27th August 2011)

258 *The British Church Newspaper,* 15th June 2012, p.4

259 *The British Church Newspaper,* 5th November 2010

260 See the Department of Health's *Abortion Statistics, England and Wales: 2010,* published 24th May 2011, at p.14: http://www.dh.gov.uk/prod_consum_dh/groups/dh_digitalassets/documents/digitalasset/dh127202.pdf (accessed 27th June 2011)

261 For more information, see "Human development from conception to birth", SPUC, at: http://www.spuc.org.uk/ethics/abortion/human-development#first (accessed 30th March 2011)

262 John R. Ling, *Responding to the Culture of Death,* Day One (2001), p.32

263 Reported on a number of websites including the following: http://www. catholic.org/politics/story.php?id=33314 (accessed 27th June 2011)

264 See: http://www.amazon.co.uk/CROSSING-LIFE-LINE-HB-AUTHOR/ dp/1414339399/ref=sr_1_1?s=books&ie=UTF8&qid=1301605297&sr= 1- 1#reader_1414339399 (accessed 27th August 2011)

265 See for example, Anand, K.J.S. and Hickey, P.R., *Pain and its effects in the human neonate and foetus, New Engl J Med* 1987; 317(21):1321-1329, available at: http://www.cirp.org/library/pain/anand (accessed 27th August 2011)

266 See the BBC News report *Scans uncover secrets of the womb* of Monday, 28th June 2004 at: http://news.bbc.co.uk/1/hi/health/3846525.stm (accessed 27th August 2011).

267 *The British Church Newspaper,* 8th April 2011, p.5

268 See the 30-year longitudinal study by David M. Fergusson, PhD, L. John Horwood, MSc and Joseph M. Boden, PhD in *The British Journal of Psychiatry* (2008) at: http://bjp.rcpsych.org/cgi/content/abstract/193/6/444 and http://bjp.rcpsych.org/cgi/content/full/194/4/377-b (accessed 11th April 2011)

269 See for example P. Shah, J. Zao, and on behalf of Knowledge Synthesis Group of Determinants of preterm/LBW births (2009), *Induced termination of pregnancy and low birth weight and preterm birth: a systematic review and meta-analyses, BJOG: An International Journal of Obstetrics & Gynaecology,* 116: 1425–1442, available at: http://onlinelibrary.wiley.com/doi/10.1111/ j.1471-0528.2009.02278.x/full (accessed 12th April 2011) and the article in the April 2010 issue of the *Canadian Journal of Psychiatry,* which reports the increased rates of substance abuse, detailed at: http://www.lifenews. com/2010/05/03/int-1531 (accessed 12th April 2011)

270 *The British Church Newspaper,* 6th April 2011, p.5

271 Because then arguably the mother's right to life outweighs that of the foetus

272 See *'I do feel happy'—living with locked-in syndrome, The Guardian,* 29th March 2011: http://www.guardian.co.uk/lifeandstyle/2011/mar/29/happy- with-locked-in-syndrome (accessed 1st April 2011)

273 [1994] 2 All ER 403

274 Letter by Veronica Stabbins, *The Daily Telegraph,* 12th December 2011

275 [2011] EWHC 2443 (Fam)

276 See Martin Beckford, *Hospitals Failing to Provide Basic Care for Elderly, The Daily Telegraph,* 26th May 2011, at: http://www.telegraph.co.uk/health/ healthnews/8536172/Hospitals-failing-to-provide-basic-care-for-elderly. html (accessed 7th June 2011)

277 John R. Ling, *The Edge of Life,* Day One (2002), Chapter 5, p.79

278 Agnes van der Heide, M.D., Ph.D. et al, *End-of-Life Practices in the Netherlands under the Euthanasia Act,* N Engl J Med 2007; 356: 1957- 65, available at: http://www.nejm.org/doi/pdf/10.1056/NEJMsa071143 (accessed 27th June 2011)

279 See report by Care Not Killing, *Dutch Euthanasia Stats,* 27th September 2007, available at: http://www.carenotkilling.org.uk/?show=435 (accessed 27th June 2011)

280   See the Care Not Killing Fact Sheet, *Holland: Termination of Life on Request and Assisted Suicide (Review Procedures)* Act at p. 2: http://www.carenotkilling.org.uk/pdf/Holland_Fact_Sheet.pdf (accessed 1st April 2011)

281   See the following reports: http://www.dailymail.co.uk/news/article-1234295/Now-Dutch-turn-legalised-mercy-killing.html and http://www.lifesitenews.com/news/archive/ldn/2009/dec/09120207 (accessed 1st April 2011)

282   *R.* (on the application of Purdy) v Director of Public Prosecutions [2009] UKHL 45

283   See: http://www.nationalarchives.gov.uk/pathways/citizenship/rise_parliament/transcripts/bill_rights.htm and Christian Concern & the Christian Legal Centre's "Response to the DPP's Consultation on Interim Policy for Prosecutors in respect of Cases of Assisted Suicide" (November 2009), p.19, available at: http://christianconcern.com/sites/default/files/docs/CCFON_and_CLC_Response_to_the_DPPs_Consultation_on_his_Interim_Policy_on_Assisted_Suicide.pdf (accessed 27th June 2011)

284   Signatures, ratifications and the text of the Convention are accessible at the Council of Europe's website: http://conventions.coe.int/Treaty/Commun/QueVoulezVous.asp?NT=164&CL=ENG (accessed 28th June 2011)

285   The text of this Additional Protocol can be viewed at the Council of Europe's website: http://conventions.coe.int/Treaty/EN/Treaties/Html/168.htm (accessed 28th June 2011)

286   The latest information on the protocol can be found at the UK Parliament's website: http://www.parliament.uk/briefing-papers/SN05963 (accessed 28th June 2011)

287   Dr. Peter Saunders, *Stem Cell Delusions— The government juggernaut rolls on, Triple Helix,* Spring 2008, p.4, available at: http://www.cmf.org.uk/publications/content.asp?context=article&id=2031 (accessed 28th June 2011)

288   *The Sunday Telegraph,* 12th February 2012

289   Quintavalle v Human Fertilisation and Embryology Authority [2005] UKHL 28, [2005] 1 WLR 1061 (28 April 2005), available at: http://www.bailii.org/uk/cases/UKHL/2005/28.html (accessed 28th June 2011).

290   See Jodi Picoult's website for further details: http://www.jodipicoult.com/my-sisters-keeper.html (accessed 7th June 2011)

291   Christian Medical Fellowship, *Hybrid hype exposed,* 5th October 2009, available at: http://www.cmf.org.uk/news/?id=146 (accessed 28th June 2011)

292   See section 59 of the Act at: http://www.legislation.gov.uk/ukpga/2008/22/part/3/crossheading/miscellaneous (accessed 28th June 2011)

293   See for example Testa, Giuseppe and Harris, John, *Ethics and Synthetic Gametes,* Bioethics, Volume 19, Number 2, 2005, available at: http://www.ifom-ieo-campus.it/research/testa_web/downloads/biot_431.pdf (accessed 28th June 2011)

294   See the transcript for the 2009 Reith Lecture Series: *A New Citizenship* at: http://www.abc.net.au/rn/bigideas/stories/2009/2616256.htm (accessed 28th June 2011)

295   Neil Scolding, *Topping and Tailing, Standpoint* magazine, January/February 2011, p.85

Chapter 12: Crime and Punishment

296   Kant, op. cit. pp.61-62

297   Tom Wright, *Virtue Reborn,* SPCK Publishing (2012), p.34

298   BBC Radio 4, 23rd September 2011

299   Peter Hitchens, op. cit. p.31

300   Lawrence Sherman, *Cam* magazine, issue 61, pp. 30 and 31

301   Pascal, Pensees, Chapter 10, No. 29, op. cit. p.187

302   Byron R. Johnson, *More God, Less Crime,* Templeton Press (2011)

303   Byron R. Johnson, op. cit. pp.165-166

304   *The Daily Telegraph,* 23rd April 2012

305   Peter Hitchens, op. cit. pp.13-15

306   *The Daily Telegraph,* 25th January 2012

307   *The Daily Telegraph,* 18th September 2012, p.2

308   *The Daily Telegraph,* 25th January 2012, p.10

309   Philip Johnston, *The Telegraph,* August 10th 2011, p.19

310   *The Metro,* 23rd May 2012, p.10

311   *The Daily Telegraph,* 31st December 2012

312   *The Daily Telegraph,* September 28th, 2012, p.2

313   An anonymous Metropolitan police officer, *The Spectator,* 28th May 2011

314   *The Evening Standard,* 10th August 2011

315   David Ruffley, *The Daily Telegraph,* August 12th 2011, p.21

316   *The Guardian,* 16th September 2010

317   *The Guardian,* 3rd March 2012, p. 43

318   *The Times,* 24th September 2012, p.7

319   *The British Church Newspaper,* June 1st 2012, p.1

320   *The British Church Newspaper,* 27th January 2012

321   *The Telegraph,* 28th September 2012, p.2

Chapter 13: Education

322   Renford Bambrough, *Reason, Truth and God,* op. cit. p.75, quoting
      Matthew Arnold, *Literature and Dogma,* Chapter 1

323   Cicero, *The Laws* I, 31, op. cit. p.107

324   Herbert Schlossberg, op. cit. p.232

325   Katherine Birbalsingh, *Standpoint magazine,* September 2011

326   See Amelia Gentleman, *UK riots: 'Being liberal is fine, but we need to
      be given the right to parent',* The Guardian, 10th August 2011, available
      at: http://www.guardian.co.uk/uk/2011/aug/10/uk-riots-liberal-right-
      parent?INTCMP=SRCH (accessed 27th August 2011)

327   Amelia Gentleman, *The Guardian,* op. cit.

328   Amelia Gentleman, *The Guardian,* op. cit.

329   *The Times,* 2nd March 2011

330   *The Guardian,* 23rd August 2011

331 *The Daily Telegraph,* 15th June, 2012, p.4

332 Speech at Southfields Community College, Wandsworth, 5th September 2011, quoted by The Family Education Trust

333 *The Daily Telegraph,* 15th June 2012

334 Bill Bonner, *Moneyweek,* 4th November 2011, p. 50

335 James Bartholomew op. cit. p.170

336 Katherine Birbalsingh, *The Daily Telegraph,* 6th April 2012, p.30

337 Katherine Birbalsingh, *The Daily Telegraph,* 1st February 2012, p.21

338 Katherine Birbalsingh, op. cit, 6th April 2012

339 *The Evening Standard,* 31st January 2011

340 Katherine Birbalsingh, op. cit.

341 *Standpoint* magazine, June 2012

342 Bagehot, *The Economist, Wanted: a schools revolution,* 24th June 2011, available at: http://www.economist.com/blogs/bagehot/2011/06/british-education (accessed 27th August 2011).

343 Oliver Lewis, *The Spectator,* 11th December, 2010, p.18

344 David Cameron, speech delivered at Witney, 15th August 2011, quoted by The Family Education Trust

345 See the Office for National Statistics' Bulletin, *Conceptions in England and Wales 2009,* published 22nd February 2011, available at: http://www.statistics.gov.uk/pdfdir/con0211.pdf (accessed 12th April 2011) and the *Telegraph* article, *Teenage pregnancies on the rise despite £286m campaign,* 20th February 2009, available at: http://www.telegraph.co.uk/health/healthnews/4734697/Teenage-pregnancies-on-the-rise-despite-286m-campaign.html (accessed 12th April 2011)

346 See the Office for National Statistics' Opinions Survey Report No. 41, *Contraception and Sexual Heath,* 2008/09, Table 5.4, at: http://www.statistics.gov.uk/downloads/theme_health/contra2008-9.pdf (accessed 12th April 2011)

347 See the Health Protection Agency's Press Release, *Sexually transmitted infections reach almost half a million,* 25th August 2010, available at: http://www.hpa.org.uk/NewsCentre/NationalPressReleases/2010PressReleases/100825STI (accessed 12th April 2011)

348 Valerie Riches: *Sex Education or Indoctrination,* Family Youth and Concern (2004), pp.11-12

349 Valerie Riches, op. cit. p.54

350 International Planned Parenthood Association: *Alert* issued in 2001, quoted in Valerie Riches, op. cit. p.22

351 *The Guardian,* 20th January 2012

352 Michael L. Brown, op. cit. p.271

353 Marshall Kirk & Hunter Madsen, *After the Ball: How America Will Conquer its Fear and Hatred of Gays in the 90's,* quoted in Michael L. Brown, op. cit. p.389

354 See Lisa Severine Nolland PhD, *Serious Concerns with Redefining Marriage* (2012), available from Anglican Mainstream

355 *A Cure for our National Amnesia,* Bishop Michael Nazir-Ali, Standpoint, November 2010, available at: http://www.standpointmag.co.uk/features-november-10-a-cure-for-our-national-amnesia-michael-nazir-ali-educational-reform-michael-gove (accessed 8th April 2011)

356 *The Daily Telegraph,* 5th March 2001

357 op. cit, loc. cit.

358 Cambridge History Faculty Newsletter, July 2012, p.4

359 *The Guardian,* 21st January 2011

360 Simon Conway Morris, in Chapter 15 of *Real Scientists, Real Faith,* edited by R. J. Berry, Monarch Books (2009), p.219

361 Simon Conway Morris, op. cit. p.221

362 Simon Conway Morris, quoted in *Cam* magazine, Issue 65, p.35

363 See F. Wood Jones, F.R.S., *Trends of Life,* Edward Arnold & Co. (1953), Chapter 7, p.76ff

364 Simon Conway Morris, op. cit, loc. cit.

365 See Patrick Sookhdeo, *Slippery Slope: The Islamisation of the UK,* Operation Nehemiah, at p.18, available from the Barnabas Fund: http://barnabasfund.org/UK/News/Barnabas-Aid-magazine/Barnabas-Aid-May-June-2011-34MB.pdf (see p.11, accessed 27th August 2011)

366 Sookhdeo, op. cit. at p.28

367 Sookhdeo, op. cit. at p.26

368 Sookhdeo, op. cit. at p.27

369 *The Daily Telegraph,* 25th August 2011

370 *The Daily Telegraph,* 11th May 2012, p.15

Chapter 14: The Family

371 *The Daily Telegraph,* 17th March 2009

372 http://www.relationshipsfoundation.org/web/content/Default.aspx?Content=144

373 *The British Church Newspaper,* 19th November 2012

374 *The Daily Telegraph,* April 30th 2012, p.2

375 Centre for Social Justice, *Breakdown Britain: Interim report on the state of the nation,* December 2006; available at: http://www.centreforsocialjustice.org.uk/client/downloads/CSJ%20FINAL%20(2).pdf

376 *The British Church Newspaper,* 17th December 2010, p.4

377 Patricia Morgan, *Family Policy, Family Changes: Sweden, Italy and Britain Compared,* Civitas (2006), available via their website: http://www.civitas.org.uk/press/prcs43.php (accessed 29th August 2011)

378 Patricia Morgan, *The War between the State and the Family,* Institute of Economic Affairs (2007), available at: http://www.iea.org.uk/publications/research/the-war-between-the-state-and-the-family (accessed 29th August 2011)

379 Patricia Morgan, op. cit. p.112

380 Newsletter from C & M Ministries, December 2011

381 Patricia Morgan, *The War between the State and the Family*, op. cit. p.79

382 Anthony Giddens, *Sociology*, 6th Edition, Polity (2009), p.335

383 *The Daily Telegraph*, 14th June 2012

384 Dean Byrd: this can be found at: http://narth.com/docs/byrdtestimony.pdf

385 Michael L. Brown, op. cit. p.590

386 This can be found at: http://www.nytimes.com/2004/03/09/opinion/a-marriage-made-in history.html?pagewanted=print&src=pm

387 *The Daily Telegraph*, 9th November 2010, p.13

388 *The Daily Telegraph*, 7th February 2012, p.3

389 Sentamu on same-sex marriage, this can be found at: http://www.dailymail.co.uk/news/article-2097305/Archbishop-John-Sentamu-receives-racist-emails-saying-ministers-allow-sex-marriage.html?printingPage=true

390 Aric Sigman, *The Spoilt Generation*, Piaktus (2009)

391 *The Daily Telegraph*, 15th September 2010, p.29

392 *The Guardian*, G2, page 3, report by Paris Lees, 24th May 2012

393 Relationships Foundation, 2.5 million families affected by Sunday Trading

Chapter 15: Freedom of Expression

394 *The Metro*, 9th November 2010

395 Munira Mirza, *The Evening Standard*, 20th September 2012, p.14

396 *The Daily Telegraph*, 4th May 2012, p.17

397 The case of Ben and Sharon Vogelenzang: see http://www.dailymail.co.uk/news/article-1234680/It-victory-free-speech-did-breakfastinsult-Muslims-faith-case-come-court.html

398 *The British Church Newspaper*, 9th September 2011, p.10

399 *The British Church Newspaper*, 24th February 2012, p.5

400 *The British church Newspaper*, 3rd December 2010, p.4

401 *The British Church Newspaper*, 9th September 2011, pp.1 and 3

402 See: http://www.huffingtonpost.co.uk/2012/10/18/facebook-post-anti-gay-marriage-adrian-smith_n_1980639.html and http://www.christianconcern.com/our-concerns/sexual-orientation/demoting-christian-over-facebook-comments-was-%E2%80%9Cover-reaction%E2%80%9D-says-l

403 DPP v Collins [2006] UKHL 40

404 *The Guardian*, 21st January 2012

405 William M. Struthers, *Wired for Intimacy. How Pornography Hijacks the Male Brain*, IVP Books (2009), p.90

406 Maggie Ellis, *Christianity magazine*, June 2012, p.31

407 *The Daily Telegraph*, 4th July 2012

408 *The Daily Mail*, 18th September 2012, p. 11

409 *The British Church Newspaper*, 3rd December 2010, p.1

410 See the report of the *Parliamentary Inquiry into Online Protection* held in Committee Room 8, 8th September 2011

411 Matthew 18:15-17, NIV

Chapter 16: The Value of Community

412 See *The Citizenship Foundation,* website: http://www.citizenshipfoundation. org.uk/main/page.php?398

413 Jim Wallis, *God's Politics,* Lion Books (2006)

414 Herbert Schlossberg, op. cit. p.192

415 Francis Fukuyama, *Trust,* Free Press Paper, Simon & Schuster (1995), p.221

416 Edmund Burke, *Reflections on the Revolution in France,* Oxford World Classics (1999)

Chapter 17: Companies and Markets

417 Paper for clients of Allen & Overy LLP, 2011

418 William T. Muhaire, op. cit.

419 James Featherby, *Of Markets and Men,* Centre for Tomorrow's Company (2012)

420 See Schluter, Michael, *Beyond Capitalism: Towards a Relational Economy,* Cambridge Papers, Volume 19, Number 1, March 2010, available at: http:// www.jubilee-centre.org/document.php?id=346 (accessed 29th August 2011)

421 Chris Blackhurst, *Want to make the world a better place? Do me a favour, The Evening Standard,* 31st January 2011, available at: http://www.thisislondon. co.uk/standard-business/article-23918863-want-to-make-the-world-a-better-place-do-me-a-favour.do (accessed 11th June 2011)

422 James Featherby, op. cit. p.21

423 *The Guardian,* 26th September 2011

424 Chandran Nair, *Consumptionomics,* Infinite Ideas (2011)

425 Max Weber, *Protestant Ethic and the Spirit of Capitalism,* Routledge Classics (2001), p.124

426 Bill Bonner, *Moneyweek,* 16th September 2011, p.46

427 Merryn Somerset Webb, *Moneyweek,* 10th June 2011, p.3

428 Tim Jackson, *Prosperity without Growth,* Earthscan Publications (2009)

429 Anthony Hilton, *The Evening Standard,* 11th October 2012, p.54, referring to William Janeway, *Doing Capitalism in the Innovation Economy,* Cambridge University Press, (2012)

Chapter 18: Debt

430 *The Financial Times,* 7th September 2012

431 See Paul Mills, *The Great Financial Crisis: A Biblical Diagnosis,* Cambridge Papers, Volume 20, Number 1, March 2011, available at: http://www. jubileecentre.org/document.php?id=414 (accessed 29th August 2011)

432 See Paul Mills, *The Ban on Interest: Dead Letter or Radical Solution?,* Cambridge Papers, Volume 1, Number 4, March 1993, available at: http:// www.jubilee-centre.org/document.php?id=3 (accessed 29th August 2011)

433 *The Daily Telegraph,* 5th March 2011 and see article by Robert Winnett, *Britain at risk of another financial crisis, Bank of England chief warns,* in the electronic edition of 4th March: http://www.telegraph.co.uk/finance/ economics/8362951/Britain-at-risk-of-another-financial-crisis-Bank-of-England-chief-warns.html (accessed 11th June 2011)

434 These quotations come from Charles Moore's article entitled, *Mervyn King interview: We prevented a Great Depression... but people have the right to be angry,* see the electronic edition of *The Daily Telegraph,* 4th March 2011 at: http://www.telegraph.co.uk/finance/economics/8362959/Mervyn-King-interview-We-prevented-a-Great-Depression...-but-people-have-the-right-to-be-angry.html (accessed 11th June 2011)

435 See Paul Mills, *The Divine Economy,* Cambridge Papers, Volume 9, Number 4, December 2000, available at: http://www.jubilee-centre.org/document.php?id=30 (accessed 29th August 2011)

436 Sajid Javid, *The Daily Telegraph,* 3rd August 2011, p.16

437 *Moneyweek,* 27th January 2012, p.8

438 Dambiso Moyo, *How the West was Lost,* Allen Lane (2011), pp.40-45

439 Dambiso Moyo, op. cit. p.83

440 See *America's Overdue Financial Crisis, The Spectator,* 6th August 2011, available at: http://www.spectator.co.uk/essays/all/7141198/americas-overdue-financial-crisis.thtml (accessed 29th August 2011)

441 *Moneyweek,* 27th February 2012, p.50

442 John Maudlin and Jonathan Tepper, *Endgame,* John Wiley & Sons (2011), p.173

443 *New Yorker,* 14th June 2010

444 Charles Dumas and Diana Choyleva, *The Bill from the China Shop,* Profile Books Ltd (2006)

445 *Moneyweek,* 5th August, 2011, p.21

446 Fraser Nelson, *The Spectator,* 11th February 2012, pp.12-13

447 *The Sunday Telegraph,* 12th December 2012

448 *The Spectator,* 15th October 2011

449 Liam Halligan, *The Sunday Telegraph,* 12th December 2012

450 Bill Bonner, *Moneyweek,* 6th May 2011, p.46

451 *The Daily Telegraph,* September 2012, p.B5, and see *The Spectator,* 22nd October 2011, p.3

452 *Moneyweek,* 2nd September 2011, p.3

Chapter 19: Nationality and Globalisation

453 Ha-Joon Chang, *Bad Samaritans,* Random House Business Books (2007), p.27

454 Charles Dumas and Diana Choylesa, op. cit.

455 James McKeigue in *Moneyweek,* 22nd June 2012, quoting Alex Brummer of *The Daily Mail*

456 *The Metro,* 19th September 2012, p.16

457 *Le Monde,* 14th June 2007 and *The Sunday Telegraph,* 1st July 2007, quoted in *The British Church Newspaper,* 5th October 2012, p.16

Chapter 20: The Environment

458 See Albert Schweitzer, *Out of My Life and Thought,* Epilogue, available at: http://www1.chapman.edu/schweitzer/sch.reading3.html (accessed 13th June 2011)

459 Quoted in Christopher Caldwell, *America's overdue financial crisis,* The Spectator, 6th August 2011, available at: http://www.spectator.co.uk/essays/all/7141198/americas-overdue-financial-crisis.thtml (accessed 30th August 2011)

460 Chandran Nair, *Consumptionomics,* op. cit.

461 See Bob Goudzwaard, *Globalization, Regionalization and Sphere-Sovereignty,* p. 10, available at: http://www.allofliferedeemed.co.uk/goudzwaard/BG76.pdf (accessed 13th June 2011)

462 Chandran Nair, op. cit. pp.91-95. This quotation is also available in Chandran Nair's *Consumption, The Banker,* January 2011, pp.124-125, at p.125: http://www.globalinstitutefortomorrow.com/files/file/20110107-The%20Banker-WEFArticle-CN.pdf (accessed 13th June 2011)

463 R.M. Carter, *The Myth of dangerous Human-Caused Climate Change,* The Aus IMM New Leaders Conference, Brisbane, QLD, May 2007

464 *The Sunday Telegraph,* 12th February 2012, p.13

465 *The Guardian,* 16th June 2012, interview with Leo Hickman

466 *The Spectator,* 15th October 2011

467 *The Guardian,* 5th September 2012

468 Simon Stuart et al. in *Conservation Theology for Conservation Biologists* in Conservation Biology, Volume 19, No. 6, December 2005

Chapter 21: International Development and Aid

469 *The Daily Telegraph,* 18th December 2012

470 See *Western aid now does more harm than good,* available at: http://www.thisislondon.co.uk/standard/article-23927633-western-aid-now-does-more-harm-than-good.do (accessed 13th June 2011)

471 Francis Fukuyama, *State Building,* Profile Book Limited (2004)

472 See Francis Fukuyama, op. cit. pp.54-55

473 Peter Grant, *Poor No More: Be Part of a Miracle,* Monarch (2008)

474 Ha-Joon Chang, op. cit.

475 *Moneyweek,* 29th June 2012

476 *The Spectator,* 18th February 2012

477 James Mc Keigue, *Moneyweek,* 5th October 2012, quoting Andrew Gilligan of *The Daily Telegraph*

Chapter 22: The Foreign Policy of States

478 Christopher Coker, op. cit. See in particular Chapter 2, *Etiquettes of Atrocity*

479 The transcript of President Bush's speech *No justice without freedom* of 20th January 2005 can be found at the CNN website: http://edition.cnn.com/2005/ALLPOLITICS/01/20/bush.transcript/index.html (accessed 13th June 2011)

480 Quoted in Daniel W. Drezner, *Does Obama Have a Grand Strategy? Foreign Affairs,* Volume 90, No. 4

481 Montesquieu, *Esprit des Lois*

482 Oliver O'Donovan and Joan Lockwood O'Donovan, *A Sourcebook in Christian Political Thought,* Eerdmans (1999), p.792

483 Christopher Coker, op. cit. p.120

484 Christopher Coker, op. cit. p.100

485 Christopher Coker, op. cit. p.101

486 Peter Hessler, *New Yorker magazine* 18th June 2012

487 Rory Stewart and Gerald Knaus, *Can Intervention Work?* W. W. Norton & Company (2011)

488 W.B Grant, *We Have a Guardian,* Covenant Books (1952) p.10

489 David C. Relf, *The British Church Newspaper,* 4th November 2011, p.15

490 Quoted In Nick Solly Megoran, *The War on Terror,* InterVarsity Press (2007), p.37

491 See Christopher Coker, op. cit. p.171

492 *League of Nations Mandate for Palestine,* available at: http://www.mfa.gov. il/MFA/Peace%20Process/Guide%20to%20the%20Peace%20Process/ The%20Mandate%20for%20Palestine (accessed 31st August 2011)

493 The *Balfour Declaration,* contained in a letter from the Secretary of State for Foreign Affairs, Arthur James Balfour to Lord Rothschild, The British Foreign Office, 2nd November 1917, available at: http://news. bbc.co.uk/1/hi/in_depth/middle_east/israel_and_the_palestinians/key_ documents/1682961.stm (accessed 31st August 2011)

494 See: Wikipedia at :http://en.wikipedia.org/wiki/William_Temple (bishop)

495 Quoted in *The World after Mubarak, The Spectator,* 5th February 2011, available at: http://www.spectator.co.uk/essays/all/6666353/part_2/the-world-after-mubarak.thtml (accessed 13th June 2011)

Chapter 23: Change and Hope for the Future

496 Clifford Denton and Paul Slennet, *Earthquake in the City,* Kingsway Publications (1997)

497 Quoted in *Texas governor gets on knees for evangelicals' help to White House, Irish Times,* 6th August 2011, available at: http://www.irishtimes.com/ newspaper/world/2011/0806/1224301950762.html, (accessed 2nd September 2011)

498 Robert Gray, *The Spectator,* 11th June 2011, p.23

499 Letter to *The Spectator,* 20th August 2011

500 *Standpoint* magazine, September 2011

501 Michael L. Brown, op.cit. p.152

502 Michael L. Brown, op.cit. p.169

503 Judges 21:25, KJV

504 Herbert Schlossberg, op. cit.

505 Patrick Kavanagh, *The Spiritual Lives of Great Composers,* Sparrow Press (1992), p.7

506 Peter Hitchens, interview with Richard Godwin, *The Evening Standard,* 11th October 2012, p.23

507 Isaiah 53:6, KJV

508 Renford Bambrough, op. cit. p.143

509 Adam Smith, The Theory of Moral Sentiments, Part VI, Section III, Penguin Classics, p.209

510 Cited in D.A. Carson, *Christ and Culture Revisited,* Apollos (IVP) (2008), p.89

Postscript

511 Arthur Bryant, *The Triumph of the West,* Collins (1959), p.458

512 Lines 68-71 and 102-110, available at: http://faculty.plattsburgh.edu/anna. battigelli/eng313/newpage3.htm (accessed 13th June 2011)

513 John 14:6, KJV